Fundamentals of Computer Education

◀ ▼ ▶ ▲ ◀ ▼ ▶ ▲ ◀ ▼ ▶ ▲ ◀ ▼ ▶ ▲ ◀ ▼ ▶ ▲ ◀ ▼ ▶ ▲

Fundamentals of

▶ ▲ ◀ ▼ ▶ ▲ ◀ ▼ ▶ ▲ ◀ ▼ ▶ ▲ ◀ ▼ ▶ ▲ ◀ ▼ ▶ ▲ ◀ ▼ ▶

Wadsworth Books in Computer Education

Fundamentals of Computer Education, Second Edition
Janice L. Flake, C. Edwin McClintock, and Sandra Turner

Computers, Curriculum, and Whole-Class Instruction: Issues and Ideas
Betty Collis

Tools for Schools: Applications Software for the Classroom
Sandra Turner and Michael Land

The Computer: A Tool for the Teacher
Edward B. Wright and Richard C. Forcier

Classroom Activities for Computer Education
Janice L. Flake, C. Edwin McClintock, Linda Edson,
Kristen Ellington, Frankie Mack, Marvel Lou Sandon, and Joanne Urrutia

Computer Education

▲ ◄ ▼ ► ▲ ◄ ▼ ► ▲ ◄ ▼ ► ▲ ◄ ▼ ► ▲ ◄ ▼ ► ▲ ◄ ▼ ► ▲ ◄ ▼ ► ▲

Second Edition

Janice L. Flake

Florida State University

C. Edwin McClintock

Florida International University

Sandra Turner

National College of Education

Wadsworth Publishing Company
Belmont, California
A Division of Wadsworth, Inc.

We dedicate this book to our families.

▶ ▲ ◀ ▼ ▶ ▲ ◀ ▼ ▶ ▲ ◀ ▼ ▶ ▲ ◀ ▼ ▶ ▲ ◀ ▼ ▶ ▲ ◀ ▼ ▶

Computer Science Editor:
Frank Ruggirello

Editorial Assistant:
Carol Carreon

Production Editor:
Patricia Brewer

Managing Designer:
James Chadwick

Print Buyer: *Barbara Britton*

Copy Editor: *Fannie Toldi*

Art Editor: *Irene Imfeld*

Computer Screen Coordinators:
Sharon Downie Cooper
and *Ann Hernandez*

Text Designer: *Detta Penna*

Cover Design: *James Chadwick*

Cover Illustration: Sarn

Signing Representative:
Leo Simcock

Apple® is a registered trademark of Apple Computer, Inc.
LogoWriter is a trademark of Logo Computer Systems, Inc.

Printed in the United States of America
1 2 3 4 5 6 7 8 9 10—94 93 92 91 90

Library of Congress Cataloging in Publication Data
Flake, Janice L.
    Fundamentals of computer education/Janice L. Flake,
  C. Edwin McClintock, Sandra Turner.—2nd ed.
      p. cm.
  ISBN 0-534-11718-X
    1. LOGO (Computer program language) 2. LogoWriter (Computer program)
  3. AppleWorks 4. Apple II (Computer)—Programming.
  I. McClintock, C. Edwin.   II. Turner, Sandra   III. Title.
  QA76.73.L63F53   1990
  004.16′024372-dc20   89-16642 CIP

Illustration Credits

Introduction *Figure 1(a, b):* Jak Dempsey (Apple IIe and IIc). *Figure 1(c):* Apple Computer, Inc. (Apple IIGS). *Figure 2(a–c):* Jak Dempsey (Apple IIe and IIc on/off switches). *Figure 6(a, b):* Jak Dempsey (Apple IIe and IIc disk drives). *Figure 6(c, d):* Apple Computer, Inc. (Apple IIe/GS disk drive and disks). *Figure 7(a–c):* Jak Dempsey (Apple II +, IIe, and IIc keyboards). *Figure 7(d):* Apple Computer, Inc. (Apple IIGS keyboard). **Chapter 1** *Figure 2:* Sharon Downie Cooper (Robot turtle). **Chapter 4** *Figure 5:* The Learning Company (*Rocky's Boots* display). *Figure 6:* The Learning Company (*Rocky's Boots* display). **Chapter 5** *Figure 1:* Sierra On-Line (*Homeword* display). **Chapter 8** *Figure 1(a):* Sharon Downie Cooper (Koala Pad). *Figure 2:* Apple Computer, Inc. (*MacPaint* display). *Figure 3:* Jak Dempsey (Apple-Mouse II). *Figure 5:* Hayes (modem). **Chapter 9** *Figure 1:* Hartley Courseware, Inc. (*Clock* display). *Figure 2:* Microsoft Consumer Products (*Olympic Decathlon* displays). *Figure 3:* MECC (*MECC Music* display). *Figure 4:* Frontier Software (*Plurals and Possessives* display). *Figure 5:* Hartley Courseware, Inc. (*Clock* display). *Figure 6 (a–c):* MECC (*MECC Elementary Volume 7* displays). **Chapter 10** *Figure 2(a–d):* EduWare (*Perception II* displays). *Figure 3:* EduWare (*Perception I* displays). *Figure 4:* EduWare (*Perception II* displays). *Figure 6:* SubLogic (*Flight Simulator II* displays). *Figure 8:* The Learning Company (*Rocky's Boots* display). *Figure 9.* Control Data Corporation (*Plato Sentences* display). **Chapter 11** *Figure 1:* MECC (*Oregon Trail* display). *Figure 2:* MECC (*Pollute* display). *Figure 3:* MECC (*Collide* display). *Figure 4:* SubLogic (*Flight Simulator II* display). **Chapter 12** *Figure 1:* Control Data Corporation (*Plato Sentences* displays). *Figure 2:* Control Data Corporation (*Plato Tenses* displays). *Figure 3:* Cambridge Development Laboratory (*Mea-*

surement displays). *Figure 4:* Adapted from L.S. Shulman, Psychological controversies in the teaching of science and mathematics, *The Science Teacher* 35: 34–38. 1968 (Task analysis diagram). **Chapter 14** *Figure 1:* MECC (*Lemonade Stand* display). *Figure 2(a):* MECC (*Lemonade Stand* display). *Figure 3:* MECC (*Odell Lake* display). *Figure 4:* Hartley Courseware, Inc. (*Clock* display). *Figure 5:* Muse (*Three Mile Island* display). *Figure 6:* MECC (*Prefixes* display). *Figure 7:* Sharon Downie Cooper; Developmental Learning Materials (*Alligator Mix* display). *Figure 8:* Educational Activities (*Compu-solve* display). *Figure 9:* Educational Activities (*Dragon Games* display). **Appendix A** *Figure 1:* Jak Dempsey (electric bar). *Figure 2(a, b):* Jak Dempsey (disks and disk drives for Apple II +, IIe, and IIc). *Figure 3 (a–c):* Jak Dempsey (disk drive doors for Apple II +, IIe, and IIc). *Figure 4(a–c):* Jak Dempsey Apple II +, IIe, and IIc keyboards). *Figure 4(d):* Apple Computer, Inc. (Apple IIGS keyboard). **Appendix D** *Figure 1:* Logo Computer System Inc. (LogoWriter, Apple version, keyboard display. *Figure 2:* Logo Computer Systems Inc. (IBM PC version). *Figure 3:* Logo Computer Systems Inc. (IBM PCJR 64 version). **Appendix F** *Figure 1(a):* Apple Computer, Inc. (Apple IIGS desktop system). *Figure 1(b, c):* Jak Dempsey (Apple Macintosh and IMB PC desktop systems). *Figure 2(b):* Jak Dempsey (6502 microprocessor). *Figure 3(a):* Apple Computer, Inc. (Apple II + motherboard). *Figure 3(b):* Jak Dempsey (Apple IIe motherboard). *Figure 3(c):* Janice Flake (Apple IIGS motherboard). *Figure 4(a, b):* Jak Dempsey (Apple II + expansion slot). *Figure 4(c, d):* Janice Flake (Apple IIGS expansion slots and backview of ports). *Figure 5(a–c):* Jak Dempsey (Epson MX 100, Okidata, Brother printer). *Figure 5(d, e):* Apple Computer, Inc. (Apple ImageWriter II and Apple LaserWriter II).

Brief Contents

Detailed Contents

Preface

◀ ▼ ▶ ▲ ◀ ▼ ▶ ▲ ◀ ▼ ▶ ▲ ◀ ▼ ▶ ▲ ◀ ▼ ▶ ▲ ◀ ▼ ▶ ▲ ◀ ▼

Computers are now common in school settings; consequently, teacher education programs are requiring students to take courses in computer education. In addition, in-service teachers are returning to college for computer education courses.

We each teach courses in computer education and felt a need for a textbook such as *Fundamentals of Computer Education*. For the first edition, verification of proposed topics and suggestions for additional topics came from a survey conducted by Wadsworth Publishing Company of 366 professional educators, including computer educators, computer scientists, psychologists, and curriculum and instruction faculty. The text was then carefully field tested, and students gave considerable input. The result was a comprehensive computer education textbook that gave educators—preservice or in-service—a solid foundation for any future study in the area.

To prepare for the second edition, we surveyed many more people concerning the field of computer education, which is rapidly growing and changing. Because of this survey we have made the following modifications for the second edition.

▶ Increased the emphasis on tool uses of the computer
▶ Increased the amount of software reviewed
▶ Included sample activities to be incorporated directly into school classrooms
▶ Added LogoWriter and Logo Plus

Because of space limitations, we then eliminated our section on BASIC.

Features of This Book

Fundamentals of Computer Education is unique in the following ways:

▶ Provides *comprehensive coverage* of computer education
▶ Emphasizes *problem solving*
▶ Draws connections between *learning theory* and *educational applications* of the computer
▶ Provides *applications* and *uses* of multiple versions of Logo, including LogoWriter
▶ Emphasizes *graphics* and the importance of *imagery* development through both programming experiences and software evaluation
▶ Discusses in detail educational computer *applications,* including in-depth analyses and evaluations of various types of educational software

> ▶ Gives concrete examples, emphasizing AppleWorks, of the computer's use as a *tool* through word processing, databases, and spreadsheets
> ▶ Includes *numerous* computer programs, exercises, and applications in a variety of subject areas
> ▶ Builds connections between the *past* and the *future* by analyzing *societal changes* brought on by *technology*
> ▶ Utilizes an *applications disk of sample programs* illustrating specific educational ideas, which is keyed to the text by a disk symbol in the text margin
> ▶ Provides *activities* and *worksheets* that can be directly applied to classroom use.

Problem Solving and Logo

Problem solving is a major focus of the book. We feel that teaching problem-solving processes is a fundamental responsibility of schools. Most educators consider problem solving to be the one stable educational goal in a rapidly changing society. Some facts and skills necessary in the past are obsolete today; problem-solving ability, in contrast, does not become obsolete.

Original programming is problem solving, requiring problem-solving processes. Effective use of process-type software and the important uses of computer tool programs involve problem solving. For example, decision-making can be facilitated by electronic spreadsheets; organizing and analyzing information to solve problems is inherent in the use of databases. In addition, commercial programs that enhance problem solving are being developed and are examined.

We consider Logo to be a fundamental computer language for use in the teaching of problem-solving processes. To help students visualize concepts, Logo uses graphics and other methods; it was developed through applications of a constructivist theory, including Piagetian theory. The logic, exploration, and problem solving inherent in the use of Logo make it an excellent tool for helping teachers to achieve fundamental educational goals. The principles of organizing, reasoning, planning, and decision-making learned through Logo transcend specific academic subjects taught in school and provide an overall framework for all school subjects. This second edition includes LogoWriter and Logo Plus. Such an active approach to learning provides motivation for the learning of all academic subjects.

Educational Theory

We consider the underlying principles of education, particularly those expounded by Gestalt, Bruner, Piaget, Polya, and Papert, to be fundamental to computer education. Chapter 12 discusses how teaching/learning theories, including those developed from the observation of *expert teachers* by K. B. Henderson and B. O. Smith, can be developed into *expert systems*, using the capabilities of the computer. This chapter also covers the designing of lessons to include the dynamic and visual aspects, as well as abstractions, of conceptual learning. The text goes on to discuss a combination of moves that builds from the *concrete* to the *iconic* (including visualization and imagery development) and finally to the *abstract*.

We consider *learning styles* to be essential in the improvement of educational practices. Tools such as computers now can enhance learning styles. Computers not only help educators to develop instructional materials that are consistent with students' learning styles but also help them to strengthen individual students' weaknesses. For example, with well-designed computer experiences, *visual* learners can develop their *verbal* learning skills, and vice versa; *impulsive* learners can become more *reflective* in learning style.

Orientation to This Book

This is a machine-specific book for the Apple® II series. We have designed it this way to aid easy entry to computers. Our data suggests that the Apple II series is the most commonly used computer in education today. Our Logo sections include M.I.T. versions (Terrapin, Krell, and Logo Plus) and LCSI versions (Apple Logo and LogoWriter) because we find that these versions are used heavily. LogoWriter is also a multiple-machine version for the Apple IIe/c and Apple IIGS, IBM PC, IBM PC$_{JR}$, and Commodore.

The book has three parts. Part One focuses on control of the computer and emphasizes programming. Its goal, to build an understanding of the computer and its power and versatility, can best be met through the readers' actual programming of the computer. We believe that people *learn* best *by doing* and have included many activities, experiences, and exercises to help guide that learning. The book will be most effective if computer time is carefully allocated.

We also stress the importance of developing problem-solving strategies. In Chapter 1, first programming experiences are with Logo, which is proving to be a very good language for beginners. Logo has many of the features of a well-designed programming language, as well as easy entry. Also using Logo, Chapter 2 develops programming concepts along with problem-solving strategies. Computer uses that are more *generalizable*, such as word processing concepts, are presented through the Logo editor in Chapter 3. *Structured programming* is examined in the writing of Logo programs and also is applied to music. The concept of *microworlds* is explored in Chapter 3. In addition to those aspects of Logo, LogoWriter includes an easy-to-use shapemaker, which allows for multiple-shaped turtles and multiple turtles (up to four); it also includes built-in music and easy-to-use systems for editing and manipulating files.

Parts Two and Three examine educational applications of the computer. Part Two, Chapters 5–8, focuses on instructional uses of word processors, databases, spreadsheets, and graphics packages; AppleWorks is emphasized. In Part Three, educational software is discussed in chapters on drill and practice (9), visualization and imagery development (10), simulations (11), tutorials (12), and computer-managed instruction (13). Chapter 14 examines software evaluation.

The final chapter of the book examines *trends* and *issues* of computer education; particular emphasis is given to the past and future societal changes generated by technology. Other issues include *computer literacy*, schools' uses of the computer, legal aspects of computer use, intelligent computers, and artificial intelligence.

We were unable to come up with a consensus on where the chapter "What Is a Computer?" should be placed. Some people prefer starting with this chapter. We prefer having students first have some successful experiences with the computer before making the computer the object of study. Because we were unable to get any consensus about placement, we moved it to an appendix (Appendix F) so that you can study it whenever it is appropriate for you.

So that the flow of the book will be smooth, the more mechanical instructions on use of the computer are built into the appendixes. These appendixes cover operating the computer, using operating systems, editing features within the Logo language, and a discussion of utility programs on the DOS 3.3, ProDOS, and GS OS MASTER DISK for the Apple II computer series. In this second edition, appendixes also describe special features of LogoWriter, Logo Plus, AppleWorks, and Apple IIGS, and Logo commands.

Also in the appendixes are two more lists that we hope will be helpful. One list is a set of computer programs used in the text and the distributors from whom they can be purchased. The second is a cross-listing of subject areas and computer programs discussed in the text.

A Note to Instructors

The materials discussed in *Fundamentals of Computer Education* can be sequenced in various ways. The chapters are organized so that students can gain confidence in controlling the machine before they examine the applications. Programming and applications also could be taught simultaneously. Adequate time must be given for students to develop appropriate problem-solving abilities; we see this as the most important objective and the one most in need of time to develop.

A Note to Students

Fundamentals of Computer Education is designed to be used actively with the computer. If you wish to develop machine skills, you need to plan time to work at a computer. Throughout the book, explorations, activities, and discussions are designed to help you gain the most from your computer experiences.

Each chapter contains *chapter objectives, important terms,* and *exercises* to help you organize your knowledge. Also included are sample activities for your students. Each of these should be examined carefully while you work through the chapter. We hope you will enjoy learning about computers, developing problem-solving abilities, and understanding computer education!

Acknowledgments

Thanks to these reviewers, whose comments were helpful in preparing this second edition: William Deaton, Auburn University; William P. Dunaway, Jacksonville State University; Gaylen Kelley, Boston University; Colin MacKinnon, United States International University; Cleborne Maddux, University of Nevada, Reno; Stephen Marcus, University of California at Santa Barbara; Albert Nous, University of Pittsburgh; Michael Simonson, Iowa State University; Wenden Waite, Boise State University; and Robert Wall, Towson State University. We also are grateful to the many students at Florida State University and Florida International University, who most graciously have given us input on the book. Thank you to the administration, faculty, and students at the Florida State University Developmental Research School.

We appreciate the contributions of reviewers and consultants for the first edition: B. J. Allen, Florida State University; Rodney Allen, Florida State University; Cheryl Anderson, University of Texas; Richard H. Austing, University of Maryland; Robert K. Bane, North Texas State University; Roy Bolduc, University of Florida; Alan Crawford, California State University, Los Angeles; Judith H. Dettre, University of Nevada; Vernon S. Gerlach, Arizona State University; Kenneth B. Henderson, Professor Emeritus, University of Illinois; Roger Johanson, Norwalk Community Schools; Thomas D. Johnsten, Oklahoma State University; Jacqueline McMahon, University of Missouri; Bonnie K. Mathies, Wright State University; Thomas E. Miller, Auburn University; David M. Moore, Virginia Polytechnic Institute and State University; Margaret L. Moore, Oregon State University; Janet Parker, University of Louisville; Charles Parson, Bemidji State University; Scott Stevens, George Mason University; Joanne Urrutia, Dade County Public Schools; Sandy Wagner; Robert Wall, Towson State University; Robert Wiedermann, Corpus Christi State University; Herbert Wills III, Florida State University; and N. Wood, Pan American University.

Thanks to those who allowed us to photograph students, teachers, facilities, and equipment: Moore Elementary School, Tallahassee, Florida; Pineview Elementary School, Tallahassee, Florida; Sears School, Kenilworth, Illinois; Cobb Middle School, Tallahassee, Florida; Florida State University, Tallahassee, Florida; National College of Education, Evanston, Illinois; and Computerland of Tallahassee, Florida.

Thanks to the people at Wadsworth who shaped the book: Frank Ruggirello, Pat Brewer, James Chadwick, Irene Imfeld, Detta Penna, and Fannie Toldi.

Introduction

▶ ▲ ◀ ▼ ▶ ▲ ◀ ▼ ▶ ▲ ◀ ▼ ▶ ▲ ◀ ▼ ▶ ▲ ◀ ▼ ▶ ▲

> When confronted with a new gadget, a new dance step, a new idea . . . first, relate what is new and to be learned to something you already know. Second, take what is new and make it your own. Make something new with it, play with it, build with it. [Papert, 1980, p. 120]

Welcome to computer education! Computers are becoming a major part of school settings. These new "gadgets" offer much potential for education. By using prepared computer materials and developing their own computer programs, students can learn content. They can also learn about computers and the influences of technology on our society. They can learn to use the computer as an effective tool. Using Papert's words, students can learn to experiment, make something new, play with it, and build with it.

As high technology rapidly changes our society, new skills will be needed for successful adaptation. One of these skills, programming the computer, can help shape thinking. Through learning to program, students can learn to control machines, and in the process learn to develop problem-solving, logical-thinking, and visualization abilities.

This is a book about computers; it is also a book about learning. We believe that the best way to learn is through experience and exploration of various ideas, such as through *writing* programs or *using* available software. One of the features of computers is their interactive nature, with immediate feedback. Throughout this book, we encourage you to use the immediate feedback: try out various ideas as you read.

We stress use of computer graphics and development of problem-solving processes. We use computer graphics to make ideas concrete and to develop your ability to make mental images. You control and manipulate the graphics displays. In some cases, you construct the graphics through programming the computer; in others, you manipulate already prepared software.

To develop content and principles, such as effective ways of using simulation or visualization materials, we provide activities and then analyze these learning experiences. We encourage you to participate in the activities. Experiment, conjecture, build knowledge. To make the best use of the book, plan to spend adequate time at the computer.

The book has three parts. Part One helps you gain control of the computer through programming and problem solving. Part One teaches you to do these tasks:

1. Program the computer through Logo
2. Identify a variety of programming concepts
3. Illustrate approaches to teaching programming concepts
4. Describe a philosophy for a learning environment
5. Describe the problem-solving process, identify a variety of problem-solving strategies, and develop your own problem-solving abilities
6. Develop some simple microworlds

Part Two explores educational tool uses of the computer, including the following:

1. Word processor
2. Database
3. Spreadsheet
4. Telecommunications
5. Graphics packages
6. Desktop publishing
7. Integrated software

Part Three is designed to explore educational software applications of the computer. Part Three teaches you to do this:

1. Identify types of instructional programs and effective ways of using them
2. Identify ways of using the computer for management
3. Evaluate software
4. Describe the influence of technology on society, and other trends and issues in computer education

Getting Started

This is a book about computers, so we will first examine a computer and its parts. If you have available *Know Your Apple* by Muse Software, place it into the **disk drive,** as shown in Figures 1 and 6. (This program is available in two versions,

Figure 1 *Sample computer systems: (a) Apple IIe, (b) Apple IIc, and (c) Apple IIGS.*

▼

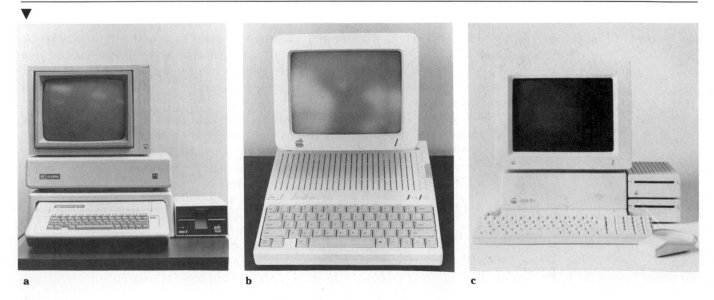

a   b   c

a

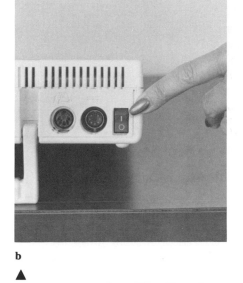

b

c

▲

Figure 2 *On/off switches with (a) back of Apple IIc, (b) pointing to on/off switch for Apple IIc, and (c) back of Apple II + and IIe with on/off switch.*

Figure 3 *Main menu of Know Your Apple IIe shows the Apple system.*

▼

Figure 4 *The monitor is displayed by the Know Your Apple program.*

▼

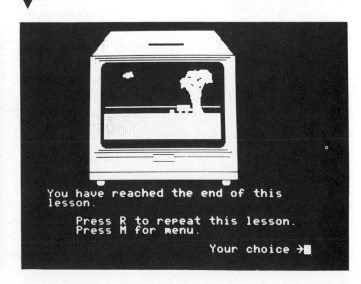

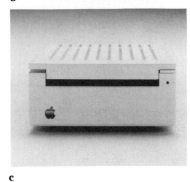

▲

Figure 5 *Sample high resolution display from Know Your Apple program.*

▲

Figure 6 *Disk drives (a) for Apple II + and IIe, (b) for Apple IIc (on the side of the machine), and (c) 3½-inch disk drive for Apple IIe/GS, (d) 5¼-inch and 3½-inch disks.*

one for the Apple II + and one for the Apple IIe. We will describe the essential ideas from this program in case you do not have it available.) If you are using the Apple IIGS, a copy of *Your Tour of the Apple IIGS* should be available. You might choose to use this program here. To get the program running, turn on the computer; Figure 2 shows the **on/off switch** for the Apple.

Now follow the discussion that appears on the screen. For those who do not have the disk, Figure 3 shows the screen displaying a picture of the Apple system. You see a **display** of the information shown by the computer on the **monitor** (Figure 4), an **output device.** The monitor will show both words and pictures. The pictures may be drawn with large dots, small dots, or very small dots (**super-high resolution**), as in the Apple IIGS. The pictures may be **static** (still) or **dynamic** (have moving parts). Figure 5 shows a high resolution picture.

Figure 6a shows a **floppy disk** (on the bottom) and a disk drive (on the top). The floppy disk (sometimes called a *diskette*) is a 5¼-inch square piece of plastic with a paper cover on which the program is stored. Figure 6b shows the disk drive for the Apple IIc, and Figure 6c shows a 3½-inch disk drive, which takes smaller disks. The smaller disk, as in Figure 6d, has a harder plastic surface and can store more data. The disk drive reads information from and records information on the floppy disk.

The typewriterlike part of the computer is called a **keyboard** (Figure 7). The keyboard is used to **input** information to the computer and to give it instructions. The keyboard is much like that of a typewriter. There are, however, some extra keys. On the right, in the second row up, is a critical key called the <RETURN> key. This is important because it allows you to transmit information to the computer. When in doubt, press <RETURN>. On the left, in the second row up, is the <CTRL> key. This key sometimes has special functions. When you use this key with another key, for example, <C>, you hold down the <CTRL> key while you press the <C> key. (This combination is written <CTRL-C>.) Also, note the <ESC> key (top row of the keyboard) that sometimes has a special purpose. It can be used to escape from a program or to erase typed characters. When you are finished with

Figure 7 *Keyboards for (a)
Apple II +, (b) Apple IIe, (c)
Apple IIc, and (d) Apple IIGS,
emphasizing* <RETURN> *key,*
<SPACE BAR>, *and*
<CONTROL> *key.*

this program, turn the machine off, take the disk out of the disk drive, and place the disk back in its cover.

If you have the *Apple Presents Apple* available, now is a good time to work with it as a keyboard tutorial. To use it, place it in the disk drive, turn on the computer, and follow the instructions given in the program.

Developing Thinking Processes through the Activities

Thinking processes can be developed through use of the activities in this book. These sections focus on problem solving, visualization/imagery development, and logical thinking. Because research indicates that many adults never reach the formal operations stage, activities in this book are specifically designed to help students progress in their intellectual development from concrete operations to early formal operations. A brief discussion of each of the three thinking processes follows.

Problem Solving

The major emphasis throughout these activities is on problem solving. We select a few problem-solving strategies and develop activities focusing on them. Because the concept of problem solving is broader than any specific subject area, we also apply these strategies to different subject areas. Students should thus learn to employ the strategies in a variety of settings. We emphasize these problem-solving strategies:

Working backward
Using a model
Estimating, predicting, and projecting (as through controlling variables)
Looking for a pattern or sequence
Decomposing (breaking things down) and recombining (organizing into new patterns)
Relating to a similar problem
Organizing and systematizing information (for example, systematic trial and error; and gathering, organizing, and representing data)

Before students apply these strategies, they must understand what the strategies involve. Some examples of these strategies follow.

Working Backward   When working backward, a person knows an end result but not how that result was obtained. For example, the end result may be a picture, a story, or a game. The thinking process involves backtracking through the sequence of events that led to the end result. See activities such as PATTERNS IN PICTURES and TRANSFORMING SHAPES.

Using a Model   Models aid students in making abstract ideas concrete. Learning how to develop and use models also builds foundations for thinking, learning, and problem solving through visualization and imagery. Examples of models are physical representations, maps, and graphs. See activities in POLYGONS TO CIRCLES and PATTERNS IN PICTURES.

Estimating, Predicting, and Projecting   Estimating, predicting, and projecting help students go beyond available data in these ways: by estimating measures of physical properties, such as length, area, volume, weight, and time; by estimating rates of change, such as speed; and by observing changes in variables, to yield predictable behavior. See POLYGONS TO CIRCLES.

Looking for a Pattern or Sequence   Patterning and sequencing are basic forms in which information is organized. They involve observing and extending existing patterns and sequences, and creating new ones. Students should be encouraged to look for patterns around them. Patterns exist in nature, in language, even in abstract structures, such as mathematics. See POLYGONS TO CIRCLES.

Decomposing and Recombining   Decomposing and recombining are basic to the understanding of structured programming. A picture can be broken into its component parts, and analysis of and design for each part given. The parts can then be recombined to form new structures that achieve a goal. Similarly, the process of composing a story can be broken into component ideas (as in an outline); each idea is developed as a subtheme, then those are recombined to form the total story. See ROBOT and EYES.

Relating to a Similar Problem   Given a difficult problem to solve, you can relate it to a similar but less complex problem. Once the original problem is compared to a related problem, the solution often becomes much easier to find. See activities such as POLYGONS TO CIRCLES and PROBLEM SOLVING.

Organizing and Systematizing Information   Strategies of systematic organization of data are important problem-solving processes. These strategies include gathering data, organizing the data into tables or charts, representing the data in some kind of a graph, and using the data to project additional information. See PETS WE HAVE AT HOME; WHAT'S IN A NAME; LETTERS IN WORDS AND SENTENCES; TV VIEWING; FOOD, CALORIE, AND NUTRITION; ORGANIZING DATA FOR SPREADSHEETS; and CODE CONTEST.

As the world's knowledge and use of technology grows, organizational strategies will greatly increase in importance. Currently, databases that hold all kinds of information are being formed. The more we know how to access that information and apply it, the more we gain command of the information explosion in process. Students need to be prepared for the future.

Visualization/Imagery Development

Visualization and imagery development should be experienced, not presented abstractly. Effective visualization and imagery development involve participation, a feeling of joining together between the person and the object being visualized. Research indicates that reasoning about sizes, shapes, and actions, is faster and more accurate when done in terms of images, and that abstract thought and logical deduction are performed faster and more accurately in terms of images and concepts. A number of aspects of visualization and imagery development follow, many of which involve working with models.

Transformations and Imagery   The concept of transformations is very important in discussions of imagery. Transformations include translation (slide), rotation (turn), reflection (flip), dilation (stretch or shrink), reversibility, and change of perspective. A brief explanation of each term follows.

A *translation* is a "slide" along a direction for a given distance. A chair can slide across the room; a pencil can slide across a table; an ice cube can slide across your back—these are all examples of translation.

Rotation is the turning of an object about a fixed point. In early stages, a child might not be conscious of a point's remaining fixed. Experiences can enhance awareness of this center and amount of rotation.

A *reflection* or "flip" is a mirror image of an object. The object is "flipped" about a line.

Dilating is making a figure larger or smaller. The object keeps the same shape but changes size.

Doing and undoing is related to *reversibility*. Examples include the following: coming into a room, then backing out of the room along the path of entry; putting objects together, then taking them apart into the same pieces; stretching and shrinking; turning left, then turning back right; going forward and going back; adding an amount, then subtracting it. Reversibility is the total undoing of action or thought, achieved by traversing the same path in reverse order and ending in the original state.

Projection, changing perspective, and *zooming* all affect our views of physical objects. Altered projection provides a different view; for instance, with one dimension hidden in shadows. A changing perspective views objects from different vantage points. Zooming is the moving closer to or farther away from an object.

Images developed through experiences with these physical actions become the vehicles for reflections on or anticipation of actions or thought. For examples of the concepts of transformations discussed here, see TRANSFORM, SHAPE CON-STRUCTION SET, and PATTERNS IN PICTURES.

Other Aspects of Imagery   Several related aspects of imagery are also considered.

To understand imagery, first differentiate between static and dynamic imagery. *Static imagery* describes only what is visible at one time. *Dynamic imagery* on the other hand uses transformations; in particular, *reversibility* of thought. The more easily a person can apply transformations of thought, the more flexible the thinking can be.

Another important aspect of imagery is the difference between reflective and anticipatory imagery. *Reflective imagery* is the image(s) derived from actions already completed, whereas *anticipatory imagery* is the image(s) arising from the thought "What will happen if." Ideally, people would have an active anticipatory imagery. People should also develop backup strategies to help them when they cannot imagine "What will happen if." Try examining concrete situations, to see what will happen in specific cases, then try to imagine "What will happen if."

Closely related to imagery and visualization is the intellectual development of *spatial* and *geometric concepts*. In studying transformational geometry, one should take care not to focus on regular shapes too early; rather, concentrate first on irregular shapes and their transformations. Then the transformations of regular shapes will be easier for students to comprehend.

Another aspect of spatial and geometric visualization is the relationship between number systems and points in space. Understanding underlying coordinate systems is important for elementary and middle school students. In this book, activities related to transformations start with a synthetic approach (with less emphasis on the underlying coordinate system); see the SHAPE CONSTRUCTION SET or TRANS-FORM (*Applications Disk*). TURTLE TRANSFORMATIONS uses Logo, with a "local-ized" polar system whose center or origin is the turtle's location on the screen; locations change by forward and back moves and right and left turns.

Other important parts of this imagery development are the concepts of chang-ing sizes and perspectives. Activities involving these concepts can promote under-standing of ratio and proportion. Consider TRANSFORM and SHAPE CONSTRUC-TION SET.

To *communicate* about the images in their minds, students can (1) draw pic-tures about the images, (2) write or tell stories about the images, or (3) discriminate or select one picture (from several) that best represents the picture in their minds. Such communication can also help sharpen the images.

Research has indicated that *explicit treatment* of imagery, that is, having the students become distinctly aware of the pictures in their minds, enhances the development of imagery. We strongly encourage you to have your students write, talk, and draw pictures about the images in their minds. If they do not have clear pictures in their minds, encourage them to illustrate their ideas through sketches or models.

Ideally, by manipulating their dynamic images, people should be able to antic-ipate future actions and relationships, and to illustrate these images through a variety of communications. The activities in this book can help students to develop such thinking processes.

Logical Thinking

Logical thinking is one of the ultimate goals of education. Much can be done to help students develop logical thinking. Several aspects of logical thinking are briefly described here.

Patterning   Being able to perceive abstract relationships generated through patterns is one feature of logical thinking. Students need to be able to identify unfamiliar patterns, extend existing patterns, and create new ones. Activities that examine patterning include GUESS MY RULE, WORD FORMING GAME, and FINDING THE BIG PICTURE.

Sequencing   The sequencing of events, ideas, objects, or programming lines, is another important part of logical thinking. A number of activities, such as SENT and WORS can aid your students in this area.

Logical Connectives   The use of logical connectives is crucial to logical thinking. Logical connectives are words, such as *and* and *or,* that join together two or more sentences. One type of logical connective is conjunctive thinking (*and*). Conjunctive thinking is the consideration of the dependency of an outcome on two (or more) events; that is, event A *and* B happens only when both event A and event B happen, or statement A and B is true only if both statement A and statement B are true.

Another type of logical connective is disjunctive thinking (use of *or*). Disjunctive thinking is considering the outcome when only one of two (or more) events happens; that is, event A *or* B happens if either event A or event B happens.

Conditional Thinking   Conditional thinking is the consideration that something will happen or be true under certain conditions. For example, consider "If the weather is nice, then we will have a picnic." Suppose the weather is nice. Then it is reasonable to conclude that we will have a picnic. If we do not have a picnic, we then could conclude that the weather is not nice. See PROBLEM SOLVING.

Actual programming experiences relate closely with logical thinking and are important to the understanding of sequencing, quantifiers, logical connectives, and conditional sentences. To get desired results, the student must be analytical about the order in which the computer processes the statements. If a program is out of sequence, the expected results might not occur. The immediate feedback capability of the computer greatly enhances this understanding.

Thinking Processes and Computers

Technology opens the doors to many exciting ideas and concepts that you can actively explore with your students. These ideas include the following:

1. Images (both mental and graphic) can be manipulated. See TRANSFORM and SHAPE CONSTRUCTION SET (*Applications Disk*), TEDDY BEAR, and THE FACTORY.
2. Data are manipulable and retrievable. See activities in SHAPE CONSTRUCTION SET, FINDING THE BIG PICTURE, WHAT'S IN A NAME, and ELECTRONIC SCAVENGER HUNT.
3. Variables are powerful and useful. See activities in Chapter 2.
4. Ratio and proportion can help explain the world about us (in graphics as well as in data). See TRANSFORM and SHAPE CONSTRUCTION SET, and exercises that involve spreadsheet experiences, projecting into the future, or interpreting from existing data.
5. Top-down design (the generation of big ideas, with smaller ideas within big ideas) helps develop analytic and synthetic abilities. See FINDING THE BIG PICTURE, PATTERNS IN PICTURES, and the work with games in Logo and BASIC.

6. Programming in itself can be a microworld rich with potential for integrating many of these thinking processes. Many of these activities provide seeds for such microworlds.

7. Algorithm formation is at the heart of the effective use of computers. One of the strengths of a computer is its ability to follow an algorithm, or set of instructions, tirelessly and ceaselessly. The best application of the human mind to the computer is the discovery of such algorithms and the writing of procedures that the computer can follow. Tools for discovering such algorithms are the processes we have listed in discussions of problem solving, visualization, and logical thinking. Through use of these processes, students can formulate algorithms, for which they can then construct procedures.

We hope that you can make use of the ideas in this book. We also hope that your students grow in their knowledge of technology and learn to make effective use of their thinking processes.

Important Terms

<CTRL>	floppy disk	monitor
disk drive	high resolution	on/off switch
display	input	output device
dynamic	keyboard	<RETURN>
<ESC>	low resolution	static

Part One

Controlling the Machine

▶ ▲ ◀ ▼ ▶ ▲ ◀ ▼ ▶ ▲ ◀ ▼ ▶ ▲ ◀ ▼ ▶ ▲ ◀ ▼ ▶ ▲

Computers are now a center of attention in most schools. It is important that you, as a teacher, be familiar and comfortable with computers in the classroom. Part One of this book will teach you how to gain control of the computer through programming and problem solving. You need to gain control of the machine for two reasons. First, you cannot effectively use the machine if you cannot control it. Second, your students, who also will want to have control of the machine, will look to you for advice and answers to their questions.

You gain control of a computer in two ways: by programming it and by understanding how it works.

In the next four chapters, you will learn a computer language: Logo. Logo is designed to help young students program, but it has many applications for people of all ages. Logo presents a good model for a programming language and is a good language with which to start your programming.

Our approach is to introduce programming through the computer's graphics capabilities, so that you can easily visualize programming concepts. We emphasize hands-on experimentation and investigation. We will also introduce you to text processing.

Chapters 1 through 3 examine the philosophy and logic systems of Logo. Chapter 4 elaborates on problem-solving exercises you have already begun, and thereby extends your problem-solving capabilities considerably.

Chapter 1

Introduction to Logo

► ▼ ◄ ▲ ► ▼ ◄ ▲ ► ▼ ◄ ▲ ► ▼ ◄ ▲ ► ▼ ◄ ▲ ► ▼ ◄

Objectives

► Operate the computer equipment
► Write and edit Logo programs using turtlegraphics commands
► Use turtlegraphics to draw geometric shapes and patterns
► Describe the philosophy of Logo
► Describe an appropriate Logo classroom environment
► Describe strategies for teaching Logo in the classroom

You are entering the world of computers. This world of computers has many entrances. The first entrance we will use is programming the computer through Logo. Logo is a computer language created to help young children program computers. Logo is a powerful educational language that can help people of all ages to learn many of the processes involved in gaining effective control over the machine.

A major feature of Logo is its graphics capabilities. Students usually are highly motivated to work with graphics. By developing graphics procedures, students learn to program computers, as well as to develop problem-solving, logical-thinking, and spatial-visualization processes. You, their teacher, will want to develop these processes so that you can enjoy teaching them to your students. Hence, we will give you problems to investigate and explore, just as you will later give your students.

Like the English language, the Logo language is a tool for thinking and expressing ideas. To tell a computer what to draw, you must first visualize what you want drawn. You must plan the sequence of steps needed to accomplish your goal. Then to communicate with the computer, you must use words it understands. As you try out your program, you may need to revise your plans. Notice that the processes used in planning, writing, and revising a computer program are very similar to the processes used in writing a report or solving a mathematics problem. These processes can be applied to solve a wide variety of problems. But to use these processes, you first need to know the language.

A **programming language** is a medium of communication between you and the computer. For the computer to understand your instructions, you must use a well-defined vocabulary of **commands.** The set of rules that apply to the use of this vocabulary is called the language's **syntax.** In this chapter, you will learn a set of commands (also called **primitives** in Logo) and will logically sequence them.

◄ ▲ ► ▼ ◄ ▲ ► ▼ ◄ ▲ ► ▼ ◄ ▲ ► ▼ ◄ ▲ ► ▼ ◄ ▲ ►

That sequence, the program, will direct the computer to perform certain tasks, such as drawing shapes, patterns, and pictures. You will then examine the philosophy and instructional strategies of Logo.

If this is your first experience with an Apple computer system, refer to Appendix A for information about proper use of the equipment. Then load the Logo language disk in the disk drive and turn on the computer. If all goes well, you should see a screen display like one in Figure 1. Throughout the Logo discussions there are six versions of Logo: Terrapin (including Logo Plus), Krell, Apple Logo, Logo II, and LogoWriter. Terrapin, Logo Plus, and Krell are MIT versions and are very similar. Apple Logo, Logo II, and LogoWriter are LCSI (Logo Computer Systems Incorporated) products and are fairly similar. As variations occur, they are indicated in the text.

Exploring with Turtlegraphics—
Direct Mode

Your study of Logo will begin with **turtlegraphics.** The word *turtlegraphics* comes from work at the Massachusetts Institute of Technology Artificial Intelligence Laboratory, in which a small turtle-shaped robot, following directions given to it through a computer, moved around on the floor. Figure 2 shows a form of the equipment used.

Children could tell the robot to go forward, turn right, and so on. The robot had a pen that it could raise or lower to draw pictures. Instead of a turtle robot, you now have a turtle represented on the video screen by a triangle. To move the turtle around on the screen, you give it commands such as FORWARD, BACK, RIGHT, and LEFT. The commands given here are for the Terrapin and Krell versions of Logo. When the Apple Logo command is different, it is shown in brackets. Box 1 suggests some typing hints.

First, type

    DRAW   [Apple Logo: CLEARSCREEN or CS, LogoWriter: CG for ClearGraphics]

and press <RETURN>. This command clears the screen and displays the triangular turtle. Next type

    FORWARD 50

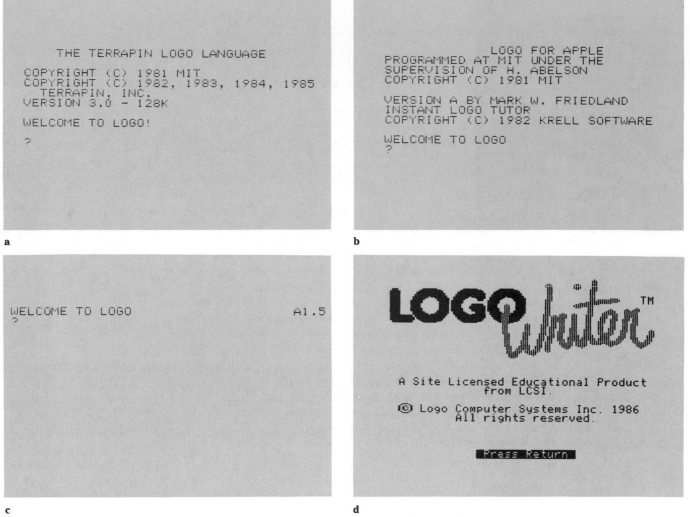

```
           THE TERRAPIN LOGO LANGUAGE                                    LOGO FOR APPLE
                                                      PROGRAMMED AT MIT UNDER THE
   COPYRIGHT (C) 1981 MIT                             SUPERVISION OF H. ABELSON
   COPYRIGHT (C) 1982, 1983, 1984, 1985              COPYRIGHT (C) 1981 MIT
      TERRAPIN, INC.
   VERSION 3.0 - 128K                                VERSION A BY MARK W. FRIEDLAND
                                                      INSTANT LOGO TUTOR
   WELCOME TO LOGO!                                  COPYRIGHT (C) 1982 KRELL SOFTWARE

   ?                                                 WELCOME TO LOGO
                                                      ?
```

a   b

```
   WELCOME TO LOGO                          A1.5
   ?
```

c   d

▲
_____

Figure 1 Screen display after
first booting up, or loading, the
Logo language: (a) Terrapin, (b)
Krell, (c) Apple Logo, and (d)
LogoWriter.

and press <RETURN>. You should get a display like the one in Figure 3. The 50
represents the distance (or units) the turtle traveled. We say the turtle moved
forward 50 turtle steps. Now type

    RIGHT 90   [abbreviated RT 90]

and press <RETURN>. Observe that in this book we are using brackets [ ] to enclose
a remark statement. You should see the turtle turn 90 degrees to the right. If you
had typed RIGHT 60 instead, the turtle would have turned 60 degrees. Next type

    FORWARD 50   [abbreviated FD 50]

and again press <RETURN>. (In the future, remember to press <RETURN> after
each statement.) You should now have a display like the one shown in Figure 4.
Continue making a square using the two commands, FORWARD and RIGHT.
(Remember to press <RETURN> at the end of each line.) Now type

    DRAW <RETURN>   [Apple Logo: CS <RETURN>, LogoWriter: CG <RETURN>]

▲

Figure 2 *Robot turtle moving around on the floor.*

Figure 3 *FD 50.*

Box 1   **Typing Hints**
1. Spaces are important in Logo. The turtle understands FD 50 but not FD50.
2. Be sure to press <RETURN> at the end of each line.
3. There is a big difference between the *number* 0 (zero) and *letter* O (oh). Often the number is written with a slash, 0, to distinguish it from the letter; this is especially true in computer manuals. Similarly, do not type the *letter* l (lowercase el) when you intend the *number* 1 (one).
4. To correct a typing mistake, backspace by using <ESC> (in Apple Logo and LogoWriter, left arrow ←; in LogoWriter the <DELETE> key erases the characters to the left).

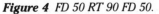

Figure 4 *FD 50 RT 90 FD 50.*

to erase the video screen and place the turtle back in the center. Now make a square that is 75 units on each side.

Remember that Logo commands are called primitives. Experiment with the primitives in Table 1. Try using large numbers. Try using negative numbers. Try using an unfamiliar word. Try PENUP and draw something. Try PENDOWN and draw something. Try to draw the letter *A*. Make your own shapes and designs. Then try to draw the pictures shown in Figure 5. If your drawing does not appear the way you expected, clear the screen with DRAW (CS, in Apple Logo; CG in LogoWriter) and try again.

Note that when a line of instructions is typed and <RETURN> is pressed, an action occurs on the screen, such as the turtle's moving or turning. This direct interaction is called the direct or immediate mode because each command is executed or processed as soon as <RETURN> is pressed. Direct mode is particularly helpful in your building an intuition about how commands behave.

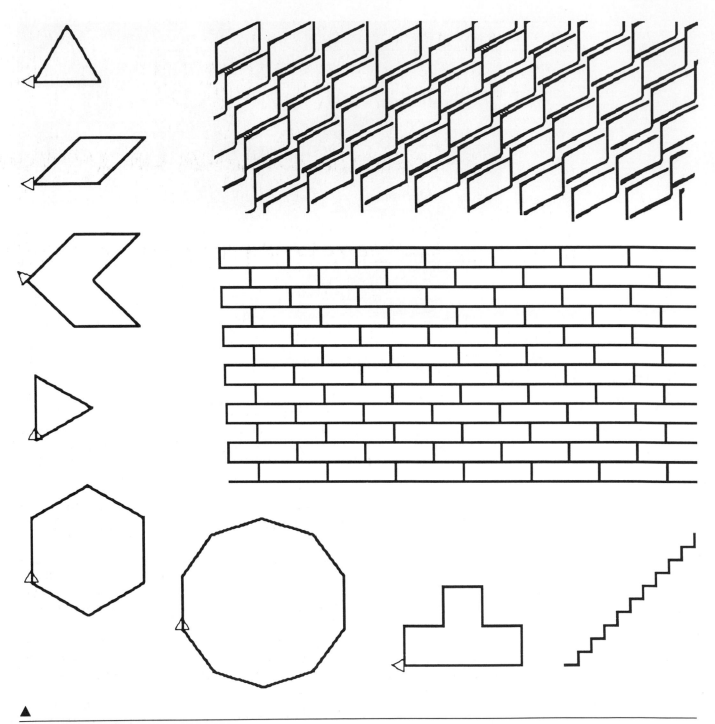

Figure 5 *Figures for you to develop.*

One advantage of direct mode is that commands are executed immediately. However, a disadvantage is that in order to vary similar commands, you must retype the entire program, as when you draw a series of squares with different side measures. Another disadvantage of direct mode is that the program cannot be saved for later use. Appendix C discusses methods of saving programs for Terrapin/Krell and Apple Logo. Appendix D discusses saving programs in LogoWriter. Appendix E discusses special features of Logo Plus.

Table 1   Some Logo Primitives

Primitive	Abbreviation	Example of Use
DRAW (CS in Apple Logo; CG in LogoWriter)	—	DRAW (CS in Apple Logo; CG in LogoWriter)
FORWARD	FD	FD 50
BACK	BK	BK 50
RIGHT	RT	RT 90
LEFT	LT	LT 90
PENUP	PU	PU
PENDOWN	PD	PD
HIDETURTLE	HT	HT
SHOWTURTLE	ST	ST
HOME	HOME	HOME

Exploring with Turtlegraphics—
Indirect Mode

An alternative to direct mode is **indirect** or programming **mode.** The indirect mode is used to write a set of instructions (a procedure) that is stored in the computer's memory for later execution. In order to use this mode, you must first give your procedure a *name*. Type

TO *name* or EDIT *name*   [where *name* is what you wish to call your procedure; for example, TO SQUARE; to flip the page for Logo-Writer, use < ⌂ -F> for Apple* or <CTRL-F> for IBM]

This will take you into the screen editor for Terrapin or Krell Logo, where you will move from direct mode, as in Figure 6b, to the edit mode, as in Figure 6c. (If you are using Apple Logo, the > prompt will appear, which indicates that you are defining a procedure outside the screen editor, as in Figure 6a. In Apple Logo, to enter the screen editor, type EDIT "SQ.)

Once you are in the screen editor you can construct procedures, or change them by adding and deleting information. The portion you will be changing will be wherever the cursor or blinking light is. (Ways of moving the cursor up, down, left, and right are discussed in Appendix B.)

After you have written your procedure you will *define* the procedure. This is done by typing <CTRL-C> which then takes you outside the screen editor. (In Apple Logo, the procedure is defined by typing END <RETURN>. In LogoWriter you must again flip the page to leave the editor and define the procedure.)

Students sometimes get confused as to where they do what. This should help you remember: for Terrapin or Krell Logo, procedures are *constructed* or modified inside the editor. They are defined by leaving the editor. The procedures are *executed* outside the editor, or back in the direct mode. (See Figure 6.) LogoWriter uses the concept of flipping the page to enter and to leave the editor.

You now know how to get into and out of the editor, so you can learn how to write a procedure in the editor. A **procedure** is a set of instructions that tells the

*The symbol ⌂ will be used for <Open-Apple>. Thus, ⌂ -F means <Open-Apple-F>.

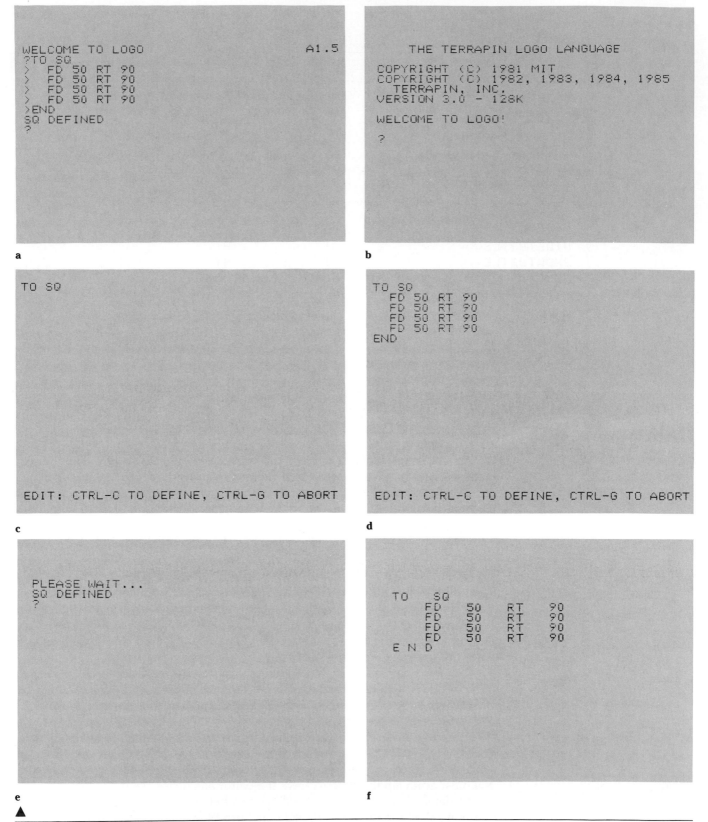

Figure 6 *Screen displays for writing a procedure called SQ in Logo for the different versions of Logo: (a) a procedure can be written in Apple Logo without entering the screen editor; (b) in Terrapin or Krell Logo, you must first enter the screen editor by typing either TO SQ or EDIT SQ (to enter the editor for the Apple Logo, type EDIT "SQ); (c) the beginning of a procedure once you have entered the editor; (d) a procedure is now written, press <CTRL-C> to define; (e) SQ is now defined (Terrapin, Krell, Apple); and (f) SQ is defined on the flip side for LogoWriter.*

computer what to do. In Logo, a procedure always starts with the word TO followed by the name of the procedure, which you create. The name must begin with a letter, have no blank spaces, and not be a Logo primitive. For example, type

```
TO SQUARE <RETURN>          [At the end of the line, press <RETURN>. On the
                            next lines, first press <SPACE BAR> a few times to
                            indent—this makes the procedure more readable.]
    FD 50                   [Remember FD is the abbreviation for FORWARD.]
    RT 90                   [RT is abbreviation for RIGHT.]
    FD 50
    RT 90
    FD 50
    RT 90
    FD 50
    RT 90
END                         [Apple Logo: A procedure always finishes with END
                            or END <RETURN>.]
```

After you finish typing a procedure in Terrapin Logo, you must define the procedure: hold down <CTRL> and press <C> (<CTRL-C>) (for Apple Logo, type END <RETURN> or flip the page for LogoWriter). You should now see SQUARE DEFINED! on the screen. Now type

```
SQUARE <RETURN>
```

A square like the one you created in the procedure will be drawn.

You can put more than one command on a line. Hence, the above program could be abbreviated as

```
TO SQUARE
    FD 50 RT 90
    FD 50 RT 90
    FD 50 RT 90
    FD 50 RT 90
END
```

Note also that the pattern FD 50 RT 90 was repeated four times. The REPEAT command shortens the program even more:

```
TO SQUARE
    REPEAT 4 [FD 50 RT 90]    [Use <SHIFT-N> for the left bracket and
                              <SHIFT-M> for the right bracket on Apple
                              II+.]
END
```

The number of times that the statements or commands inside the brackets are repeated must be designated by a whole number larger than 0, after the command REPEAT. On the Apple II +, the <[> symbol is created by <SHIFT-N> (hold down <SHIFT> and press <N>), and the <]> symbol is created by <SHIFT-M>. On the Apple IIe/IIGS, the brackets are on the keyboard. (Careful: <SHIFT-[> on the Apple IIe may display a left bracket on the video screen, but the computer will read it as an error; be sure not to press <SHIFT>.)

To run this program, first exit from the Logo editor: <CTRL-C> (or END <RETURN> in Apple Logo). After the screen displays SQUARE DEFINED, type

```
SQUARE <RETURN>
```

If the display does not show the correct figure, you need to start troubleshooting. The problem may be that you did not type the information correctly. One nice feature of computers is that typing errors usually can be corrected relatively easily, as is discussed in Appendix B for the Logo editor. Appendix D discusses LogoWriter.

Exploring Shapes and Patterns

Now that you know how to use the editor and write some simple procedures, try using turtlegraphics to make (define) various shapes and patterns. Before reading further, try drawing an equilateral triangle. Many people encounter a problem when they turn RIGHT 60 to make a triangle; try it. The result is shown in Figure 7. The RIGHT 60 command does not work, so can you think of another possible candidate? If you were to walk a path forming an equilateral triangle, what degree of turns would you need to make?

To clear the screen use the CLEARSCREEN (CS) primitive, which leaves the turtle in the last location. To move the turtle to the center of the screen, use the HOME primitive. The DRAW primitive combines both the HOME and the CLEAR-SCREEN (for Apple Logo, CLEAN; for LogoWriter, CG) commands. (CS sends the turtle HOME and clears the screen in Apple Logo.)

To move the turtle on the screen without leaving a trail, use the PENUP or PU primitive. This lifts the turtle's pen. To place the pen back down, use PENDOWN or PD. Now, to move back to the center, use the DRAW command, then use the PU and PD commands to make three triangles on the screen.

To draw the triangle, you can use the following

```
TO TRIANGLE                          [Remember to press <RETURN> even
                                     though we will stop telling you every
                                     time.]
    REPEAT 3 [FD 50 RT 120]
END
```

Now make a regular hexagon (six-sided figure with all sides and all angles of the same measure)

```
TO HEXAGON
    REPEAT 6 [FD 50 RT 60]
END
```

You can generate a regular polygon with side measure of 50 with the following, where _ is the number of sides

Figure 7 *Screen display of FD 50 RT 60 FD 50, a common error people make when trying to draw an equilateral triangle.*

▼

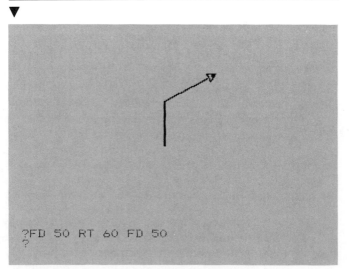

```
?FD 50 RT 60 FD 50
?
```

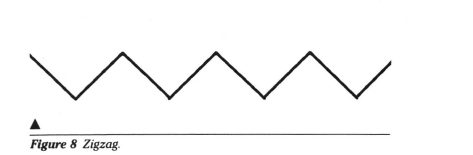

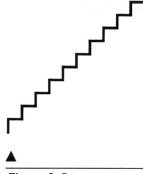

Figure 8 *Zigzag.*

Figure 9 *Steps.*

```
TO POLYGON
    REPEAT _[FD 50 RT 360/_]        [Observe that a new symbol "/" is used,
                                     for divided by.]
END
```

To generate different figures, fill in the blanks with appropriate whole-number values. Try using a 3. Leave the editor. Type

```
POLYGON
```

Return to the editor by typing

```
EDIT POLYGON     [Apple Logo: EDIT "POLYGON, LogoWriter: flip the page]
```

Now put a 4 in each blank. Exit the editor. Type

```
POLYGON
```

Repeat, filling the blanks with 6, 7, and 10.
  Draw different types of patterns. For example, try the procedure,

```
TO ZIGZAG
    RT 45
    REPEAT 15 [FD 49.5 RT 90 FD 49.5 LT 90]
END
```

You should get the pattern shown in Figure 8.
  Or try this procedure

```
TO STEPS
    REPEAT 10 [FD 10 RT 90 FD 10 LT 90]
END
```

This should create a pattern like the one in Figure 9. You should try to look at such a procedure and *predict* the drawing by hand tracing the pattern on a piece of paper. Try to form the habit of predicting the picture before having Logo produce it.

Exploring Colors

Try this procedure

```
TO CROSS
    REPEAT 4 [FD 10 RT 90 FD 10 LT 90 FD 10 RT 90]
```
  [In typing the above line, do not press <RETURN> when you reach the edge of the screen. The computer will automatically "wrap around" the last word to the next line and insert a ! at the right edge of your screen indicating that a line is continued.]
```
END
```

Apple Pen-Colors	
Pen color	**Number**
Black	0
White	1
Green	2
Violet	3
Orange	4
Blue	5
Reverse	6 (not available in Apple Logo)

By adding colors, you can change the appearance of the patterns you design (provided, of course, that you have a color monitor or television). You can change the colors of both the lines and the background. To change the pen's color, use the PENCOLOR (abbreviated as PC; Apple Logo uses SETPC; LogoWriter uses SETC) and a number according to the key shown at left. IBM, however, has four pen-colors and sixteen background colors.

An example might be

```
PC 5          [Apple Logo: SETPC 5, LogoWriter: SETC 5]
CROSS1
```

Now try

```
BG 1          [Apple Logo and LogoWriter: SETBG 1]
PC 5          [Apple Logo: SETPC 5, LogoWriter: SETC 5]
SQUARE
```

BG (or BACKGROUND) allows you to select the color of the background. Explore combinations of the PC (SETPC or SETC) and BG (SETBG) color settings and see which colors you get on the screen and which combinations result in no picture being generated. Some color combinations cause bleeding. When the pen color is the same as the background color, you will not see a picture.

To return to the original white on black, use

```
BG 0          [Apple Logo and LogoWriter: SETBG 0]
PC 1          [Apple Logo: SETPC 1, LogoWriter: SETC 1]
```

Building with Procedures

As we work with Logo, we teach it new procedures. These new procedures are like new words in the vocabulary of Logo, and they are useful for other creative work. We will illustrate this idea. Make sure that you have the procedures *Square* and *Triangle* in memory: to see what procedures are in memory, type POTS for *print out titles* (except for LogoWriter). (Logo uses a **workspace,** which is where Logo keeps track of procedures and variables that you define. Those procedures will stay there until you erase them, turn off the machine, or leave Logo. See Appendix D for LogoWriter.)

Now try to draw the house pictured in Figure 10. Make use of the procedures *Square* and *Triangle* in your drawing.

Once you have finished the house picture, try to build extensions onto your house. Maybe you will wish to add a garage, a door, a window, a chimney, or all of these. Figure 11 shows an example of a house created by extending the original.

It is fun to try to draw new designs. It is also helpful to plan the way in which the new designs will be drawn. First, however, it is a good idea to experiment; you can then organize the results of your experiments into a well-planned sequence.

For example, earlier we drew a cross; now suppose we wish to use SQUARE to draw the cross shown in Figure 12. (If this next procedure is more complex than you are ready for now, come back to it after you have worked through Chapter 2.) You could experiment in this way. First, draw the SQUARE with the turtle in HOME position. Then turn LT 90, and then SQUARE again. This is a good start for a cross design. Observe, however, that the pattern you have generated suggests another way of breaking the cross into parts. Hint: observe that a square is drawn on each side of the original square. You may wish to complete it before reading further.

A square that is drawn to the left (outside) of the original square is what we need. Thus, if we write a procedure *Lsquare* ("square with left turns"), and call it each time we draw a leg of the original square, we will have the cross. (To **call a**

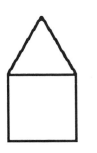

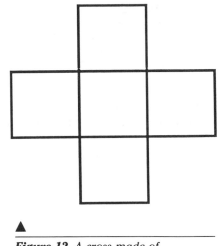

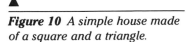

Figure 10 *A simple house made of a square and a triangle.*

Figure 11 *A creative extension to a house.*

Figure 12 *A cross made of squares.*

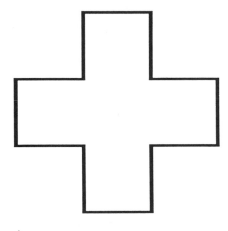

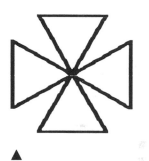

Figure 13 *A cross made without the inside square showing.*

Figure 14 *A cross made of triangles.*

procedure means to tell the computer to use a procedure you have already defined and stored in memory.) LSQUARE provides a clear, simple, and elegant solution

```
TO LSQUARE
    REPEAT 4 [FD 50 LT 90]
END
TO CROSS
    REPEAT 4 [LSQUARE FD 50 RT 90]
END
```

The cross is simply the original SQUARE with LSQUARE inserted at the beginning of each repetition. Once you understand how well LSQUARE works, design a procedure that will generate the same drawing in another way. It is always useful to try doing the same thing in several ways; the next time you need to solve a design problem, one of your alternative approaches may provide the answer. So, first find one solution, then look for more elegant solutions to your problems.

A variation of the cross problem involves attempting to draw the cross without showing the original square. Figure 13 shows such a cross. Develop a number of approaches, and experiment to determine which ones are helpful. Hint: you may use a particular PENCOLOR to help.

Now try another variation: a cross like the one pictured in Figure 14. You might wish to use the similarity of this drawing to the cross made of squares; see if the same approach will work. A slight variation, involving a rotation at the beginning, will be necessary.

Now make drawings of your own choice. See if you can design several creative drawings.

Exploring with Inputs

To get a feeling for **inputs,** be sure you have the Logo language in memory, then insert the *Applications Disk* for *Fundamentals of Computer Education.* (LogoWriter and Logo Plus programs are on the second side of the *Applications Disk.*) Be sure you have LogoWriter in memory, then put the second side of the disk face up into the disk drive and press <ESC>. (Appendixes C and D discuss using Logo programs on the disk.) Type

    READ "HOUSE   [Apple Logo: LOAD "AHOUSE, LogoWriter: use ↑ or ↓ arrow on
                     Contents Page]

The procedure *House* allows for different inputs. To explore this capability, type the name of the procedure, *House,* followed by two numbers, each separated by a space (*House* requires two inputs). For example

    HOUSE 100 50

Now, to see if you can create pictures like those in Figure 15, try other pairs of inputs to *House.* To produce other shapes, also try using different combinations of inputs. After finishing *House,* type: GOODBYE!

Figure 15 *Variations of House with different inputs.*

▼

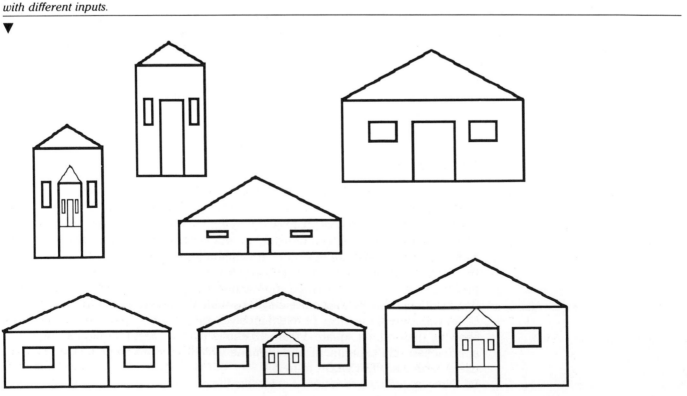

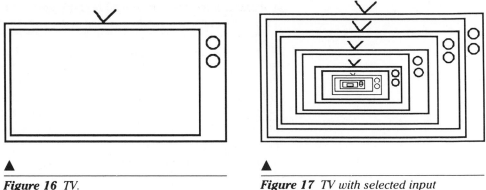

Figure 16 *TV.*

Figure 17 *TV with selected input values illustrating recursion.*

Now explore another procedure that accepts inputs. First type

READ "TV   [Apple Logo: LOAD "ATV, LogoWriter: use ↑ or ↓ arrow on Contents Page]

Now, explore TV as you did *House.* TV also takes two inputs, such as

TV 60 50

See Figure 16 as a potential television set. By using a particular combination of inputs, you can also create a magic television, as pictured in Figure 17.

Logo Philosophy

For many people, Logo is a philosophy of education as well as a programming language. It was created under the direction of Seymour Papert at the Artificial Intelligence Laboratory of the Massachusetts Institute of Technology. The purpose of learning Logo is not to turn the learners into professional computer programmers, but rather for them to use the computer as a tool for developing thinking processes, emphasizing the mind rather than the machine.

We briefly summarize the Logo philosophy; we suggest that you read the complete discussion in Papert (1980) at a convenient time.

Piagetian Orientation

The orientation of Logo grew out of Piaget's theories. Four aspects of these theories are dominant in Logo's characteristics. One is that spatial orientation, considered very important for developing the child's imagery (the pictures in his or her mind), is used in Logo, as the user draws or anticipates pictures on the video screen. The second is that children learn best from their own actions—they learn by doing; in using Logo they make decisions about how pictures are drawn, or explore various ways of drawing pictures. Further, the primitives of Logo are in paired opposites, allowing reversibility and thus inviting experimentation. The third and overall aspect is the constructivist theory, that is, that children learn best through constructing their own knowledge, such as through building their own programs to develop their own designs. The fourth aspect is that a language should live, so that communication is a natural process; Logo meets this requirement as well.

A Language for Exploration

Logo is designed as a language for exploration by all people. The intent is to get students to use the language to experiment, investigate, and form hypotheses for further investigation. For example, in drawing a triangle you first visualize how the turtle turns. You then manipulate the turtlegraphics to form display images that stimulate you to build further mental images. At first your mental images are **reflective;** they are based on what has already happened. Eventually, however, they become **anticipatory;** you can anticipate in your mind what will happen when you try various experiments.

It takes time to form mental images. Be careful not to rush your development of images. Free exploration (the ability to explore without constraint) is a very important part of imagery development. If people are rushed too fast through exploring shapes and spatial relationships, their learning becomes strictly imitative and, therefore, is not constructed. Invest time in careful development of images so that additional learning will be built on a solid foundation of coordinated learning.

Often teachers ask how much free exploration their students should be allowed, and how much students should be shown. Such questions are not easy to answer. The trick is to strike a compromise between offering students appropriate models to follow and allowing free exploration. If people have no models to follow, they do not know where to start. On the other hand, they should be able to change, modify, and create new variations from examples. Ultimately, they should create their own examples.

Student–Teacher Relationship

The relationship between the student and the teacher, using Logo, should be different from that in a more traditional classroom, in which the teacher has well-organized lesson plans for students. When they use computers in a less restrictive manner, students learn through their own investigations rather than through being taught all information. The teacher becomes more of a *facilitator* or resource person rather than the distributor of knowledge. Students often ask teachers questions that the two can, ideally, investigate together. As a teacher, you do not need to know all the answers (sometimes you will not); what you do need to know is how to investigate with the student and how to nurture your students' intellectual development.

Child Controlling Computer versus Computer Controlling Child

Computers can be used for traditional instruction, in which children interact with prepared materials. For example, children might fill in a missing word or number in a sentence or solve an exercise on the screen, much as they would use a workbook. The child's response is virtually controlled by the computer. The computer makes decisions based on the child's response and the programmer's analysis of what the child should do next. In these applications, the computer, not the child, has made the decision.

The intent of Logo is to allow students to make their own decisions: they construct their own pictures and conduct their own investigations. One of the important skills that students need to develop is effective decision making. If someone else always makes decisions for children, children do not learn how to make decisions themselves. Furthermore, students are highly motivated to gain control of the machine by programming it themselves.

Thinking about Thinking

A very important part of Logo is its reflective aspect. You work on a set of experiences and then *reflect* on them, to abstract underlying properties. To manipulate the turtle, you must reflect on your own thinking; this is how you finally figured out how to make a triangle or construct the patterns in Figure 5. The intent of Logo is to make students analyze what has happened, and what will happen under certain conditions, as they construct their own drawings.

The Fallacy of a Right-or-Wrong Environment

Papert (1980) stresses that our society is too right-or-wrong–oriented. This orientation inhibits rather than enhances learning. One of the advantages to programming computers, Papert claims, is that the odds of doing everything correctly the first time are very slim. The important question is not whether the program is *correct,* but whether it is *fixable.* Fixing a program is **debugging,** the process of removing **bugs** or errors from programs. Debugging can be thought of as a form of assimilation and accommodation as described in Piagetian literature. Strategies for debugging are discussed in the next chapter.

Geometry and Turtlegraphics

Some people think that in order to work with Logo, you need to know a lot of geometry; this is not true. On the contrary, Logo is a tool for learning, through investigation, various geometric properties. In our earlier investigations, you learned how to generalize properties of regular polygons. Similar investigations can help you to explore other geometric properties. The intent is not to teach you all of geometry, but to encourage you to develop ways of learning geometry. (Note, however, that Logo's use is not restricted to geometry.) The graphics portion of Logo is a tool for investigating the physical world. Furthermore, physical coordination with geometry in the children's environment may also enhance their understanding of the Logo environment.

Implications for Hemispheric Brain Functioning

The bimodal functioning of the brain is well known. Right-hemisphere functioning is predominantly visual, spatial, holistic, metamorphic, and synthetic; left-hemisphere functioning is predominantly logical, sequential, verbal, and analytical. Many people believe that our schools have been too left-hemisphere–oriented; research has shown, for example, that a number of factors highly correlated with mathematical achievement are strongly right-hemisphere functions (Flake, 1983). (See Chapter 10 for further discussion.)

Logo could be a vehicle for beginning whole-brain development. Children are highly motivated by working with computer graphics. They create pictures in their minds (right-hemisphere activity) that they want to create on the video screen; they use analytic skills to break the picture down into pieces and write programs sequentially (left-hemisphere activity). In the process, they may force communication between the right and left hemispheres.

Strategies for Teaching Logo

A number of people have been successful in teaching Logo to children. A few suggestions for instructional strategies follow.

Playing Turtle: Using Students' Bodies as Models

One method for helping children understand turtle movements is to actually walk out the paths that they want the turtle to follow on the video screen. Much of the computer–child interaction should be second-stage work; that is, they should use Logo after they have had an opportunity to explore similar ideas in real life, such as walking out square or triangular paths. Using perceptual and motor skills can help to develop the child's mental image of an action or behavior such as walking a path.

Explicit Imagery Instruction

Explicitly make your students aware of the pictures that they are forming in their minds. Use finger tracings or body movements to make them aware of how those pictures are formed, and have them talk or write about the pictures in their minds.

Displaying Students' Work

Just as it is important to display children's art work in other settings, it also is important to display their Logo graphics. Appendixes C, D, and E discuss how to load and save programs and pictures, and how to print out saved pictures. After learning to make their own printouts of pictures, students can then display them in the classroom or hallway, on the school bulletin board, or at home. Displaying graphics is extremely important because it creates considerable motivation for students to continue to improve their drawings. Examples of other children's work (and perhaps some of your own) will help them think of new routines to explore.

Using Transparencies

Transparencies can be used in several ways to enhance the concepts in Logo. On a transparency, make a maze that the turtle is to move through. Make a grid of turtle steps that can be placed over the video screen, to help the students initially get a better feeling of the size of the steps.

Figure 18 *Logo compass.*

▼

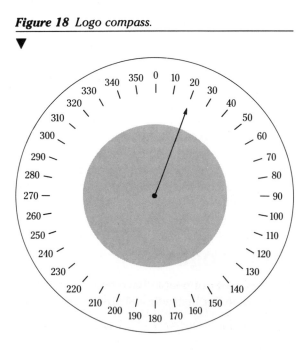

Making a Logo Compass

To make a Logo compass, create a circle and mark off appropriate units (perhaps every 10 degrees). Make a second circle (perhaps of clear plastic) that has one arrow on it pointed from the center in one direction (Figure 18). Fasten the two pieces together in the center with a fastener that will allow for easy movement. Point the arrow in the direction in which the turtle's head is to be pointed. Then move the compass around until the 0 degree is lined up with the turtle's head. The angle in which the turtle should turn is thus identified by the compass. You can construct both a right compass and a left compass.

► ▲ ◄ ▼ ► ▲ ◄ ▼ ► ▲ ◄ ▼ ► ▲ ◄ ▼ ► ▲ ◄ ▼ ► ▲

Summary

This chapter introduced Logo and its philosophy. You used turtlegraphics to make shapes and patterns in both direct and indirect mode. Logo philosophy was discussed, and some instructional strategies for teaching Logo were introduced.

The following procedures were described in this chapter:

Square	*Steps*	*House*
Polygon	*Cross*	*TV*
Zigzag	*Lsquare*	

Important Terms

You should know what each of these terms means when you finish this chapter.

Abort*	<CTRL-X>*	PENCOLOR PC (SET PC) [SETC]
Anticipatory	Debugging	
BACK BK	Define	PENDOWN PD
BACKGROUND BG (SETBG)	Direct mode	PENUP PU
	DRAW (CS) [CG]	Primitive
Bug	EDIT *name* (EDIT "*name*) [♂F]	Procedure
Call		Programming language
CLEARSCREEN CS (CLEAN) [CG]†	END	Reflective
	<ESC> (←) [*delete key*]	REPEAT
Command		RIGHT RT
<CTRL-C> [♂F]‡ (END <RETURN>)	Execute	Syntax
	FORWARD FD	TO
<CTRL-D>* (n.a.)	HOME	TO *name*
<CTRL-G>* [♂S]§	Indirect mode	Turtlegraphics
<CTRL-N>* [↓]	Inputs	→*
<CTRL-P>* [↑]	LEFT LT	←

Exercises

1. Write a procedure that draws a regular octagon (eight-sided figure with all sides having the same measure).

---

*Discussed in Appendixes B and D.

†Commands in [ ] refer to variations for LogoWriter.

‡<CTRL-F> for IBM for LogoWriter.

§<CTRL-Break> for IBM PC or <Fn-Break> for IBM PCjr for LogoWriter.

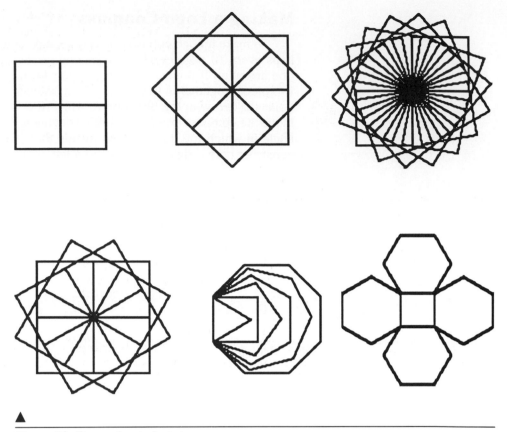

Figure 19 *Figures for students to develop.*

2. Write a procedure that draws a regular pentagon (five-sided figure with all sides having the same measure).

3. Change some of the procedures in this chapter by replacing RT with LT, and LT with RT. What is (are) the result(s)?

4. Change some of the procedures in this chapter by replacing FD with BK, and BK with FD. What is (are) the result(s)?

5. Change some of the procedures in this chapter by making the changes in both Exercise 3 and Exercise 4.

6. Write procedures that draw the patterns shown in Figure 19.

7. What is the difference between a Logo *primitive* and a Logo *procedure*?

8. Explain why the following procedure does not draw an equilateral triangle.

```
TO TRIAN
   REPEAT 3[FD 50 RT 60]
END
```

9. Without using the computer, analyze the following procedure and show what it draws.

```
TO BOXES
   RT 90 PU BK 100 PD
   REPEAT 4 [SQUARE FD 100]
END
```

10. Suppose you are drawing with a white pen color on a black background. You type RT 90 FD 70 LT 90 in the direct mode, and then you change your mind. What can you type to erase that line without erasing the entire screen? (Hint: change the pen color and reverse your steps.)

11. What is the difference between POTS and CATALOG? (See Appendix C.)

12. Insert the *Applications Disk* and type:

> READ "C   [Apple Logo: LOAD "AC, LogoWriter: use ↑ or ↓ arrow for Contents Page]

This will give you a procedure for drawing arcs of a circle when you input two numbers for the radius and number of degrees. For example, try: C 50 60. Explore various combinations of uses of this procedure to make interesting designs.

13. **Making and using shapes.** To make a shape, follow these instructions:
    a. Go to the shapes page on your LogoWriter disk and flip the page. You will see a blowup of shape 1. To advance through the shapes use < ⌘ →> for the Apple or <PgDn> for the IBM. Go to shape 9.
    b. Now use the up–down and left–right arrows to move about on the screen. To make or remove a dot, press the <SPACE BAR>. Now move about to make a shape of your choice. Then flip the page, view the shape in its normal size, and if you are happy with it, exit by pressing the <ESC> key.
    c. Now go to a file in which you are going to use the shape you have constructed.
    d. Next type:

    > SETSH 9   [which sets the shape of the turtle to shape number 9] [Terrapin: SETSHAPE]
    >
    > ST   [which shows the turtle with the new shape]

14. **Changing the shape of the turtle.** To change the shape of your turtle, you simply use the SETSH command again. For example, suppose you follow the instructions in Exercise 13, to make the mirror image of your shape 9 in shape 10. Return to the page or file in which you plan to use the shape, and type the following:

> REPEAT 20 [SETSH 9 ST WAIT 5 SETSH 10 ST WAIT 5] [Terrapin: SETSHAPE]

The WAIT command allows for some control of timing. If this is too slow, replace the 5 with a smaller number; if it is too fast, replace the 5 with a larger number.

15. **Using multiple turtles.** Up to four turtles, called 0, 1, 2, and 3, are allowed. You communicate with them through the TELL command. For example, try the following commands:

```
TELL 0
SETSH 9
TELL 1
SETSH 10
TELL 2
SETSH 25
TELL 3
SETSH 26
TELL all
ST
```

16. **Stamping the turtle.** By using the STAMP command, you can freeze a picture of a turtle shape on the video screen. (Note: be sure your turtle's pen is down before you stamp.) For example, try

```
SETSH 25
ST PD
STAMP PU
FD 50
ST PD
STAMP
```

or

```
CG SETSH 26 REPEAT 6[FD 50 ST STAMP RT 60]
```

Now make a design that uses several turtle shapes.

17. **Creating motion effects.** Motion effects can be created by having the turtle move across the screen. For example, try these commands:

```
RT 90 PU BK 100 REPEAT 200 [FD 1]
```

or

```
RT 90 PU BK 100 REPEAT 40 [FD 5]
```

Note the difference in the effects of these two. Experiment to see if you can make it go faster or slower. To have the turtle leave a path, simply use PD (for PENDOWN) before the repeat command.

18. Now put together Exercises 13–17, to make a nice dynamic picture with moving, changing, and stamping shapes.

References

Flake, J. L. (1983). Brain hemispheric considerations for a developmental approach to diagnosing mathematics concepts for children. *Research monograph.* Kent, Ohio: Research Council for Diagnostic and Prescriptive Mathematics.

Hart, L. A. (1983). *Human brain and human learning.* New York: Longman.

Papert, S. (1980). *Mindstorms: children, computers, and powerful ideas.* New York: Basic Books.

Chapter 2

Writing Turtlegraphics Programs

▲ ▶ ▼ ◀ ▲ ▶ ▼ ◀ ▲ ▶ ▼ ◀ ▲ ▶ ▼ ◀ ▲ ▶ ▼ ◀ ▲ ▶

Objectives

- ▶ Identify and use problem-solving strategies for writing turtlegraphics programs
- ▶ Use the Logo operating system to save pictures and to retrieve programs or sets of procedures
- ▶ Print out hardcopy of program listings and pictures
- ▶ Distinguish between Logo primitives and procedures
- ▶ Write well-structured procedures using other procedures, recursion, and inputs in turtlegraphics
- ▶ Use rectangular coordinate systems in Logo
- ▶ Describe strategies for teaching Logo in the classroom
- ▶ Explore uses of computers for teaching very young children

The last chapter introduced Logo, turtlegraphics, and the Logo philosophy. In this chapter, attention is given to writing more powerful Logo programs, with an emphasis on problem-solving strategies. One of the major aspects of Logo is its use of problem-solving strategies. The exercises at the end of the chapter will give you many opportunities to apply these strategies. As you help your students write Logo programs, you can use Logo as a tool in problem solving, logical thinking, and spatial visualization. To help you in those processes, we will discuss a number of ideas, including uses of Logo in the classroom and techniques for appropriate program structuring. We also provide programs and suggestions for uses of Logo with young children.

First, you may wish to read Appendixes C, D, and E to learn how to load and save Logo programs that you create. Also in these appendixes are discussions of how to print out Logo pictures.

Extending Logo

Primitives and procedures were briefly mentioned in the previous chapter. A *primitive* is a command that is naturally understood by Logo, such as RIGHT and FORWARD. A *procedure* is a sequence of steps, commands, and/or primitives that allows new commands to be defined in terms of primitives. In the last chapter, for example, the procedure *Square* was defined in terms of the Logo primitives RT and FD. Writing procedures extends the Logo language, because new procedures can be defined in terms of primitives and previously defined procedures. For procedures to be available, they must all be in the **workspace,** the part of the computer's memory reserved for storing procedures. As you will recall from Chapter 1, primitives include such commands as FORWARD, RIGHT, and REPEAT, whereas examples of procedures are *Square, Triangle,* and *Polygon.*

Calling Procedures within a Procedure

An interesting feature of Logo is its ability to call one procedure within another procedure. A language-building analogy might be to start with certain words, for example *points, lines, planes,* then use those initial terms (which are similar to primitives in Logo) to define some new terms, such as *intersecting lines* and *perpendicular lines;* then define additional terms using these previously defined terms.

An example of a procedure that is called within another procedure is *Moresquares,* which calls *Square* during execution. (Note: if you did not save *Square* from the previous chapter and have turned the machine off since using it, reenter it now.) *Moresquares* is defined as, turning RIGHT 20 degrees (a Logo primitive), then calling *Square* (a procedure in Logo we defined in the previous chapter); after that is completed, the same pattern repeats several more times:

```
TO MORESQUARES
    RT 20
    SQUARE
    RT 20
    SQUARE
    RT 20
    SQUARE
END
```

Figure 1 illustrates the pattern drawn by *Moresquares.* Using the technique of calling a procedure is important for children. It helps them learn to break programs or pictures into component parts and develop each component part. A concern of many people is that youngsters learning to program computers write very long, inefficient programs. They develop bad programming habits that are difficult to break. Students should instead develop the habit of writing short programs that can combine to have the computer do big jobs, such as *Cross* and *Boxes* in Chapter 1 and *Moresquares* in this chapter. This process emphasizes the power of the human mind to make effective use of mechanical devices.

▲

Figure 1 *Moresquares.*

Input Variables

An understanding of **variables** is important to the effective use of computers. In Chapter 1, while exploring *House* and *TV,* you used inputs to variables. In computers, a variable is a memory location, like a mail box address. The name of the mail box is the variable's name, such as SIDE. If the value of SIDE is 50, then whenever the value of SIDE is indicated in a program, the value 50 will be inserted. Through varying the values of variables, one procedure can generate several different figures. For example, consider *Square* as used in the last chapter. Instead of making a square of side measures of 50, you can make a square of 100, or 30, or 75; simply use a variable and change its value.

In Logo, the *value* of a variable is indicated by use of a colon in front of the *name* of the variable (for example, :SIDE, sometimes read "DOT SIDE"). A space must occur before the colon, and no space can occur between the variable's name and the colon. Two procedures for making squares, one with side measure of 50 and another with side measure of 100, can be condensed into one procedure by use of a variable name:

```
TO SQ :SIDE
   REPEAT 4[FD :SIDE RT 90]
END
```

To execute this procedure, you then type the name of the procedure, a space, and an input for the variable:

```
SQ 50 <RETURN>
SQ 100 <RETURN>
```

Try SQ <RETURN>; this should give an error message that

```
SQ NEEDS MORE INPUTS     [Apple Logo: NOT ENOUGH INPUTS TO SQ]
```

Now you know that the input must be included. Try SQ :50 <RETURN>. This should give an error message that

```
THERE IS NO NAME 50     [Apple Logo and LogoWriter: 50 HAS NO VALUE]
```

Now you know that the colon should not be given with the value.

The number after SQ is the *input* to the variable, which becomes the value of the variable. Hence, 50, in the first case, or 100, in the second case, is the value used for SIDE in SQ. Make a square whose side is one-half that of SQ 50. Make a square whose side is 10 units bigger than that of SQ 50.

Recall that in Chapter 1, we wrote a procedure for a polygon that had blanks in it, so that if 3 was substituted in the blanks, a triangle was formed; if a 4 was substituted into the blanks, a square was formed, and so on. Instead of blanks you can use variables, and thus make the procedure general. Try to execute

```
TO POLYGON1  :N
   REPEAT  :N[FD 50 RT 360/:N]
END
```

Then

```
TO POLYGON  :N :SIDE
   REPEAT  :N[FD :SIDE RT 360/:N]
END
```

In this case, values of two variables are used; :N for the number of sides and :SIDE for the length of the side. The procedure can then be called by typing

```
POLYGON 5 30
```

which generates a regular pentagon (five-sided polygon) with side measures of 30 (Figure 2). Another example is:

```
POLYGON 8 20
```

which is pictured in Figure 3.

Experiment with different values of N and SIDE to see if you can make a circle. Note that as the value of N becomes larger, the number of sides increases. If you find how to make a circle, see if you can make circles of different sizes.

▲

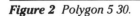

Figure 2 *Polygon 5 30.*

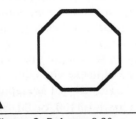

▲

Figure 3 *Polygon 8 20.*

An important part of thinking involves relational concepts, which include thinking about increasing or decreasing quantities. Logo can be very helpful in the exploration and development of relational thinking. Consider the values of two variables such as :N and :SIDE in *Polygon,* as examples. Think about what happens when the values for both variables increase. Try to predict what happens if the value of one increases and the other decreases. Predict the outcome if both decrease. Also, think about other combinations such as the effect obtained if one variable is kept the same value, and the other is changed. (The section called "Screen Commands" in Appendix C and parts of Appendix D might be useful if you would like more information on screen control.)

Using Simple Recursion

A powerful feature of Logo is the ability of a program to call itself. In Chapter 1, did you discover how to draw the TV? The process used there is called **recursion** and can occur in either **infinite loops,** in which calling of the procedure can continue forever, or in **finite loops,** in which the calling stops after a certain number of calls. Papert (1980) commented,

> Of all ideas I introduced to children, recursion stands out as the one idea that is particularly able to evoke an excited response. I think this is partly because the idea of going on forever touches on every child's fantasies and partly because recursion itself has roots in popular culture. For example, there is the recursion riddle: If you have two wishes what is the second? (Two more wishes.) And that is the evocative picture of a label with a picture of itself [pp. 71, 74].

Infinite Loops

The following program is an example of recursion that continues on until you tell it to stop (or pull the plug on the computer). After typing the program into the computer and executing it, type <CTRL-G> when you have decided that you have seen enough. (Use of this procedure assumes that you have the procedure SQ in memory.)

```
TO MORESQUARES1   :SIDE        [To stop, use <CTRL-G>. In LogoWriter, use
   RT 20                        < ⌘-S> for Apple, <CTRL-Break> for IBM,
   SQ :SIDE                     and <Fn-Break> for IBM PC_JR.]
   MORESQUARES1   :SIDE
END
```

Observe that this procedure calls for a rotation of 20 degrees, calls the procedure SQ to draw a square, then calls a copy of itself repeatedly (Figure 4).

Observe that *Moresquares1,* an example of infinite looping, also demonstrates how the value of a variable can be passed from procedure to procedure. The *Moresquares1 :Side* procedure requires an input (try 50). Type

```
MORESQUARES1 50
```

to run the procedure. The value, 50, will be placed in the memory location called SIDE and the 50 will be used as the input whenever :SIDE occurs in the procedure. Examine the program line by line. In the first line the turtle will turn right 20 degrees. In the second line, the procedure SQ is called with an input of :SIDE (50 in this case). The third line calls *Moresquares1* all over again, again with :SIDE, in this case 50. This is recursion: a procedure is used as a subprocedure of itself. The effect is to loop back and start the procedure again (until you press <CTRL-G> for Terrapin;

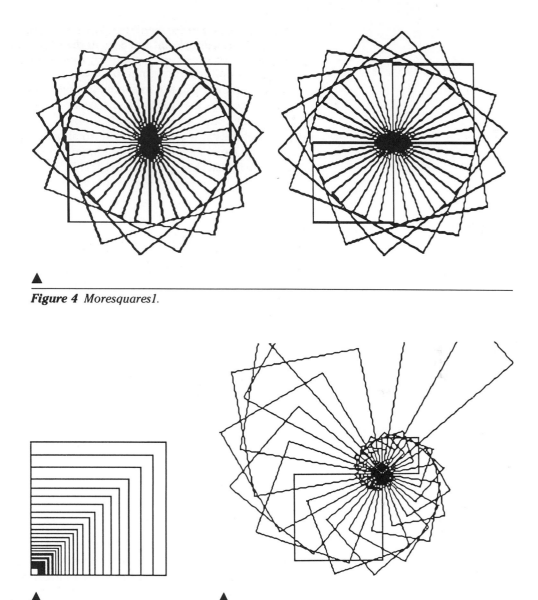

▲

Figure 4 *Moresquares1.*

▲

Figure 5 *Csquare 100.*   ▲

Figure 6 *Dsquare 1.*

for LogoWriter, use < ♿ -S> for Apple, <CTRL-Break> for IBM PC, and <Fn-Break> for IBM PC_JR).

Examine the next two procedures and describe ways in which they behave differently from the earlier procedures and from each other (Figures 5 and 6). Box 1 shows you how to have some control over the screen.

```
TO CSQUARE :SIDE                    [* is used for "multiply by"]
   SQ :SIDE
   CSQUARE :SIDE * .9
END

TO DSQUARE :SIDE
   RT 20
   SQ :SIDE
   DSQUARE :SIDE * 1.1
END
```

Box 1   Controlling What You See on the Screen

To keep a picture from going off the screen, use the NOWRAP command (in Apple Logo, FENCE; not available in LogoWriter). This will stop the drawing when it gets to the limit of the screen. To undo NOWRAP (FENCE, in Apple Logo), use the WRAP command.

Sometimes you want the turtle to show, other times you do not. To keep the turtle from showing use the command HIDETURTLE, abbreviated HT. To undo HIDETURTLE, use SHOWTURTLE, abbreviated ST.

Finite loops (using IF . . . THEN STOP)

The recursive procedures described in the last section will continue forever. However, there are times when it is an advantage to have a recursive procedure stop. To accomplish this, insert after the line SQ :SIDE in *Csquare* the line (Figure 7):

```
IF :SIDE <5 THEN STOP     [Apple Logo and LogoWriter: IF :SIDE < 5 [STOP]]
```

Make similar changes in *Dsquare*.

In *Csquare,* the squares become smaller and smaller because each time the new :SIDE is .9 times the old :SIDE. The value for stopping should be a small number, such as 5 used in the above case, and the program should stop when the :SIDE becomes less than that number.

Dsquare, on the other hand, generates squares that are larger and larger because the new :SIDE is 1.1 times the last :SIDE measure. Hence, the value for stopping should be a larger number (try 100); the procedure stops when :SIDE becomes greater than that number.

The name *Csquare* indicates *convergent squares; Dsquare* indicates *divergent squares.*

Using relational thinking is important here, too. As you think about the value of SIDE changing, you realize that the stopping value must be large if the value of SIDE is increasing but small if the value of SIDE is decreasing.

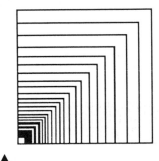

▲

Figure 7 *Csquare stopped after :side < 5.*

Using More Complex Recursion

In the last section you learned that **recursion** is a procedure that calls a copy of itself as a subprocedure. Recursion has repetition; the original procedure is a part of the repetition. Whenever a Logo procedure calls itself at the end of the procedure (called **tail recursion**), the effect is much the same as iteration (as in *Csquare*). However, if it calls itself in the middle of a procedure, it is more powerful then and contrasts sharply with iteration. Consider these procedures:

Terrapin Logo

```
TO TRI :SIDE
   IF :SIDE < 10 STOP
   REPEAT 3[FD :SIDE RT 120] TRI :SIDE/2
END
```

Apple Logo

```
TO TRI :SIDE
   IF :SIDE <10 [STOP]
   REPEAT 3[FD :SIDE RT 120] TRI :SIDE/2
END
```

The procedure draws a triangle with other triangles inside it, as shown in Figure 8. Now consider

Terrapin Logo

```
TO TRIS :SIDE
   IF :SIDE < 10 STOP
   REPEAT 3[FD :SIDE RT 120 TRIS :SIDE/2]
END
```

Apple Logo/LogoWriter

```
TO TRIS :SIDE
   IF :SIDE < 10 [STOP]
   REPEAT 3[FD :SIDE RT 120 TRIS :SIDE/2]
END
```

We get a very different, more interesting result. The recursive call to *Tris* occurs within a REPEAT cycle. Type TRIS 100<RETURN> to see the effect.

Another way of writing the procedure, which emphasizes the positioning of the recursive call (showing it is not at the end), follows:

Terrapin Logo

```
TO TRIS :SIDE
   IF :SIDE < 10 STOP
   FD :SIDE RT 120
   TRIS :SIDE/2
   FD :SIDE RT 120
   TRIS :SIDE/2
   FD :SIDE RT 120
   TRIS :SIDE/2
END
```

Apple Logo/LogoWriter

```
TO TRIS :SIDE
   IF :SIDE < 10 [STOP]
   FD :SIDE RT 120
   TRIS :SIDE/2
   FD :SIDE RT 120
   TRIS :SIDE/2
   FD :SIDE RT 120
   TRIS :SIDE/2
END
```

This shows that the procedure is definitely not tail recursion. It also illustrates how to dissect a procedure, to study process and order.

Consider the sequence of the drawing. First a triangle of 100 units per side is drawn. Then, at the end of the first leg, a triangle of 50 units on a side is drawn. Then one of 25 units and finally one of 12.5 units are drawn. These lengths are determined by a continued halving of :SIDE. When 10 is reached (:SIDE<10 forces a STOP) the lowest level has been achieved. The procedure then begins to do the triple repetition, then comes up a level to complete the next to shortest side, and so on. Study the sequence and attempt to predict the outcome. Figure 9 shows the completed pattern. Figure 10 shows a step for step evolution of the picture.

We have illustrated in this example these characteristics of recursion:

1. The procedure calls itself as a subprocedure.
2. The repetition of "self" can bring deeper and deeper "introspection."
3. When the deepest level of introspection is complete, unfolding begins from that level.
4. Each level of introspection is completed from the lowest level outward; completion occurs during the return from the deepest level.

Examine these Logo tail-recursive procedures:

```
TO CIRCLES :R
   POLYGON 360 :R
   CIRCLES :R * 1.1
END
```

```
TO POLYGON  :N  :R
   REPEAT :N[FD :R RT 360/:N]
END
```

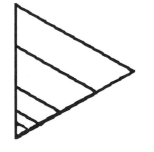

Figure 8 *Triangles produced by Tri.*

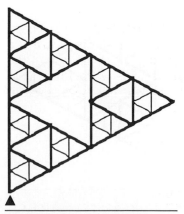

Figure 9 *Recursive triangle produced by Tris.*

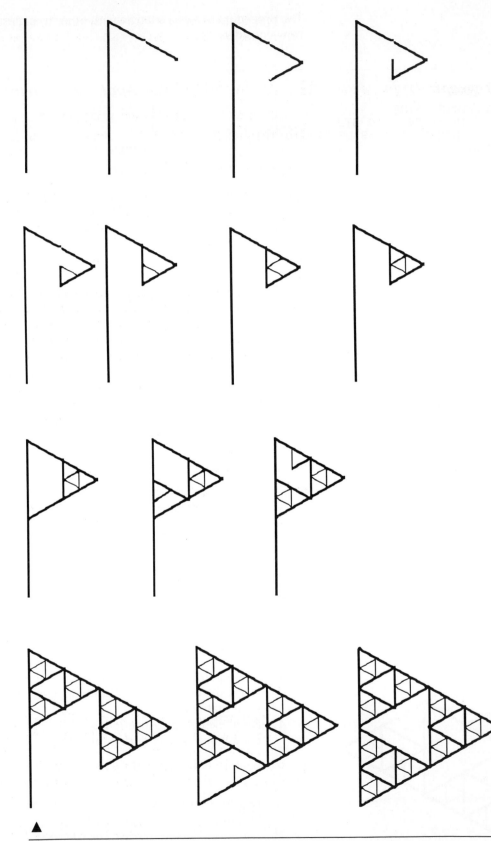

Figure 10 *Sequence of patterns produced by Tris.*

Note that characteristic (1) is illustrated, as is (2) to a limited extent. However, characteristics (3) and (4) are not found in tail recursion.

Teaching Logo—More Strategies

Chapter 1 discussed some strategies for teaching Logo. Here are additional strategies for you to consider.

Structuring Programs

One aspect of computer programming receiving considerable attention is **structured programming,** which involves breaking a difficult problem down into simpler problems. Suppose in turtlegraphics you want to make a complex picture; if you break it down into a simple picture or pictures, these can be drawn one at a time and then put together. The process, called **top-down analysis,** starts with a final desired product (the complex picture), breaks it down into smaller parts, then puts it back together. This is an important problem-solving technique that can be generalized: to solve a problem, first break it down into component parts.

Another important part of structured programming is **modularization,** which involves writing individual procedures to accomplish each component of the program goal. Such modules can be used as subprocedures in a number of programs. Instead of troubleshooting a huge program, you can debug individual modules or procedures. The small procedures can then be put together into a main procedure. Each procedure is called one at a time. Structured programming was used to create Figure 11. In this picture, a small left circle, a large left circle, a small right circle, and a large right circle are combined to form *Eyes*.

Consider the procedure for a circle:

```
TO CIRCLE :R
    HT    [This hides the turtle to give faster circles]
    REPEAT 36 [FD :R * 2 RT 10]
    ST
END
```

Using the Logo editor, make a procedure *Lcircle* by adding an L to the CIRCLE and changing the RT command to a LT command. The following procedure can then create the eyes in Figure 11:

```
TO EYES
    CIRCLE 5
    LCIRCLE 5
    CIRCLE 2
    LCIRCLE 2
END
```

Create *Lpolygon* in a way analogous to the creation of *Lcircle*.

Robot is another Logo application to develop a complex figure. The object is to draw a picture of a robot, as presented in Figure 12. To construct such a big picture, consider the different subparts. Our *Robot* needs a head, a body, right and left arms, and right and left legs and feet. The main program is

```
TO ROBOT
    FULLSCREEN         [not available in LogoWriter]
    DRAW               [Apple Logo: CLEARSCREEN, LogoWriter: CG]
    HEAD
    BODY
```

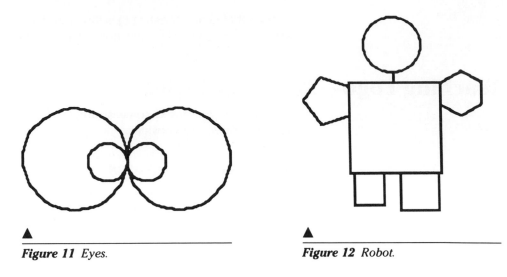

Figure 11 *Eyes.*   **Figure 12** *Robot.*

```
        LARM
        RARM
        RFOOT
        LFOOT
    END
```

Think of ways to write each subprocedure that will take advantage of the procedures you already know. Observe the shape created for each part, and the turtle's movements from one shape or part to another. Before reading on, see if you can make the *Robot* on your own.

The following procedures were generated to develop the robot in Figure 12.

```
TO MOVE :X :Y
    PU
    FD :Y
    RT 90
    FD :X
    LT 90
    PD
END
```

The move procedure simply allows the turtle to move around the screen. The pen is lifted with PU. The turtle is moved forward (up) :Y units. It is then turned right 90 degrees. The turtle is moved forward :X units, then turned left 90 degrees to bring its orientation back to its original direction. The pen is then put down with PD to do the next drawing.

```
TO HEAD
    MOVE 0 30
    FD 6
    LT 90
    POLYGON 20 7
    PU HOME PD
END

TO BODY
    MOVE (-30)(-30)
    POLYGON 4 60
    PU HOME PD
END
```

```
TO LARM
    MOVE (-30)15
    LPOLYGON 5 15
    PU HOME PD
END

TO RARM
    MOVE 30 15
    POLYGON 6 12
    PU HOME PD
END

TO RFOOT
    MOVE 25 (-30)
    RT 180
    POLYGON 4 24
    PU HOME PD
END

TO LFOOT
    MOVE (-10)(-30)
    RT 180
    POLYGON 4 18
    PU HOME PD
END
```

These subprocedures use the previously developed procedures *Polygon* and *Lpolygon*. Specific values of *Polygon* and *Lpolygon* are used in the new procedures.

Sometimes it is helpful to use variables when you are creating a procedure. Figure 13 shows a picture created by use of a variable. A program for generating that picture is,

```
TO CIRCLES :R
    CIRCLE :R
    CIRCLES :R * 1.1
END
```

In each of these programs, the big picture is composed of a series of simpler pictures, and subprocedures are used to generate the simpler pictures.

Figure 13 *Circles.*
▼

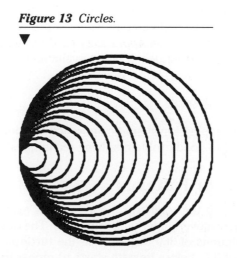

State-Transparent Procedures

The procedures used in the *Robot, Eyes,* and *Circles* were designed so that each part started and finished at HOME (the center of the screen with a top-of-screen turtle orientation). Exercise 13 at the end of this chapter incorporates translation to an arbitrary center anywhere on the screen. Procedures that start and finish at HOME are called **state transparent.** State transparency is an aid to modularization. In generating the *Robot,* the parts can be called in any order. You can first draw the head, then the right foot, left arm, and so on.

Debugging—a Tool for Problem Solving

Debugging is the process by which bugs or errors are removed from programs. As mentioned in Chapter 1, this is an important part of programming. There are a number of debugging techniques, including these:

1. Using body movements as a model, particularly in turtlegraphics.
2. Hand tracing or working through the program, doing each step by hand: drawing or computing results for each of the variables involved. The hand-tracing results are compared to the machine's results.
3. Checking your overall logic. Be sure you have carefully thought through each step and all possible alternatives.
4. Printing out the values of the variables in question to see if an error is occurring. (See Appendixes C, D, and E for instructions on use of the printer. Execute the program with the values of the variables printed on the screen, or turn on the printer and print the values.)
5. Printing out values of variables so that the results obtained from different values can be identified.
6. Isolating and controlling variables: assign a constant to one or more variable(s) and observe the effects of the constant on the remaining variable(s). For example, search out, explore, and input values of POLYGON that give a close approximation to a circle. Keep the value of SIDE fixed, and examine the effects of different values of N.
7. Performing machine tracing. Type the word

   TRACE

   and execute the program. Each step is displayed, and Logo waits for you to press <RETURN> before it continues to the next step. You may wish to compare your machine-traced program with your hand-checked program. (The TRACE command is not available in Apple Logo or Terrapin Logo, but it is on *Apple Logo Tool Kit,* a supplementary disk that accompanies Apple Logo. It is not available for LogoWriter.) In order to remove the machine tracing, type

   NOTRACE

   Developing a systematic approach to good debugging techniques can lead to good problem-solving techniques.

Looking for Patterns

Discovering the total trip theorem is an example of ways in which you can explore and discover underlying principles. The question to be investigated is: How many revolutions of 360 degrees will the turtle need to make for given values of SIDE and ANGLE, before its path starts to repeat itself?

```
TO TTT :SIDE :ANGLE
    FD :SIDE
    RT :ANGLE
    TTT :SIDE :ANGLE
END
```

First, enter the program. Then type

```
TTT 50 90
```

This should produce the familiar square; the path starts repeating after one 360-degree revolution. Now try:

```
TTT 50 80
```

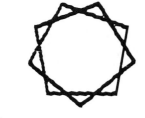

Figure 14 *TTT 50 80.*

After two revolutions, the turtle starts to repeat its path (Figure 14). Try walking out the path and see how many times you actually turn around. Do you find that it is the :ANGLE, and not the :SIDE, that makes the difference? Consider these values for ANGLE: 30, 100, 60, 45, 32, 64, 144.

In your exploration, consider the debugging techniques discussed earlier, such as using *Trace,* isolating and controlling variables, and printing out values of variables. The task is to find a general relationship that could be used to predict how many trips it would take for any value of ANGLE. A hint: the greatest common divisor (abbreviated gcd) of two numbers is the largest number that divides into both numbers a whole number of times. To illustrate this idea, the gcd of 4 and 6 is 2, because 2 is the largest number that divides into both 4 and 6. Similarly, the gcd of 90 and 360 is 90, because 90 is the largest number that divides into both 360 and 90.

One technique of problem solving is to organize your data into tables, so that you can examine the data for patterns. Table 1 suggests an organization for your data. When you have organized your data, look for some general pattern.

To help students see other relationships, you can use similar techniques. For the TTT problem, you provide a procedure, some simple examples, and some less simple examples. Provide guidance about setting up a table, perhaps suggesting headings. (Ultimately, the students should have to ponder upon headings to choose.)

Table 1 Organizing Data from the Total Trip Theorem Problem			
:ANGLE Measure	**GCD of 360 and :ANGLE**	**:ANGLE/ GCD**	**Number of 360 Degree Revolutions**
90	90	1	1
80	40	2	2
30	30	1	1
100	20	5	
60			
45			
32			
64			
.			
.			
.			

Chunking

There is a magic number, called **Miller's number,** which is the number of pieces of information that the human being can hold in his or her short-term memory at one time (Miller, 1956). The number is 7 plus or minus 2, or a range from 5 to 9. It has been found that to hold larger numbers of data in their short-term memory, people can chunk pieces of information. That is, if you need to remember 35 pieces of information, break them down into seven categories of information with five items in each category, or into some other subsystem. This is called **chunking.**

One goal of Logo is to help children learn to break problems into subparts, or, as Papert (1980) calls it, mind-size bites, and to write procedures so that they learn structured programming concepts. Miller's number can serve as a guide for you and your students to choose the sizes of chunks. If a decomposition has more than nine parts, some other way of breaking down the problem might be more appropriate. One reason why many computer scientists prefer that children begin programming in Logo rather than in BASIC is that the children using Logo begin developing structured programming approaches. Nonetheless, we have found that children (and adults) can develop just as many bad habits in Logo as in BASIC, unless they are carefully taught proper strategies.

Using Logo with Young Children

Young children (under the age of 7 years) do not have a concrete concept of large numbers such as 50 and 100. They do enjoy drawing pictures in Logo and can benefit from many of the experiences that older children have while learning to program. To help young children, several programs are useful. Enter these programs and save them onto your disk, or read them into the computer memory from the *Applications Disk* for *Fundamentals of Computer Education* (stored under YOUNG).

Start with *Blogo,* which simply allows the child to use single keystrokes to move the turtle around on the screen. It uses large-scale movement. F moves the turtle *forward* 10 steps. R turns the turtle *right* 10 degrees. T *turns* the turtle 30 degrees.

You can choose the level of directions you wish to be displayed on the video screen. If you, another adult, or an older child will be at the machine with the young child, oral directions can suffice. You can start with only a couple of commands, such as F and T. Three procedures are given here, one for large motions (10 dots for each step forward and 30 degrees for each turn), one for small motions (1 dot for each step forward and 1 degree for each turn), and one with a move procedure similar to that used in *Robot.* The small-motions procedure is given because young children like the large motions at times but also want finer motions. They can learn to call the smaller motions procedure by typing S.

Terrapin Logo/Krell

```
TO DIRECTIONS
    PRINT [F FOR FORWARD-T FOR TURN-R
    FOR RIGHT]
    PRINT [L FOR LEFT-K FOR BACK]
    PRINT [S FOR SMALL STEPS-B FOR
    BIG STEPS]
    PRINT [D FOR DRAW-Q FOR QUIT]
    MAKE "X READCHARACTER
    BLOGO
END
```

Apple Logo/LogoWriter

```
TO DIRECTIONS
[LogoWriter: add a line CT CG CC]
    PRINT [F FOR FORWARD-T FOR TURN-R
    FOR RIGHT]      [LogoWriter: throughout
                    replace PRINT with TYPE]
    PRINT [L FOR LEFT-K FOR BACK]
    PRINT [S FOR SMALL STEPS-B FOR
    BIG STEPS]
    PRINT [C FOR CLEARSCREEN-Q FOR
    QUIT]
    MAKE "X RC      [LogoWriter: replace RC with
                    READCHAR]
BLOGO
END
```

Terrapin Logo/Krell

```
TO BLOGO
    MAKE "X READCHARACTER
    TMOVE 10 10
    IF :X = "S THEN SLOGO
    IF :X = "Q THEN STOP
    BLOGO
END
```

Apple Logo/LogoWriter

```
TO BLOGO
    MAKE "X RC
    TMOVE 10 10
    IF :X = "S [SLOGO]
    IF :X = "Q [STOP]
    BLOGO
END
```

Terrapin Logo/Krell

```
TO TMOVE :D :A
    IF :X = "F FD :D
    IF :X = "T RT 3 * :A
    IF :X = "R RT :A
    IF :X = "L LT :A
    IF :X = "K BK :D
    IF :X = "D DRAW
END
```

Apple Logo/LogoWriter

```
TO TMOVE :D :A
    IF :X = "F [FD :D]
    IF :X = "T [RT 3 * :A]
    IF :X = "R [RT :A]
    IF :X = "L [LT :A]
    IF :X = "K [BK :D]
    IF :X = "C [CS];     [LogoWriter: replace
                          CS with CG]
END
```

Terrapin Logo/Krell

```
TO SLOGO
    MAKE "X READCHARACTER
    TMOVE 1 1
    IF :X = "B THEN BLOGO
    IF :X = "Q THEN STOP
    SLOGO
END
```

Apple Logo/LogoWriter

```
TO SLOGO
    MAKE "X RC      [LogoWriter: replace RC with
                     READCHAR]
    TMOVE 1 1
    IF :X = "B [BLOGO]
    IF :X = "Q [STOP]
    SLOGO
END
```

Observe that several new primitives are introduced in this program. One is the PRINT command; it simply prints what appears between the brackets [   ].

Another new command is MAKE "X, a way of *assigning a value* to a variable. The variable, X, is determined by another command, READCHARACTER or READ-CHAR. After READCHARACTER or READCHAR reads the keyboard, it assigns the value to the variable X.

Observe that this variation of Logo requires only single keystrokes and only small numbers in order to get some interesting pictures. Note also that the switch between small movements and big movements can help the children develop a sense of grouping structures. Rather than doing lots of small movements, you can use big movements until you have almost completed the part, then switch to smaller motions to complete it. Similar ideas can be applied to other subjects, such as arithmetic. If you need to count a large number of objects, for example, it would be easier to count out groupings of 10 (or 100 or 1000) as far as possible before switching to smaller units (1).

Rectangular Coordinate Systems

Thus far, the Logo examples have used relative polar coordinates, involving angles, rotations, and distances; the examples used variations of going forward and turning left or right. The developers of Logo found that it is initially easier for young children to understand these movements than the more common rectangular coordinates, consisting of distances in the horizontal and vertical directions. However, provisions for the use of rectangular coordinates are built into Logo. Eventually, children should work with both rectangular coordinate and relative polar coordinate systems.

The rectangular coordinate system for Terrapin Logo is sketched below:

```
-140 120              . . .              139 120
                      . . .
                   . . .O. . .
                      . . .
-140(-79)             . . .              139(-79)
              (End of split screen)
                      . . .
                      . . .
-140(-119)            . . .              139(-119)
```

Using the information below, experiment to find the coordinate system of your system. The following commands are part of the rectangular coordinate system in Logo: SETXY (SETPOS), SETX, SETY, XCOR, and YCOR. To see how these commands work, type

▲

Figure 15 SETXY 40 50 through SETXY 40 (−50).

SETXY 40 50	[Apple Logo and LogoWriter: SETPOS [40 50]] [This should move the turtle 40 units to the right and 50 units up from the center of the screen, the origin.]
SETXY -40 50	[Apple Logo and LogoWriter: SETPOS [− 40 50]] [This should move the turtle from the previous point, 40 50, to the new point, 40 units to the left of the origin and 50 units above the center.]
SETXY (-40)(-50)	[Apple Logo and LogoWriter: SETPOS [−40 −50]] [Use parentheses if second component is negative.]
SETXY 40(-50)	[Apple Logo and LogoWriter: SETPOS [40 −50]] [Try to figure out where this should be.]
SETXY 40 50	[Apple Logo and LogoWriter: SETPOS [40 50]] [You now should have completed the rectangle shown in Figure 15.]

SETX and SETY behave like SETXY except that the former each sets the value of only one coordinate. SETX and SETY are not primitives in LogoWriter.

XCOR and YCOR give the current location values of the turtle. XCOR and YCOR are not primitives in LogoWriter (although they are included tools) but POS will give both coordinates. To get the individual coordinates, use the following:

MAKE "X FIRST POS	[See Chapter 3 for explanation of FIRST.]
MAKE "Y LAST POS	[See Chapter 3 for explanation of LAST.]

One application of rectangular coordinates is given in the RANDOM.WALK program. A random walk is a path generated by random numbers, designated one for a turn and another for a forward distance. Thus, the turtle walks in random paths on the video screen.

Terrapin Logo/Krell

```
TO RANDOM.WALK :N
    MAKE "X RANDOM 140
    MAKE "A RANDOM 2
    IF :A < 1 MAKE "X (-:X)
    MAKE "Y RANDOM 120
    MAKE "B RANDOM 2
    IF :B < 1 MAKE "Y (-:Y)
    SETXY :X :Y
    IF :N < 50 RANDOM.WALK :N + 1
END
```

Apple Logo/LogoWriter

```
TO RANDOM.WALK :N
    MAKE "X RANDOM 140      [Replace 140 with a
                            number to fit your
                            system if needed]
    MAKE "A RANDOM 2
    IF :A < 1 [MAKE "X -:X]
    MAKE "Y RANDOM 120
    MAKE "B RANDOM 2
    IF :B < 1 [MAKE "Y -:Y]
    SETPOS SE :X :Y
    IF :N < 50 [RANDOM.WALK :N + 1]
END
```

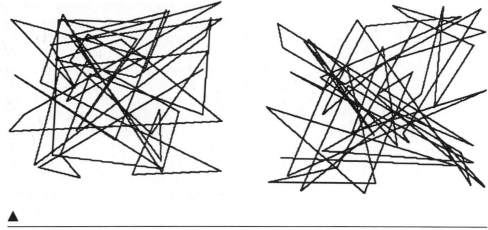

▲

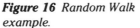

Figure 16 *Random Walk*
example.

Another command or primitive introduced in addition to SETXY (SETPOS) is RANDOM. RANDOM 140 will randomly select a number between 0 and 139 (inclusive). RANDOM 2 will randomly select a number between 0 and 1 (inclusive). In the random walk example, :X is a number between 0 and 139. :A is either 0 or 1. If :A is 0, :X will be assigned its negative value; if it is 9 it will become −9. (This programming technique is often used for making approximately one-half of the values negative.) Figure 16 shows two random walks generated by this program. The procedure starts at the middle of the screen, randomly generates the coordinates for the next point, and draws a line segment between the two next points. The process continues for the number of steps input when RANDOM.WALK is called.

Perhaps you want to know the direction the turtle is pointing. A command that will help you is HEADING, which gives the angle direction of the turtle. To set the turtle in a direction, use the command SETHEADING followed by the angle desired.

Many of the experiences in this chapter can be done with your students. Following the exercises are additional sample activities.

Comments from Research

Before continuing, we want to make a few comments about our approach. Several years ago there were claims that the main focus of computer use should be the development of problem-solving abilities. There seemed to be the belief that if students did anything with computers, then problem-solving skills would immediately develop. Taking the claims of Papert (1980) even further, some people concluded that fabulous thinking processes would immediately follow. Then research, such as Pea (1983) and Pea and Kurland (1983), started producing sobering facts.

Papert claims that Logo provides an environment for powerful experiential learning (in the Piagetian sense), and enhances learning and problem-solving abilities, which emphasize the activities of the student rather than the tasks to be accomplished. Delclos, Littlefield, and Bransford (1984), however, found that the learning process was more complex and that the learning method was also very important. A particularly effective method was a mediated style, in which the teacher made specific and conscious attempts to frame learnings from the Logo lesson in a broader context, and to bridge specific principles of learning to other applications. They found that a structured mediated approach to Logo was more effective than open-ended discovery. They concluded that Logo is an exciting, rich environment in which computer programming and problem-solving processes can be learned, but that the environment cannot succeed on its own. To achieve lasting, generalizable effects, the teacher must pay serious attention to the instructional method. A carefully structured, mediated method seems to promise good results.

The effects of using Logo might not be immediately obvious. For example, Clements (1987), to examine the delayed effects of learning Logo, studied nine third-graders who had learned Logo as first-graders. The students in the Logo group were given instruction for three months in the first grade. Their skills were then compared with students of equivalent age and ability, who had been given computer-assisted instruction also in first grade but not Logo. Eighteen months after the training, all of the students were tested on achievement and cognitive abilities. Five months after that testing, the children were interviewed. The results indicated that using Logo programming had affected particular areas of cognitive functioning and achievement. These effects were not simple or straightforward. Interviews with the children from both groups indicated that experience with Logo might have provided the children with schemata that helped them choose the "correct" answer for some items on standardized mathematics achievement tests, but misled them on other items (especially geometry). Clements suggests that teachers working with Logo programming should be aware of the ideas that the children are forming, such as circle and angle, and should assist them in building complete and mathematically correct schemata.

Some researchers have examined expert and novice programmers' thinking processes. To see the various patterns of learning that different students bring to the programming environment, Perkins et al. (1986) made clinical investigations of novice programmers. Mandinach and Linn (1987) studied achievements of experienced and talented programmers. Turble (1984) reports on a careful eight-year study of people who use computers. These researchers found that some types of instruction foster better learning practices that enable students to acquire a full repertoire of programming skills.

We have deliberately tried to build many of those practices into our instruction, at appropriate places. We intentionally develop problem-solving processes and build them for the transfer of learning processes; these are two very important procedures that do not necessarily happen automatically. Further, some research suggests that it would be good for you to learn in an environment with cooperative, small groups. (The role of social effects is examined further in Chapter 15.)

Because of its easy entry, Logo seems to be an appropriate language for students developing programming concepts to use. The language is a nice introduction not only for young children but also for middle school or secondary level students, as well as adults. Not only does it have an easy entry, but it is also a powerful language that can take users into considerable depth. Robinson et al. (1984) reported on children's use of Logo to direct their own learning to program a computer and engage in problem-solving skills, as well as develop logical, sequential-thinking, and planning skills. They found that children will set specific goals and work very hard to achieve them. However, they caution that slotting Logo into a prescribed Logo curriculum for each grade imposes an order contrary to Papert's intent. Further, these researchers point out that restricting Logo to the elementary grades wastes Logo's potential as an aid to geometry students in the middle and high schools, as well as to many adult uses.

Should programming be a part of a fundamental computer-education book? This question is not easy to answer. Our opinion is that it should be. Our goals are to provide a tool for developing higher-order thinking and to empower people with control over their computers. We are not trying to develop professional programmers, but rather to use programming as a microworld through which understanding of the computer and means to control it can be achieved. We also use computer graphics as a means for integrating spatial and numerical concepts. Further discussion of programming, particularly Logo, is given in Chapter 15. If interested, you might read that chapter now. The additional discussion is placed there rather than here because it might be more meaningful after you have completed active learning and in-depth problem-solving experiences in a Logo environment.

▶ ▼ ◀ ▲ ▶ ▼ ◀ ▲ ▶ ▼ ◀ ▲ ▶ ▼ ◀ ▲ ▶ ▼ ◀ ▲ ▶ ▼

Summary

In discussions of writing Logo programs, this chapter emphasized applications of problem-solving techniques and the use of turtlegraphics as a visualization tool. Logo primitives, procedures, and the calling of procedures within procedures were discussed with various techniques for programming. We mentioned the importance of structured programming and recursion. We suggested instructional strategies and procedures used for teaching Logo to very young children. A survey of research and sample activities complete the chapter.

The following procedures were described in this chapter:

Moresquares	*Body*
Sq :Side	*Larm*
Polygon :N :Side	*Rarm*
Moresquares1 :Side	*Rfoot*
Csquare :Side	*Lfoot*
Dsquare :Side	*Circles :R*
Circle :R	*TTT :Side :Angle*
Lcircle :R	*Blogo*
Robot	*Tmove :D :A*
Move :X :Y	*Slogo*
Head	*Random.walk :N*

Important Terms

CATALOG* [pagelist]	NOWRAP (FENCE)
Chunking	OUTDEV (.PRINTER)†
<CTRL-F>*[n.a.]	[PRINTNAMES]‡
<CTRL-G> In LogoWriter, use < - S> for Apple, <CTRL-Break> for IBM PC, <FN-Break> for IBM PC_{JR}]	PRINTOUT PO†[n.a.]
	PRINTOUT TITLES POTS†[n.a.]
<CTRL-S>*[n.a.]	[PRINTSCREEN]‡
<CTRL-T>*[n.a.]	[PRINTTEXT]‡
ERASE ER†	[PRINTTEXT80]‡
ERASEFILE,ERASEPICT†	RANDOM
Finite loops	READ,READPICT**
HEADING	READCHARACTER (RC)
HIDETURTLE HT	[READCHAR]
IF ... THEN ...	[READLISTCC]
Infinite loops	Recursion
MAKE	SAVE,SAVEPICT**
Miller's number	SETHEADING (SETH)
Modularization	SETXY (SETPOS)
	SETX

*Discussed in Appendixes C and D.

†Discussed in Appendix C.

**These commands are not available on Apple Logo, but they are on Apple Logo Tool Kit, a disk that accompanies Apple Logo.

‡Discussed in Appendix D.

```
SETY                              Variables
SHOWTURTLE ST                     [VCAT]§
State transparent                 Workspace
STOP ([STOP])                     WRAP [n.a.]
Structured programming            XCOR]
Top-down analysis                 YCOR} [POS]
TRACE NOTRACE*[n.a.]
```

Exercises

1. Write a program that will generate a picture you like and, if possible, make a hard copy of it.

2. Read the following program, and work through it by hand tracing each step. Once after you feel confident with the picture you have generated, run it on the computer and compare your drawings.

```
TO THIG :SIDE
    FD :SIDE
    RT 45
    THIG :SIDE
END
```

3. Select some of the programs in this chapter and change: (a) all LT's to RT's and vice versa, (b) all FD's to BK's and vice versa, (c) all RT's to LT's, LT's to RT's, FD's to BK's, and BK's to FD's. In each case predict what will happen, then make the changes and see if your prediction is correct.

4. Consider using SQ 10 to introduce multiplicative relationships. Make a square whose side measure is twice as big as SQ 10, then three times as big, then ten times as big.

5. Consider using SQ 100 to introduce fractional values. Make a square whose side measure is one-half of SQ 100, then one-fourth, one-third, one-fifth, one-tenth, and nine-tenths.

6. Consider using SQ 100 to introduce decimal values. First, work with exercises such as Exercise 5 until you are comfortable with those ideas. Use decimal notation, such as .1 instead of $\frac{1}{10}$. Then explore squares, in which the side measure is .5 of the side measure in SQ 100, then try .3, .2, .8, .1, .9, 1.5, and .25.

7. Use SQ 10 to explore the area of a figure. For example, draw SQ 20. Now use SQ 10 to make squares that cover SQ 20 but do not overlap, as in Figure 17. Now find how many squares of SQ 10 it would take to cover SQ 30, SQ 50, SQ 40, and SQ 100.

8. Write programs that will generate the pictures in Figure 18.

9. The pictures in Figure 19 were all generated by the same procedure. Can you find one procedure that would generate all of these pictures?
   Hint: Consider the following questions:
   a. How many variables seem to be involved?
   b. Once the value(s) of the variable(s) have been input, do any seem to remain the same throughout the program? Do any seem to be changing?

10. Make a list of pedagogical principles (principles of teaching) that have been discussed in this book. Make a list of problem-solving principles discussed.

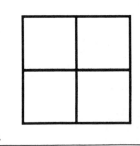

▲

Figure 17 SQ 20 "covered" by SQ 10.

§Discussed in Appendix E.

▲

Figure 18 *Sample Logo programs: Challenges.*

Figure 19 *Pictures all drawn by one procedure. Find the procedure.*

▼

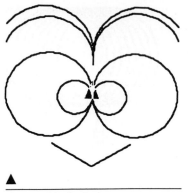

Figure 20 *Owl.*

11. The picture in Figure 20 is a good example of an application of structured programming. Some of the procedures that generated the figure follow. Using the editor and concepts of symmetry, see if you can modify these to generate the figure.

```
TO REYE
    REPEAT 20 [FD 11 RT 18]
END

TO REYB
    REPEAT 20 [FD 7 RT 18]
END

TO REYBR
    PU FD 40 PD
    REPEAT 10 [FD 10 RT 18]
    REPEAT 8 [BK 12 LT 18]
    SETHEADING 0 BK 10        [Apple Logo and LogoWriter:
    PU HOME PD                replace with SETH 0 BK 10]
END

TO RBEAK
    PU BK 70 PD
    LT 45 FD 40 BK 40 RT 45
    PU HOME PD
END

TO OWL
    ND HT        [LogoWriter: ND is not available; replace with CT CG]
    REYE
    LEYE
    REYB
    LEYB
    REYBR
    LEYBR
    RBEAK
    LBEAK
END
```

12. Recall that the pictures in Figure 15 in Chapter 1 for *House* were all drawn by the same procedure, using different values of the variables. Without looking at the HOUSE procedure, see if you can make procedures that will generate such figures.

13. The following exercise will guide you into constructing transformations of figures; first you will transform the *Robot* picture. Be sure that your robot procedure is in a file that you can use. Now load it into memory.

   A. Scaling. To change the size of :S of the robot,

   i. Go through your procedures to identify the values that represent lengths. Multiply each of those values by :S (that is, insert * :S for each length used). (Caution: When using *Polygon* and *Lpolygon,* discern the values that represent lengths and those that represent the number of sides. Change only the ones representing lengths. Also be careful not to change values of angles.) Note that you will change the values calling the procedures of *Move, Polygon,* and *Lpolygon,* so you do not need to insert the * :S within these procedures.

ii. Next go through your main procedures and add inputs of :S as well as call the procedures within ROBOT; for example,

```
TO ROBOT :S
   CLEARSCREEN        [or CG]
   HEAD :S
   BODY :S
   LARM :S
   RARM :S
   RFOOT :S
   LFOOT :S
END
```

iii. Now try the following:

ROBOT 1	[This is a good test to see if you get exactly what you had before, or if you have introduced some bugs into the process.]
ROBOT .5	[This robot should be one-half the size of the original robot.]
ROBOT 1.2	[This robot should be a little larger than the original.]

B. **Translating.** To move the robot to various locations represented by :X1 :Y1,

i. Write a procedure called *Ho,*

Terrapin/Krell

```
TO HO :X1 :Y1
   SETXY :X1 :Y1
   SETHEADING 0
END
```

Apple Logo/LogoWriter

```
TO HO :X1 :Y1
   SETPOS LIST :X1 :Y1
   SETH 0
END
```

---

ii. Next change the HOME command throughout the procedures to HO :X1 :Y1.

iii. Going through the procedures, insert inputs :X1 and :Y1 as inputs to the procedures and call these procedures within ROBOT. For example, the ROBOT procedure now becomes:

```
TO ROBOT :S :X1 :Y1
   CLEARSCREEN             [or CG]
   PU HO :X1 :Y1 PD
   HEAD :S :X1 :Y1
   BODY :S :X1 :Y1
   LARM :S :X1 :Y1
   RARM :S :X1 :Y1
   RFOOT :S :X1 :Y1
   LFOOT :S :X1 :Y1
END
```

iv. Now, to check that these changes are correct, try

ROBOT 1 0 0	[Again, this should give you the original robot; by comparing them, you can see if you have introduced new bugs.]
ROBOT 1 30 20	[This should give you a copy of the robot in its original size, shifted 30 units to the right and 20 units up.]

```
ROBOT .5 (-50) (-20)
```
[This should give you a robot one-half the size of the original robot, and shifted 50 units to the left and 20 units down.]

C. **Rotating.** To rotate the robot by an angle of :a units,

    i. Change the *Ho* procedure to:

Terrapin/Krell

```
TO HO :X1 :Y1 :A
   SETXY :X1 :Y1
   SETHEADING :A
END
```

Apple Logo/LogoWriter

```
TO HO :X1 :Y1 :A
   SETPOS LIST :X1 :Y1
   SETH :A
END
```

---

    ii. Go through the procedures and insert the :A as an input for the *Ho* procedure.

    iii. Insert :A as an input for the main procedures and call those procedures within *Robot*. For example,

```
TO ROBOT :S :X1 :Y1 :A
   CLEARSCREEN                [or CG]
   PU HO :X1 :Y1 :A PD
   HEAD :S :X1 :Y1 :A
   BODY :S :X1 :Y1 :A
   LARM :S :X1 :Y1 :A
   RARM :S :X1 :Y1 :A
   RFOOT :S :X1 :Y1 :A
   LFOOT :S :X1 :Y1 :A
END
```

    iv. Next try the following:

```
ROBOT 1 0 0 0              [Why these values?]
ROBOT .5 (-30) (-40) 45
ROBOT .3 70 50 180
```

D. **Reflecting.** To flip or make a "reflection" of the robot,

    i. Go through the procedures and make comparable left procedures as you did in *Lcircle* and *Lpolygon* to make a main procedure called *Lrobot*.

    (Suggestion for LogoWriter users: Go to a file containing *Robot*. Use the NAMEPAGE command from that file to make a new file, say NP "LROBOT. This will make a copy of the entire *Robot* collection of procedures and will leave the procedures created above in the first file. To create the reflected robot, make appropriate changes in the second file. Press the <ESC> key to save the new file. Now go to the first file or another file and merge these files by typing

```
LOAD "LROBOT
```

This will put both *Robots* in the same file. An alternative method is to use a tool file.)

    ii. Now try:

```
ROBOT :S :X1 :Y1 :A
LROBOT :S :X1 :Y1 :A
```

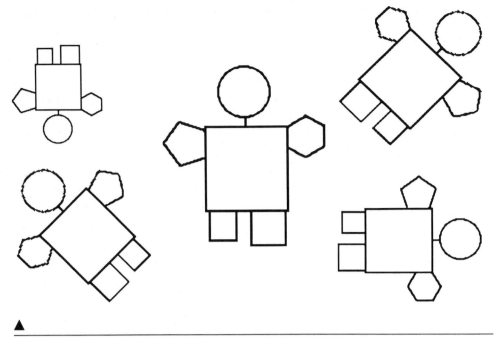

Figure 21 *Transforming* Robot.

E. **Building a composite picture.** To build a collection of such transformations,
    i.   Erase the clearscreen or CG primitive in each of the individual robot procedures.
    ii. Next write a composite procedure for building a collage of various robots transformed. For example,

```
TO COMPOSE.ROBOT
   CG
   ROBOT 1 0 0 0
   LROBOT .6 (-80) (-20) -45
   LROBOT .5 90 20 60
   ROBOT .4 75 (-50) 90
   ROBOT .3 (-90) 70 180
END
```

Now execute and make a printout of your picture (Figure 21).

F. **Modifying the shape of the robot.** Note that the original robot has one arm that is a pentagon; the other is a hexagon. Also, one leg is shorter than the other. Modify the various parts to make a differently shaped robot.

G. **Practicing.** Now make your own figure, transform it in several different ways, and make a printout of your composite figure.

References

Abelson, H. (1982). *Logo for the Apple II.* Peterborough, NH: BYTE McGraw-Hill.

Abelson, H., & Klotz, L., Jr. (1982). *Logo technical manual for the Apple II.* Cambridge, MA: Terrapin.

Burnett, J. D. (1982). *Logo: An introduction.* Morris Plains, NJ: Creative Computing Press.

Clayson, J. (1988). *Visual modeling with Logo: A structural approach to seeing.* Cambridge, MA: The MIT Press.

Clements, D. H. (1987). Longitudinal study of the effects of Logo programming on cognitive abilities and achievement. *Journal of Educational Computing Research, 3*(1), 73–94.

The Computing Teacher, 11. (1983–1984). 3–5, 7, 12–86. (Entire issue devoted to Logo.)

Delclos, V. R., Littlefield, J., & Bransford, J. D. (1984). *Teaching thinking through Logo: The importance of method.* Technical Report Series, Report No. 84.1.2. ERIC ED 262 756.

Forman, G., & Pufall, P. B. (Eds.). (1988). *Constructivism in the computer age.* Hillsdale, NJ: Lawrence Erlbaum Associates.

Grammer, V. C., & Goldenberg, E. P. (1988). *Logo Plus: The Terrapin Logo language for the Apple II: Tutorial.* Cambridge, MA: Terrapin.

Guntermann, E., & Tovar, M. (1987). Collaborative problem-solving with Logo: Effects of group size and group composition. *Journal of Educational Computing Research, 3*(3), 313–334.

Klein, E. (Ed.). (1985). *Children and computers: New directions for child development* (no. 28). San Francisco: Jossey-Bass.

Mandinach, E. B., & Linn, M. C. (1987). Cognitive consequences of programming: Achievements of experienced and talented programmers. *Journal of Educational Computing Research, 3*(1), 53–72.

Miller, G. A. (1956). The magic number seven, plus or minus two: Some limits on our capacity for processing information. *Psychology Review, 63,* 81–97.

Morgan, C. (1982, August). *BYTE: The small systems journal, 7,* 57–340. (Special issue focusing on Logo.)

Papert, S. (1980). *Mindstorms: Children, computers, and powerful ideas.* New York: Basic Books.

Pea, R. D. (1983). *Logo programming and problem solving.* (Technical Report Number 12.) New York: Bank Street College of Education, Center for Children and Technology.

Pea, R. D., & Kurland, D. M. (1983). *On the cognitive effects of learning computer programming.* (Technical Report Number 9.) New York: Bank Street College of Education, Center for Children and Technology.

Perkins, D. N., Hancock, C., Hobbs, R., Martin, F., & Simmons, R. (1986). Conditions of learning in novice programmers. *Journal of Educational Computing Research, 2*(1), 37–55.

Robinson, L., Moyer, L., & Odell, K. (1984). *Where does Logo fit in?* Paper presented at a meeting of the National Association of Laboratory Schools, Chicago. ERIC ED 278 379.

Salomon, G., & Perkins, D. N. (1987). Transfer of cognitive skills from programming: When and how? *Journal of Educational Computing Research, 3*(2), 149–169.

Thornburg, D. D. (1983). *Discovering Apple Logo: An invitation to the art and pattern of nature.* Reading, MA: Addison-Wesley.

Turkle, S. (1984). *The second self: Computers and the human spirit.* New York: Simon & Schuster.

Watt, D. (1983). *Learning with Logo.* New York: McGraw-Hill.

Zinn, K. L. (Ed.). (1982). Full speed ahead: A learner driven language. *The Computing Teacher, 10,* 12–69. (Entire issue devoted to Logo.)

▶ ▲ ◀ ▼ ▶ ▲ ◀ ▼ ▶ ▲ ◀ ▼ ▶ ▲ ◀ ▼ ▶ ▲ ◀ ▼ ▶ ▲

Activity Polygons to Circles

Type	Machine
Level	Intermediate
Objective	To use estimating, predicting, and projecting abilities, apply *Polygon* program to generation of other figures.
Prerequisite(s)	Work with turtlegraphics
Materials needed	None other than Logo
Activity	After loading the Logo language in the computer, use the *Polygon* procedure:

```
TO POLYGON    :N :SIDE
    REPEAT :N [FD :SIDE RT 360/:N]
END
```

First, to explore the effects of each of the inputs, have the students keep one of the values fixed and change the other. Next, see if they can make figures with a specific number of sides. Then have them try to make a circle using the *Polygon* procedure (see the figure below).

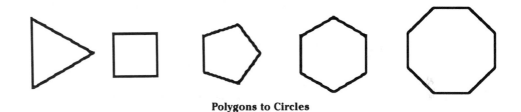

Polygons to Circles

Variations   Have them use the *Polygon* procedure to make a polygon inscribed in a circle, to circumscribe a polygon around the circle, and to circumscribe a circle around the outer polygon.

Activity General Bear

1. Start with a picture of the teddy bear and sample procedures such as *Circle, Rear, Reye,* and *Rsmile* (give students a printout of *Tedhead*). Emphasize building with the pieces. For example, start with the face and the right ear and add the left ear. (See Figure 22.) Use related problems (recall SQUARE.CROSS, which uses RT <---> LT, and FD <----> BK).
2. Once the teddy bear's head is outlined (without eyes and mouth), solve the problem of drawing the body. Note that the body is a reflection of the head

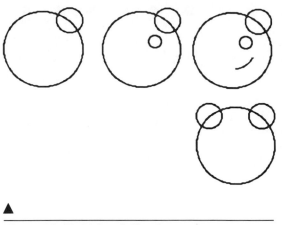

▲
_____

Figure 22 *Teddybear's Head.*

(and ears). This is why we will do the eyes and a mouth later (see *Teddybear's head*).

3. Solve the problem of the eyes and mouth. Note that the mouth is a part of a circle; thus, use part of the number of repetitions used in making a circle.

    Notice how symmetry and similarity are used to create the teddy bear. This method illustrates how to create any type of animal, or other complex figure. The parts are developed separately, then put together to form the whole. Here we see how two or more procedures are used to draw a picture.

    The intent is to form a perfect model. That perfect model can then be scaled, to form figures of the same shape but different sizes. We then generalize the model teddy bear. Start with a sample and use it as a model. For example, explain how to divide dimensions by 10 and insert :X to vary the size of the teddy bear's head. Add analogous changes for the other parts. Break the problem into subproblems.

4. Shown in Figure 23 is the *Threebears* picture, suggesting a way to generalize location (use printout of *Threebears*). Employ the model to create *Fourbears* (Figure 24).

5. Work on a procedure that provides directions and has inputs for location and size. (The *Applications Disk* contains the intended results, *Somebears* or *Asomebears*.) The outcome should be a procedure that explores placement and size, used to make well-proportioned pictures.

Figure 23 *Threebears (and Baby).*

▼

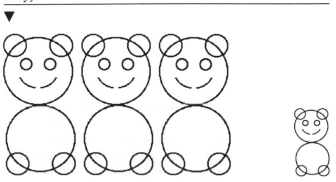

▲

Figure 24 *Fourbears (and Giant).*

We introduce variables to maintain *proportionality*. To help understand proportionality, make a specific example that is "perfect." Then use variables to scale the model. This use of variables will guarantee that all copies, regardless of size, are perfectly shaped.

Note that in the above procedures a PU SETX :L PD was introduced in many cases, so that we could move the turtle to make several bears in a row or place them wherever we wanted. Further, we could make bears of different sizes. These procedures are very general; we can do many things with them.

6. Problem variations include:

> A shelf full of bears all the same
> A collection of bears of many different sizes
> Bears that are arranged from smallest to largest, starting at the left
> Bears that are arranged from largest to smallest, starting at the left
> A family of bears

Your imagination can suggest many other possibilities.

In doing this construction, your students can learn many concepts of natural language and mathematics. For example, the idea of largest, smallest, to the left of, and so on, are taught by experience. Further, the most important mathematical concept might be that of proportionality (a very sophisticated idea). It isn't necessary to deliberately talk about proportionality, because the students experience the concept. This innate experience is what Papert, the creator of Logo, really wanted the language to help provide.

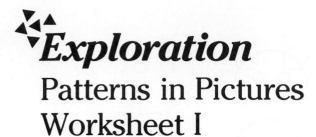
Exploration
Patterns in Pictures
Worksheet I

Consider how you would use Logo to draw the examples of gothic art shown below. First, you need to be able to draw circles of different sizes. The following procedure will do that. Further, it will allow you to move the circle around on the screen.

```
TO CI: R
  PU LT 90 FD :R RT 90 PD
  REPEAT 50[FD :R*SIN 360/50 RT 360/50]
  PU HOME PD
END
```

1. Use the procedure *Ci* to draw the pictures below.

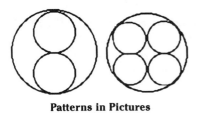

Patterns in Pictures

2. Try using the procedure *Ci* to draw a snowman.

Snowman

62

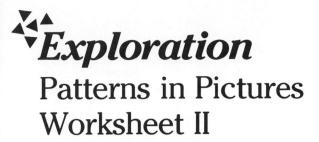

Exploration

Patterns in Pictures
Worksheet II

1. Make *Rabbit* and *Butterfly* procedures using the Logo file *Generalize* (*Ageneralize*) catalog entry. Generalize these procedures to form scale models of the rabbit or butterflies (see the patterns in pictures below).

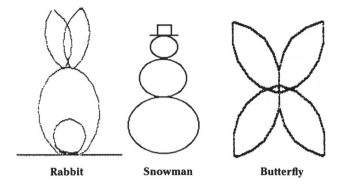

Rabbit **Snowman** **Butterfly**

2. Look back at the *Snowman* procedure. Generalize it so that you can produce different sizes of snowmen, placed at different locations on the screen.

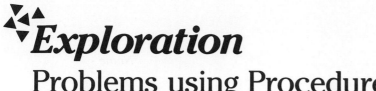 *Exploration*

Problems using Procedures
Worksheet I

1. The two procedures given below (in the file *Generalize* on the *Applications Disk*) can be used to draw many different pictures. See the variety that you can create in your pictures. To start, see if you can draw the three pictures in *Recursive crosses* (below).

```
TO GENPOL :SIDE :N :DIV :MIN
    IF :SIDE < :MIN STOP     [Apple Logo and LogoWriter: IF :SIDE < :MIN
                            [STOP]]
    REPEAT :N [ FD :SIDE RT 360/:N GENPOL :SIDE/:DIV :N :MIN]
END


TO LOC.GEN.POL :LIST.COORD :SIDE :N :DIV :MIN
    PU SETXY :FIRST :LIST.COORD LAST :LIST.COORD
    GENPOL :SIDE :N :DIV :MIN
END
```

Recursive Crosses

2. Seek ways of placing your pictures at various locations on the screen. Draw copies of the same picture at different locations, and get printouts of them.

▲ *Exploration*

Problems using Procedures Worksheet II

1. The *Rectree* procedure given below (in the file *Generalize*) can be used to draw many different pictures. Explore the variety of pictures you can get. To start, see if you can draw the picture in TREE STRUCTURES below.

```
TO RECTREE :SIDE :ANGLE :DIV :MIN
   IF :SIDE < :MIN STOP

   LT :ANGLE FD :SIDE
   RECTREE :SIDE/:DIV :ANGLE :DIV :MIN
   BK :SIDE
   RT 2*:ANGLE FD :SIDE
   RECTREE :SIDE/:DIV :ANGLE :DIV :MIN
   BK :SIDE
   LT :ANGLE
END
```

[Apple Logo and LogoWriter: IF :SIDE < :MIN [STOP]]

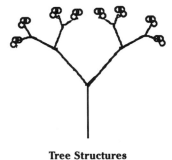

Tree Structures

2. You may be able to get trees from your picture. (Hint: use values such as 2 or 3 for :DIV. Also try numbers such as .8 or .9 for :DIV.) Or put leaves or cherries on the trees. Write a procedure for a leaf or a cherry and call it within RECTREE, at appropriate places.

Chapter 3

Beyond Turtlegraphics

▶ ▲ ◀ ▼ ▶ ▲ ◀ ▼ ▶ ▲ ◀ ▼ ▶ ▲ ◀ ▼ ▶ ▲ ◀ ▼ ▶ ▲ ◀

Objectives

▶ Predict results of an interactive graphics program
▶ Write interactive programs in Logo using words and lists to create sentences
▶ Modify procedures for the generation of patterns and variations on patterns
▶ Write interactive Logo procedures involving mathematical and logical primitives
▶ Perform readiness activities for problem solving
▶ Use the Logo editor to perform word processing tasks
▶ Experiment with predesigned microworlds; create a microenvironment for inquiry learning
▶ Use and create music in Logo
▶ Describe features and classroom uses of the Lego-Logo system

This chapter extends your knowledge of the Logo language beyond turtlegraphics. After several lessons with Logo turtlegraphics, you and your students will typically ask, "What else can we do with Logo?" This is normal curiosity about computers and the language Logo. To start our answer, we will work through two exercises.

Load Logo into the computer. Then follow the instructions in Table 1.

As you play the game, notice how well the computer remembers what you teach it. Try to pick an animal that you think the program should already know. Now try to pick an unusual animal, one you are fairly sure that the program will not already know. After answering all questions about an animal that is unknown, try the same animal again and see what happens. The *Music* and *Animal* programs (ANIMAL.GAME, in Apple Logo) suggest that Logo can do much more than turtlegraphics.

Logo is an all-purpose language. In this chapter, we will introduce interactive procedures in graphic and nongraphic forms, pattern generation and variation, readiness activities for problem solving, the Logo editor as a word processor, the design and use of microworlds, and music. We will also extend the computing concepts of procedures within procedures, recursion, and use of variables.

▼ ► ▲ ◄ ▼ ► ▲ ◄ ▼ ► ▲ ◄ ▼ ► ▲ ◄ ▼ ► ▲ ◄ ▼ ► ▲

Introduction to Interaction

Logo is an **interactive** computer language. Interactive computer languages make it easy to exchange ideas during a program's execution. A few primitives are necessary for interaction; a few techniques help to produce the next program.

Words as Inputs

The Logo primitive REQUEST (READLIST, abbreviated RL, in Apple Logo; use the full word READLIST in LogoWriter) is fundamental to interactive procedures. This primitive allows the user to supply information at the keyboard during a program's execution. Typically, a question is asked, and the program waits for an answer. Logo accepts and might store responses. Uses made of responses include

Table 1 Two Exercises in Logo

Terrapin Logo	Apple Logo	LogoWriter
Load appropriate disk into the computer.		
1. Logo Utilities Disk (comes with the language)	Apple Logo Tool Kit (should have with the language)	*Applications Disk,* Side 2 (comes with this book)
2. Type: READ "MUSIC	Type: LOAD "MUSIC	Move cursor to THE.ENTERTAINER and press \<RETURN>
3. Type: SET UP \<RETURN> FRERE	When computer is ready, type: FRERE	Wait. It will automatically load and play, making use of a START UP command.
After finishing the music exercise:		
4. Type: GOODBYE	Type: ERALL	
5. Type: READ "ANIMAL	Type: LOAD "ANIMAL.GAME	

echoing the responses back to the user at an appropriate time, using the responses to choose among alternatives, and using the responses as data for later analysis.

Putting together the components of interactive programs will illustrate the way Logo uses responses entered at the keyboard. We will need some new Logo primitives. SENTENCE (SE) takes two or more inputs and forms a sentence of the inputs. If more than two inputs are used, SENTENCE and its inputs must be enclosed in parentheses. Another is PRINT [　], which prints the data within brackets (we must use brackets, not parentheses or other grouping symbols) exactly as it appears.

A third is MAKE "NAME, which assigns a value to the memory location called NAME. The value may be a number, a word, or a set of words called a **list.** Finally, the primitive REQUEST (RL in Apple Logo, READLIST in LogoWriter) is needed. REQUEST (RL in Apple Logo, READLIST in LogoWriter) takes data input at the keyboard and forms a list from them. FIRST is used to select the first word of a list.

Echoing the Response

Enter *Hi* into workspace:

Terrapin Logo/Krell

```
TO HI
   CLEARTEXT
   PRINT [PLEASE ENTER YOUR FIRST
   NAME.]
   MAKE "NAME REQUEST

   PRINT (SE [HI, ] FIRST :NAME [
   ,ARE YOU SURE THAT'S YOU?])
END
```

Apple Logo/LogoWriter

```
TO HI
   CLEARTEXT     [LogoWriter: CT]
   PRINT [PLEASE ENTER YOUR FIRST
   NAME.]
   MAKE "NAME RL     [LogoWriter: READLIST
                      instead of RL]
   PRINT (SE [HI, ] FIRST :NAME [
   ,ARE YOU SURE THAT'S YOU?])
END
```

Now execute this procedure by typing

```
HI <RETURN>
```

Your name response is stored in a memory location, NAME. When the procedure calls for it again, a copy of the value, the first word in NAME, is printed in the sentence. SENTENCE (SE) has three inputs: two are lists, [HI] and [ARE YOU SURE THAT'S YOU?], and one is the value of NAME. Note that NAME as a label of the memory location is purely arbitrary. To convince yourself that NAME is arbitrary, replace NAME with X every place it occurs. After completing this replacement, execute *Hi* again. It should function just as it did before the change.

Names and Values of Variables

X·is the name (or label) for a memory location, whereas :X is the value, or content, of that memory location. The X is analogous to a name on a mailbox, whereas :X is analogous to a post card in the mailbox X. Be aware that the " preceding the X is a part of the syntax for use of MAKE.

Interactive Graphics

Now we will examine an interactive graphics procedure. It allows the user to input a number that chooses a picture to be drawn on the video screen. Before the drawing appears on the screen, however, screen instructions appear. To enter the program from the *Applications Disk,* type READ "FINAL <RETURN> (LOAD "AFINAL in Apple Logo). To execute the program, type

```
FINAL
```

You should first see the following screen display:

```
PLEASE TYPE IN A NUMBER.
WE'LL DRAW A PICTURE.

THEN TYPE ANOTHER.
AND WE'LL DRAW ANOTHER PICTURE.

THERE'LL BE A PAUSE AFTER THE DRAWING.
ENTER A NUMBER . . . 4 OR 5 . . . OR 12.
```

After reading the instructions, you should follow them. We suggest you try *4.* Type 4   <RETURN>. Figure 1 shows the picture drawn on the screen. Get a copy of the set of procedures used by *Final.* The procedures are

```
FINAL
INST
CHOICE
TIME
PAT
MOVE
TRI
```

These procedures are used together. *Final* is the main procedure; the others are subprocedures. Their relationship to each other is diagrammed in Figure 2, which is a structure chart. A **structure chart** shows how procedures in a program are linked (see Hassell & Law, 1982). Thus, executing *Final* starts the program. Each procedure is called by the procedure linked to it. Note that the diagram does not describe an order in which the subprocedures are executed; it only shows relationships.

Figure 3 shows some outputs of this program. Experiment with the procedures. First determine how to execute the procedures so that the individual parts of Figure 4 are obtained. After studying *Final* enough that you can determine the inputs that produced each picture in Figure 4 and the pictures that cannot be obtained with *Final,* study the procedures that make up *Final.* The list was given above; you will want to get a printout from the disk for study.

▲

Figure 1 *Screen display of Final, with input of 4.*

Figure 2 *Final structure chart.*

▼

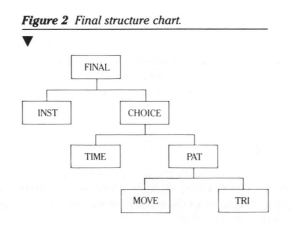

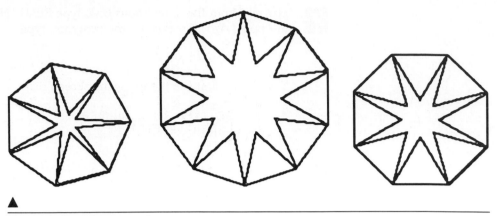

▲

Figure 3 *Sample outputs from Final.*

Interaction means communication with (not to) another. Although what occurs in these Logo procedures is not really interaction in this sense, the raw material (primitives and techniques) of interactive programs are established. With these raw materials, building truly interactive programs is easy. Also note that each response represents a choice made among alternatives; this use of choices illustrates a second use of REQUEST (RL).

Using Words and Lists for Interactive Programs

Logo is an all-purpose language, so it provides many programming capabilities beyond turtlegraphics.

Although turtlegraphics is a unique and motivating opening to the language, we now examine how Logo provides for **text programming.** Type the following:

```
PRINT ["MINDSTORMS" IS A BOOK BY S. PAPERT.] <RETURN>
```

The exact message enclosed in the brackets [   ] is printed on the screen. When PRINT is in the **immediate execution mode,** it is executed immediately after you press <RETURN>. PRINT can also execute from the **delayed execution mode.**

Drawing Inferences

Drawing inferences involves, among other things, reasoning from examples and patterns. Frequently, such conclusions drawn from experiments are more intuitive and meaningful than a definition or law. To infer the meaning of some new primitives, we experiment with a procedure. Start with *Words:*

```
TO WORDS
    REPEAT 4 [PRINT [LOGO IS FUN!]]
END
```

Execute *Words* (type WORDS <RETURN>). The message LOGO IS FUN! appears on the screen four times. Now we will vary what is printed. Edit *Words* and change the name to *Wording:*

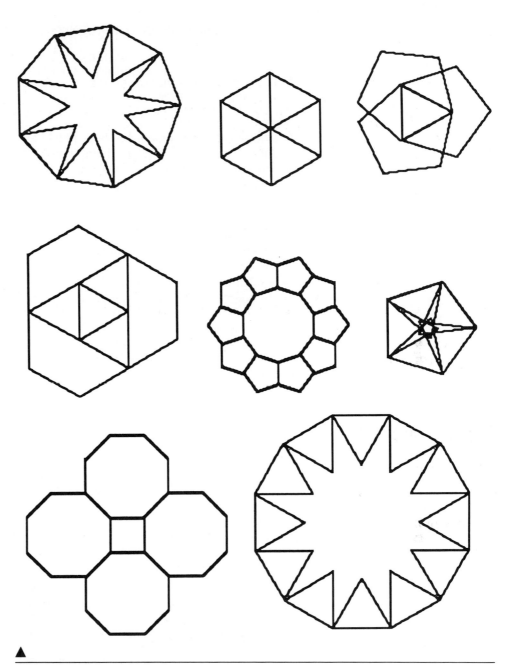

▲

Figure 4 *Determine the inputs for Final needed to produce each figure. Collect those that Final cannot produce and write one procedure to make them all.*

Terrapin Logo/Krell

```
TO WORDING
    REPEAT 4[PRINT ["LOGO IS A FUN
    LANGUAGE!"]]
    REPEAT 3[PRINT1 [LOGO!! ' ']]
END
```

Apple Logo/LogoWriter

```
TO WORDING
    REPEAT 4[PRINT ["LOGO IS A FUN
    LANGUAGE!"]]
    REPEAT 3 [TYPE [LOGO!! \ \ ]]
```
[Apple IIe: Use <CTRL-Q> to produce a backslash, Apple IIGS: has a backslash]
```
END
```

Now upon typing WORDING <RETURN> we see the following on the video screen:

```
"LOGO IS A FUN LANGUAGE!"
"LOGO IS A FUN LANGUAGE!"
"LOGO IS A FUN LANGUAGE!"
"LOGO IS A FUN LANGUAGE!"
LOGO!! LOGO!! LOGO!!
```

The output tells us something about PRINT and PRINT1 (TYPE in Apple Logo and INSERT in LogoWriter). (Note: TYPE is used differently in LogoWriter; it puts the text in the command center—bottom of the screen.)

Our observations suggest that PRINT and PRINT1 (TYPE in Apple Logo and INSERT in LogoWriter) affect the form of the output. PRINT apparently causes not only printing on the screen, but also a carriage return: the second printing of "LOGO IS A FUN LANGUAGE!" occurred at the left edge of the screen.

Note that the second and third copies of LOGO!! were printed on the same line as the first copy. The cause was possibly the PRINT1 (TYPE in Apple Logo, and INSERT in LogoWriter) or the ' '. To test this hypothesis about PRINT1 (TYPE in Apple Logo, and INSERT in LogoWriter) and ' ' (\ \ in Apple Logo), first edit so that ' ' (\ \ in Apple Logo) is not present, then execute the procedure. Draw a conclusion about the effect of ' ' (\ \ in Apple Logo). Also draw some conclusions about the difference between PRINT and PRINT1 (TYPE in Apple Logo, INSERT in LogoWriter). Further testing of PRINT and PRINT1 (TYPE in Apple Logo, INSERT in LogoWriter) might be appropriate. An interesting way of experimenting with PRINT and PRINT1 is to edit NAMING to the following:

Terrapin Logo/Krell

```
TO NAMING
   REPEAT 4[PRINT1 ["LOGO IS A FUN
   LANGUAGE."
   ' ']]
   REPEAT 3[PRINT [LOGO!!]]
END
```

Apple Logo/LogoWriter

```
TO NAMING
   REPEAT 4[TYPE ["LOGO IS A FUN
   LANGUAGE."
   \ \ \ ]]        [LogoWriter: need only use
                    one backspace]
   REPEAT 3[PRINT [LOGO!!]]
END
```

Anticipate the output. Write down what you think the output will be, then <RETURN>:

```
"LOGO IS A FUN LANGUAGE!" "LOGO IS A FUN LANGUAGE!" "LOGO
IS A FUN LANGUAGE!" "LOGO IS A FUN LANGUAGE!" LOGO!!
LOGO!!
LOGO!!
```

Recursion in Text Mode

Let us return to a simple form of recursion, the powerful tool using repetition. Enter the following procedure:

```
TO REP
   PRINT [GOOD COMPUTERS SPEAK LOGO.]
   REP
END
```

Now <CTRL-C> <RETURN> and see on the screen:

```
PLEASE WAIT . . .
REP DEFINED
```

Type:

```
REP <RETURN>
```

The output will be an infinite continuation of the following (or it will be infinite if something does not stop it!):

```
GOOD COMPUTERS SPEAK LOGO.
GOOD COMPUTERS SPEAK LOGO.
GOOD COMPUTERS SPEAK LOGO.
GOOD COMPUTERS SPEAK LOGO.
GOOD COMPUTERS SPEAK LOGO.
GOOD COMPUTERS SPEAK LOGO.
GOOD COMPUTERS SPEAK LOGO.
GOOD COMPUTERS SPEAK LOGO.
```

[<CTRL-G> to stop this.] [Apple version: <⌂-S>, IBM version of LogoWriter: <CTRL-Break>, IBM PC_JR version of LogoWriter: <Fn-Break>]

The abort (stop) command will not only stop the operation of a procedure, it also aborts the process of defining a procedure. The result of this command depends on *when* it is used. If used in the edit mode, it aborts the defining of the procedure; if used during execution, it stops the execution.

Another example of recursion follows:

Terrapin Logo/Krell	*Apple Logo/LogoWriter*
| ```
TO VOCAB :V
   PRINT :V
   MAKE "V BUTLAST :V
   IF NOT (:V = []) THEN VOCAB :V
END
``` | ```
TO VOCAB :V
   PRINT :V
   MAKE "V BUTLAST :V
   IF NOT (:V = []) [VOCAB :V]
END
``` |

If you type

```
VOCAB [TOM GEORGE MARY SAM BILL SUSAN]
```

the sample output would be:

```
TOM GEORGE MARY SAM BILL SUSAN
TOM GEORGE MARY SAM BILL
TOM GEORGE MARY SAM
TOM GEORGE MARY
TOM GEORGE
TOM
```

Terrapin Logo/Krell	*Apple Logo/LogoWriter*
| ```
TO LVOCAB :V
   PRINT :V
   MAKE "V BUTFIRST :V
   IF NOT (:V = []) THEN LVOCAB :V
END
``` | ```
TO LVOCAB :V
   PRINT :V
   MAKE "V BUTFIRST :V
   IF NOT (:V = []) [LVOCAB :V]
END
``` |

If you type

```
LVOCAB [TOM GEORGE MARY SAM BILL SUSAN]
```

the sample output would be:

```
TOM GEORGE MARY SAM BILL SUSAN
GEORGE MARY SAM BILL SUSAN
MARY SAM BILL SUSAN
SAM BILL SUSAN
BILL SUSAN
SUSAN
```

These procedures illustrate the use of BUTFIRST and BUTLAST. FIRST gives the first word of a list; BUTFIRST gives all but the first word of the list. LAST gives the last word of a list; BUTLAST gives all but the last word of the list.

Developing Interactive Programs

Final (and its associated procedures) is an example of a graphics interactive program. To further illustrate the concept of *interaction,* we will play a simple mathematical game. The procedure of the game uses a few mathematical and logical primitives.

An Interactive Mathematics Program

After you READ "GG from the *Applications Disk* (or LOAD "AGG for Apple Logo; go to GG on *LogoWriter Applications Disk*), execute GG. You will see the following screen:

```
1   CHOOSE A FIXED NUMBER,
2   USE A RANDOM NUMBER,
```

Press 1 and you will see:

```
ENTER NUMBER YOU WISH,
```

Enter 100 <RETURN>.

```
TOUCH ANY KEY TO BEGIN,
```

Touch a key; then you'll see the game's instructions. The screen will look like this:

```
LET'S PLAY A GAME,

I'LL CHOOSE A NUMBER,

THEN I'LL DIVIDE IT INTO 100,

I'LL TELL YOU THE QUOTIENT,
I'LL TELL YOU THE REMAINDER,

YOU GUESS THE NUMBER,

THE QUOTIENT IS 22,
THE REMAINDER IS 12,

, , , DIVIDED INTO 100,
```

At this point, enter your guess. For example, if you enter 6 you'll get feedback such as YOU'RE 2–5 AWAY. GET CLOSER. You will be given more feedback for each guess. Some other examples of feedback are YOU'RE CLOSE, GUESS AGAIN, YOU'RE MORE THAN 6 AWAY. One of the objectives of the game is to figure out exactly what the feedback tells you. By playing the game several times, you will find that more information is given than you had initially realized.

When you get the right answer, you will see GREAT!!! Options of continuing the game will also appear.

Now study the program, particularly the **documentation** that follows the ";" in the procedures statements. These documentation statements tell you what action is performed by the primitive or procedure of that line.

The program has the following procedures:

```
AB          READNUMBER      AGAIN      CHECK
GUESDIV     DIRECTIONS      GG         AB
SPACE       CHOOSEDIVIDEND
```

Get a printout of these procedures and study them. (See Appendixes C and D for printing procedures.) Draw a structure chart for GG.

An Interactive Language Arts Program

An interactive program, *Wordgame (Awordgame* in Apple Logo), is provided on the *Applications Disk*. This set of procedures provides practice in the use of prefixes. It is designed so that any prefix, together with words containing it, can be added to the program. The general pattern and examples are provided. Extensions are easy to make by analogy. Execute the file *Wordgame* from the *Applications Disk*.

Study the procedures that make up the file Wordgame. Printout (list the procedure on the screen) the procedures individually. Examine the procedures in the following order (to examine all the procedures, first type POTS, n.a. in LogoWriter):

```
INTRO
GAME
UNWORDS
UN
SUBWORD
SUB
PREWORD
PRE
```

These procedures are related as shown in Figure 5. To obtain individual listings, try the Logo instruction PO (short for PRINTOUT) GAME (PO "GAME, in Apple Logo;

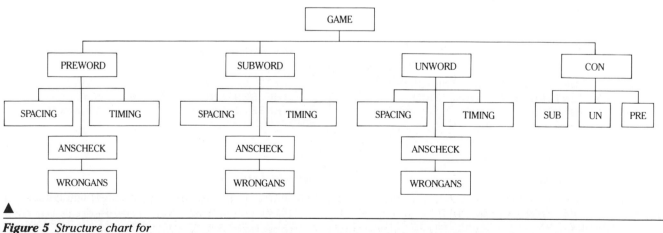

Figure 5 *Structure chart for Wordgame.*

see Appendix D for LogoWriter). After studying the printout of *Game,* get printouts of *Intro* by typing PO INTRO (PO "INTRO, in Apple Logo), and so on.

The earlier procedure *Hi* simply introduced the fundamentals (the raw materials) of interactive programming. The more recently discussed interactive programs (GG and *Game*) are nearer to a useful classroom learning tool. It is easy to see that you could develop a useful piece of software with the computing skills you already have.

Integrating Graphics and Text (in LogoWriter)

LogoWriter and Logo Plus have the capability of integrating text with graphics. To use this capability in LogoWriter, first move the turtle to the graphics location; use commands such as SETPOS to indicate the beginning of the text. Next use the LABEL command for LogoWriter (or GPRINT for Logo Plus) in the same manner as you use a print command. For example,

```
LABEL [GUESS WHERE THIS IS]
```

The Edit Mode as a Word Processor

Word processing is one of the most common uses of microcomputers. The Logo editor (edit mode of Logo) performs most of the important functions of a **word processor** (**text editor**). Experience with the Logo editor will give you practice in using four major word-processing capabilities, and will also give you a sense of the power and utility of Logo editor. The capabilities are

1. Block moves
2. Duplication and simplification of text
3. Correction of errors or editing
4. Storage and retrieval

Block Moves

A block move changes the position of a segment of text (a paragraph, a sentence, or a page). For example, the last paragraph of a story could be moved to become the first paragraph. To illustrate this capability, we use *Par1* and *Par2.* Enter these Logo programs:

Terrapin Logo/Krell

```
TO PAR1
    PRINT1 [WE INTERCHANGE THE ORDER
    OF THE SENTENCES SO THAT THEY
    MAKE SENSE.]
END
```

Apple Logo/LogoWriter

```
TO PAR1
    TYPE [WE INTERCHANGE THE ORDER OF
    THE SENTENCES SO THAT THEY MAKE
    SENSE.] [LogoWriter: replace TYPE with PRINT]
END
```

Terrapin Logo/Krell

```
TO PAR2
    PRINT1 [WE HAVE TYPED SOME
    SENTENCES. WE DECIDE AFTER TYPING
    THEM THAT THEY ARE NOT IN GOOD
    ORDER.]
END
```

Apple Logo/LogoWriter

```
TO PAR2    [LogoWriter: replace TYPE with PRINT]
    TYPE [WE HAVE TYPED SOME
    SENTENCES. WE DECIDE AFTER TYPING
    THEM THAT THEY ARE NOT IN GOOD
    ORDER.]
END
```

Now put the two procedures together to form a paragraph. For example, enter and execute the following:

```
TO PARAGRAPH
    PAR1
    PAR2
END
```

The paragraph made of the sentences does not make sense, because the order of the sentences is wrong. To improve the paragraph, try the procedure below

```
TO BETTERORDER
    PAR2
    PAR1
END
```

The paragraph now makes more sense. The reversal of the order of the sentences is a block move.

Duplication and Simplification

Duplicating similar or identical text can be done in several ways. For example, a procedure can call the desired number of copies of the text. We can use an analogy to illustrate the process.

Consider how a musical tune is sung. You describe it as: verse1, chorus, verse2, chorus, verse3, chorus. The procedure *Tune* will "sing" the entire tune:

```
TO TUNE
    VERSE1 CHORUS
    VERSE2 CHORUS
    VERSE3 CHORUS
END
```

In the same manner that CHORUS was repeated in *Tune,* blocks of text can be replicated. When you use a word processor, you do not have to retype identical passages; type them once and duplicate them at will. You can also save time on typing similar material; simply duplicate the passage and edit it as necessary.

Editing

Many editing commands were introduced in earlier chapters. Recall the keystrokes <ESC>, (<CTRL-X>, in Terrapin 2.0 version), <CTRL-D>, <CTRL-N>, and so on, that you used for debugging. Look at the Important Terms section for an organized set of editing commands.

Storing, Retrieving, and Combining

The techniques of storage and retrieval are discussed in Appendixes C, D, and E. For example, SAVE "NAME and READ "NAME (LOAD "NAME, in Apple Logo) are discussed there. However, some ways of combining storage and retrieval techniques will be useful here and will illustrate analogous features in word processing. When you are using word processing, you often need to combine documents. Because Logo allows there to be multiple procedures in workspace, it is possible to READ "PROC1 READ "PROC2 READ "PROC3 (in Apple Logo and LogoWriter LOAD "PROC1 LOAD "PROC2 LOAD "PROC3); the three procedures are then concurrently in workspace. This capability is essential to the combining of documents. All that remains is to edit them into a single document (procedure).

To illustrate combining techniques, we will use two *pseudoprocedures* (things that look like procedures). They represent two different paragraphs that need combining.

Terrapin Logo/Krell

```
TO LOGO
    PRINT1 ['      'THUS FAR IN THE
COURSE WE HAVE LEARNED MUCH ABOUT
LOGO. IT IS A FUN, ALL-PURPOSE
LANGUAGE. SO IT CAN DO THINGS
OTHER LANGUAGES CAN DO. IN
ADDITION, IT IS AN "EDUCATION"
LANGUAGE DEVELOPED FROM PIAGETIAN
THEORY.]
END
```

Apple Logo/LogoWriter

```
TO LOGO
    TYPE [ \  \  \  \  \   THUS FAR
IN THE COURSE WE HAVE LEARNED A
GREAT DEAL ABOUT LOGO. IT IS A
FUN, ALL-PURPOSE LANGUAGE. SO IT
CAN DO MOST THINGS THAT OTHER
LANGUAGES CAN DO. IN ADDITION, IT
IS AN "EDUCATION" LANGUAGE
DEVELOPED FROM PIAGETIAN THEORY.]
              [LogoWriter: replace TYPE with PRINT]
END
```

Now save this "text":

        SAVE "LOG   [LogoWriter: Use NAMEPAGE "LOG, then press <ESC> key]

Later, erase it from memory:

        ER ALL   [ERALL, in Apple Logo, will automatically erase the memory and save
                       the file in LogoWriter, when the <ESC> key is pressed.]

The second pseudoprocedure should be entered now:

Terrapin Logo/Krell

```
TO BASIC
    PRINT1 ['      'BASIC IS ALSO AN
ALL-PURPOSE LANGUAGE. IT IS A
SEQUENTIAL LANGUAGE, WITH
NUMBERED LINES. THIS NUMBERING
DICTATES THE ORDER OF
"INSTRUCTIONS." IT IS A WIDELY
AVAILABLE LANGUAGE FOR
MICROCOMPUTERS. SOME ARGUE THAT
IT IS NOT "LOGICAL" SINCE IT
ALLOWS JUMPING AROUND, WHICH
CREATES CONFUSION.]
END
```

Apple Logo/LogoWriter

```
TO BASIC
    TYPE [ \  \  \  \  \   BASIC IS
ALSO AN ALL-PURPOSE LANGUAGE. IT
IS A SEQUENTIAL LANGUAGE, WITH
NUMBERED LINES. THIS NUMBERING
DICTATES THE ORDER OF
"INSTRUCTIONS." IT IS A WIDELY
AVAILABLE LANGUAGE FOR
MICROCOMPUTERS. SOME ARGUE THAT
IT IS NOT "LOGICAL" SINCE IT
ALLOWS JUMPING AROUND, WHICH
CREATES CONFUSION.]    [LogoWriter:
                        replace TYPE with
                        PRINT.]
END
```

Save this pseudoprocedure:

        SAVE "BAS   [For LogoWriter, use NP "BAS, then press <ESC> key.]

With workspace still containing the first pseudoprocedure, simply READ "LOG (LOAD "LOG, in Apple Logo; for LogoWriter, go to the file BAS, then type NP "LOG.) Now both pseudoprocedures are in workspace. To see that they are, type EDIT ALL (ED [LOGO BASIC], in Apple Logo). To create the document, remove the END and the TO BASIC, and pull the two pseudoprocedures together. Workspace should now show:

Terrapin Logo/Krell

```
TO LOGO
    PRINT 1 ['    ' THUS FAR IN THE
    COURSE WE HAVE LEARNED A GREAT
    DEAL ABOUT LOGO. IT IS A FUN,
    ALL-PURPOSE LANGUAGE. SO IT CAN
    DO THINGS OTHER LANGUAGES CAN DO.
    IN ADDITION, IT IS AN "EDUCATION"
    LANGUAGE DEVELOPED FROM PIAGETIAN
    THEORY.]
    PRINT1 ['    ' BASIC IS ALSO AN
    ALL PURPOSE LANGUAGE. IT IS A
    SEQUENTIAL LANGUAGE, WITH
    NUMBERED LINES. THIS NUMBERING
    DICTATES THE ORDER OF
    "INSTRUCTIONS." IT IS A WIDELY
    AVAILABLE LANGUAGE FOR
    MICROCOMPUTERS. SOME ARGUE THAT
    IT IS NOT "LOGICAL" SINCE IT
    ALLOWS JUMPING AROUND, WHICH
    CREATES CONFUSION.]
END
```

Apple Logo/LogoWriter

```
TO LOGO
    TYPE [ \   \   \   \   \   THUS FAR
    IN THE COURSE WE HAVE LEARNED A
    GREAT DEAL ABOUT LOGO. IT IS A
    FUN, ALL-PURPOSE LANGUAGE. SO IT
    CAN DO MOST THINGS THAT OTHER
    LANGUAGES CAN DO. IN ADDITION, IT
    IS AN "EDUCATION" LANGUAGE
    DEVELOPED FROM PIAGETIAN THEORY.]
                        [LogoWriter: PRINT for TYPE.]
    TYPE [ \   \   \   \   BASIC IS
    ALSO AN ALL-PURPOSE LANGUAGE. IT
    IS A SEQUENTIAL LANGUAGE, WITH
    NUMBERED LINES. THIS NUMBERING
    DICTATES THE ORDER OF
    "INSTRUCTIONS." IT IS A WIDELY
    AVAILABLE LANGUAGE FOR
    MICROCOMPUTERS. SOME ARGUE THAT
    IT IS NOT "LOGICAL" SINCE IT
    ALLOWS JUMPING AROUND, WHICH
    CREATES CONFUSION.]    [LogoWriter:
                              PRINT for TYPE.]
END
```

To do word processing, LogoWriter can also be used without using procedures. Simply go to a file, press < ⌂ -U> for Apple or <CTRL-U> for IBM, and start writing. Press return only when starting a new line. When done, press < ⌂ -D> for Apple or <CTRL-D> for IBM, turn your printer on, and type PRINTTEXT (for 40 columns) or PRINTTEXT80 (for 80 columns). Also, there are tools, called *Formtools,* available on the LogoWriter disk put out by LCSI, for setting the margins at different values.

This introduction to the concepts of word processing should help you to know what to expect from word processors. It further provides you with practice in transferable editing skills.

Microworlds

The *Logo Utilities Disk* for Terrapin Logo and the *Apple Logo Sample Programs Disk* contain a program *Dynatrack (Dynaturtle* in Apple Logo and on the Applications Disk for LogoWriter). The program illustrates the development of concepts and principles through experiences, rather than through verbal abstractions. Before continuing in this section, you might want to experiment with this program. The following discussion is partly based on the description of microworlds given by Papert, as he describes Dynaturtle as an example of a microworld.

According to Papert (1980), **microworlds** are "explorable and manipulable environments" (p. 129). He says that the purpose of Dynaturtle involves "putting students in a simulated world where they have direct access to Newtonian motion" (p. 124). The purpose of a microworld is to put students in a simulated world in which they can directly build their intuitive sense of the concepts and principles of a discipline. They should be able to act directly and see the consequences of their actions; the microworld should also allow for assimilation and accommodation. Papert points out that "instead of waiting for equations, it [Dynaturtle] can motivate and facilitate [students'] acquisition of [an] intuitively well understood context for their use" (p. 124). Microworlds provide rich environments in which an intuitive understanding of a discipline's concepts and important principles can be developed. The design criteria include that there be very simple and accessible instances of laws, and the possibility of activities (games, art, and so on) that made activities in the microworld matter. Further, Newtonian laws should use concepts that are outside most people's experiences; for example, the concept of *state*.

Though described within the context of a particular microworld, Papert's design criteria are general and hence provide meaning to the term *microworld*. Further, Papert suggests, in referring to the Turtle World (turtlegraphics) that "The microworld was an incubator. . . . The design of the microworld makes it a 'growing place' for a specific species of powerful ideas or intellectual structures" (Papert, 1980, p. 125).

Characteristics of Microworlds

Lawler (1982), in describing Papert's conception, attributes four characteristics to microworlds. These characteristics are

1. Simple
2. Useful
3. General
4. Syntonic

A microworld is *simple,* but it hides deep, profound ideas within it. It is easy to understand, but also contains more than is obvious. The intuition developed from its use and the patterns seen within it, can produce a foundation for learning and understanding. A microworld is *useful* for the development of knowledge with understanding. A microworld is *general:* it is extensive in scope and includes cases that cover all variations of the concepts and laws. Finally, a microworld is *syntonic. Syntonic* implies a sense of harmony. A dictionary defines syntonic as possessing resonance; resonance is the "intensification and enriching . . . by supplementary effect, increasing to greater stability." Oneness and wholeness are essential components of syntonic environments.

Sample Microworld Candidates

To understand better the concept of a microworld, you can consider several candidates for microworlds:

Dr, microworld candidate I, (given below) requires two inputs. To execute, type DR 4 5, for example. Make sure you type just the name DR, then a space, then a number (3 through 15), a space, and then another number (3 through 15).

Terrapin Logo/Krell

```
TO DR :N :M
   ND HT FULLSCREEN
   REPEAT :N[BK 20 REPEAT :M[FD 20
   LT 360/:M] LT 360/:N]
END
```

Apple Logo/LogoWriter

```
TO DR :N :M
   CLEAN HT FULLSCREEN    [LogoWriter:
                          replace this line
                          with CT HT]

   REPEAT :N [BK 20 REPEAT :M [FD 20
   LT 360/:M] LT 360/:N]
END
```

It is advisable to execute *Dr* many times, so you see the pattern of figures produced and eventually become able to predict the next figure. Try some of these, for example:

```
DR 3 4     DR 6 4     DR 3 6
DR 3 5     DR 6 5     DR 4 6
DR 3 6     DR 6 6     DR 5 6
DR 3 7     DR 6 7     DR 6 6
```

Once you have spent sufficient time exploring *Dr,* it can be either saved to a data disk (SAVE "DR) or erased from memory (ER ALL) or (ERALL, in Apple Logo; (use NP "DR and press <ESC> in LogoWriter).

Now is a good time to enter and explore *Pop,* our second microworld candidate. To do so, enter the procedure *Pop* below, and type POP 4 50. Two numbers are required as inputs; of course, the 4 and 50 are just examples of inputs for you to try. Enter many different number combinations as inputs to *Pop.* Before concluding with *Pop,* try to determine the effects of N(:N) and S (:S) on the drawing. The goal is to visualize a figure (that *Pop* can draw) and to know the inputs that will produce the figure.

Terrapin Logo/Krell

```
TO POP :N :S
   ND HT FULLSCREEN
   REPEAT :N[RT 180/:N REPEAT :N[FD
   :S RT 360/:N] REPEAT :N[BK :S RT
   360/:N]]
END
```

Apple Logo/LogoWriter

```
TO POP :N :S
   CLEARSCREEN HT FULLSCREEN
      [LogoWriter: replace this line with CT CG HT]
   REPEAT :N[RT 180/:N REPEAT :N [FD
   :S RT 360/:N] REPEAT :N [BK :S RT
   360/:N]]
END
```

A third microworld candidate is the context created for the exploration of a sociological problem and its associated procedures. In the country of Salaj, the family is considered complete when the first son is born. In fact, a law of the land states:

> The birth of a son signals the completion of the family; therefore, it is hereby forbidden to have other children after the birth of a son.

What is the eventual effect of this law on the population of Salaj? Will there be considerably more females than males in Salaj? Will the country's population decrease, possibly to extinction? Or, will there be so few males that the country will have to begin to practice polygamy to survive? (Salaj's current laws require monogamy.) What do you think sociologists would say?

The following procedures are provided for you to use in exploring the Salaj problem. Experiment with them to see how they relate to the main question. *Many-pop* allows you to input a number of families to be examined. To execute, enter MANYPOP 100, and look at the data produced.

Terrapin Logo/Krell

```
TO COPOPU
   MAKE "X RANDOM 2
   IF :X = 0 THEN MAKE "C :C + 1
   MAKE "G :G + 1 PRINT1 [G '    ']
   COPOPU ELSE MAKE "C :C + 1 PRINT
   [B '    ']<RETURN>
   END
```

Apple Logo/LogoWriter

```
TO COPOPU
   MAKE "X RANDOM 2
   IF :X = 0 [MAKE "C :C + 1 MAKE "G
   :G + 1 TYPE [G \  \  ] COPOPU]
   [MAKE "C :C + 1 PRINT
   [B \  \  ]]
```
   [LogoWriter: replace IF with IFELSE, TYPE with PRINT, and PRINT with INSERT]
```
   END
```

[Type lines 3 to 6 continuously without a RETURN. Hit <RETURN> after last bracket.]

Terrapin Logo/Krell	*Apple Logo/LogoWriter*
| ```
TO MANYPOP :N
   MAKE "C 0 MAKE "G 0
   REPEAT :N [COPOPU]
   PRINT ( SE [THE TOTAL NUMBER OF
   CHILDREN WAS] :C [.])
   PRINT ( SE [THERE WERE] :G [GIRLS.])
END
``` | ```
TO MANYPOP :N
   MAKE "C 0 MAKE "G 0
   REPEAT :N [COPOPU]
   PRINT ( SE [THE TOTAL NUMBER OF
   CHILDREN WAS] :C [.])
   PRINT ( SE [THERE WERE] :G [GIRLS.])
END
``` |

Thoroughly explore these microworld candidates. Make it your goal to develop some system for organizing your exploration, after you have had a comfortable amount of free play.

A microworld is a "small world." The term is inherently constructivist in that it assumes that persons living in the full world explore, experiment, and give meaning to that world through their activities and interactions. Thus a computer microworld is an environment in which persons can explore, conjecture, and engage in computer activities such as constructing and analyzing patterns and relations in programming environments. Box 1 summarizes the characteristics of a microworld.

Dynatrack, Music and *Lego-Logo* are examples of microworlds. Dynatrack is conceptually based in the motion and acceleration laws of physics: The structures of these laws are the testable elements of the game. Because experimentation and the feedback are available, conjectures about the laws can be made and tested. It is intrinsically interesting, to the point that people of all ages will enjoy it for hours. By reflecting on your experiments, this extended play and conjecturing helps to facilitate abstractions.

Music is a natural environment in which the elements of music can be studied. Surely it is conceptually based and is conducive to experimental learning. Feedback is available as the music is played back to you. Cognitive restructuring and reflective abstraction are possible with work in *Music;* however, the question of intrinsic interest depends on individuals. Some might enjoy and persist in using *Music* to the point that they begin to explore and interact with others and think about principles of music. Others might not.

Lego-Logo is the clearest example of a microworld among the three. It is highly interesting and motivating, an environment for exploration of a wide variety of conceptually based principles, and it makes exploration and learning exciting. Constructing and conjecturing occurs naturally, leading to abstractions through reflection. The concreteness of the *Lego-Logo* equipment and the symbolism of the commands to create motion are a natural small world of reflection. The cars, blinking lights, and sensors that provide the mechanisms of motion and action are quite concrete representations of their real-world analogs. Experimentation with them is controlled experimentation with "the world." The abstractions build from the concrete and from more fundamental abstractions.

Turtlegraphics of Logo is a microworld. All of the properties are clearly present. The principles of geometry provide a strong conceptual base and a structure for the content; feedback is abundant, both in error messages and particularly in visual clues from output of constructed graphics. It is intrinsically interesting and involving, and has plenty of room for experimentation and exploration. The feedback leads naturally to reflective thought and eventually to abstractions of the principles of programming and geometry. Turtlegraphics is syntonic, general, and specifically designed for experimental learning. Working within the environment leads naturally to reflection and then to reflective abstraction. The construction of knowledge is a natural part of the turtlegraphics environment.

Box 1 Checklist for Microworlds

---

1. Allows for experimental learning, including explorations, investigations, and building hunches
2. Is conceptually based
3. Contains underlying structure of the content to be explored
4. Allows major cognitive restructuring and the facility for students to meaningfully construct knowledge
5. Allows students to generate feedback from which they can judge the efficacy of their methods of thinking
6. Is intrinsically interesting enough for students to want to discuss alternative strategies with other students about explorations, hence allowing social constructions
7. Facilitates reflective abstractions
8. Are easy to get started

None of *Dr, Pop,* nor *Salaj* is a microworld. Their main deficiency is their lack of sufficient intrinsic interest. They are not really syntonic. Though they are reasonable for experimentation and investigation and are conceptually based, the extent of their underlying structure is insufficient to lead to any depth of cognitive restructuring.

Music in Logo

In the introduction to this chapter, you used the *Logo Utilities Disk (Apple Logo Tool Kit)* to play a musical tune, "Frere Jacquès" or "Twinkle, Twinkle, Little Star," which is created in Logo. Incorporating music into a program and exploring the development of music can be fun. Neither knowledge of music nor understanding of musical notation is necessary for the exploration and creation of music. You can explore familiar computing concepts—such as recursion, procedures within procedures, and top-down planning—within the music environment. First, be sure you have appropriate utilities for music in memory.

Coding Music in Logo

Table 2 provides a translation for musical notes to the numerical form that Logo uses in playing music. Use the table for translation.

In order to program a tune in Logo, you write a procedure. First you need to know a new Logo primitive, *Play. Play* takes two lists as inputs; to designate a musical note, these two lists state its two components, its name and its duration. The first list includes the values of the notes, as translated from Table 2. The list ranges over more than three octaves. Middle C is denoted by the number value 8. One octave above middle C has a value of 8+ (C') and one octave below middle C has a value of 8− (C' '). Figure 6 shows an example of notes on the staff and their number values.

Table 3 translates durations, the time values of the notes and rests, to computer code. If 100 is taken as a whole note, then 50 is a half note.

Likewise, in Apple Logo, the "." before the code letter adds half again the duration of the note.

To change the tempo of the music, change the values of the duration list. For example, in DO.RE.MI given below, if you wish to slow down or speed up the tempo of the song, you provide a new second (duration) list. Remember that the idea is to experiment with the musical part of Logo; it is not to create specific musical

Table 2   Translation of Musical Notes to Computer Code

Notes		Terrapin and Krell Logo	Apple Logo*	Notes		Terrapin and Krell Logo	Apple Logo*
Octave −1				*Octave 0*			
F		1−	F''	F		1	F
F♯	G♭	2−	F#''G%''	F♯	G♭	2	F# G%
G		3−	G''	G		3	G
G♯	A♭	4−	G#''A%''	G♯	A♭	4	G# A%
A		5−	A''	A		5	A
A♯	B♭	6−	A#''B%''	A♯	B♭	6	A# B%
B		7−	B''	B		7	B
C		8−	C''	C		8	C
C♯	D♭	9−	C#''D%''	C♯	D♭	9	C# D%
D		10−	D''	D		10	D
D♯	E♭	11−	D#''E%''	D♯	E♭	11	D# E%
E		12−	E''	E		12	E
F		13−	F''	F		13	F
Octave 1				*Octave 2*			
F		1+	F''	F♯	G♭	14+	F#''G%''
F♯	G♭	2+	F#''G%''	G		15+	G''
G		3+	G''	G♯	A♭	16+	G#''A%''
G♯	A♭	4+	G#''A%''	A		17+	A''
A		5+	A''	A♯	B♭	18+	A#''B%''
A♯	B♭	6+	A#''B%''	B		19+	B''
B		7+	B''	C		20+	C''
C		8+	C''	C♯	D♭	21+	C#''D%''
C♯	D♭	9+	C#''D%''	D		22+	D''
D		10+	D''	D♯	E♭	23+	D#''E%''
D♯	E♭	11+	D#''E%''	E		24+	E''
E		12+	E''	F		13−(1+)	F''
F		13+ (1)	F''				

*See *LogoWriter Applications Disk* and Appendix D in this text.

Table 3   Translation of Musical Duration to Computer Code

Durations	Terrapin and Krell Logo	Apple Logo*
Eighth	12.5	EI
Quarter	25	Q
Half	50	H
Three-quarters	75	.H
Whole	100	W
One and one-half	150	.W

*See *LogoWriter Applications Disk* and Appendix D in this text.

Figure 6 *Notes on staff for DO.RE.MI.*

scores. In fact, it probably would be advisable to look at a small part of DO.RE.MI and experiment with it before you try to enter the entire tune. Start with the first seven notes, entered as a subroutine; then enter another set of seven notes as a second subroutine, and so on. By modularizing the song in this way, you facilitate experimentation.

Terrapin Logo/Krell	**Apple Logo/LogoWriter**

``
TO DO.RE.MI
    DO.RE.MI1
    DO.RE.MI2
    DO.RE.MI3
    DO.RE.MI4
    DO.RE.MI5
    DO.RE.MI6
    DO.RE.MI7
    DO.RE.MI8
    DO.RE.MI9
END
``
	``
	TO DO.RE.MI
	    DO.RE.MI1
	    DO.RE.MI2
	    DO.RE.MI3
	    DO.RE.MI4
	    DO.RE.MI5
	    DO.RE.MI6
	    DO.RE.MI7
	    DO.RE.MI8
	    DO.RE.MI9
	END
	``

(continued)	*(continued)*

Terrapin Logo/Krell, continued

```
TO DO.RE.MI1
    PLAY [8+ 10+ 12+ 8+ 12+ 8+
    12+][75 25 75 25 50 50 100]
END

TO DO.RE.MI2
    PLAY [10+ 12+ 13+ 13+ 12+ 10+
    13+][75 25 25 25 25 25 100]
END

TO DO.RE.MI3
    PLAY [12+ 13+ 15+ 12+ 15+ 12+
    15+][75 25 75 25 50 50 100]
END

TO DO.RE.MI4
    PLAY [13+ 15+ 17+ 17+ 15+ 13+
    17+][75 25 25 25 25 25 100]
END

TO DO.RE.MI5
    PLAY [15+ 8+ 10+ 12+ 13+ 15+
    17+][75 25 25 25 25 25 100]
END

TO DO.RE.MI6
    PLAY [17+ 10+ 12+ 13+ 15+ 17+
    19+][75 25 25 25 25 25 100]
END

TO DO.RE.MI7
    PLAY [19+ 12+ 13+ 15+ 17+ 19+
    20+][75 25 25 25 25 25 100]
END

TO DO.RE.MI8
    PLAY [20+ 19+ 17+ 13+ 19+ 15+
    20+][75 75 75 75 75 75 100]
END

TO DO.RE.MI9
    PLAY [8+ 10+ 12+ 13+ 15+ 17+ 19+
    20+ 15+ 20+][25 25 25 25 25 25 50
    50 50 50]
END
```

Apple Logo/Logo Writer, continued

```
TO DO.RE.MI1
    PLAY [C D E C E C E] [.H Q .H Q H
    H W]
END

TO DO.RE.MI2
    PLAY [D E F F E D F] [.H Q Q Q Q
    Q W]
END

TO DO.RE.MI3
    PLAY [E F G E G E G] [.H Q .H Q H
    H W]
END

TO DO.RE.MI4
    PLAY [F G A A G F A] [.H Q Q Q Q
    Q W]
END

TO DO.RE.MI5
    PLAY [G C D E F G A] [.H Q Q Q Q
    Q W]
END

TO DO.RE.MI6
    PLAY [A D E F G A B] [.H Q Q Q Q
    Q W]
END

TO DO.RE.MI7
    PLAY [B E F G A B C'] [.H Q Q Q Q
    Q W]
END

TO DO.RE.MI8
    PLAY [C' B A F B G C'] [.H .H .H
    .H .H .H W]
END

TO DO.RE.MI9
    PLAY [C D E F G A B C' G C'] [Q Q
    Q Q Q H H H H]
END
```

Structured Music

As is true when you create any type of Logo program, it is easier to plan the program and to build it with modules. Building a program into modules is efficient and organized. It provides an easy way of reading, extending, and modifying the program. These advantages are, of course, supplemental advantages beyond those of the ease of the initial development, which is facilitated by the initial planning. To illustrate this planning and modularization process, we use a sample from the song "The Entertainer" (Figure 7). Note that the main program presents three specific measures. To play "The Entertainer," enter it with MUSIC read in from the *Terrapin Utility Disk* (*Apple Logo Tool Kit,* in Apple Logo). Remember the SETUP must be executed also (this step is not done in Apple Logo). Once the four procedures associated with "The Entertainer" are entered, simply call it by typing THE.ENTERTAINER.

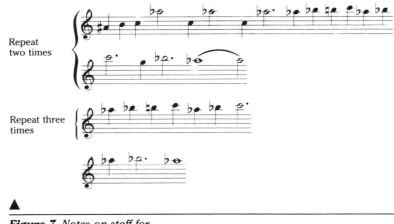

Repeat two times

Repeat three times

▲

Figure 7 *Notes on staff for The entertainer.*

Terrapin Logo/Krell

```
TO THE.ENTERTAINER
   REPEAT 2[ENT.1]
   REPEAT 3[ENT.2]
   ENT.3
END

TO ENT.3
   PLAY [16+ 18+ 16+][25 75 100]
END

TO ENT.1
   PLAY [6+ 7+ 8+ 16+ 8+ 16+ 8+ 16+
   16+ 18+ 19+ 20+ 16+ 18+ 20+ 15+
   18+ 16+] [25 25 25 75 25 75 25
   100 25 25 25 25 25 25 75 25 75
   150]
END

TO ENT.2
   PLAY [16+ 18+ 19+ 20+ 16+ 18+
   20+][25 25 25 25 25 25 75]
END
```

Apple Logo/LogoWriter

```
TO THE.ENTERTAINER
   REPEAT 2 [ENT.1]
   REPEAT 3 [ENT.2]
   ENT.3
END

TO ENT.3
   PLAY [A%' B%' A%'] [Q .H W]
END

TO ENT.1
   PLAY [A# B C' A%' C' A%' C' A%'
   A%' B%' B' C'' A%' B%' C'' G'
   B%' A%'] [Q Q Q .H Q .H Q W Q Q Q
   Q Q Q .H Q .H .W]
END

TO ENT.2
   PLAY [A%' B%' B' C'' A%' B%'
   C''] [Q Q Q Q Q Q .H]
END
```

Lego-Logo

Another exciting feature of Logo is Lego-Logo. This expands the computer's reach into the three-dimensional world in a very dynamic way, even more dynamic than the original robot-turtle on the floor. Lego-Logo allows students to use computers to control the manipulation of special Lego blocks. Students can build Lego figures that use motors and sensors—touch and light sensors, plugged into an interface box. Through creating and constructing meaningful products, students can learn the behavior of machines, electronics, and motion; they can also find meaningful problems with which to explore the problem-solving process. Students learn to break complex problems or complex machines, electronic components, or motions into simple machines, electronics, and/or motion. For example, students can learn about the motion of cars by comparing light/heavy cars or small/large wheels. They can explore ways of transforming rotary motion to linear motion, or the effects of friction on the motion.

Students type Logo commands that give their toys motion. Through conducting experiments the students can learn about different types of measurement, standard units of measure, rate-distance-time relationships, and the processes of collecting, representing, and analyzing data. Students can also learn about more complex concepts such as mechanical advantage.

These exercises combine the manipulation of concrete materials with the manipulation of symbolic representations, such as the names and definitions of Logo procedures. Thus students learn to connect the concrete and the abstract. Further, to learn to express their ideas, students can write reports about their projects and use word-processing capabilities. Through such processes students can learn to build connections between the right and left hemispheres of their brains; they also learn the processes by which knowledge is constructed. Microworlds can truly come alive in such environments.

Observations of fifth graders working with Lego-Logo indicate that indeed Lego-Logo is highly motivational. It increases interest in both Lego blocks and the achievement of building mechanisms that work. To get their machines to move, both boys and girls will work with gears and pulleys.

A Lego-Logo starter pack comes with an Apple IIe and Apple IIGS or IBM slot card and cable, an operating disk, reference guides, a transformer and interface box, and a starter set of 450 elements, including two 4.5 volt motors, one optosensor, one counting disk, two touch sensors, four light bricks, seven sets of building instructions for different models, and learning and teaching materials. The LEGO® TC Logo is produced by the Educational Products Department of LEGO Systems, Inc. and can be purchased through LCSI (Logo Computer Systems, Inc.). The form of the Logo follows the form of LogoWriter (for example, it uses the concept of flipping the page to enter and exit the editor), and some find that it is helpful for students to have prior experience with LogoWriter. The starter kit costs about $485 and contains enough materials for about four or five students. It could work nicely for a learning center.

▶ ▲ ◀ ▼ ▶ ▲ ◀ ▼ ▶ ▲ ◀ ▼ ▶ ▲ ◀ ▼ ▶ ▲ ◀ ▼ ▶ ▲

Summary

This chapter explored the all-purpose nature of Logo. We developed some interactive programs (*Final, Gg, Wordgame*). We also learned that Logo produces music, does mathematics, manipulates logic concepts, and serves as a tool for linguistic analysis (list processing).

We discussed ideas related to lists, words, numbers, and sentences, and introduced programs that use these concepts in interactive procedures. Interactive learning activities in mathematics and language arts provided examples of uses for Logo in your classroom. We showed how the text-editing capabilities of the edit mode of Logo can be used to write paragraphs and print them on paper. Finally, we examined the concept of microworlds and explored sample materials related to microworlds.

The following procedures were described in this chapter:

MUSIC	AGAIN	POP
FRERE	CHECK	SALAJ
ANIMAL	GUESDIV	COPOPU
HI	WORDGAME	MANYPOP
FINAL	GAME	PLAY
INST	SENTENCE	DO.RE.MI
CHOICE	UNWORD	DO.RE.MI1
TIME	SUBWORD	DO.RE.MI2
PAT	PREWORD	DO.RE.MI3
MOVE	PAR1	DO.RE.MI4

```
TRI           PAR2          DO.RE.MI5
WORDS         PARAGRAPH     DO.RE.MI6
WORDING       BETTERORDER   DO.RE.MI7
NAMING        TUNE          DO.RE.MI8
REP           PROC1         DO.RE.MI9
VOCAB         PROC2         THE.ENTERTAINER
LVOCAB        PROC3         ENT.1
GG            LOGO          ENT.2
DIRECTIONS    BASIC         ENT.3
SP            DYNATRACK
```

Important Terms

BUTFIRST [BF]
BUTLAST [BL]
CLEARTEXT [CT for LogoWriter]
<CTRL-K> [⌂6 for LogoWriter]
CURSOR
Delayed execution mode
Documentation
Echoing
<ESC>
FIRST
IF... THEN... ELSE
  [IFELSE]
Immediate execution mode
Interactive
LABEL in LogoWriter, GPRINT in
  LogoPlus
LAST
List
MAKE"
Microworld
PRINT

NODRAW (CLEARSCREEN, in Apple
  Logo) [n.a.]
PRINT1 (TYPE, in Apple Logo,
  INSERT in LogoWriter)
PRINTOUT [PO] [n.a.]
QUOTIENT [n.a. in LogoWriter]
RANDOM
REMAINDER
REQUEST (READLIST, in Apple
  Logo and LogoWriter)
SENTENCE[SE]
SETHEADING (SETH)
Structure chart
Text editor
Text programming
Thing
WORD
Word processor
[' '] (\ \ in Apple Logo,
  the backslash is created by
  <CTRL-Q>)

Exercises

1. Write a Logo procedure to print your first name ten times, so that each name prints under the previous one and at the left edge of the screen.

2. Write a Logo procedure to print your first name ten times, one name after the other on the same line *except* whenever the line becomes filled.

3. Modify the procedure in (2) so that three spaces are inserted between each printing of your name.

4. Write a procedure to accept your first and last names (with a space between them). To separate the names as words in a list, assign each to a variable. Include in the program a printing of your names in the following orders:

   ```
   FIRST LAST
   LAST FIRST
   LAST, FIRST
   ```

5. Modify the procedure of (4) to include a middle name. Extend the printing program accordingly.

6. Consider the procedure *Final*. Decompose it and pull out the following subprocedures:

   ```
   TO TRI
      REPEAT 3[FD 50 RT 120]
   END
   ```

```
TO SQ
   REPEAT 4[FD 50 RT 90]
END
```

Recombine these procedures into a procedure that produces the drawings in Figure 1 (p. 69).

7. Make two, three, and four copies of Figure 1. Get Logo to read coordinates of corners, to use in positioning the turtle for a second copy after a first copy is completed.

8. Restructure the procedures (UNWORDS, PREWORD, SUBWORD) of *Word.game* so that the repetition is consolidated into a single procedure.

9. Study *Word.game*. To add another prefix, add appropriate procedures and lines to existing procedures. For example, write procedures for *Biword* and *Bi*. (Save the new program on your disk.)

10. Design a microworld. (Do not program it.) Choose the concepts and principles of a discipline to be experienced. Describe the activities and the environment that provide the experience.

11. Test *Dr* against the characteristics of microworlds described by Lawler. Describe, in writing, whether and why the procedure is or is not simple, useful, general, and syntonic.

12. Use Papert's discussion of microworlds as a basis for a "proof" that *Dr* is (or is not) a microworld.

13. Repeat Exercise 11 for the procedure *Pop*.

14. Repeat Exercise 11 for the sociological exploration (including *Copopu* and *Manypop*).

15. Use the Logo editor to write three separate, brief paragraphs (call them PAR1, PAR2, and PAR3). Change the order of the paragraphs in workspace into PAR3, PAR2, PAR1. Merge the paragraphs into a single unit. Print the unit on paper.

16. The *Logo Utilities Disk* contains a *Text.editor* procedure. Using this procedure and the Logo utilities manual, write, edit, and print out a letter.

17. There are conventions governing the order in which the operations ($+$, $-$, $*$, $/$) are performed. To predict the outcomes, experiment with the following; then type each in, and precede each with the word PRINT:

```
3 * 4 + 5 * 6
4 + 4 / 2 * 2
10 / 5 * 2 + 3
9 + 6 / 3 - 1
(9 + 6) / 3 - 1
(9 + 6) / (3 - 1)
5 - 3 + 2 * 5 / 2 + 5
3 * 4 + 6
3 + 4 * 6
(3 + 4) * 6
6 + 4 * 3
```

Have you figured out the rules? Try using some more expressions, to see if you can predict the outcomes. Build some generalizations about how the grouping conventions work.

Exercises 18–21 use LogoWriter and Logo Plus.

18. Making careful use of structured programming techniques, construct a video story that integrates text, graphics, multiple turtles, motion, and

music. An optional feature could be to allow for branching within the story.

19. (For LogoWriter) On your *Applications Disk* is a file called *Game.* Go to that file, print out the program, and play the game. Observe uses of random numbers, multiple turtles, motion graphics, judging routines, scoring devices, and feedback to create an interactive video game. Making use of each of these features, create your own video game.

20. Examine the numerical patterns for frequencies given in Table 1 of Appendix D; for example, consider applying a multiplier of about 1.059699 within each column, starting from the bottom and going up. Observe there are 12 steps in each octave—on a piano keyboard those steps would be the 7 white and 5 black keys. You might try the following procedures:

```
TO EXP :N
    CT CG HT
    MAKE "FACTOR 1.059699
    MAKE "FREQ 65
    MEXP :N 1
END

TO MEXP :N :M
    IF :N < :M [STOP]
    MAKE "FREQ :FACTOR * :FREQ
    PR SE :M :FREQ + .5
    TONE :FREQ + .5
    MEXP :N :M+1
END
```

Also look across each row for a pattern. Music is built around numerical patterns. See your music teacher or read a book on music theory for further discussion.

21. Examine the way in which the tool musictool on your *LogoWriter* disk is designed. Notice how inputs are used in the LogoWriter versions of *Do.re.mi* and *The.entertainer.* Now let's think about some analogies between musical transformations and the transformations of graphics discussed in Chapter 2.

   a. Translating might be like changing keys or *transposing* the music, as could be done in *The.entertainer* by variations in the first input. If you change the first input from 1 to 2, you have shifted the range one octave. If you change it to a 3, you have shifted it two octaves. The key would remain the same. On the other hand, if you replace the 1 with a 1.25, you have shifted only one-fourth of an octave—this shift will change the key. Ask your music teacher or consult some music theory books for further information on this.

   b. *Dilating* in graphics means keeping a figure's original form as you change its size. The analogous transformation in music might be to change the *timing.* To change the timing of *The.entertainer,* change the second input. Experiment with different values for this input.

   c. Reflecting could be compared to playing a song backward. What might a song played backward sound like? The sample songs could be written as lists like those written for the other versions of Logo. To play the song normally, use the FIRST and BUTFIRST commands. To play a song backward, you could use LAST and BUT-LAST instead. This reflection is called *retrograde* in music.

   d. Rotating is less clear. Perhaps you can figure out a meaningful interpretation.

References

Abelson, H. (1982). *Logo for the Apple II.* Peterborough, NH: BYTE McGraw-Hill.

Abelson, H., & Klotz, L., Jr. (1982). *Logo technical manual for the Apple II.* Cambridge, MA: Terrapin.

Ackermann, E. (1987). *Lego-Logo activities: A formative evaluation.* Boston, MA: Massachusetts Institute of Technology, The Media Laboratory.

Bearden, D. (1987). Sixth grade software developers. *The Computing Teacher, 15,* 8–10.

di Sessa, A. A. (1985, June). Learning about learning. In E. L. Klein, (Ed.). *Children and computers.* New Directions for Child Development. San Francisco: Jossey-Bass, *28,* 97–124.

Faltis, C. (1987). Pre-Logo writing activities. *The Computing Teacher, 15,* 20–22, 43.

Forman, G., & Pufall, P. B. (1988). *Constructivism in the computer age.* Hillsdale, NJ: Lawrence Erlbaum Associates.

Goldenberg, E. P., & Feurzeig, W. (1988). *Exploring language with Logo.* Cambridge, MA: The MIT Press.

Hassell, J., & Law, V. J. (1982). Tutorial on structure charts as an algorithm design tool. *ACM SIGCSE Bulletin, 14,* 211–223.

Ivanier, P., et al. (1987). *LEGO programmable bricks.* (Technical memo.) Boston, MA: Massachusetts Institute of Technology, Artificial Intelligence Laboratory.

Lawler, R. W. (1982). Designing computer-based microworlds. *BYTE: The Small Systems Journal, 7,* 138–160.

Ocko, S., & Resnick, M. (1987). Integrating Lego and Logo: Making connections with computers and children. Boston, MA: Massachusetts Institute of Technology, The Media Laboratory.

Papert, S. (1980). *Mindstorms: Children, computers, and powerful ideas.* New York: Basic Books.

Piaget, J., & Inhelder, B. (1967). *The child's conception of space.* New York: Norton.

Resnick, M., & Ocko, S. (1987). *Lego-Logo and science education.* (Technical memo). Boston, MA: Massachusetts Institute of Technology, Artificial Intelligence Laboratory.

Rosen, M. (1987). But wait, there's more: One teacher tells what happens when you put LogoWriter in the hands of young people. *Classroom Computer Learning, 8*(2), 50–55.

Shimabukuro, G. (1989). A class act: Junior high students, Lego and Logo. *The Computing Teacher, 16*(5), 37–39.

Thompson, P. W. (1985). Experience, problem solving, and learning mathematics: Considerations in developing mathematics curricula. In E. A. Silver (Ed.). *Teaching and learning mathematical problem solving: Multiple research perspectives.* Hillsdale, NJ: Lawrence Erlbaum Associates.

Turkle, S. (1984). *The second self: Computers and the human spirit.* New York: Simon & Schuster.

Weir, S. (1987). *Cultivating minds.* New York: Harper & Row.

Weir, S. (1987). Lego-Logo: A vehicle for learning. Boston, MA: Massachusetts Institute of Technology, Media Laboratory.

Activity Stars or Polygons

Type	Machine
Objective	Look for patterns and use them to classify stars and polygons.
Prerequisite(s)	Work with turtlegraphics
Materials needed	*Logo* language *Star.poly* Table for data organization (worksheet)
Activity	After loading Logo, load the file *Star.poly.* Use the *Stars* procedure for this investigation.

First, to explore the effects of the inputs to STARS, students should keep one variable fixed and change the other. Next see if they can make two different seven-pointed stars. Then have them determine the pattern of numbers that will produce the sequence of "stars" below. Discuss the effect of each variable, and encourage students to predict the star that will result from given inputs.

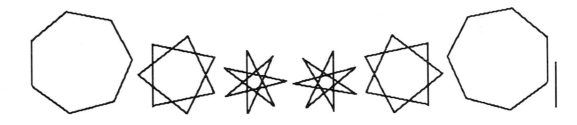

The students should make a table (see the worksheet) to organize and classify the stars and their corresponding inputs. Using that table, they should predict the patterns of inputs that produce the polygons of *N* sides. What about the reflections of the polygons to the left of the screen? What can be observed about the values of *M* that produce stars of the same shape?

For example, consider the value $N = 7$. Let *M* vary and see the patterns of numbers that correspond to each pattern of seven-pointed stars. Using the pattern above draw the stars given by STARS 7 12, STARS 7 16, STARS 7 17. What input to STARS will produce the stars shown below?

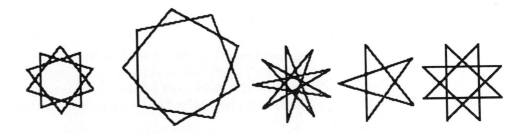

Variation(s)	Develop another procedure that will produce the same sets of stars but with different "formulae." See if students using the new procedure can predict and draw any stars requested.
Worksheet	See page 96.

Activity Word-Forming Game

Type	Machine
Level	Intermediate
Objective	Apply decomposing and recombining skills to language patterns, to form words (In Variation(s), the ability to work backwards is helpful.)
Prerequisite(s)	Experience in providing input in Logo
Materials needed	*Wors* on the *Applications Disk* *Sent* on the *Applications Disk* (for variation)
Activity	By inputting letters, one at a time, two or more teams (or individuals) compete to form words. The loser is the player or team that cannot continue adding letters to the word any further. To use the WORS procedure:

```
READ "WORS
```

from the disk. Execute by typing

```
INTRO
```

To play the game, type

```
WORS
```

In a typical game each team alternately chooses a letter and types it in as requested. Suppose the letters are chosen as follows:

```
Team 1        Team 2
   U             N
   L             I
   K             E
```

The word thus builds on the screen:

```
U
UN
UNL
UNLI
UNLIK
UNLIKE
```

As the students become familiar with the game, they should begin to develop strategies for playing. For example, they can decompose words into "blocks," perhaps in terms of prefixes, root words, and suffixes. Ask them what the prefix in the word in the sample game is. Did they consider -(E)D and -(E)LY as alternate endings?

Variation(s) Rather than using *Wors* and forming words from first to last letter, the students can work backwards: words are formed from last letter to first. The Worsback program can be used. As a second variation, the *Sent* procedure from the *Applications Disk* is a similar game played with sentences instead of words (but cannot be worked backwards).

Activity   Extending *Sent*

Type	Machine
Level	Advanced
Objective	Apply decomposing and recombining skills to language patterns and use analogy to extend Logo procedures
Prerequisite(s)	Some experience in programming with Logo
Materials needed	*Wors* on the *Applications Disk* *Sent* on the *Applications Disk* (for variation)
Activity	Have the students study the procedures that make up the games *Wors, Worsback,* and *Sent,* particularly the uses of the primitives *LPUT, FPUT, LAST,* and *FIRST.* Discuss how *Wors* was modified to make the game *Worsback.* By employing analogy, see if they can decompose *Sent* to program a new game (called *Sentback*) that creates sentences, last word to first word, just as *Worsback* created words from last letter to first letter. Suggest working backwards as a strategy in playing *Worsback* and *Sentback.* Why?
Variation(s)	Have the students create a different set of rules for *Wors* (or *Worsback, Sent,* or *Sentback*) and modify the program to fit the new rules.

◢◣ Exploration

Stars or Polygons Worksheet

Using the procedure below, sketch pictures of the stars with various inputs, and identify the pairs of inputs that produce a polygon (P), a star (S), or a type of star (T). Record P, S, or T in the chart below for the respective :M and :N.

```
TO STARS :M :N
    REPEAT :N[FD 50 RT 360 * :M/:N]
END
```

N/M = 1   2   3   4   5   6   7   8   9   . . .

1

2

3

4

5

6

7

8

9

.

.

.

Chapter 4

Problem Solving:
Looking Back

▶ ▲ ◀ ▼ ▶ ▲ ◀ ▼ ▶ ▲ ◀ ▼ ▶ ▲ ◀ ▼ ▶ ▲ ◀ ▼ ▶ ▲

Objectives

▶ Describe characteristics of problem solving
▶ Identify problem-solving strategies
▶ Use problem-solving strategies to develop computer programs
▶ Describe computer-related activities for developing problem-solving skills

What is problem solving? Many answers to this question have been suggested; however, problem solving as a process cannot be understood unless it is experienced. Reading what others have written provides only a partial view and incomplete understanding. Solving problems yourself and reflecting upon the process of solution are crucial.

Problem solving involves intellectual curiosity. It is wanting to find out: to find answers to questions, to find ways to overcome difficulties, to find solutions to puzzles, and to find ways of accomplishing goals. Problem solving is doing rather than receiving. A problem solver is more likely to try out an idea and experiment with it than to ask someone for an answer or an explanation. This problem-solving attitude is a part of the person's personality pattern. Problem solvers approach learning by doing and experimenting. They try to understand a concept more deeply and try to create something new with the concept. You should develop this attitude.

Logo primitive LPUT works with words and lists. Here is an example:

```
PRINT LPUT "A [B C]
```

Now explore the meaning of LPUT. Try to see how many different uses it has. Write a program that makes use of LPUT. If you suppose that there is also such a thing as FPUT, it could also be explored as an analogy to LPUT; use what you have already learned about LPUT.

Characterizing Problem Solving

A problem is a function of the problem solver. What is a problem for one person is child's play for another and can be overwhelming for a third person.

A problem for a person is one of the following:

1. A question for which the answer is not easily obtained and for which the problem solver must search for, deliberate on, and create a valid answer.
2. A difficulty that must be overcome, for which resources must be marshalled or created, and for which the resolution must be invented (a strong desire is present for overcoming the difficulty).
3. A goal that is obstructed, but for which motivation is present. To achieve the goal, the problem solver must creatively develop a way of overcoming the obstacle.

These views suggest that learning how to solve problems is different from learning skills and concepts. Learning to solve problems requires different teaching and learning strategies. These methods are developed later in this chapter.

Productive Rather than Reproductive Thought

Much of initial learning in a discipline involves defining rules, memorizing lists, and practicing skills. These lead to **reproductive thought.** However, isolated facts and rules, devoid of an organized scheme, are difficult to remember. Miller (1956) conjectures, according to evidence, that information of this sort can be retained in memory only briefly and in small quantities.

Reproductive thought involves repetition of what is known. It can be application of a rule that the user has seen applied. Thus the rule is a fact to be remembered. For example, having heard the rule "*i* before *e* except after *c*" and having seen it applied to the spelling of the word "ceiling," you could involve reproductive thought to use it again (Wertheimer, 1959).

In contrast, problem solving is more consistent with **productive thought.** Productive thought is the production of something *new* out of the old. Productive thought goes beyond known patterns to unknown patterns (that is, patterns unknown to the problem solver). For example, someone who listened analytically to "The Battle Hymn of the Republic" and concluded that the song was written during a particular battle of the Civil War would be using productive thought.

Use of a Model to Solve a Real-World Problem

Most disciplines have some sort of theoretical base. Translating a real situation into a theoretical base that can be analyzed is **applied problem solving.** One illustration of this process is describing the effects of nuclear explosion, according to a theoretical base in physics and materials engineering. Fortunately, the destructive power of nuclear explosions in populated areas has not been documented in many specific cases. Yet, science provides formulas and other theory that allow the real-world situation, which has distances, quantities, and physical environments, to be **modeled** and predicted. To give a picture of likely results, the theory can be translated back into the real world.

Heuristic Processes

Heuristics are guiding and organizing thoughts that suggest possible courses of action in a problem situation. Individual thought processes (for example, generalizing, working backward) are among the easier parts of problem solving, and are heuristic in that they are reasonable activities to use in trying to solve problems. You read about and worked through some of those processes in earlier chapters. They are listed and described in Box 1. No single process works in every situation, but at least one should provide a key to the analysis of any new situation. Learning to be a good problem solver, in one sense, is learning to use heuristics effectively.

> **Box 1 Heuristics**
>
> ▶ **Analogy:** An analysis that is based on the similarities of two or more problems or representations
> ▶ **Decomposition:** The process of breaking down a problem situation into a series of simpler parts that, when put together, achieve the goal
> ▶ **Generalization:** The process of extending a pattern to other situations, so that the pattern is more complete and inclusive
> ▶ **Recombination:** The process of putting together the decomposed parts of a problem situation so that the new pattern achieves the goal
> ▶ **Simpler, related problem:** A problem related to the main problem whose solution contributes to the solution of the main problem
> ▶ **Symmetry:** Identical parts of a problem that, viewed from different perspectives, aid in solving the problem
> ▶ **Working backward:** The form of reasoning that starts with the goal and asks, What is sufficient to yield the goal?, or What subgoals yield the goal?

The thought processes are very general and are applicable in quite different situations. Think how often you use generalizing and analogy.

```
TO ZIG
    RT 90
        FD 15 LT 90
        FD 15 RT 90
        FD 15 LT 90
        FD 15 RT 90 FD 15
END
```

To practice **working backward,** move the turtle through the ZIG pattern, as shown. In our ZIG example, working backward is what we could try since the turtle is at the end of a sequence of moves and turns. If the turtle backed through its moves and turns, it would get back to the starting point. This process is heuristic in that it is a reasonable thing to try; it may help to solve the problem.

To practice the reversal of thought, consider the problem of developing a Logo procedure to produce a screen display of names in a list. For example, suppose you have names in a Logo list [ADA JANE SUZI TONY BILL] and wish to produce a list consisting of [ADA JANE TONY BILL]. Devise a way of doing this. Make sure it is general, so that the specific names, the number of names in the list, and the name(s) to be eliminated can vary.

To experience **decomposition** and **recombination** processes, ponder this problem. Consider the task of drawing a cube (assume a square base or front is the starting point) (Figure 1). Draw the cube in the manner that shows the clearest, most structured form. Analyze the drawing of the cube and break it into subprocedures. Make full use of patterns that can be repeated. Later in the chapter, we will discuss some related ideas.

Figure 2 pictures a visual pattern. It can be decomposed into a series of simpler patterns that can be recombined to form the pattern. Use decomposition and recombination skills and skills of programming to create the visual pattern. To tie together your earlier learning and experiences, create a structure diagram and a structured program for this pattern.

The use of **symmetry** is an important technique using heuristic hypotheses. Consider the problem of providing directions with enough clarity and simplicity that a robot can follow them. Think about the challenge of directing a robot to trace an oval (ellipse), with emphasis on the symmetry of the patterns created. Specifically, write a structured set of procedures (hold them to a minimum, maybe two)

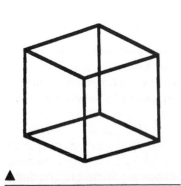

Figure 1 *A cube.*

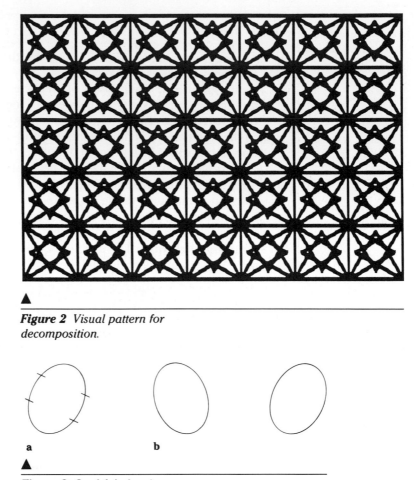

▲

Figure 2 *Visual pattern for decomposition.*

Figure 3 *Oval (a) showing symmetry, and (b) reflecting its mirror-image.*

that can be used repeatedly to draw an oval, and that emphasize the symmetry of the oval (Figure 3a).

A second, related challenge is to **reflect** the oval (describe the reflection, the mirror-image) about a straight line (Figure 3b). The description should be general enough that the oval could be reflected about any line requested of you.

Approaching Problem-Solving Experiences

Learning and teaching problem-solving processes require systematic approaches. Solving problems is a uniquely human mental process. Assuming that it is innate and cannot be taught leaves it available to only those few who manage to learn it on their own. This section is devoted to ways of developing the mental processes appropriate to systematic problem solving.

Problem-Solving Models

Humans have exhibited much ingenuity in problem solving, including the development of the concept of a computer and the electronic circuitry that made it

---

Box 2   Questions Guiding Problem-Solving Thought

Orienting or Getting Started
- ▶ Can I restate the problem (in my own words)?
- ▶ Do I know all concepts (technical terms)?
- ▶ What is given?
- ▶ What is the goal? (Guess the result.)
- ▶ What connections can I make between given and goal?

Planning or Design
- ▶ In what ways can I decompose the problem into simpler problems?
- ▶ What are appropriate subgoals?
- ▶ Which subgoals need further decomposition?
- ▶ Does the set of subgoals accomplish the goal?
- ▶ What thought processes can help (now) to generate the subgoals?

Modeling or Execution
- ▶ What processes or other problems are related to the subgoals?
- ▶ Can I use analogy, simpler problems, working backward, or generalizing? How?
- ▶ Can I generate a path to achieve each subgoal (create an algorithm)?

Verification or Looking Back
- ▶ Have I completely achieved the goal?
- ▶ Can I simplify the process? Generalize it? Structure it?
- ▶ Can I verify each subgoal?
- ▶ Can I generate a contrasting process to verify the results?

---

possible to implement this idea. From this and other examples of problem solving, models of problem solving are abstracted. Most of these models have common stages (Polya, 1957; Wertheimer, 1959):

1. Orienting or getting started
2. Planning or designing
3. Modeling or executing
4. Verifying or looking back

Problem-Solving Strategies

Some general approaches to solving problems provide a basis for an attack on any problem. These approaches usually are either not taught to students or are not mastered by them. Almost every teacher has heard students say things such as: "If I knew the formula, I could have solved the problem." "If I could think of an idea, I could write the theme." "If I could remember the date, I could figure out the cause of this historical event."

The common difficulty underlying these obstacles to the problem's solution is lacking a start: simply not knowing how to approach the problem. The first step is for students to know how to start to solve a problem, to learn **orienting.**

A few questions provide a way of getting started. Working with these questions and learning to pose them to yourself during problem solving can help you overcome the difficulty of getting started. Eventually, however, the solution plan evolves through the use of heuristic thought. Box 2 shows a set of questions useful in problem solving.

Teaching and Learning Strategies

Teaching and learning strategies parallel the functions of reasoning and heuristics. By teaching with and about analogy, uses of analogy are learned. The same may be said about teaching with and about generalization, decomposition and recombination, **inductive and deductive reasoning,** working backward, and so on. It seems reasonable that seeing a process used in a variety of ways and seeing its usefulness in a variety of situations are part of learning the process. Seeing the concept's uses across disciplines while seeing the shades of differences shows the power of that concept.

To illustrate teaching and learning strategies, we present the idea of **generalization.** This process can combine disciplines and simplify learning across them (and thereby shows its power). For example, start with the concept *structure* and note its generality across disciplines. The theme's outline, the plan of an experiment (the scientific method) in science, the game plan in an athletic event, the program or, more specifically, the acts of a play in a performing arts event all represent the same concept, the *structure.* One aspect of generalizing is seeing the patterns of key ideas, which appear in and are useful to many subject areas. Another aspect, as has been exemplified, is seeing patterns in English sentences (He speaks. He walks.) or geometric designs (TRIANGLE 3 . . . 120, SQUARE 4 . . . 90, PENTAGON 5 . . . 72).

Hints and Partial Solutions

In this section, we focus on experimenting with the problem-solving attitude, the willingness to try, and the strength to ignore what others may think. Your problem-solving trials will be individual, and you will do them at the computer. Feel free to try over and over again; work a little while, then do something else, then work a little while again. As a start, consider the following problem.

Suppose there are two cups, one filled (almost) with coffee and one with milk. The cups are the same size and are filled to the same level. A spoonful of milk is taken from the milk cup and transferred to the coffee cup (and mixed in thoroughly). Then a spoonful of the mixture in the coffee cup is taken from the coffee cup and mixed into the milk cup. Is there more milk in the coffee cup or more coffee in the milk cup?

Hint: use analogy. Suppose there are equal numbers of white marbles and black marbles in separate containers. By analogy, the marbles are transferred in the same way as were the coffee and the milk. Use actual marbles (or other counters) as you experiment with the problem.

Exploration

The process of problem solving involves exploration. Trial and error should be encouraged, not ridiculed. Trials and improving approximations are a natural part of any problem-solving process. By trying a sequence of options, you allow the emergence of a clearer formulation of the goal and means to the goal, together with a possible solution strategy. Exploration with computers allows for the rapid development and testing of hypotheses. Building and testing hypotheses is crucial to problem solving.

Another form of exploration involves building physical models to simulate the problem situation. Consider the following:

A monkey is holding on to a rope that passes round a frictionless pulley and supports at the other end a weight that is just as heavy as the monkey. The monkey now starts to climb the rope. What happens?

Exploring, in this case, should involve building a physical model. Get a pulley (or something that serves the same purpose) and put equally weighted objects to represent the weight and the monkey on a string. Model the situation and see the results.

Independent Learning

Problem solving requires independence, the attitude or belief that one can do things without help. Experiencing and gaining confidence in problem solving increase independence and perseverance. Computers can be tools for developing independence. In particular, programming in a language that provides good error messages (aids to debugging) and encourages trial and error allows for experimentation without fear of ridicule. This process can help remove the right-or-wrong attitude that forms dependence; further, programming encourages an attitude of wanting to learn rather than having to know.

It is appropriate to reexamine the problems *Salaj* and *Cointoss*. What is the relationship between them? Does it suggest that the problems have the same solution? Is either of them more easily solved analytically? If so, the process of restating a problem as an equivalent problem that is more concrete hints at the problem's solutions. Execute the two procedures that simulate these problems. Do they produce essentially the same results? Now examine the simulations' procedures. How are they related?

Consider three programs (*PS.1, PS.2, PS.3*) on the *Applications Disk*. (Type INTRO to run.) They contain problem statements and programs for exploring the problems. First consider the statements of the problems. Attempt to reformulate the problems into models that more closely fit your way of thinking (a sample of such reformulation is contained in the hints on the *Applications Disk*). As time permits, continue to explore the problems without assistance. Whenever necessary, request hints (provided on the *Applications Disk*). This problem-solving set provides sufficient hints and solutions. As you experiment with the problem-solving samples, attempt to produce analytic solutions.

Programming versus Problem Solving

Creating original programs in any language is problem solving. However, programming that is reproductive rather than productive is not problem solving. Thus, some but not all programming is problem solving. Whenever you design a program that requires novel usage of existing programming knowledge and that accomplishes a predetermined goal you use problem solving.

The forms of reasoning that contribute to problem solving are also necessary for programming. Analogy, decomposition, the use of simpler related problems, and working backward are common to problem solving and programming. However, learning their use in a programming environment does not necessarily mean that a student will generalize them to other problem-solving situations.

Problem solving and programming are similar in that each attempts to solve a problem. Some computer educators describe programming as using the computer as a tool for solving problems. They define a *program* as *a computerized solution to a problem:* the conclusion that programming is problem solving follows. However, consider their basic assumption carefully before accepting that definition.

Computer Uses in Problem Solving

Computers can be used in several ways to aid in problem solving. Computer-generated data may suggest hypotheses from which solutions can be worked out analytically. Computers can be programmed to generate complete solutions if conceptual structures have been developed beforehand. Problem-solving exploration with computers involves data organization and analysis, including simulation of real-world situations.

The *Salaj* microworld problem illustrates a good use of decomposition, of one complex problem to simpler, related problems. Recall the statement of the problem in Chapter 3:

> The birth of a son signals the completion of the family. Therefore, it is hereby forbidden to have other children after the birth of a son.
>
> What is the eventual effect of this law on the population of *Salaj?* Will there be considerably more females than males in *Salaj?* Will the country's population decrease, possibly to extinction? Will there be so few males that the country will have to begin to practice polygamy to survive (Salaj's current laws require monogamy)? What would the sociologists conclude?

When the procedure is executed, data are generated. Some problem solvers may see an analysis that can solve the problem in a few executions. If you do not, it might be helpful to make crucial observations about the data, or to tabulate and analyze the data generated from several executions. An example of tabulated data is given in Table 1.

The executions with small numbers of families (10, 10, 10, 20, 20) seem to provide no definite patterns. However, suppose the totals across all ten executions in Table 1 are examined. You can draw some conclusions from these data. (We give you hints, but do not provide solutions. Problem solving provides ways of thinking through a situation, not the completed paths. If we gave you the answer, your thought about the problem would be considerably curtailed, if not stopped altogether.)

Decomposing Problems: Structured Programming

A crucial aspect of problem solving involves breaking down the problem into a series of subproblems (or reducing the goal to a series of intermediate goals). This decomposition of a problem is analogous to the decomposition of a procedure into a series of subprocedures that, when taken together, will achieve the same end

Table 1 Data from *Salaj* Executions			
Families	**Boys**	**Girls**	**Totals**
10	10	6	16
10	10	13	23
10	10	18	28
20	20	18	38
20	20	25	45
100	100	115	215
100	100	84	184
500	500	463	963
500	500	560	1060
1000	1000	1009	2009

as the original procedure. This is the essence of structured programming. Decomposing and recombining is the analogous method of problem solving: structured programming is to programming as decomposing and recombining are to problem solving. Consider the following problem:

> The player of a game is permitted to toss a penny until a head appears. For each toss, one dollar is awarded. How much, on the average, would the player receive for playing the game once?

It is easier first to look at a single game than to think about the average of several games. Examine some examples of how individual games could turn out (each line represents a game):

H	($1)
TH	($2)
TTTTH	($5)
TTH	($3)
TTTH	($4)
TTTTTTTTTTTH	($12)
TTTTTH	($6)

We now ask how the single-game examples can be used to solve the original problem.

A computer procedure to simulate the single-game simplification of the problem could be written. That procedure could then be used as a subprocedure in a simulation of the original problem. To further analyze the game and solve it, use the procedure *Cointoss* on the *Applications Disk.*

Inductive and Deductive Reasoning

Problem solving generally requires both inductive and deductive reasoning. Some examples of these reasoning forms have been illustrated already. Although sometimes associated with mathematics and science, inductive and deductive reasoning are at least as important to the development of understanding and learning of other disciplines as well.

Inductive Reasoning   The process of seeing patterns and inferring a general pattern (a conclusion about the pattern) is crucial to organizing and storing knowledge. It also is effective in learning and in problem solving. Consider the following pattern of sentences in Spanish and English.

> "Él habla" means "He talks."
> "Él pasea" means "He walks."
> "Él baila" means "He dances."
> "Él canta" means "He sings."
> "Él maneja" means "He drives."
> "Él mira" means "He looks."
> "Él escucha" means "He listens."

A computer is powerful in speed, repetition, and storage and retrieval. Because of the computer's easy use of repetition, it is a good tool for learning through inductive processes. For example, to look at these language patterns, you could use this Logo program:

```
TO ES
    CLEARTEXT    [LogoWriter: CT]
    MAKE "SLIST [HABLA PASEA BAILA CANTA MANEJA MIRA
    ESCUCHA]
    MAKE "ELIST [TALKS WALKS DANCES SINGS DRIVES LOOKS
    LISTENS]
    ENGL.SPANISH
END
```

```
TO ENGL.SPANISH
   IF:SLIST = [] STOP ELSE MAKE "S FIRST :SLIST MAKE "E
   FIRST :ELIST    [LogoWriter: IFELSE :SLIST = [  ] [STOP] MAKE "S FIRST
                                :SLIST MAKE "E FIRST :ELIST]
      PRINT (SE ["EL] WORD :S "." [ MEANS "HE] WORD :E
   "." )
   MAKE "SLIST BUTFIRST :SLIST
   MAKE "ELIST BUTFIRST :ELIST
   ENGL.SPANISH
END
```

The difficulty of learning through inductive reasoning lies in generating and organizing patterns. There also must be many similar single items that can be identified, to make the general pattern evident. Further, patterns must be studied for limitations on generality. The pattern in our example is limited to regular Spanish verbs ending in "-ar." The characteristic examples and repetition can be easily organized by computers. Thus, computers contribute to the usefulness of inductive reasoning processes. A byproduct of learning about inductive processes with computers is that both general problem-solving ability and understanding of structured programming are strengthened.

Deductive Reasoning   Deductive reasoning, on the other hand, starts from the general and draws specific conclusions. For example, by definition, a *verb* is a *word that shows action or state of being.* From this definition, it is clear that *dances, sings, walks, talks,* and so on in *Es* are verbs; these words show action.

Comparing Top-Down and Bottom-Up Programming

Top-down programming involves first developing the structure of a program, then creating the program. **Bottom-up programming** involves writing a program and then structuring it. **Middle-out programming** is a combination of top-down and bottom-up programming. Actually, it may be more accurate to call these **top-down planning** and **bottom-up planning.** It is the problem-solving process of planning that initiates good programming. Ideally, planning before the fact makes structure easier to achieve; planning during or after the fact is necessary and appropriate at times. Turkle (1984) relates these different styles of programming to various types of people. She identifies the *hard masters* who prefer the top-down approach and the *soft masters* who prefer a more intuitive approach.

Owl, an exercise in Chapter 2, illustrates the results of top-down planning. The programming proceeded as follows:

1. The goal is established (the picture of the owl is the goal).
2. The parts of the owl (those chosen to be considered separate components) are determined.
3. The plan is written.
4. The parts of the plan (the subprocedures outlined in the plan) are developed individually.
5. The individual subprocedures are debugged.
6. The plan is evaluated (the program is executed and the output is checked against the goal).

```
TO OVAL :S1 :S2
   REPEAT 2[C1 :S1 C2 :S2]
END
```

```
TO C1 :S1
    REPEAT 5[FD :S1 RT 18]
END

TO C2 :S2
    REPEAT 5[FD :S2 RT 18]
END
```

By contrast, the developments of *Circle, Lcircle,* and *Eyes* illustrate bottom-up planning. That is, the sequence of writing and the process of accomplishing the goal evolved in a less determined way. Recall the process:

1. *Circle* is written (the procedure is defined).
2. *Lcircle* is written.
3. After these two procedures are written, *Eyes* is structured.
4. The subprocedures of *Eyes* are developed and debugged.
5. The procedure *Eyes* is verified (by executing, the output is compared to the goal).

In this example, the procedure is created from the pieces (the procedures *Circle* and *Lcircle*). The picture of the eyes is not defined as the final goal, nor is there a complete plan developed prior to the development of the subprocedures.

Top-Down Plan of an Oval

Suppose you want a diagram of an ellipse (Figure 4). First you make a freehand drawing of the oval with paper and pencil. You note from the sketch that the top and bottom halves are symmetrical (mirror reflections of each other). Further, you note that the top half (like the bottom half) is made of:

1. A sharply curving arc (SHARP.ARC)
2. A smooth or slowly curving arc (SMOOTH.ARC)
3. A sharply curving arc identical to the first one (SHARP.ARC)

The top-down plan, created from the analysis of the goal, is

```
TO OVAL
    SHARP.ARC
    SMOOTH.ARC
    SHARP.ARC
    SHARP.ARC
    SMOOTH.ARC
    SHARP.ARC
END
```

Although this plan should work, once the individual arcs SHARP.ARC and SMOOTH.ARC are defined, the procedure is not well structured. Consider the following as a structure that is more consistent with the visual image of the oval itself:

```
TO OVAL
    SHARP.ARC SMOOTH.ARC SHARP.ARC
    SHARP.ARC SMOOTH.ARC SHARP.ARC
END
```

or

```
TO OVAL
    REPEAT 2[SHARP.ARC SMOOTH.ARC SHARP.ARC]
END
```

Now that a well-structured plan for *Oval* is completed, the individual subprocedures that are called in the main procedure must be written and debugged. When you

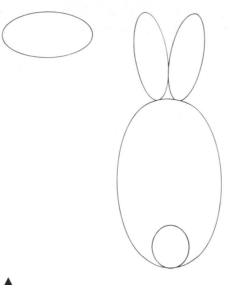

▲

Figure 4 *(a) Ellipse created by Oval. (b) By using procedures with a variable that creates an oval, graphics such as the bunny rabbit can be created.*

have accomplished this, the procedure will be complete and the goal accomplished (upon execution and verification).

To write the first of these subprocedures, we realize that *Sharp.arc* is part of a small circle (small in a relative sense), so the related procedure for a circle would be a good thing to consider first. When we experiment, we can first consider describing a fourth or an eighth of a circle. A starting point is

```
TO SHARP.ARC
    REPEAT 12[FD 3 RT 5]
END
```

Now it is your turn to use *Sharp.arc* and finish *Oval:* write and debug the related procedure *Smooth.arc.*

The observations necessary for the completion of *Sharp.arc* and *Smooth.arc* are:

1. That there is top and bottom symmetry suggests that each half should contain total turns of 180 degrees.
2. The *(Sharp.arc)* sharp turn suggests that short steps are needed between turns (FD 3).
3. The *(Smooth.arc)* slow-or-smooth turn suggests that (relatively) long steps are needed between turns, hence (FD ? . . .you determine).
4. The repetition of *Sharp.arc* at the end of the top half of the oval is due to the symmetry of the left and right halves.

Bottom-Up Plan of a Cube

The planning that follows illustrates bottom-up planning. Suppose the goal is to draw a cube on the screen. Knowing that a square is an essential part of a cube, we write the procedure for a square as a starting point:

```
TO SQUARE
    REPEAT 4[FD 50 RT 90]
END
```

From there, we decide that the edge of the cube beginning at the bottom left corner of the face (*Square*) is to be drawn next:

```
TO EDGE
    LT 45 FD .707*50 BK .707*50 SETH 0
END
```

(SETH stands for SETHEADING; it sets the direction for the turtle.) Then we decide to draw the parallel sides together in a particular pairing:

```
TO PARALLELSIDES
    EDGE FD 50 EDGE
    PU HOME PD
END
```

From there, the other parallel sides (*Otherparallelsides*) and the back face (*Backsquare*) are finally accomplished after experimentation. The end result is then structured as follows:

```
TO CUBE
    SQUARE
    PARALLELSIDES
    OTHERPARALLELSIDES
    BACKSQUARE
END

TO SQUARE
    REPEAT 4[FD 50 RT 90]
END

TO PARALLELSIDES
    EDGE FD 50 EDGE
END

TO EDGE
    LT 45 FD .707*50 BK .707*50 SETH 0
END

TO OTHERPARALLELSIDES
    RT 90 FD 50 LT 90
    PARALLELSIDES
END

TO BACKSQUARE
    LT 45 FD .707*50 RT 45
    SQUARE
    PU HOME PD
END
```

Although this goal might not be easy to accomplish, the actual building of the procedure starts with a component of the desired picture. Using that as a base, the building proceeds to develop additional parts. Organization and structuring occur as the results approach the goal. The subgoals are typically determined by experimentation, as different subgoals contribute to the final goal. For example, during the design of *Cube* it is likely that a procedure (accomplished subgoal) for drawing an edge (a side between the front and back faces) is needed. Chances are good that attempts were made to call the procedure for the edge within the procedure that draws the square.

The point is that bottom-up planning is frequently appropriate, especially when the desired results can be analyzed in many different ways and when some of the subgoals are difficult to achieve.

Applications to the Use of Software

The concept of problem solving can be seen not only in programming techniques, but also in the use of some types of software. For example, consider the following software and their uses of problem-solving processes. (Also see Chapter 10, for more examples.)

***The Pond: Strategies in Problem Solving* (Sunburst)**   Students, in grades two and up, help a frog jump along a path of lily pads; without falling into the water, the frog must reach the magic lily pad. In this game, the students practice and develop skills in directionality, pattern recognition, hypothesis formulation, and logic. First the student must identify the pattern of lily pads, then use that knowledge. Because there are several different levels of difficulty, the software does allow for real growth.

***The King's Rule* and *The Royal Rules* (Sunburst)**   As they seek to discover numerical rules for number patterns, students (from grade four through adult) apply their problem-solving processes to the generation and testing of working hypotheses. The students can advance through progressive levels of difficulty. The rules of the later levels are quite challenging. The final level now allows students to create their own library of rules, disguise examples to look as if they fit another rule, and save them on a data disk. They can then challenge other students to solve their created rules.

***Rocky's Boots* and *Robot Odyssey I* (The Learning Company)**   Through active involvement in the commercial program *Rocky's Boots,* the user explores concepts of electrical circuitry. After demonstrating examples and skill practice, *Rocky's Boots* involves problem solving. The challenge is that the user must create circuitry to fulfill a particular goal. The *create circuitry* example in *Rocky's Boots* illustrates that facts and processes are both essential for successful problem solving. Figures 5 and 6 show the progression in complexity. *Rocky's Boots* develops logical thinking

Figure 5 *Screen display of Rocky's Boots.*

Figure 6 *Screen display of Rocky's Boots, showing a more complex circuitry.*

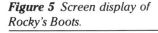

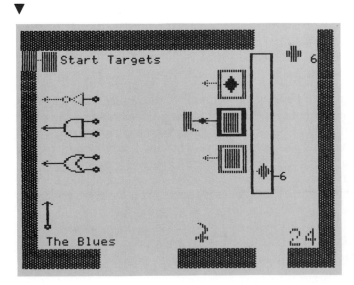

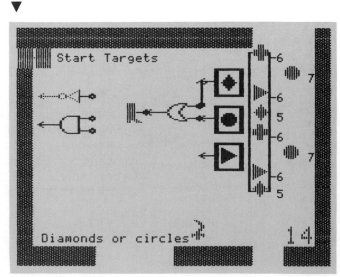

and problem-solving processes in students (in grades four and up), as they build switching circuits and logic designs, embedded in a gaming format. *Robot Odyssey* I lets students (in grades seven and up) program their own robots to navigate obstacles, sneak past sentries, solve intricate puzzles, and unlock the secret exit.

***Gertrude's Secrets* and *Gertrude's Puzzles* (The Learning Company)**   This software uses Gertrude, the Goose, to help students learn important skills in classification, grouping, sequencing, and organizing. *Gertrude's Secrets* is for students in grades K–four. For students in grades four through seven, *Gertrude's Puzzles* seeks to extend these logic skills; carefully developed games build a child's critical thinking and problem-solving processes.

▶ ▲ ◀ ▼ ▶ ▲ ◀ ▼ ▶ ▲ ◀ ▼ ▶ ▲ ◀ ▼ ▶ ▲ ◀ ▼ ▶ ▲

Summary

Problem solving is probably the major factor in successful computer use; therefore, teaching problem solving is a major goal of computer education. Writing an original program is problem solving; the planning that leads to a program is problem solving. In fact, from one point of view, the problem must be solved before the program is written. Creative uses of computers require problem-solving processes.

In general, problem solving is likely to become more central to education as society becomes more complex. Advanced technology requires sophisticated problem solving; at the same time, it provides the tools for sophisticated problem solving. The rapid alterations in today's world suggest that the form and the goals of education are changing. Some skills that used to be drilled for considerable periods are now replaced by the skills of an inexpensive calculator. Rather than being memorized, some facts can be called from a computer's database. In modern society, knowing only facts, formulas, and specific solutions is not enough, because those can quickly become obsolete. Knowledge of how to approach and solve new problems, on the other hand, always will be applicable. Learning how to learn may become the focus of educational programs designed for changing societal needs. Problem solving as a way of learning is not likely to become obsolete.

The following procedures and programs were described in this chapter:

PS.1	*Sharp.arc*	*The Pond*
PS.2	*Smooth.arc*	*The King's Rule*
PS.3	*Square*	*The Royal Rules*
ES	*Edge*	*Rocky's Boots*
Engl.Spanish	*Parallelsides*	*Gertrude's Secrets*
Owl	*Otherparallelsides*	*Gertrude's Puzzles*
Eyes	*Backsquare*	
Oval	*Cube*	

Important Terms

Analogy	Middle-out programming
Applied problem solving	Modeling
Bottom-up planning	Orienting
Decomposition	Planning
Deductive reasoning	Productive thought
Generalization	Recombination
Heuristics	Reflect
Inductive reasoning	Related problems

Reproductive thought   Verifying
Symmetry   Working backward
Top-down planning

Figure 7 *Initial pattern to be decomposed.*

Exercises

1. Decompose the picture in Figure 7 and recombine those fragments to produce it.

2. Decompose the picture in Figure 8 and recombine those fragments to produce it.

3. Decompose the picture in Figure 9 and recombine those fragments to produce it.

4. Using a process analogous to the following program, teach Logo a new word, according to the goals listed in (a) and (b).

```
TO ERNS :LNAME
    IF :LNAME = [] STOP
    RUN LIST "ERNAME FIRST :LNAME
    ERNS BUTFIRST :LNAME
END
```

a.   Teach Logo a new word, *Erps,* that will erase all procedures input as a list.

Figure 8 *Intermediate pattern to be decomposed.*

Figure 9 *Final pattern to be recombined.*

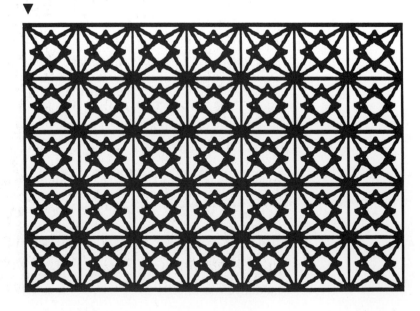

b.   Teach Logo a new word, *Pops,* that will place on the screen all procedures input as a list.

5.   Teach Logo a new word, *Erasure,* that will erase the most recently drawn line of turtlegraphics.

6.   Decompose a set of ten pentagons rotated through 36 degrees, and recombine the resulting elements. (Figure 10 shows the pattern you want to produce.)

7.   Determine the symmetry of the picture in Figure 10. Can the symmetry be used in another way of drawing the picture?

8.   The reflection problem may be stated as follows: Given a left half of a picture, construct the right half. Create an algorithm for such a reflection of symmetrical patterns.

9.   Write a procedure to count words in a list.

10.   Teach Logo the word WAIT, which takes a number, :N, as input and produces a wait of :N/60 seconds.

11.   Prepare an essay to answer one of these questions:

   ▶ What is structured programming?
   ▶ What is bottom-up planning?
   ▶ What is top-down planning?

For your essay, do thorough structuring, including (a) an outline of major and minor headings, (b) an outline with topic sentences, (c) four or five defenses for each topic sentence.

12.   How could a fishing rod that is 12 feet long be transported by Newmail Express, which limits all packages to no more than 10 feet long and 8 feet wide? Hint: consider related problems. Think of ways to package objects. Physically model the situation (use a scale model).

13.   Draw a circle. Transform copies of it to develop a sphere. Describe, in a structured way, the major features of the building of the sphere.

14.   Examine one of the microworlds discussed in Chapter 3. By experimenting with it, predict the outcome it will produce from specific inputs. What does this prediction have to do with problem solving?

Figure 10 *Designs to be decomposed and recombined.*

▼

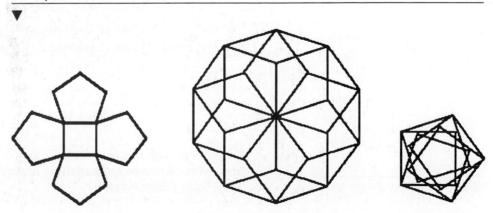

15. Compare the pair of Logo procedures:

```
TO TRIANG
   REPEAT 3[FD 50 LT 120]
END

TO TRIANG
   REPEAT 3[LT 120 FD 50]
END
```

Enter and execute the procedures. Is one the reverse of the other? (Is each process reversed and the order of the processes reversed?)

16. Compare the pair of Logo procedures:

```
TO TRIANG
   REPEAT 3[FD 50 LT 120]
END

TO UNTRIANG
   REPEAT 3[BK 50 RT 120]
END
```

Enter and execute the procedures. Is there true reversibility between the pair? (Are the process and order reversed?)

17. By modifying *Triang,* create *Untriang,* in which the turtle reverses the order, movement, and rotation used in Triang. Compare this newly created procedure to the procedure that reversed *Square.*

18. Explore FPUT, a primitive of Logo. Its syntax is FPUT "C [A B].

19. a. How are problem solving and imagery related to the skills and concepts involved in the making of generalizations?
   b. Describe how the best, commercially available programs help develop problem-solving ability and the use of heuristics.
   c. Describe how programming Logo teaches students how to generalize.
   d. Choose a brain teaser to solve. Describe the evolution of your thought in solving the brain teaser.
   e. Choose another brain teaser to solve. Ask yourself the thought-generating questions in Box 2 as you solve the brain teaser. Write an analysis of the effect of this process on your solution.
   f. Draw a three-dimensional object. As you organize the process of drawing, emphasize repeated patterns in the drawing's structure (for example, the squares in *Cube*). Describe the imagery that you used during this process.
   g. Keep a diary of work that you performed during a day. Make notes on your attempts to use top-down planning. Write an analysis of the effectiveness of this top-down planning.

20. Write a top-down plan to draw the sailboat in Figure 11.

21. The pictures in Figure 12 were all drawn by this procedure:

```
TO CURVE :Y :A
   FD 5
   RT :Y
   CURVE :Y + :A :A
END
```

Experiment with this procedure until you can predict the figure you get. See if you can make some of these unusual shapes. (This procedure is sometimes called *Polyspi.*)

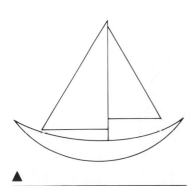

Figure 11 Sailboat design.

Figure 12 Sample results of
Curve.

continued

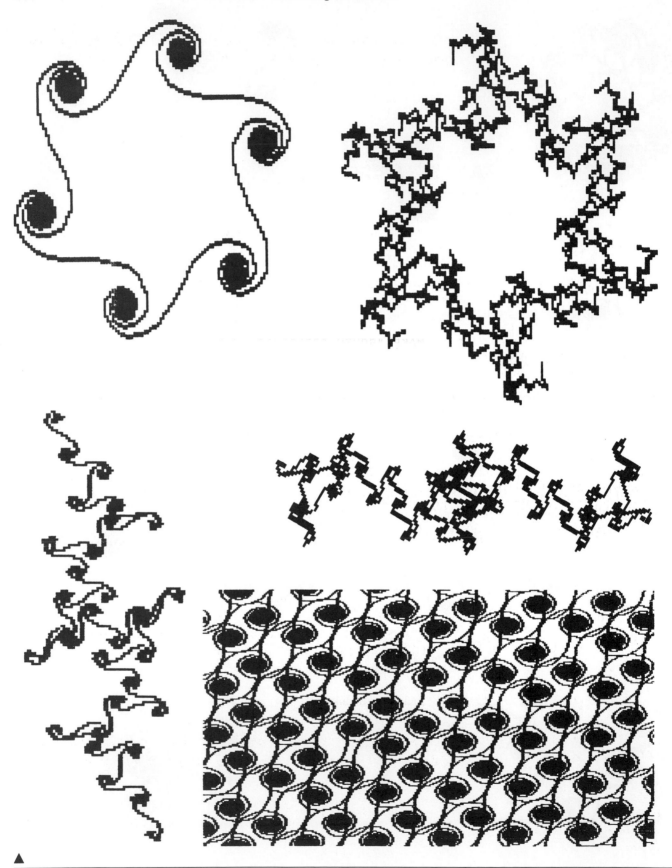

Figure 12 *Continued*

22. To explore the meanings of *global* and *local variables,* use the following procedures (and others that you create):

```
TO SQUARE :SIDE
    REPEAT 4[FD :SIDE RT 90]
    CIRCLE
END

TO CIRCLE
    REPEAT 30[FD :SIDE RT 12]
END

MAKE "SIDE 8
```

You may wish to place print statements at judicious places, as you develop hypotheses about global and local variables. Justify the hypotheses with evidence.

23. Explore the linguistic implications of WORD (the Logo primitive). You may begin with

```
MAKE "H ( WORD "S "OUT "H )
MAKE "SOUTH [OPPOSITE NORTH]
PRINT :H
PRINT :SOUTH
```

Develop hypotheses about how WORD (the Logo primitive) works. Provide evidence to justify your hypotheses.

24. Explore the meaning of *lists.* You may wish to begin with

```
TO J :S :T
    MAKE "L SE :S :T
    PRINT :L
END

TO J1 :S :T
    MAKE "L LIST :S :T
    PRINT :L
END
```

Develop hypotheses about how *lists* work. Provide evidence to justify your hypotheses.

25. Find a way to place multiple or single words from a list into a sentence. For example, suppose sentences such as these,

John is smart.
John is tall.
John is good looking.

were to be constructed by the selection of *smart, tall,* and *good looking* from a list of predicate adjectives. How could this construction be done?

26. Consider the following alternate procedure for drawing a cube:

```
TO CUBE
    SQUARE EDGE1 SQUARE 2
    PU HOME PD
    FD 50 EDGE
    RT 90 FD 50 LT 90 EDGE
    BK 50 EDGE
    PU HOME PD
END
```

```
TO SQUARE
   REPEAT 4[FD 50 RT 90]
END

TO EDGE1
   LT 45 FD.707*50 SETH 0
END

TO SQUARE 2
   REPEAT 4[LT 90 BK 50]
END

TO EDGE
   LT 45 FD .707*50 BK .707*50 SETH 0
END
```

Write a description of the differences between this program and *To Cube*.

27. Consider the following generalized cube:

```
TO CUBE :SIDE
   SQ :SIDE
   SEG1 :SIDE/SQRT ( 2 ) 45 0 0
   SQ :SIDE
   SEG :SIDE/SQRT ( 2 ) 45 0 :SIDE
   SEG :SIDE/SQRT ( 2 ) 45 45 :SIDE
   SEG :SIDE/SQRT ( 2 ) 45 :SIDE 0
END

TO SEG :L :ANGLE :X :Y
   MOVE :X :Y
   RT :ANGLE
   FD :L
   PU HOME
END

TO MOVE :X :Y
   PU
   FD :Y RT 90
   FD :X LT 90
   PD
END

TO SEG1 :L :ANGLE :X :Y
   MOVE :X :Y
   RT :ANGLE
   FD :L
   SETH 0
   SQ :SIDE
   PU HOME PD
END

TO SQ :SIDE
   REPEAT 4[FD :SIDE RT 90]
END
```

Which cube, presented within the chapter or the one in Exercise 26, has the process that more closely resembles that of this generalized *Cube*?

28. An alternative way of building a cube would be to use the side faces, which appear to be rhomboid. A procedure using this approach follows.

```
TO RHOMBUS :SIDE :ANGLE
   PD
   REPEAT 2[FD :SIDE RT :ANGLE FD :SIDE RT 180 - :ANGLE]
   PU HOME
END

TO CUBE :SIDE
   RHOMBUS :SIDE 90
   RHOMBUS :SIDE 60
   MOVE 0 :SIDE
   RT 60
   RHOMBUS :SIDE 30
   MOVE :SIDE 0
   RHOMBUS :SIDE 60
   RT 60
   RHOMBUS :SIDE 30
END

TO MOVE :X :Y
   PU
   FD :Y RT 90
   FD :X LT 90
   PD
END
```

To draw a specific version of this cube, choose values for the variables. Before executing this procedure, predict the precise order in which the edges of the cube will be drawn.

References

Buswell, G. (1956). *Patterns of thinking in problem solving.* University of California Publications in Education, No. 2. Berkeley, CA: University of California Press.

Duncker, K. (1945). Problem solving. *Psychological Monographs, 58* (entire issue).

Feigenbaum, E. A., & Feldman, J. (1963). *Computers and thought.* New York: McGraw-Hill.

Goldin, G. A., & McClintock, C. E. (1980). The theme of problem symmetry. In *Problem solving in school mathematics,* pp. 178–194. National Council of Teachers of Mathematics (NCTM) 1980 Yearbook. Reston, VA: NCTM.

McClintock, C. E. (1982). Problem solving: Some means and some ends. In *Problem solving in the mathematics classroom.* Rachlin, S. (Ed.). The Mathematics Council of the Alberta Teachers' Association (Math Monograph No. 7). Alberta, Canada: Barnett House.

Miller, G. A. (1956). The magic seven, plus or minus two: Some limitations on our capacity for processing information. *Psychology Review, 63,* 81–91.

Polya, G. (1957). *How to solve it.* 2nd ed. New York: Doubleday.

Polya, G. (1965). *Mathematical discovery.* Vol. 2. *On understanding, learning and teaching problem solving.* New York: Wiley.

Turkle, S. (1984). *The second self: Computers and the human spirit.* New York: Simon & Schuster.

Wertheimer, M. (1959). *Productive thinking.* New York: Harper.

Wickelgren, W. (1974). *How to solve problems.* New York: W. H. Freeman.

Part Two

Tool Uses of the Computer

▶ ▲ ◀ ▼ ▶ ▲ ◀ ▼ ▶ ▲ ◀ ▼ ▶ ▲ ◀ ▼ ▶ ▲ ◀ ▼ ▶ ▲

Computers are valuable for many uses, including computations, instruction, accounting, and programming. The wide variety of tool uses of computers are important to society and to education. We discuss and provide activities in these uses: word processing, database management, spreadsheet use, telecommunications, and a selection of other tools. The four chapters that make up Part Two give you first-hand experience in working with these tools. A particular word processor, database program, or spreadsheet is not required, even though AppleWorks is cited frequently. The activities can easily be adapted to any similar tool. Also included are some activities for school students using these tools.

Chapter 5 explores what is probably the most commonly used tool, word processing. We look at a simple and a more versatile word processor, and we discuss the features that are now available in word processors.

Chapter 6 focuses on uses of databases. Various uses of databases are demonstrated. Some databases are used to solve problems and some are created from scratch. Hands-on activities illustrate creating, experimenting with, and solving problems involving data. As an example, *Data Manager II* is presented on the *Applications Disk*. AppleWorks is also used extensively. *dBASE IV* is discussed.

Chapter 7 presents spreadsheets as tools for the investigation of numerical data. AppleWorks is a suggested tool, but similar spreadsheets could be used instead. The discussion and activities help you learn what spreadsheets are, what they can do, how they work, and how to make them from scratch.

Chapter 8 includes several other tools. Telecommunications is examined extensively. Likewise, networking discussions help you set up and use networks in your school and home. Finally, *CAD-CAM* and other graphics programs are presented. Two or three programs for creating bar graphs and graphics are included on the *Applications Disk*. AppleWorks GS is examined. A sample interactive video disk system for science is also discussed.

Chapter 5

Word Processing

▶ ▲ ◀ ▼ ▶ ▲ ◀ ▼ ▶ ▲ ◀ ▼ ▶ ▲ ◀ ▼ ▶ ▲ ◀ ▼ ▶ ▲ ◀ ▼ ▶ ▲

Objectives

▶ Identify the important characteristics of a word processor
▶ Develop skill in using one or more word processors
▶ Write, edit, format, and print a document on a word processor
▶ Compare and contrast at least two word processors

The single most popular tool application of microcomputers is word processing. For this reason, there are more word processors on the market than any other application. Students, teachers, business people, and families all make substantial use of word processors. Because our society is becoming increasingly reliant on information, this trend toward substantial use of word processors is likely to continue.

Features of a Word Processor

Word processing is a tool for verbal communication. Word processing packages are the most popular microcomputer software both in the office and at home. Schools are starting to realize the instructional potential of word processing. It can be used in the language arts classroom to teach writing skills or in the business classroom to teach typing. Students can use word processing as they write term papers, reports, and essays for all their classes. Word processing can simplify the task of producing a school newspaper or literary magazine.

Over 1,000 programs are available. A few, such as *Bank Street Writer* and *Homeword,* have been designed specifically with young students in mind. All of the word processors on the market perform certain basic functions. They can insert, delete, move, or copy blocks of text, search for and replace a word or phrase, center a title, set margins, and print the finished document. In addition, a variety of special features make some word processors more powerful or easier to use than others.

Word processors are changing and improving virtually by the month. Examples of constructive changes include On-disk tutorials; *help* that is accessible as you work; dictionaries and other references, including spelling checkers and thesauruses; grammar checkers; processes to produce outlines, indexes, tables of content, footnotes, headers and footers, endnotes, and boilerplates; processes to merge mail and to set style; fundamental desktop publishing units and graphics production (including bit-maps); windowing capabilities; and finally, "intelligent" anticipating and typing ahead of the writer. These capabilities only indicate the directions that word processors such as Microsoft *Word, WordPerfect, ZenWord,* and *WordStar* are taking.

Selecting a Word Processor

The features of a word processor can be divided into three general categories. The **text-editing** functions determine how easily you can write and make changes in your document. The **print-formatting** functions dictate the format in which the document will be printed on paper. **Screen display** involves the text that you see on the screen.

Text Editing   To use some word processors, you compose text in the write mode, then switch to an edit mode (by pressing <ESC>, for example) to move the cursor, and then return to the write mode to insert or delete text. Word processors that allow you to write and edit in the same mode can be easier to use. Switching between modes is cumbersome, especially if you make many changes.

To replace existing text, you can either write over text to be deleted or you can insert new text and delete old. Many word processors are capable of both and leave the choice to you. Overwriting is faster, but you should use it with care.

More powerful word processors allow you to delete not only characters but also whole words, lines, sentences, or paragraphs. In addition, you can move blocks of information, such as paragraphs or series of paragraphs. Another useful feature is the ability to merge a text file saved on your disk with the one you are currently writing.

Some word processors permit you to use the shift key to capitalize letters as you normally do on a typewriter. (To use the shift key, you need an inexpensive shift key modification for the Apple II + but not for the Apple IIe, IIc, or IIGS.)

Print-Formatting   Print-formatting functions direct the printer about the arrangement of the text on the printed page. The best word processors are able to center a line, indent a paragraph, underline, justify the right margin, set tab stops, number the pages, and change to a new page, different margins, or different line spacing in the middle of the document. More sophisticated programs can also print in boldface or italics and can print subscripts, superscripts, or special symbols. Of course, to

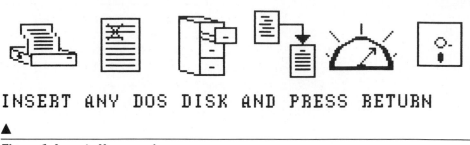

Figure 1 *Icons in Homeword.*

take advantage of these features, your printer must also be capable of handling them.

Screen Display   Some word processors display text one way as you type and edit it, but then print it differently. For example, although the screen display is 40 columns across, the printed page could be 70 columns. The screen might show all upper-case letters even though the printout has upper and lower case. Several word processors display your text on the screen exactly as it will appear on the printed page, including centering, justification, underlining, and even boldface. This is called the "what you see is what you get" feature.

Another type of screen display has options for different modes. For example, *Homeword* displays icons, or small drawings, as options for type of mode, as shown in Figure 1.

Support Materials   No matter how easy the operation of a word processor is, you will sometimes need help. Some programs have an onscreen *help* command that explains some commands. Many programs include a summary of the commands on a *quick-reference card* that you can keep next to the computer. One feature of *Bank Street Writer* that makes it easy to use is that the commands are always displayed at the top of the screen so you do not need to remember them (Figure 2). Tutorials on using the program—either on disk or in print—can be helpful in getting started. In addition, the manual should be clearly written and indexed for easy reference. Finally, some word processors have a built-in dictionary, thesaurus, or grammar checkers. Others can integrate addresses, graphics, and other special tools, into text.

Safety Features   Word processors should include safety features so that you do not lose data when you accidentally press the wrong key. One such safety feature is that text to be deleted is highlighted. You may be asked, "Are you sure?" when you are erasing a file from disk or clearing the computer's memory. You may be able to move back or undelete text that you have moved or deleted. Is a backup copy included? What is the publisher's warranty? These safety features are especially important to the word processor to be used in the classroom.

Loading   Another feature to be considered is whether the whole program can be loaded into memory and the disk removed. If so, the same disk can be used with several computers in the same classroom. (First check the program maker's policy on loading; some allow it, but others consider it an infringement on their rights.)

Box 1   Using One Word Processor: *Bank Street Writer* (Apple IIe/c versions)

The *Bank Street Writer* is a versatile word processor that is also easy to use. Its tutorial, *The Bank Street Writer Tutorial,* can be quickly learned. Its ease of use makes it a good word processor for young children (third or fourth grade and above); its versatility makes it a good first word processor for anyone to learn how to use.

There are three basic screens in the *Bank Street Writer.* When booted, the word processor immediately displays the writing screen (see Figure 3). The information on the screen tells you how to do almost anything you need to do. You see how to erase, how to move the cursor, and how to find editing functions.

By displaying the main editing functions, the editing screen (Figure 4) reminds you constantly of what you can do in editing. To select the editing function, you choose from the *menu* given at the top of the screen. (The program is *menu-driven.*) Putting your wishes into effect is essentially automatic.

A third screen provided in *Bank Street Writer* helps communication with the disk (Figure 5). The menu used on this *help* screen lets you save and retrieve files from the disk, initialize the disk from within *Bank Street Writer,* or delete or rename a file on the disk. To use the menu, use <TAB> and <SPACE BAR> to move the highlighter to your menu choice, then press <RETURN>. To prevent errors, the program asks guiding questions.

Word processors are designed to have maximum power but ease of use. Sometimes sophisticated features can make a word processor more difficult to learn and use. In selecting a word processor for the classroom, first identify the features that are important and then select the program that has those features and is easiest to use. Before making your choice, try out and compare several word processors.

Figure 2 *Screen display of the Bank Street Writer help page.*

▼

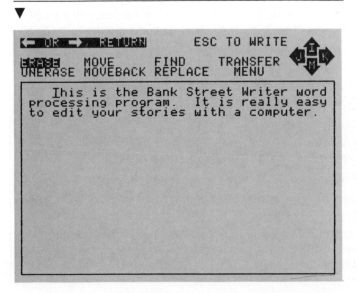

Figure 3 *Screen display of Bank Street Writer.*

▼

Box 2 Working with AppleWorks: A Hands-On Word Processing Activity

---

In this activity you will do a little writing, save it on a disk (formatted in *ProDOS*), and get a printout of it. Then you will re-format the writing to change its appearance on the printed page: you will italicize and underline certain titles and key words in the essay, and get another printout. You will also explore other features of the word-processing capabilities of AppleWorks, so that you can use it effectively. This word processor allows you to create lesson plans, and to lead students to write essays, term papers, poems, reports, event chronologies for social studies, and whatever else you might wish your students to do on a typewriter.

AppleWorks comes in a set of two, $5\frac{1}{4}$ inch disks. One of these is called the *AppleWorks Boot-up Disk* and the other is called the *AppleWorks Program Disk*. AppleWorks is also available in a single disk form on the Uni-disk (a $3\frac{1}{2}$ inch disk), available for Apple IIe, Apple IIc, and Apple IIGS.

To get AppleWorks booted up, first insert *AppleWorks Boot-up Disk* into Disk Drive 1. Turn on the computer. Soon you will get this message: Insert the *AppleWorks Program Disk*. After doing this, press <RETURN>. You will then be asked to type in today's date. You may do this or simply touch <RETURN>. Then the AppleWorks software is loaded into the computer. You see the screen shown in Figure 6.

From the *Main Menu,* choose option 1 (<1 RETURN>). This option allows you to get out the materials you need for writing the essay. After your choice, you see another menu on the screen (Figure 7a). From this menu, choose option 3 (<3 RETURN>), which brings up a menu (Figure 7b) for choosing a new file from scratch or selecting another text file. Choose option 1 (<1 RETURN>) to make a new file from scratch.

You are now ready to type the *Gettysburg Address*. The cursor (a small blinking dash, like an underline mark) indicates where your next character will be typed. You can start typing; use normal capitalization keys and the arrows to move the cursor in the direction desired. Type the excerpt shown in Figure 8 into the word processor.

After you have entered the *Gettysburg Address,* typing < ⌂ -H > will give an immediate hardcopy of exactly what you see on the screen (including border information). Or, you can type < ⌂ -P >, which will print out (or give a hardcopy) of the address without the border. Note the format of your *Gettysburg Address.* You may wish to dress it up. For example, try the following:

a. Center *The Gettysburg Address* title; also print it in boldface (heavy type).

b. Cause the address to shrink on the page so that the margins are two inches from each edge.

c. Underline *Civil War.*

d. Increase the number of characters per inch to 15. This will make the characters smaller.

e. Change the line spacing to double space, to see how that works.

f. Try out the proportional spacing to compare and contrast with regular spacing.

Typing < ⌂ -O > provides a menu of options for screen and printout formats. Explore those options as you work with the word processor, database, or spreadsheet applications.

ERASE   MOVE   FIND   TRANSFER
UNERASE MOVEBACK REPLACE   MENU

RETRIEVE   DELETE   PRINT-DRAFT QUIT
SAVE   INIT   RENAME   PRINT-FINAL CLEAR

▲

Figure 4 *Editing display of Bank Street Writer.*

▲

Figure 5 *The help screen, used for communication with the disk, in Bank Street Writer.*

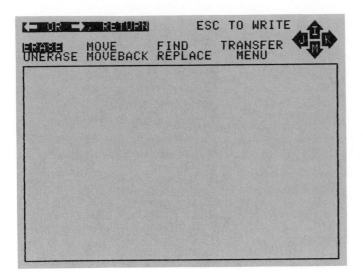

```
Disk: Disk 1 (Slot 6)                    MAIN MENU
   ┌─Main Menu──────────────────┐
   │                            │
   │   1.  Add files to the Desktop
   │   2.  Work with one of the files on the Desktop
   │   3.  Save Desktop files to disk
   │   4.  Remove files from the Desktop
   │   5.  Other Activities
   │   6.  Quit
   │
   └────────────────────────────

Type number, or use arrows, then press Return        A-? for Help
```

▲

Figure 6 *After booting up AppleWorks, you see this screen.*

Using Word Processors in the Classroom

Learning to write is a very important (but often neglected) part of the curriculum. Many young writers become discouraged about writing because their handwriting is messy. They tend to equate messiness with lack of knowledge. The word processor can give students pride in their writing because the final product is neatly printed, clean, and professional looking.

Another stumbling block to writing is that students do not like to revise and edit their work. They are reluctant to mess up their compositions with changes and insertions. Word processing can help children view their work as part of a drafting process instead of finished copy. When students do not have to worry so much about their mistakes, they can focus on the content and expression of their writing. They are more free to express themselves and to experiment.

Figure 7 *Word processor menus in AppleWorks.*

▼

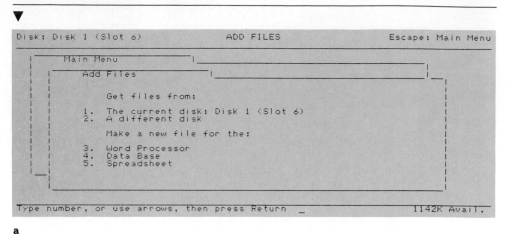

```
Disk: Disk 1 (Slot 6)              ADD FILES              Escape: Main Menu

     | Main Menu                   |
     | | Add Files                 |                                        |_
     | |                                                                      |
     | |      Get files from:                                                 |
     | |                                                                      |
     | |   1.  The current disk: Disk 1 (Slot 6)                              |
     | |   2.  A different disk                                               |
     | |                                                                      |
     | |      Make a new file for the:                                        |
     | |                                                                      |
     | |   3.  Word Processor                                                 |
     | |   4.  Data Base                                                      |
     | |   5.  Spreadsheet                                                    |
     |_|                                                                      |
     |                                                                        |
     |                                                                        |

Type number, or use arrows, then press Return  _           1142K Avail.
```

a

```
Disk: Drive 1                   WORD PROCESSOR              Escape: Add Files
_____

   | Main Menu                 |
   | | Add Files               |                                        |_
   | | | Word Processor         |                                       |_
   | | |                                                                  |
   | | | Make a new file:                                                 |
   | | |                                                                  |
   | | | --> From scratch                                                 |
   | | |                                                                  |
   | | | 2.  From a text (ASCII) file                                     |
   | | |                                                                  |
   | | |                                                                  |
   | | |                                                                  |
   | |_|                                                                  |
   |   |                                                                  |
   |_|                                                                    |
     |                                                                    |

Type a name for this new file:                         55K Avail.
```

b

Figure 8 *The Gettysburg Address, as entered into an AppleWorks word processor.*

▼

```
File: ADDRESS                  REVIEW/ADD/CHANGE            Escape: Main Menu
====|====|====|====|====|====|====|====|====|====|====|====|====|====|====|===
The Gettysburg Address:
Four score and seven years ago our forefathers brought forth
on this continent a new nation, conceived in liberty and
dedicated to the proposition that all men are created equal.
Now we are engaged in a great civil war testing whether that
nation or any other so conceived and so dedicated can long
endure...

Abraham Lincoln




--------------------------------------------------------------------------
Type entry or use A commands            Line 9  Column 16        A-? for Help
```

Word processing has a variety of uses in school. Language instructors see the word processor as a tool that leads to effective writing habits. Science and social studies teachers see the word processor as a tool for helping students write reports. The word processor has many additional uses for the overall educational process.

Using word processing in the classroom is not without its problems. At first, students' lack of familiarity with the keyboard will make text entry slow. In many schools, keyboarding skills and touch typing are being introduced in the elementary school curriculum. Even when students can type reasonably well, word processing requires a lot of individual computer time. And giving adequate computer time can be a problem, because few elementary schools have more than one or two computers per classroom. Also, having something go wrong on the word processor can be frustrating to students. Selecting software with plenty of safety features can minimize problems, and peer instruction can relieve pressure on the teacher.

▶ ▲ ◀ ▼ ▶ ▲ ◀ ▼ ▶ ▲ ◀ ▼ ▶ ▲ ◀ ▼ ▶ ▲ ◀ ▼ ▶ ▲

Summary

This chapter discussed the features and uses of a word processor. Among the new developments in word processors are built-in resources (such as "Help," a dictionary, a thesaurus, and a grammar-checker) and text-editing features that can aid not only in rewriting and recombining text, but also in producing indexes and outlines. Print-formatting features and sophisticated screen displays aid in the design of textual elements. Steps in using *Bank Street Writer* and the AppleWorks word processor were presented in detail. Word processors have many applications in the classroom: Because students can easily revise their writing, they can both focus on content and feel free to experiment. Activities demonstrate that creative uses of the word processor can help students understand the structures of book reports, poetry, and stories, as they write.

Software discussed in this chapter:

Microsoft Word	*Bank Street Writer*
WordPerfect	*Homeword*
ZenWord	*Plot File*
WordStar	

Important Terms

Print-formatting functions
Screen display
Text-editing functions

Exercises

1. Use the word processor of your choice. Create a book report form like the *Plot Book Report* form on the disk. Provide within it a chance for users to find and replace text and edit text. Supply questions to answer.

2. Use the word processor of your choice. Create a form with which a report can be written. This may be a science or social studies report or any one of your choice. Ask the user to edit and properly format the printed output.

3. Use a word processor to create an outline for a report. Using the formatting capability of word processors, be sure that the outline is in proper outline form:

I.
    A.
    B.

4. Use the word processor to write a four- to six-page library research paper comparing and contrasting two of the most advanced word processors that were described in the literature.

5. Use the word processor to write a four- to six-page library research paper describing the ten most important characteristics of an ideal word processor. The characteristics can be combinations of the best or most important characteristics of the word processors you have studied.

6. Use a word processor of your choice to write a three- to five-page library research paper comparing and contrasting two of the most advanced database programs that you found described in the literature.

7. Use a word processor of your choice to write a three- to five-page library research paper comparing and contrasting two of the most practical and realistic word-processing programs that you located in the literature; use programs that your potential students could use for their writing assignments.

8. Use a word processor of your choice to write a three- to five-page library research paper comparing and contrasting two of the most "advanced" spreadsheet programs that you have located in the literature.

9. Use a word processor to write a four- to six-page library research paper comparing and contrasting the most important features of telecommunications hardware and software. In your comparison, use the two most highly rated telecommunications materials.

References

Apple Computer, Inc. (1986). *AppleWorks tutorial—Apple II*. Cupertino, CA: Apple Computer, Inc.

Apple Computer, Inc. (1986). *Using AppleWorks—Apple II*. Cupertino, CA: Apple Computer, Inc.

Bell, J. (1988, April). WordPerfect's Mac gamble. *Personal Computing*, pp. 224–226.

Feigenson, W. (1988, March). WordPerfect: Then and now. *Personal Computing*, pp. 108–109.

Kasnic, M. J., & Stefano, S. (1987). More than a spelling checker. *The Computing Teacher, 15*, 31–32.

Madian, J. (1986). Word processing and curriculum renewal. *The Computing Teacher, 14*, 17–19.

Microsoft Corporation. (1988). *Microsoft Word—Reference to Microsoft Word word processing program version 4.1. IBM personal computers and compatibles*. Redmond, WA: Microsoft Corporation.

Microsoft Corporation. (1988). *Microsoft Word—Reference to Microsoft Word word processing program version 4.1. Apple-Macintosh*. Redmond, WA: Microsoft Corporation.

O'Malley, C. (1987, October). The best get better: Subtle differences in full-featured programs. *Personal Computing*, pp. 80–86.

Strehlo, C. (1988, March). A first look at WordPerfect 5.0. *Personal Computing*, pp. 104–105.

▶ ▲ ◀ ▼ ▶ ▲ ◀ ▼ ▶ ▲ ◀ ▼ ▶ ▲ ◀ ▼ ▶ ▲ ◀ ▼ ▶ ▲

Activity   Finding the Big Picture

Type   Machine

Objective   By applying decomposing and recombining techniques, make an outline from which students then write a story.

Prerequisite(s)   Ability to work with a word processor to move text

Materials Needed Word processor
Terms (such as listed below) already organized on a disk to use with a word processor

Activity   Students can employ word processors to help them develop key ideas for a story. Students are to (1) cluster the words in the *Terms* list around key ideas, (2) write an outline around the key ideas, and (3) write a story based on the outline. The list of words should already be entered on a disk to use with the word processor. Students can then reorganize the words into no more than five main topic clusters. Have them make no more than five subclusters within each cluster, then no more than five sub-subclusters within the subcluster, and so on. Through this process the students group the terms into topic clusters that form the basis for their outlines and subsequent stories.

Terms

airplanes	gondola	San Francisco
American Airlines	handlebars	Sydney
Amtrack	Johannesburg	seating capacity
arrival time	kilometers/hour	ships
Atlanta	London	speedometer
boats	local travel	steering wheel
Buenos Aires	miles/hour	tires
bicycles	miles	tracks
canoes	Moscow	trains
cars	motion	transportation
Chicago	New York	TWA
Denver	oar	United Airlines
departure time	Pan Am Airlines	walk
distance from home	Paris	wheels
distance from ?	PBA (or a local	wings
distance between	airline near you)	(your town)
distance traveled	Piedmont Airlines	(several cities close
Eastern Airlines	Rome	to your town)
feet		

Variation(s)   The preceding list could be varied by the addition of more or different cities, vehicles, and so on. Another variation could include a time dimension, with the use of such terms as horse, pony express, and buggy; hence, you could use it to study the history of transportation. The strategy, of course, could be applied to many different topics.

Activity   A Book Report on Plot

Type	Machine
Objective	Use story plot and patterns to predict events. Use a word processor to decompose and recombine story elements.
Prerequisite(s)	Some experience with a word processor
Materials Needed	Word processor *Plot File* on the *Applications Disk* Worksheet
Activity	Using *Plot File* improves some of the word processing skills used in the writing of a book report. Students should (1) find and replace the name, book title, and date with their own name, title, and date, (2) answer the questions about the story in the *Plot File,* as on the next worksheet, (3) delete the questions and revise the text so that sentences and paragraphs are well written, and (4) edit the report and prepare it for grading. We suggest that students first try this exercise when they have finished about one-third of the book, again after about half of the book, and once more about two-thirds of the way through. By so doing, they get experience in predicting plots according to slowly revealed information. By using the word processor, they can easily make corrections, updates, and modifications. Also, students can eventually produce a neatly typed and edited document.
Variation(s)	A similar report based on character development could be done. As they progress through a book, students answer specific questions about their favorite character and predict what will happen to the character or how the character will change during the story.
Worksheet	See p. 134.

Activity Poetry: Cinquain

Type

Machine

Objective

Apply recombining and patterning with variables to create poetry.

Prerequisite(s)

Experience with word processor
Poetry introduction

Materials Needed

Word processor

Activity

Using a pattern and an example of the poetry form *cinquain* (basically, five-part poetry), introduce students to ways in which a variety of meaningful poems can be created. Consider the following form of a cinquain and the example on the right.

Noun	Mountain
Adjective 1, adjective 2	Rugged, majestic
-ing Verb 1, -ing verb 2, -ing verb 3	Rising, peaking, shining
Word 1, word 2, word 3, word 4	Guardian of green valley
Noun (same as starting noun)	Mountain

Using the word processor, students can replace the noun, adjectives, -ing verbs, and so on, with words of their choice, but the words must be the types required.

Variation(s)

An alternative poetic form, in the shape of a diamond, is the *diamante*, which also can be used to systematically create poetry.

Noun	Summer
Adjective 1, adjective 2	Fun, free
-ing Verb 1, -ing verb 2, -ing verb 3	Snorkeling, surfing, sailing
Noun 1, noun 2—Verb 1, verb 2	August, September—Relax, enjoy
-ing Verb 4, -ing verb 5, -ing verb 6	Toiling, studying, competing
Adjective 3, adjective 4	Dreary, confined
Antonym of line 1 (Noun)	Winter

▲◄▲
▼Exploration
A Book Report on Plot Worksheet

Sample copy of *Plot File* on the *Applications Disk*

Name: John Doe

Date: _____   Title: _____

    The plot of a book is one element that keeps a reader's interest. It is the story line, the events of the story, or, simply stated, what happens in the story.

    Answer the following questions about a book you are reading. Answer these questions well before you finish the book.

1. Tell what has happened so far in the book. Be brief, covering only main points.

2. Tell what you think will happen next in the story.

3. Tell how you think the story will end. Discuss what you think will be the status of the plot at the story's end.

4. When you have finished the story, draw a diagram or chart of the plot. Using the plot diagram, compare your predictions to the actual outcome of the story.

Chapter 6

Database Management

▶ ▲ ◀ ▼ ▶ ▲ ◀ ▼ ▶ ▲ ◀ ▼ ▶ ▲ ◀ ▼ ▶ ▲ ◀ ▼ ▶ ▲

Objectives

▶ To solve some problems, use a database
▶ Use given databases to answer questions
▶ Fill in a database form
▶ Prepare a database from scratch

A database is similar to a filing system. It is useful for compiling non-numerical data that is to be used as a basis for a list (like a mailing list), that is to be sorted, or to be a source of information. For example, a database is a good tool for sorting and preparing a mailing list, and it is a particularly good tool for performing special operations on the list. For example, if you wanted to mail the same letter to many people (maybe 100 or more) with different addresses and have each correct address typed on each letter, or if you wanted to sort the letters alphabetically or according to zip code and produce mailing labels as well, then a database program is what you need.

Databases are used in schools to keep records on students (including names, addresses, phone numbers, and data on parents), records of class schedules (for a student or the entire school), and for book inventories and other records. For instruction, databases could be used in all subjects. Social studies could use banks of information about the presidents and countries of the world; science studies could use banks of information about spacecrafts, planets, bones of the body, complete properties of chemical elements or compounds, or animals and their young; physical education instructors could use records about conference teams, types and amounts of physical activity, and inventories of equipment used by the class.

Features of Database Management

Database programs have characteristics as varied and changing as those in word processors. Educational users must know these characteristics so that we do not initially purchase programs that are more complex than is needed nor find greater needs after so much time and money have been invested. Characteristic

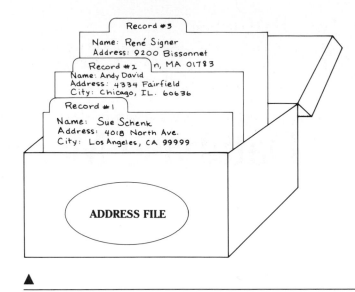

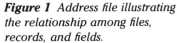

Figure 1 *Address file illustrating
the relationship among files,
records, and fields.*

processes include the movement of records between databases and among types
of documents, label and table formatting, relational and conditional searches with
built in logical functions, and mail merging. The characteristics of database management systems are evolving and expanding; those are among the ones developing
in *dBASE IV*, *Microsoft Works,* and *Microsoft File.*

A **database** is an organized collection of information. Your grade book, an
address book, and a library card catalog are examples of databases. Many databases
are stored in filing cabinets; others are computerized and stored on magnetic tape
or floppy disks. Very large databases can be stored on mainframe computers and
accessed online from terminals around the country. In this section, we will discuss
database management on a microcomputer and examine how databases can be
used in instruction.

Files, Records, and Fields

The software of database management allows you to create a database and
then store, retrieve, and update your information. In a database, information is
stored in individually named **files.** If you have a computerized grade book, for
example, you might have separate files for each group of students you teach.

A file is divided into **records.** A record is a set of information about one subject
in the file. In your gradebook database, all the information about a particular student
forms a record.

Records are further subdivided into **fields.** Your grade book might have one
field for name, one for book number, one for student number, five fields for test
grades, and twenty fields for homework grades. The **field length** is the maximum
number of characters that can be stored in that field. When you buy an address
book, the fields (name, address, city, state, zip, telephone number) are already
printed in the book for you, and the field length is determined by the amount of
space left for you to write in the information. When you set up a file yourself, you
must identify the fields you need and specify the length of each field. Figure 1
illustrates the relationship among files, records, and fields in a database.

Creating Your Own Database

A simple database-management program is included on the *Applications Disk.* To learn how to create your own database, insert the disk (side 1) and type

```
RUN DATA MANAGER II
```

You should see a menu that looks something like this:

```
DATA MANAGER
    MENU

<1> CREATE A NEW FILE
<2> FIND A RECORD
<3> ADD A RECORD
<4> CHANGE A RECORD
<5> DELETE A RECORD
<6> LIST ALL RECORDS
<7> SORT RECORDS
<8> QUIT


YOUR CHOICE?
```

To create a new file, first select option <1>. You must name the file, determine the fields that you need, and specify the length of each field. Call your file *Address* and then set up these fields:

Field Order	Field Name	Field Length
1	LAST NAME	10
2	FIRST NAME	10
3	ADDRESS	20
4	CITY	10
5	STATE	2
6	ZIP	5
7	TELEPHONE NUMBER	10

When you are asked for the eighth field, type DONE. (If you make a mistake and want to start again, just type DONE and you will be able to enter the fields again.)

After your file is created on the disk, you will be returned to the main menu. Now, to add information to the file, select option <3>. Type in your own name, address, and telephone number, and continue adding records for other people until you have five to ten records in the file.

Now that you have several records in your file, use option <6> to list all records and verify that everything was saved as you intended. Note the record numbers of those records that need correcting, and use option <4> to make the necessary changes. Because this is a very simple database program written for the purpose of demonstration, the CHANGE option is not very sophisticated. Not only do you need to know the record number, but you must type all the information in the record over again (or copy it, as in editing) even though only one item is incorrect. Commercial programs are more flexible.

Option <2> demonstrates the power of a database to search for specific records. To find all the people with the last name of Smith, you would search the LAST NAME field for SMITH. To find all the people in a particular zip code, search the ZIP field for that zip code number. More sophisticated database-management programs are able to search for all the records satisfying two or more field conditions, such as the people with zip code 98435 *and* last name Smith. Most programs also can delete records, alphabetize by any field, and direct a printer to make hard copy.

Boxes 1–3 illustrate some uses of the AppleWorks database-management system.

Box 1   Using Existing Databases: A Hands-On Activity with AppleWorks

---

In this activity you use existing databases, one entitled *Presidents* and one entitled *States*. These databases are large files containing information about the presidents of the United States (when they were born and where, dates of inauguration, and so on), and the states in the United States (their size, population, date into union, chief industries, and so on). These databases are sources of information for questions such as "What is the population of Vermont?", "Which state is the largest in land area?", "What states have manufacturing as one of their chief industries?", "Who was the sixteenth president of the U.S.?", "What presidents were under 50 years old when elected?", and so on. Of much greater significance are the more complex relationships that you can explore with databases. For example, you could determine if there is a relationship among such variables as the size of a state and its principal industries. Or, is there a tendency to elect presidents today who are younger than those of earlier years?

To work with these databases in AppleWorks, first choose the *Presidents* file from the *AppleWorks File Disk* (have the *AppleWorks Program Disk* in Drive 1 and the *AppleWorks File Disk* in Drive 2). From the *Main Menu* (see Figure 2) choose option 1, *Add files to Desktop*. A menu will appear that will allow you to choose which file to add to the desktop. It will look like the screen in Figure 3.

To choose *Presidents* from this menu (see Figure 3), move the up-down arrows until the *Presidents* line is highlighted. While you are at it, also add *States* to the desktop. To do this, you will need to touch the <ESC> once in order to return to the *Main Menu;* then repeat the process that was used for adding *Presidents* to the desktop. Once these two files are on the desktop, touch option 2, *Work with one of the files on Desktop,* from the *Main Menu.* You will then see a screen insert that lets you choose *1. Presidents* or *2. States.* Choose *States* (in the normal way, by using up and down arrow keys and hitting <RETURN>). Then you will see the screen shown in Figure 4.

Now you should try some data manipulation and analysis. Bring the cursor to the first column in Figure 4 (the arrow keys and the tab key let you move the cursor about). Type <CTRL-A>, which allows you to *Arrange the States.* You see an option screen that looks like Figure 5.

This display indicates that to arrange the *States* category alphabetically, you choose option 1. (You could also arrange them in reverse alphabetical order, or, if appropriate, from largest to smallest or from smallest to largest numbers.)

Now arrange the data according to other categories (variables), and use the database to answer these questions:

a. What state has the largest population?
b. What state has the largest land area?
c. What states have *north* in their nickname?

Now work with the *Presidents* database. (Use <ESC> to get back to the *Main Menu.* Choose option 2; then choose *Presidents* in the insert menu.)

< ⌂ -Z> lets you zoom in (or out) from the individual record to the file of presidents (see Figure 6). Notice the fields in a *Presidents* record. They include *Name, Number* (1st, 2nd, 3rd, and so on, president), *Political Party,* and *Birth Year.* These are variables (or categories) on which we can arrange, search, compare, or in other ways manipulate the data. This format shows you how a database is created. After the categories are specified and given

Figure 2 *The AppleWorks Main Menu.*

▼

```
Disk: Disk 1 (Slot 6)                MAIN MENU

    |  Main Menu               |
    |                          |
    |   1.  Add files to the Desktop                           |
    |                                                          |
    |   2.  Work with one of the files on the Desktop          |
    |                                                          |
    |   3.  Save Desktop files to disk                         |
    |                                                          |
    |   4.  Remove files from the Desktop                      |
    |                                                          |
    |   5.  Other Activities                                   |
    |                                                          |
    |   6.  Quit                                               |
    |                                                          |

Type number, or use arrows, then press Return          A-? for Help
```

Figure 3 *The AppleWorks menu of files that you can add to the desktop.*

▼

```
Disk: Disk 1 (Slot 6)         APPLEWORKS FILES          Escape: Add Files

   |  Main Menu              |
   |   | Add Files            |
   |   |  | AppleWorks files   |
   |   |  | Disk volume /INTERMEDIATE has 42K available
   |   |  |  Name            Type of file   Size   Date     Time
   |   |  | ====================================================
   |   |  | User Group Memo  Word Processor   1K   6/20/86  5:10 pm
   |   |  | Members          Data Base        4K   6/20/86  5:08 pm
   |   |  | Personnel        Data Base        4K   6/20/86  5:09 pm
   |   |  | Presidents       Data Base        5K   6/20/86  5:09 pm
   |   |  | Rolodex          Data Base        4K   6/20/86  5:09 pm
   |   |  | States           Data Base       13K   6/20/86  5:09 pm
   |   |  | Valuables        Data Base        3K   6/20/86  5:10 pm
   |_ |  | Balance Sheet    Spreadsheet       8K   6/20/86  5:07 pm
      |  | Grade Book1      Spreadsheet       2K   6/20/86  5:07 pm
      |  | Grade Book2      Spreadsheet      19K   6/20/86  5:07 pm
      |                        More
Use Right Arrow to choose files, Left Arrow to undo  _      1142K Avail.
```

Figure 4 *The file States.*

▼

```
File: States               REVIEW/ADD/CHANGE          Escape: Main Menu
Selection: All records

State           Official Nickna Population      Total Area    Principal Indus
=========================================================================
Alabama         Heart of Dixie, 3,959,000       51,609        Paper, chemical
Alaska          None            479,000         586,412       Oil, gas, touri
Arizona         Grand Canyon St 2,963,000       113,909       Manufacturing,
Arkansas        Land of Opportu 2,328,000       53,104        Manufacturing,
California      Golden State    25,174,000      158,693       Agriculture, ae
Colorado        Centennial Stat 3,139,000       104,247       Manufacturing,
Connecticut     Constitution St 3,138,000       5,009         Manufacturing,
Delaware        First State, Di 606,000         2,057         Chemistry, agri
Florida         Sunshine State  10,680,000      58,560        Services, trade
Georgia         Empire State of 5,732,000       58,876        Manufacturing,
Hawaii          The Aloha State 1,023,000       6,450         Tourism, defens
Idaho           Gem State       989,000         83,557        Agriculture, to
Illinois        The Inland Empi 11,486,000      56,400        Manufacturing,
Indiana         Hoosier State   5,479,000       36,291        Manufacturing,
Iowa            Hawkeye State   2,905,000       56,290        Manufacturing,
-------------------------------------------------------------------------
Type entry or use A commands                             A-? for Help
```

Box 1   Continued:

names, you have a *form* into which data is entered. Each entry into the form creates a record, as indicated by the example.

A variety of problem-solving activities could be created for use of a particular database. These activities could include setting up patterns and then having students study the data to discern the pattern; finally, they could prove that their noted pattern will in fact select the particular records. For example, what rule will produce the selection of states shown in Figure 7?

Box 2   Creating and Using an Instructional Database: A Hands-On Activity Using AppleWorks

In this activity you will design a database containing information about African countries and use the database to answer questions. When you use this activity in your class, design the format of the database and have students research and enter the information. Notice that the database is useful for answering simple questions like "What is the capital of Nigeria?" and more complex questions like "Do countries with larger per capita income have higher literacy rates?" (See Beverly Hunter's *My Students Use Computers* for other related activities.)

1. Designing the database
   a. Boot the AppleWorks program.
   b. Select *1. Add files to the Desktop.*
   c. Select *4. Database* from the *Add Files* menu.
   d. Select *1. From Scratch* from the *Database* menu.
   e. $< \circlearrowleft -E>$ (erase) to overwrite the *Category 1* label. Type COUNTRY.
   f. Now that you are ready to design a blank form, type the category names:

   ```
   COUNTRY:
   CAPITAL:
   AREA (SQ KM):
   POPULATION:
   LANGUAGE:
   LIFE EXPECTANCY (YRS):
   LITERACY RATE:
   INDUSTRIES:
   EXPORT CROPS:
   PER CAPITA INCOME:
   ```

   When you are finished and want to stop entering new categories, use <ESC>.

   g. To put information into the file, touch <SPACEBAR>.

   h. You are now ready to fill in the form with the information about the countries:

   ```
   COUNTRY: Botswana
   CAPITAL: Gaborone
   AREA (SQ KM): 600,372
   POPULATION: 1,112,000
   LANGUAGE: English, Setswana
   LIFE EXPECTANCY (YRS): 48
   LITERACY RATE: 35%
   ```

Figure 5 *Optional ways in which*
States can be alphabetized.

▼

```
File: States                    ARRANGE (SORT)          Escape: Review/Add/Change
Selection: All records


========================================================================
              This file will be arranged on
              this category: State

              Arrangement order:

                   1.   From A to Z
                   2.   From Z to A
                   3.   From 0 to 9
                   4.   From 9 to 0




------------------------------------------------------------------------
Type number, or use arrows, then press Return              1124K Avail.
```

Figure 6 *The record of George*
Washington, in the file of
Presidents.

▼

```
File: Presidents                REVIEW/ADD/CHANGE           Escape: Main Menu
Selection: All records


Record 1 of 40
========================================================================
Name: George Washington
Number: 1
Political Party: Fed
Birth Year: 1732
Birthdate: Feb 22
Birthplace: Va
Inauguration Date: 1789
Inauguration Age: 57
Year of Death: 1799
Date of Death: Dec 14
Age at Death: 67
Vice President: John Adams



------------------------------------------------------------------------
Type entry or use A commands                                 A-? for Help
```

Figure 7 *A selection from the*
States file.

▼

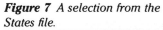

```
File: States                    REVIEW/ADD/CHANGE           Escape: Main Menu
Selection: Population is greater than 5,000,000
   through  Population is less than 6,000,000
State           Official Nickna Population        Total Area    Principal Indus
========================================================================
Georgia         Empire State of 5,732,000         58,876        Manufacturing,
Indiana         Hoosier State   5,479,000         36,291        Manufacturing,
Massachusetts   Bay State, Old  5,767,000         8,257         Electronics, ma
Virginia        Old Dominion    5,550,000         40,817        Government, tra




------------------------------------------------------------------------
Type entry or use A commands                                 A-? for Help
```

Box 2   Continued:

```
INDUSTRIES: Diamonds, Copper, Nickel, Meat Processing
EXPORT CROPS: Cotton, Peanuts, Sunflower Seed
PER CAPITA INCOME: $720.
```

When you have finished entering this information, use <ESC> to stop entering new data.

2. Use the database to answer simple questions: search the *Africa* database to answer these questions.

   a. What is the capital of Botswana?
   Solution. Use < Ó -R> and choose *1. Country.*

   b. What countries are French speaking?
   Solution: Use <ESC> so that you can change the record rule. Answer *No* to the question *Select All Files.* Use < Ó -R> and choose *5. Languages.* Use arrow keys to select *Contains* and type FRENCH. Touch <ESC> to finish selection rule. All countries that have French as one of their languages are displayed.

   c. What countries are more populous than Kenya?
   Solution: < Ó -R> (*Choose record . . .*) To select *Population,* move the down-arrow. Choose *is greater than* for the relation. For the comparison, enter the population of Kenya.

   d. Do any countries have a population less than 100,000?

   e. What languages are spoken in Ethiopia?

   f. What countries are larger in area than South Africa?

   g. In what countries are there diamond mines?

   h. What countries export coffee?

   i. Are there more English-speaking than French-speaking countries in Africa?

3. Using the database to sort and find relationships

   a. Using the printing and sorting features of AppleWorks, answer these questions.
      i. Print out the African countries in order of their population.
      Solution: First use < Ó -A> to arrange the countries in alphabetical order. Next, use < Ó -H> to get a hard copy of the list of countries.
      ii. Alphabetize the countries' capitals and print the list.
      iii. What country has the highest per capita income?
      iv. Alphabetize all countries with populations over 1,000,000 and print the list.
      v. Alphabetize all countries that have both populations exceeding 800,000 and diamond mines; print the list.

   b. Using the printing and sorting features, explore these relationships.
      i. Do countries with large areas tend to have large populations?
      Solution: Sort the countries according to their areas. Print each country's name, its area, and its population. (Use < Ó -H> hardcopy once the countries are sorted and displayed on the screen.) Another option is to use the < Ó -O> (Display print options) for the printout.
      ii. Do countries with larger per capita income have higher literacy rates?
      iii. Do countries with larger per capita income have higher life expectancies?

Box 3   Working with AppleWorks: Creating Your Own Database Template

Now we will create your own database. Your example is a *Cities* database. Because it contains a variety of information about cities on the North American continent, it is useful in solving problems and developing relationships among variables.

To create your database, you need to use <ESC> to get back to the menu shown in Figure 8. You will choose option 4, *Make a new file from the Database.* After you have made this choice, you will be given a form for making the new database. It will say *Enter categories.* You will need to erase this and then start entering the categories. Figure 9 will show how you should start the database. See Exercise 8, at the end of this chapter; then add three or four other categories that will help you answer those questions.

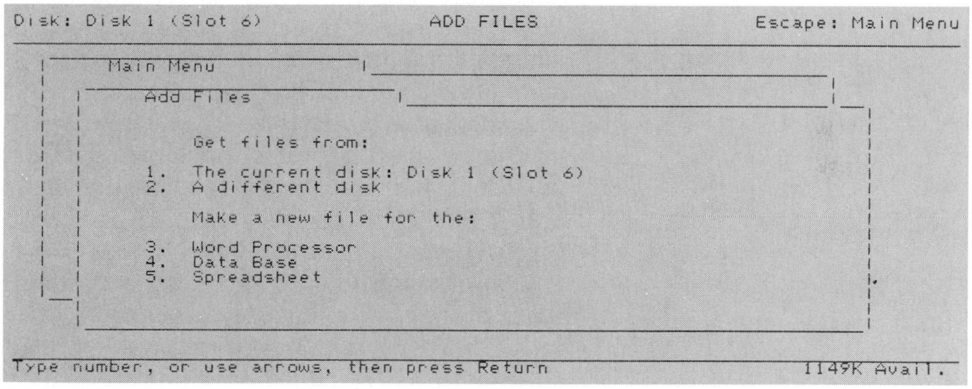

▲

Figure 8 *This menu is the first step in creating a new database.*

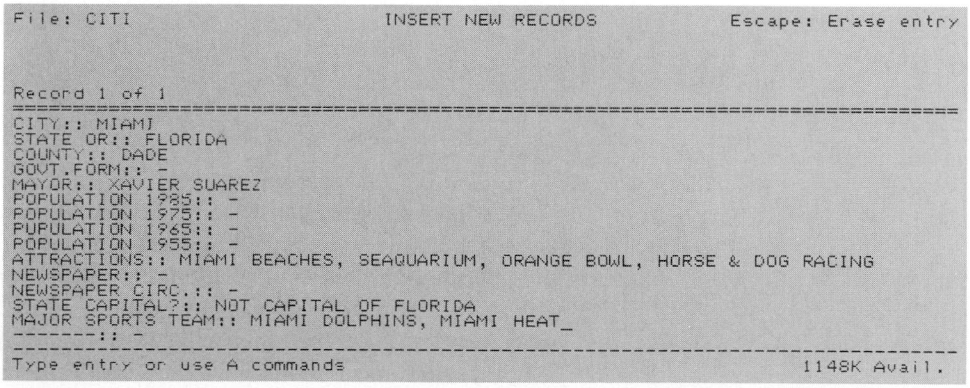

▲

Figure 9 *A database being made.*

Using Databases in the Classroom

Database programs have many instructional applications in the classroom. Students can use a database created by their teacher to find answers to specific questions and to explore relationships, or they can work together sharing and researching information to create their own database.

The noncomputer-based activities at the end of this chapter will help your students understand what is contained in a database, how to set one up, and how to get information from it. These activities use a simple questionnaire and card-sort process that is analogous to a computer's database.

A simplified database system, *Data Manager* II, is included on the *Applications Disk.* The sample databases, *What names?* and *Food and Nutrients,* will also help students get acquainted with databases. Database programs such as *Data manager II, AppleWorks,* and many others serve as tools for setting up databases.

Sunburst is also developing a number of educational databases that coordinate with the *Bank Street School Filer.* Included in the available databases are *North America, United States, Animal life, Endangered species, Space,* and *Astronomy. North America,* which includes Central America, Canada, and the West Indies, has information on the people, climate, demography, culture, economy, and government of each nation. The database on the United States includes geographic, political, and historical information for each state. The *Animal Life* database has information on the physical characteristics, classifications, behavior, food habitat, reproductive characteristics, and adaptations of warm- and cold-blooded vertebrates. *Endangered Species* has database files on all endangered mammals in the United States, animals that have become extinct since 1600, and some of the most critical endangered species worldwide. Information on manned space missions, space probes, and a timeline file of important events in the history of space exploration, make up the *Space* databases. Information on the planets; weekly logs of solar, lunar, tidal, and temperature data; and a timeline of important events in the history of astronomy comprise the databases for astronomy.

▶ ▲ ◀ ▼ ▶ ▲ ◀ ▼ ▶ ▲ ◀ ▼ ▶ ▲ ◀ ▼ ▶ ▲ ◀ ▼ ▶ ▲

Summary

We have suggested a number of organizational aids and activities, for data such as pets, names and meanings, favorite television shows, and nutrition in our diets. In performing these activities, students gain experience in determining the variables within a situation and in classifying (both serial and hierarchical), organizing, and analyzing data. This basis for instructional computing considers the vocational uses of computers and encourages the development of computer awareness development. Students' experiences with databases will be valuable as they use computers in their schoolwork and later make career decisions.

This chapter made reference to the following programs:

Data Manager II	*AppleWorks*
Bargraph	*Food and Nutrients*
Bank Street School Filer	*Color Average*
dBASE IV	*First Name and Meaning*
Microsoft Works	*What Name*
Microsoft File	

Important Terms

Database	File Disk
Field	Record
File	Template

Exercises

1. Research and summarize the five most important characteristics of a database program.

2. Describe two important types of databases. What are the characteristics of each?

3. Use the *States* database to
   a. Arrange the states in order from smallest to largest population.
   b. Arrange the states in order from smallest to largest area.
   c. Select states with populations greater than 4 million.
   d. Find answers to five other questions of your choice.

4. Use the *Presidents* database to find the
   a. Names of all presidents whose first names begin with *A*.
   b. Birthdays of all presidents whose last names begin with *W*.
   c. All presidents who were neither Democrats nor Republicans.
   d. Find answers to five other questions of your devising.

5. Use the form like that used for Botswana (see Box 2) to compile a record for each of five other African countries.

6. Add Kenya, Ethiopia, and South Africa to the *Africa* database.
   a. Arrange the African countries according to population, from largest to smallest.
   b. Arrange the African countries according to area, from largest to smallest.

7. Do library research and complete records for five cities in the *Cities* database.

8. Combine all students' entries in the *Cities* database into a single database. Do the following activities for the combined *Cities* database.
   a. Arrange the cities according to population, from smallest to largest.
   b. Select all cities with professional football teams.
   c. Select cities with populations greater than 1 million.
   d. Select all cities with professional football and basketball teams.
   e. Study the population trends for the largest 5 cities for the last 30 years. Which is growing fastest? Slowest? Ask and answer two other questions about the population statistics in the *Cities* database.
   f. Name the state and county of as many cities as you know. Use *Search* to find the state and county of each one that you did not already know.
   g. Create a *Cities* database for cities in some other country (for example, Brazil). Pose and answer four questions that this database can answer for you.

9. Add 10 names to the file *What Name?* Search the file for the French version of your own first name.

References

Apple Computer, Inc. (1986). *AppleWorks tutorial—Apple II.* Cupertino, CA: Apple Computer, Inc.

Apple Computer, Inc. (1986). *Using AppleWorks—Apple II.* Cupertino, CA: Apple Computer, Inc.

Blankenbaker, R. (1987). Databases in the English class: A valuable lesson. *The Computing Teacher, 15,* 17–18.

Hannah, L. (1987). Teaching database search strategies. *The Computing Teacher, 14,* 16–23.

Hannah, L. (1987). The database: Getting to know you. *The Computing Teacher, 15,* 17–18, 41.

Hunter, B. (1983). *My students use computers: Learning activities for computer literacy.* Reston, VA: Reston Publishing Company, a Prentice-Hall Company.

Hunter, B. (1985). Problem solving with databases. *The Computing Teacher, 12,* 20–27.

Microsoft Corporation. (1988). *Microsoft Word—Reference to Microsoft Word word processing program version 4.1. IBM personal computers and compatibles.* Redmond, WA: Microsoft Corporation.

Microsoft Corporation. (1988). *Microsoft Word—Reference to Microsoft Word word processing program version 4.1. Apple-Macintosh.* Redmond, WA: Microsoft Corporation.

Withycombe, E. G. (1986). *The Oxford dictionary of English Christian names,* 3rd ed. New York: Oxford University Press.

▶ ▲ ◀ ▼ ▶ ▲ ◀ ▼ ▶ ▲ ◀ ▼ ▶ ▲ ◀ ▼ ▶ ▲ ◀ ▼ ▶ ▲

Activity Pets We Have at Home

Type	Preparatory
Objective	Collect and organize data on pets and create a database on cards.
Prerequisite(s)	None
Materials Needed	Cards or mimeographed forms (worksheet) *Bargraph* on the *Applications Disk*
Activity	Students work together to collect information about their pets. They each take home a card and with their parents and siblings fill the cards out. Gather the information together and answer some of the following questions.

What pets do members of the class have?
How many have dogs?
How many have cats?
How many have birds?
How many have fish?
How many have hamsters?
How many have another type of pet?
What is the most common pet?
What is the second most common pet?
What pets are third, fourth, and fifth most common?

Worksheet See p. 152.

Make a graph or stack of blocks to show the number of each type of animal.

Variation(s)   Using the *Bargraph* program on the *Applications Disk,* enter the number of each kind of animal.

Get a printout of the graph. Write the corresponding kind of animal under each column in the graph. Post the graph on the bulletin board; challenge another class to do a pet survey and compare results.

Databases, to be stored on cards, may be compiled from a number of items—books in a home library, comic books, items in stamp and coin collections, and so on.

Activity   What's in a Name?

Type   Machine

Objective   Provide experience in organizing information for databases

Prerequisite(s)   Previously used databases

Materials needed   *Data Manager II* on the *Applications Disk*
First Name and Meaning on the *Applications Disk*
What Name on the *Applications Disk*

Activity   The database *First Name and Meaning* contains a few first (given or Christian) names. It also contains the meaning of each name and the same name in another language. Have the students examine the database to see the names that are there. To do so, they must type RUN DATA MANAGER II and select the file *First Name and Meaning.* From the menu they can choose *Sort Records, Sorting on Name,* and *List All Records* so that they see the records in alphabetical order.

If a particular name is not there (the student's name, for example), select *Add a Record* from the menu. Students might have to search for some information, such as the meaning of the name or the name in another language. One source is *The Oxford Dictionary of English Christian Names* by Withycombe, but other sources may be required. If a record is incomplete or incorrect, the student can alter it through *Change a Record.* And *Find a Record* can be used to determine the person's name that means, for example, *crown.* Allow the students time for experimentation to see how information is retrieved.

Students can create a new file containing their friends' names and information about their names. Have them research the meanings and Spanish, German, and Hebrew equivalents of their friends' names and set up a database.

Variation(s)   Using the database *What Name* or one that the students have created, enter data about names and their roots. This database is more extensive than *First Name and Meaning* and develops the etymologies (origins) and histories of given names and equivalents in other languages.

Activity   Letters . . . Words . . . Sentences

Type	Preparatory
Level	Introductory
Objective	Apply skills in collecting, organizing, and analyzing data, to words and sentences
Prerequisite(s)	None
Materials Needed	Newspapers
	Magazines
	Textbooks
	BarGraph on the *Applications Disk*

Activity Students will employ printed materials as they collect data to be organized and analyzed. Some ideas for questions to be answered are: What word length occurs most often in the newspaper? Which letter of the alphabet is used most (and least) frequently? What is the most common number of words in a sentence (paragraph) in magazines, newspapers, or textbooks? Discuss with the students the methods they will use in collecting their data and designing a graph to organize their data.

Collect and represent data in a chart like the one at the left, for the sentence "How now brown cow?"

Explain to the students that they can use a calculator or computer to help them with calculations. After the students have collected their data, examine how they can represent their findings with a bar graph, as shown in the figure.

**Data for the Sentence
"How Now Brown Cow?"**

Letter	Number of Appearances in Sentence
H	1
O	4
W	4
N	2
B	1
R	1
C	1

Variation(s) Involve the students in averaging their grades. Run *Color Average* from the *Applications Disk* (side 1), and compute averages. After they have completed the graphs, encourage the students to analyze their data in writing, for instance, on a word processor. Introduce the idea of variables. What grade would be needed to significantly raise or lower the average? Investigate ways in which a computer could be used for this investigation.

Activity   Animals and Their Young

Type   Machine

Objective   Collect and organize data on animals and their young, for a database.

Prerequisite(s) Experience in using *Search* procedure with data cards

Materials Needed A database manager
Source of information, such as encyclopedia

Activity   By searching through sources such as encyclopedias, the students prepare a card file on a wide variety of animals. On each card have them list the name of the animal (popular and biological, if desired), the name given to the young (for example, *bear: cub*), the number of offspring per birth, the average size of the animal, the country or countries in which the animal lives, and any other information they choose. They can place this information on index cards for ease of reference. Then they should transfer the information to a database program (such as *Data Manager* II, or AppleWorks) and use the computer as a search-and-sort tool to answer questions about the set of animals. For example, what animals typically have two offspring per birth? What animals have cubs (or kids) as their offspring? What is the name of the offspring of cats (or goats)? In what country or countries would students be able to find pheasants?

Variation(s)   This activity could also (or alternatively) develop a database for use in classification; classes contained in the system could overlap. For example, your students could build a database on the types of airplanes, or Olympic events and their medal-winners over the years.

Activity　TV Viewing

Type	Machine
Level	Advanced
Objective	Collect, analyze, display, and report information; develop serial and hierarchical classification skills
Prerequisite(s)	Experience with a database program
Materials Needed	Database software *Bargraph* on the *Applications Disk*
Activity	This activity develops a database to be used in the analysis of group preferences for types of TV programs and of favorite programs within each type. The most important step is to determine the fields in the data record. You will probably wish to use *Data Manager II,* although AppleWorks and other programs, if available, would be more powerful.

Prepare students to keep records over a period of time. Specifically, ask them to record their TV viewing for one week—the name of each program, the hours during which the program is shown, and the time spent watching the program. Place their viewing record on a 4-by-6-inch card. Be sure to organize the data collection so that all necessary information is gathered. Assign this activity on a Friday and have students start recording their viewing over the weekend and continue to Friday of the following week. During the week, ask them to do group activities for organizing and summarizing the data. Enter the information collected into a database, so that it can be analyzed. Group programs by type and compare the programs within each type to see which are most popular. Discuss how a person can compare programs that are different in type. What is the most popular type of program? How can the database be used to support the answer to the question?

Use a word processor to report the results. Can the data summary be used in the report? Using the *Bargraph* program, show the viewing records for the top ten programs. Explain the specific computer steps needed to incorporate the data in the report.

Variation(s)	Use the methods developed here to conduct a survey about such topics as students' spending habits, the ways in which they spend their time, and the amount of time they spend in studying each subject.

Have students collect information for a week on their mothers' or fathers' activities (work, TV viewing, movies, exercise, household chores, and so on).

Activity   Food, Calorie, Group, and Nutrition

Type Machine

Objective Use skills in organizing, searching, and selecting to analyze diet and to measure caloric intake and extent to which diet is balanced.

Prerequisite(s) Experience with a database program

Materials Needed *Data Manager II* (or AppleWorks, or database software of your choice)

Food and Nutrients, a sample database on the *Applications Disk*

Activity First, using a brainstorming session, have students name as many foods as they can; then categorize the foods in some workable fashion. Next have students research these foods to complete the data on their lists. The *Food and Nutrients* database sample is a good example of the type of information needed. Then the students should enter the data into the database; they should make sure that the entry is accurate and systematic (that is, that all data are entered in exactly the same way). The data should be entered into *Foods* or a variation of that database. Note that the program should be *Data Manager II* (or AppleWorks or an alternative of your choice). Note also that there is a limit of one hundred entries in *Data Manager II,* so be prepared to categorize and produce sub-databases. (For example, *Foods.vegetables, Foods.meats, Foods.desserts, Foods.breads, Foods.salads,* and *Foods.drinks* can be used as subcategories.)

As they did for *TV viewing,* students can record their eating habits for one week. Then have them develop a *Food and nutrients* database to use in the analysis of their eating habits. Finally, ask them to propose a change in their diets that would improve nutrition while maintaining the enjoyment of eating.

Variation(s) Analyzing the data that was collected, determine the favorite foods of a given food group (favorite vegetables, desserts, and so on).

Using the methods developed here, conduct a survey of types of diets and their nutritional value.

Have students use a word processor to prepare a menu for a week and print it out. Analyze the menu in terms of balance, nutrition, and so on. (There are computer programs that can rapidly compute this information.)

Exploration

Pets We Have at Home Worksheet

Name _____

Pet _____ Age _____

How many? _____

Care required _____

Other animals _____

Pet _____ Age _____

Care required _____

Pet (Circle One)							**Pet's name**
Dogs	1	2	3	4	5	6	_____
Cats	1	2	3	4	5	6	_____
Birds	1	2	3	4	5	6	_____
Horses	1	2	3	4	5	6	_____
Rabbits	1	2	3	4	5	6	_____
Gerbils	1	2	3	4	5	6	_____
Fish	1	2	3	4	5	6	_____
Other	1	2	3	4	5	6	_____

Chapter 7

Electronic Spreadsheets

▲ ▶ ▼ ◀ ▲ ▶ ▼ ◀ ▲ ▶ ▼ ◀ ▲ ▶ ▼ ◀ ▲ ▶ ▼ ◀ ▲ ▶

Objectives

▶ Use a spreadsheet in solving some problems
▶ Use a spreadsheet to answer questions
▶ Create at least one spreadsheet template
▶ Prepare a spreadsheet from scratch

The variety and power of spreadsheets are substantial. Like those of word processors, the characteristics of spreadsheets are changing rapidly. These changes are made in many different capabilities, including these: capacity; availability of formulas; calculational possibilities; formatting and stylesetting options, including headers and footers; search and choose capabilities; editing; options for the order in which operations are performed; windowing; use of macros; and choices of functions and formulas. These changes are typical of the evolution taking place and emerging in such spreadsheets as *Microsoft Works, Lotus 1-2-3,* and *Framework II.*

A spreadsheet is similar to an accountant's ledger. It is useful for the compilation of numerical data that is to be used in any type of computation. A spreadsheet would be a good tool, for example, for averaging or adding grades. It would be especially useful for averaging the grades of each of 30 or 50 students. Show the machine how to average one set and, almost with the touch of a button, they are all averaged immediately.

A variety of spreadsheets is available. *AppleWorks* has a spreadsheet, as does *First Choice; dBase IV, Microsoft Works, Framework II, VisiCalc, SuperCalc, Jazz, Lotus 1-2-3,* and *Symphony* are all examples of spreadsheets. Several spreadsheets have simple word processors or databases "within" them, although their main use is as spreadsheets.

Features of a Spreadsheet

An electronic spreadsheet is a ledgerlike worksheet. Data are entered and operations are performed on them. For example, the test scores and averages for each pupil in a class could be kept on a spreadsheet. A spreadsheet is to numbers as a word processor is to words; each allows for easy manipulation and transformation of data.

An electronic spreadsheet is like a bookkeeper's ledger, divided into rows and columns, and can be used in the making of numerical calculations. It is easy to use for data tabulation, organization, and analysis. We will list several possible ways in which spreadsheets can be used for teaching purposes, and we will demonstrate the use of one such way.

1. **Bookkeeping** A spreadsheet is designed for bookkeeping and the projection of budgets, so it is ideal for a bookkeeping class, as well as other business classes that include working with columns of numbers.

2. **Health records** Names, health statistics, and personal data can be entered for students in a class studying health. For example, the students' weight and height could be entered for each two-week period, and analysis, such as a graph of weight, could be done with a spreadsheet.

3. **Physical education studies** To study the effects of exercise on cardiovascular activity, a physical education class could enter data on heart rates before, during, and after a particular exercise. To chart changes in physical conditioning, these data could be kept and studied over a semester.

4. **Analysis of data of health and social issues** An analysis such as the relationship of smoking, or being in a room with smokers, to pulse rate and blood pressure is developed more fully in the next section.

5. **Building tables of related information** A language class can use a spreadsheet to list words and their translations or to set up matching questions for a test. This use does not involve the manipulation of numerical data; however, a spreadsheet sets up rows and columns and thus provides an easy means by which information of all types can be organized.

6. **Generating math and science problems** By using formulas to set up a spreadsheet, students could generate sets of questions of a particular type (quadratics with rational roots; ballistics examples with whole-number maxima) and their answers. These questions can be automatically generated in seconds.

7. **Instruction-related record-keeping** Spreadsheets can be used for a variety of record-keeping uses, including roll books, attendance reports, and the like. These are discussed more fully later.

Using a Spreadsheet— The Effects of Smoke

An issue in today's society is the effect of smoking upon health. Many sites of public transportation, communications, entertainment, and employment either do not permit smoking or partition off nonsmoking areas. What effects do cigar and cigarette smoke have on various bodily functions? We will examine data collected under three conditions: there is no smoke in the room, there is smoke in the room but subjects are not smoking, and subjects are smoking. The heart rate and blood pressure of subjects under each condition will be recorded.

Figure 1 shows the spreadsheet on which data will be organized. The names of the participants are listed down the left column. The first block in the top row is for heart rate, and the second block is for blood pressure. Within the first block at top, there are columns for data on *no smoking, smoke in room,* and *smoking* conditions. The same three columns are also organized for data on blood pressure.

	Heart Rate			Blood Pressure		
	No Smoking	Smoke in Room	Smoking	No Smoking	Smoke in Room	Smoking
ALPINE, ANA						
BENSON, HEDG						
CAMEL, CARRY						
CARLTON, CID						
LUCKY, LUCY						
MARLB, MARY						
KOOL, KARL						
PALL, MA						
PLAYERS, PAL						
SALEM, SAL						
STERLING, SI						
TRUE, TED						
VANTAGE, VAN						
VICE, ROY						
WINSTON, WIL						
AVERAGE OF PERSONS SAMPLED						

▲

Figure 1 *Spreadsheet framework for data on smoke effects.*

Figure 2 shows the organizational scheme with data inserted for heart rates sampled under the conditions of *no smoke* and *smoke in room*. This figure also shows the rounded average of the heart rate for all persons sampled under the *no smoking* and *smoke in room* conditions. The data show that heart rates increased an average of nine beats per minute when there was smoke in the room. To obtain the averages, we used the *Average* function of a spreadsheet. When data are added or corrected, the corresponding correction of all totals is automatic.

Figure 3 shows the completed set of data. It provides the data in labeled columns and the averages under the specified conditions. The data show that there is a difference in heart rate between the *no smoke* and the other two conditions, *smoke in room* and *smoking*. There is little difference between the heart rates in the *smoking* and *smoke in the room* conditions. However, the data show that there is a difference among the blood pressures for all of the conditions: between each, there is a significant increase in blood pressure.

This sample illustrates the use of spreadsheets in classroom activities. Of course, much more complete and elaborate examinations of issues are possible. For example, we could study more carefully the effects of the amount of smoke in a room (10 cigarettes lit in a room that has 800 cubic feet, versus 10 cigarettes lit in a room that has 1800 cubic feet), the effect of chain smoking on heart rate and blood pressure, or the effect of smoke penetration into the nonsmoking regions of a restaurant or an airplane.

	Heart Rate			Blood Pressure		
	No Smoking	Smoke in Room	Smoking	No Smoking	Smoke in Room	Smoking
ALPINE, ANA	68	74				
BENSON, HEDG	55	77				
CAMEL, CARRY	70	78				
CARLTON, CID	65	74				
LUCKY, LUCY	78	83				
MARLB, MARY	72	82				
KOOL, KARL	60	67				
PALL, MA	55	64				
PLAYERS, PAL	54	59				
SALEM, SAL	62	70				
STERLING, SI	70	78				
TRUE, TED	66	64				
VANTAGE, VAN	64	78				
VICE, ROY	58	72				
WINSTON, WIL	70	77				
AVERAGE OF PERSONS SAMPLED	64	73				

▲

Figure 2 *Spreadsheet with data for heart rates sampled under "no smoking" and "smoke in room" conditions, and a computed average.*

Administrative Uses of a Spreadsheet

There are a number of ways in which electronic spreadsheets, database programs, and word processing can be used for record-keeping and other administrative tasks. The following are some of these tasks.

1. **Roll book:** Names, personal data, notes, grades, averages, attendance data, and like information can be entered into a spreadsheet. This sets up an electronic grade book, which can be saved on a disk and updated as needed.
2. **School club financial records:** The financial records of a club or other budgetary records can be entered and updated as needed. A spreadsheet will balance books for you. It will also make corrections in all dependent records if an error is corrected in any one entry.
3. **Attendance reports:** A spreadsheet can be used to organize names and other data for daily or monthly attendance records. You can then select attendance records and easily form a report such as the daily attendance sheet or the monthly attendance register. A spreadsheet can produce the statistical summaries that you need.

	Heart Rate			Blood Pressure		
	No Smoking	Smoke in Room	Smoking	No Smoking	Smoke in Room	Smoking
ALPINE, ANA	68	74	75	130	140	150
BENSON, HEDG	55	77	78	125	140	145
CAMEL, CARRY	70	78	79	118	130	140
CARLTON, CID	65	74	75	130	140	140
LUCKY, LUCY	78	83	80	122	130	135
MARLB, MARY	72	82	81	110	125	130
KOOL, KARL	60	67	69	120	125	135
PALL, MA	55	64	67	115	130	140
PLAYERS, PAL	54	59	61	115	120	115
SALEM, SAL	62	70	72	140	145	150
STERLING, SI	70	78	79	135	140	150
TRUE, TED	66	64	66	120	125	130
VANTAGE, VAN	64	78	75	110	130	135
VICE, ROY	58	72	76	100	120	125
WINSTON, WIL	70	77	78	125	140	135
AVERAGE OF PERSONS SAMPLED	64	73	74	121	133	137

▲

Figure 3 *Complete spreadsheet for "smoking effects" data.*

4. **Inventories:** Inventories of supplies, equipment, and books can be managed by a spreadsheet. For comparison, both old and updated records can be saved.
5. **Budgets:** A sample budget can be prepared and modified, and additional budgets generated so that you can examine a number of potential budgets.
6. **Word processing:** Word processing can be helpful for writing communications, keeping information, and preparing mailing lists. Teachers can also make effective use of the word processor for preparing tests, writing course materials, or preparing lesson plans. Previously used materials can be modified, updated, and maintained.
7. **Records of library books:** The spreadsheet can easily record which books are presently in the library and which books have been checked out to whom.
8. **Schedules:** School schedules and individual student schedules can be prepared. Storage of, search for, and retrieval of schedule-related data can be accomplished easily.

By examining the roll book in some detail, we will show ways in which a spreadsheet can be used to develop it. Our purpose is to show the working of a spreadsheet. Figure 4 shows an initial screen display of a grade book using a spreadsheet. It shows the basic entries: the names and types of grades to be recorded. The framework for the grade book has been established but can be adjusted in many

GRADES	Test 1	Quiz 1	Test 2	Quiz 2	Quiz 3	Test 3	Test 4	Final Exam	TOTAL PTS	AVERAGE
Student Names										
ADE, ADAM										
CART, CAL										
EARP, EARL										
GALT, GAIL										
IRR, IRMA										
KURT, KARL										
MANN, MARK										
ORR, OLLIE										
QUIN, QUAD										
SAAS, SUE										
URR, ULAH										
WATT, WADE										
YENN, YAS										

▲

Figure 4 *Grade book setup on a spreadsheet.*

GRADES	Test 1	Quiz 1	Test 2	Quiz 2	Quiz 3	Test 3	Test 4	Final Exam	TOTAL PTS	AVERAGE
Student Names										
ADE, ADAM	98									
CART, CAL	93									
EARP, EARL	89									
GALT, GAIL	79									
IRR, IRMA	69									
KURT, KARL	63									
MANN, MARK	94									
ORR, OLLIE	74									
QUIN, QUAD	97									
SAAS, SUE	83									
URR, ULAH	59									
WATT, WADE	90									
YENN, YAS	58									

▲

Figure 5 *Grade book using a spreadsheet entered with some grades.*

ways. For example, a new row or column can be added at any location. Thus, if a new person enters the class, you can easily start a file for that person in a position of your choice on the spreadsheet. For example, you could insert Joe Jonn in proper alphabetical position. Figure 5 shows the next stage of data entry in our grade book; some grades have been entered. A spreadsheet has a built-in sum function: it can add a student's scores. Figure 6 shows the total produced by the sum function. Finally, a spreadsheet can perform calculations on the test and quiz scores. It will

GRADES	Test 1	Quiz 1	Test 2	Quiz 2	Quiz 3	Test 3	Test 4	Final Exam	TOTAL PTS	AVERAGE
Student Names										
ADE, ADAM	98	38	95	22	48	92	89	94	576	
CART, CAL	93	49	88	25	36	74	94	89	548	
EARP, EARL	89	36	89	19	50	88	94	60	525	
GALT, GAIL	79	38	89	23	29	86	88	86	518	
IRR, IRMA	69	50	79	15	38	70	72	93	486	
KURT, KARL	63	48	81	18	50	95	94	68	517	
MANN, MARK	94	50	89	25	41	93	91	83	566	
ORR, OLLIE	74	45	90	9	44	96	90	94	542	
QUIN, QUAD	97	50	82	12	50	50	83	82	506	
SAAS, SUE	83	48	90	21	25	70	81	75	493	
URR, ULAH	59	49	95	18	39	99	94	60	513	
WATT, WADE	90	49	70	20	38	70	91	95	493	
YENN, YAS	58	36	69	25	30	83	55	83	439	

▲

Figure 6 *Grade book with grades entered and sum function used.*

GRADES	Test 1	Quiz 1	Test 2	Quiz 2	Quiz 3	Test 3	Test 4	Final Exam	TOTAL PTS	AVERAGE
Student Names										
ADE, ADAM	98	38	95	22	48	92	89	94	576	91
CART, CAL	93	49	88	25	36	74	94	89	548	86
EARP, EARL	89	36	89	19	50	88	94	60	525	70
GALT, GAIL	79	38	89	23	29	86	88	86	518	82
IRR, IRMA	69	50	79	15	38	70	72	93	486	84
KURT, KARL	63	48	81	18	50	95	94	68	517	74
MANN, MARK	94	50	89	25	41	93	91	83	566	85
ORR, OLLIE	74	45	90	9	44	96	90	94	542	88
QUIN, QUAD	97	50	82	12	50	50	83	82	506	80
SAAS, SUE	83	48	90	21	25	70	81	75	493	75
URR, ULAH	59	49	95	18	39	99	94	60	513	69
WATT, WADE	90	49	70	20	38	70	61	95	493	85
YENN, YAS	58	36	69	25	30	83	55	83	439	75

▲

Figure 7 *Completed grade book with grades entered and sum function used.*

automatically weight scores, average quizzes and tests, and then perform total averages by whatever formula you choose. Figure 7 shows the grade book with a final average, which was calculated by having the final exam count four parts, the test average count two parts, and the quiz average count one part. If we wished to recalculate with the final counting two parts, tests counting three parts, and quiz averages counting one, the reformulation could be done automatically and would require only one or two minutes of work.

Box 1   Working with AppleWorks: Creating Your Spreadsheet Template

Now we will create a spreadsheet: a grade book, similar to that of the spreadsheet example in the chapter. This spreadsheet will allow you to create your own record-keeping system, one that will work with any of your classes. One of its advantages is that you can have AppleWorks do all of the averaging and other computations for you.

To create your spreadsheet, you will need to use the <ESC> to get back to the menu shown in Figure 8. You will choose option *5. Make a new file from the spreadsheet.* After you have indicated this choice, you will be given a form for the spreadsheet.

Spreadsheet Tools for Record Keeping

Building the spreadsheet to be used as a tool is a valuable experience (see Box 1). You can then use your skills to create, for example, your own record-keeping systems. To become skilled with building spreadsheets, we will work with some spreadsheets from the *Sample disk* for AppleWorks. We can then work toward building some **templates,** which are overlays for calculations that you may have to do repeatedly. By inserting different data into the form or template, you can quickly and easily do many calculations. As we work with the files on the sample disk, look back and forth between the data and the formulas that perform the calculations. This switching is accomplished by the use of $<\circlearrowleft\text{-Z}>$, for zoom.

Use $<\circlearrowleft\text{-Z}>$ to zoom into *Mom's apple pie company* (the *Organic Growth* file) spreadsheet. You will see something like Figures 9 and 10 on the screen. To experiment with the *form* of Figure 10, change the value in the *Oct.* column and *Expected* row to 400; see what other numbers change. Change it to 100 and see what other numbers change. Try to explain the changes that occur. The columns are labeled (D, for example) and the rows are labeled (7, for example). The calculation in column E and row 8, for example, is 1.5 times the value in column D, row 8. What is the calculation that is being done in column D, row 7? You are right, it is .8 times the value in column D, row 8. So you see that the value of column D, row 7, is .8 × 300 = 240. This is the way calculations are described in spreadsheets. The labels are variables for the computations; D8*.8 is the value based on the variable (or changing number) in column D, row 8.

To compare and contrast the uses of applications like spreadsheets and databases, we will examine the file *Organic pies*. First, load the *Organic pies* file from the *Sample disk*. (Recall that to do this you use the *Main Menu,* and select *Add a file to the desktop.* To get to the *Main Menu,* if you have been working with files in AppleWorks, you can use <ESC>, maybe a few times.) For example, consider the information shown in Figure 11. Would you want to set this up as a spreadsheet or as a database? Is this question answerable before you know the use of the data? Suppose you wanted to average the number of units sold. Which application would you want to use? Suppose you wanted to arrange the information in the *Date Introduced* column. Which application would you want to use?

The file is a database file. However, it might be more useful for it to have been a spreadsheet file. You may wish to look at Exercise 9 (at the end of this chapter), for practice in the transfer of data among applications. The process might be a bit difficult, so you might prefer to simply add it into the other application, especially because there is only a small amount of data to be moved. (The transfer of data from one application to another is discussed in the next section.)

We will now experiment with the record *Apple Light.* Use $<\circlearrowleft\text{-Z}>$ to zoom into the specific record; you can see the individual record in Figure 12. Recall that,

Figure 8 *The first step in creating a spreadsheet is to get back to this menu.*

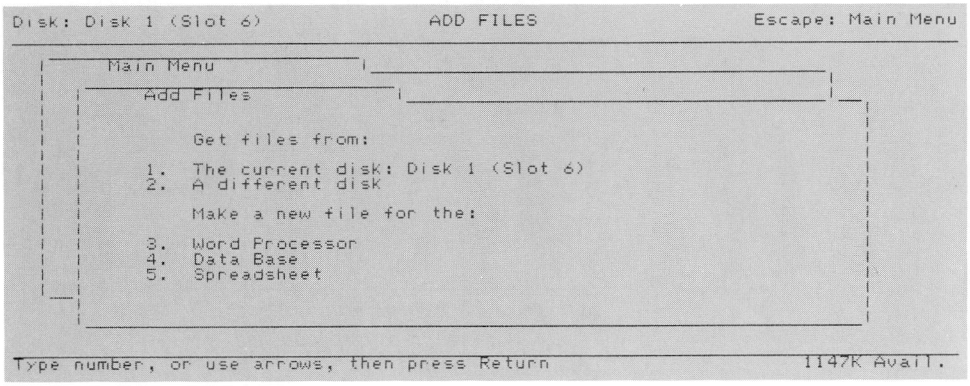

▼

```
Disk: Disk 1 (Slot 6)                    ADD FILES              Escape: Main Menu

  |‾‾‾‾‾Main Menu‾‾‾‾‾‾‾‾‾‾‾|‾‾‾‾‾‾‾‾‾‾‾‾‾‾‾‾‾‾‾‾‾‾‾‾‾‾‾‾‾‾‾‾‾‾‾‾‾
  |    |‾‾‾‾Add Files‾‾‾‾‾‾‾‾‾‾|‾‾‾‾‾‾‾‾‾‾‾‾‾‾‾‾‾‾‾‾‾‾‾‾‾‾‾‾‾‾‾|
  |    |                                                      |
  |    |       Get files from:                                |
  |    |                                                      |
  |    |       1.  The current disk: Disk 1 (Slot 6)          |
  |    |       2.  A different disk                           |
  |    |                                                      |
  |    |       Make a new file for the:                       |
  |    |                                                      |
  |    |       3.  Word Processor                             |
  |    |       4.  Data Base                                  |
  |    |       5.  Spreadsheet                                |
  |__|                                                        |
  |__|                                                        |
     ‾‾‾‾‾‾‾‾‾‾‾‾‾‾‾‾‾‾‾‾‾‾‾‾‾‾‾‾‾‾‾‾‾‾‾‾‾‾‾‾‾‾‾‾‾‾‾‾‾‾‾‾‾‾‾‾

Type number, or use arrows, then press Return            1147K Avail.
```

Figure 9 *A sample spreadsheet screen.*

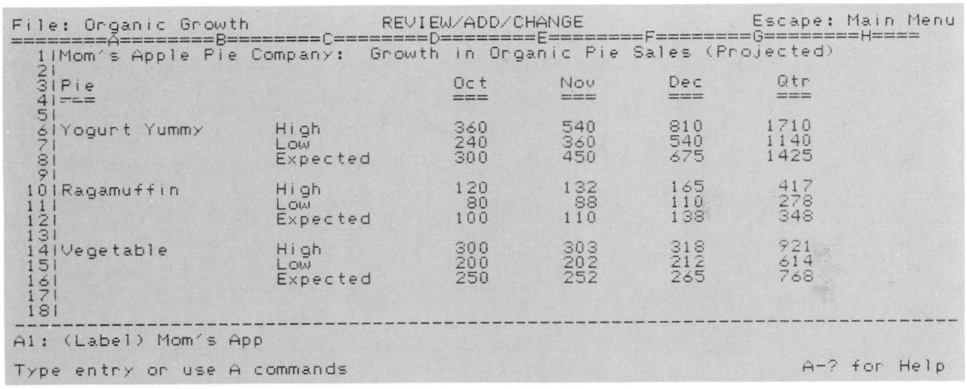

▼

```
File: Organic Growth              REVIEW/ADD/CHANGE            Escape: Main Menu
=========A=========B=========C=========D=========E=========F=========G=========H=====
  1|Mom's Apple Pie Company:  Growth in Organic Pie Sales (Projected)
  2|
  3|Pie                             Oct      Nov      Dec      Qtr
  4|===                             ===      ===      ===      ===
  5|
  6|Yogurt Yummy      High          360      540      810     1710
  7|                  Low           240      360      540     1140
  8|                  Expected      300      450      675     1425
  9|
 10|Ragamuffin        High          120      132      165      417
 11|                  Low            80       88      110      278
 12|                  Expected      100      110      138      348
 13|
 14|Vegetable         High          300      303      318      921
 15|                  Low           200      202      212      614
 16|                  Expected      250      252      265      768
 17|
 18|
-----------------------------------------------------------------------------
A1: (Label) Mom's App

Type entry or use A commands                              A-? for Help
```

Figure 10 *You can manipulate this spreadsheet in many ways.*

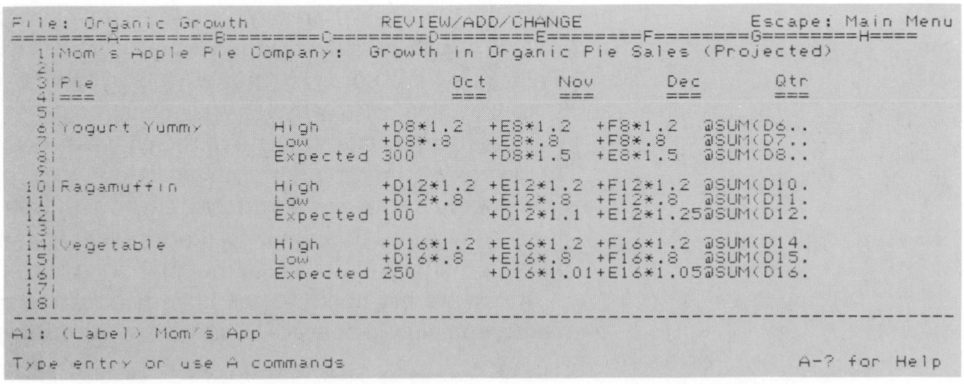

▼

```
File: Organic Growth              REVIEW/ADD/CHANGE            Escape: Main Menu
=========A=========B=========C=========D=========E=========F=========G=========H=====
  1|Mom's Apple Pie Company:  Growth in Organic Pie Sales (Projected)
  2|
  3|Pie                             Oct      Nov      Dec      Qtr
  4|===                             ===      ===      ===      ===
  5|
  6|Yogurt Yummy      High      +D8*1.2  +E8*1.2  +F8*1.2  @SUM(D6..
  7|                  Low       +D8*.8   +E8*.8   +F8*.8   @SUM(D7..
  8|                  Expected  300      +D8*1.5  +E8*1.5  @SUM(D8..
  9|
 10|Ragamuffin        High      +D12*1.2 +E12*1.2 +F12*1.2 @SUM(D10.
 11|                  Low       +D12*.8  +E12*.8  +F12*.8  @SUM(D11.
 12|                  Expected  100      +D12*1.1 +E12*1.25@SUM(D12.
 13|
 14|Vegetable         High      +D16*1.2 +E16*1.2 +F16*1.2 @SUM(D14.
 15|                  Low       +D16*.8  +E16*.8  +F16*.8  @SUM(D15.
 16|                  Expected  250      +D16*1.01+E16*1.05@SUM(D16.
 17|
 18|
-----------------------------------------------------------------------------
A1: (Label) Mom's App

Type entry or use A commands                              A-? for Help
```

```
File: Organic Pies                REVIEW/ADD/CHANGE            Escape: Main Menu
Selection: All records


Pie Name          Units Sold        Units/Month      Date Introduced Total Sales
================================================================================
Apple Light       4000              2000             Jul   4 84      $16,000
Carob Crunch      3600              900              May   5 84      $14,000
Coconut Custard   2800              700              May   5 84      $12,000
Crispy Cotton     20                20               Aug  14 84      $80
Granola Pudding   200               50               May   5 84      $800
Kumquat           600               150              May   5 84      $3,600
Pisco             5                 3                Jul   4 84      $20
Pure Peach        800               400              Jul   4 84      $3,200
Ragamuffin        500               250              Jul   4 84      $2,000
Rhubarb           400               200              Jul   4 84      $1,600
Squash Blossom    400               200              Jul   4 84      $1,600
Strawberry Strip  460               200              Aug  14 84      $1,600
Vegetable         285               100              Jul   4 84      $1,200
Very Berry        6000              1500             May   5 84      $24,000
Yogurt Yummy      1250              300              Jul   4 84      $3,675
                                                                    ------------
Type entry or use A commands                                        A-? for Help
```

▲

Figure 11 *Information that
could be set up as a spreadsheet
or as a database.*

```
File: Organic Pies          REVIEW/ADD/CHANGE    Escape: Restore former entry
Selection: All records


Record 1 of 16
================================================================================
Pie Name: Apple Light
Units Sold: 4000
Units/Month: 2000
Date Introduced: Jul   4 84
Total Sales: $16,000
Total Profit: $4,800
Price/Unit: $4.00
Cost/Unit: $2.80
Profit/Unit: $1.20




           -------------------------------------------------------------------
Type entry or use A commands                                     1143K Avail.
```

▲

Figure 12 *The record Apple
Light.*

because the database is easily manipulated, it easily can be sorted or re-arranged. For example, you can easily search for particular information or order items alphabetically. In particular, you can arrange the dates in sequence by months of the year and by days within each month (Date Introduced). A technique not used before, < ⌘-A>, will allow you to make this change. The data in *Units Sold, Units/Month, Total Sales,* and so on are numerical and can therefore be used in any computations that were needed to answer your questions.

The exercises at the end of the chapter request that you set up a form like this to serve as a grade book or as an attendance keeper. Working with the values in the columns and rows will permit you to set up the appropriate calculations. Remember, the *AppleWorks Tutorial* will also be valuable for you to use in completing the calculations and the templates of the requested spreadsheets.

Now we are going to see how a companion to AppleWorks, called *Visualizer,* can graphically display data so that relationships are clear.

Working with Visualizer: A Companion to AppleWorks Spreadsheets

Visualizer is a companion to AppleWorks, in that data of an *AppleWorks* spreadsheet can be visualized with the aid of graphs made by *Visualizer*. Pie graphs, bar graphs, line and dot graphs, and three-dimensional graphs are easy to make with *Visualizer*. As a teacher you may wish to examine the trends in a group's performance or to graphically present data in a report you are writing. *Visualizer* is ideal for such purposes. You will probably enjoy your experience with this piece of software. (AppleWorks GS incorporates the capabilities of *Visualizer*.)

Using *Visualizer,* you can take files from *AppleWorks* and convert them into a display. For an example, use the *AppleWorks* file contained on the tutorial disk for *Visualizer*. First boot *Prodos* as you would with *AppleWorks*. Then from the desktop, choose *Add File to Desktop*.

Like those in AppleWorks, the < ⌘ -?> keys give help. After you have returned to the spreadsheet, choose < ⌘ -A>. It suggests that you highlight the data you wish to plot, beginning with the first line of data. You should then choose < ⌘ -G> to draw the graph. A typical screen display is shown in Figure 13.

That first figure can be easily modified to Figure 14, in which a particular "slice of the pie" is emphasized. The directions with *Visualizer* make it easy for users to pull out a slice of the pie. To choose the section to be pulled, use the arrow key for movement around the graph. It's nice to know that the slices of the pie are lettered in clockwise order from the top; the top one is labeled *A*. Options presented on the screen permit you to move a piece of the pie: You touch <RETURN> and the piece is moved automatically.

Figure 13 *Typical screen display of Visualizer.*
▼

Figure 14 *A modification that has pulled a "piece" from the "pie."*
▼

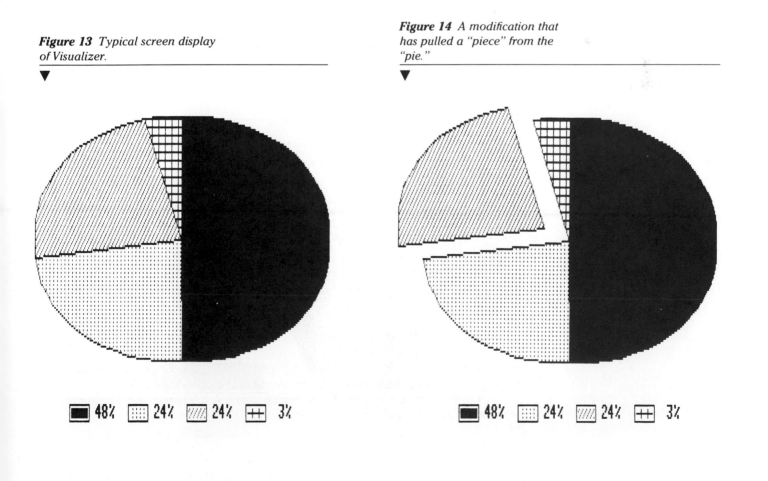

Figure 15 *Visualizer Main Menu.*

▼

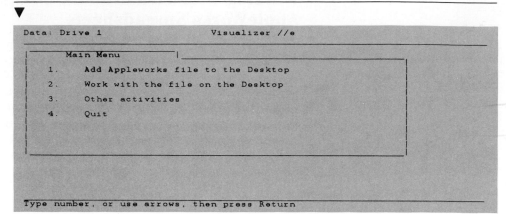

```
Data: Drive 1                      Visualizer //e
_____
   | Main Menu                  |
   1.      Add Appleworks file to the Desktop
   2.      Work with the file on the Desktop
   3.      Other activities
   4.      Quit




Type number, or use arrows, then press Return
```

Figure 16 *Typical options menu
for Visualizer.*

▼

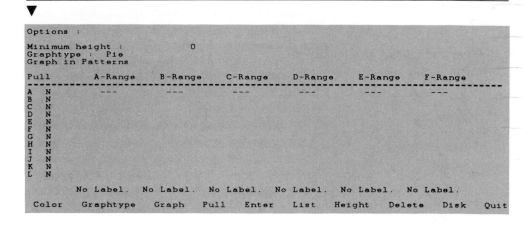

```
Options :

Minimum height :              0
Graphtype :  Pie
Graph in Patterns

Pull       A-Range     B-Range     C-Range     D-Range     E-Range     F-Range
------------------------------------------------------------------------------
A   N        ---         ---         ---         ---         ---         ---
B   N
C   N
D   N
E   N
F   N
G   N
H   N
I   N
J   N
K   N
L   N

         No Label.  No Label.  No Label.  No Label.  No Label.  No Label.
  Color   Graphtype   Graph    Pull    Enter    List   Height   Delete   Disk   Quit
```

Figure 17 *See if you can use the
AppleWorks spreadsheet and
Visualizer to make this bar
graph.*

▼

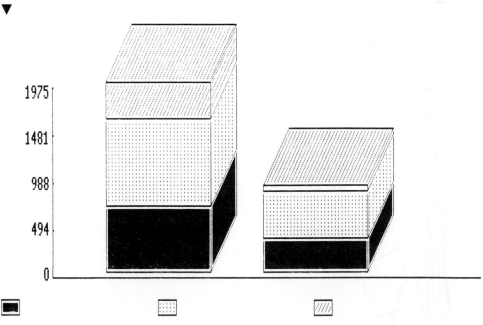

A particularly pleasant feature of integrated software such as AppleWorks is the ease with which you can transfer data among the applications. In AppleWorks, typically one would <Ô-C> to cut and paste. However, when you move a graph (made with Visualizer, for example) into text, or move an item from a spreadsheet to a word processor, you can choose <Ô-P> and the picture or table will be moved to the clipboard. After the item is moved to the Clipboard, simply locate the position in the other document to place the information and it will be pasted there with an <Ô-P> selection. This is how a Visualizer graph would be moved into a word processed document.

The Main Menu for *Visualizer* is shown when you boot Visualizer (Figure 15). It tells you the options of uses of *Visualizer*. The Graph Options Screen shows the types of graphs you can make with *Visualizer* (Figure 16). Using AppleWorks spreadsheet, see if you can make the choices necessary to draw the bar graph (Figure 17).

▲ ▶ ▼ ◀ ▲ ▶ ▼ ◀ ▲ ▶ ▼ ◀ ▲ ▶ ▼ ◀ ▲ ▶ ▼ ◀ ▲ ▶

Summary

Spreadsheets are tools for performing arithmetic or numerical operations on data. AppleWorks is a popular spreadsheet for the Apple II family of computers. Activities in this chapter illustrate the use of AppleWorks in varied examples. *Visualizer* is a graphics companion to AppleWorks.

These software programs were referenced in this chapter.

AppleWorks	*VisiCalc*
Visualizer	*SuperCalc*
Microsoft Works	*Jazz*
Lotus 1-2-3	*Symphony*
Framework II	*Apple Light*
dBase IV	

Important Terms

Spreadsheet	File
Template	Data transfer among applications

Exercises

1. Using AppleWorks, create a spreadsheet template for a grade book for a 9-week grading period. Include room for 40 students, 10 test grades, 10 quiz grades, 30 homework grades, a final-exam grade, and the final grade. Calculate the final grade as a total of the following: 50% for tests, 15% for quizzes, 15% for homework, and 20% for final exam basis.

2. Using AppleWorks, create a spreadsheet template for attendance records for a month's attendance. Provide opportunities for absences (excused), absences (unexcused), and tardies to be recorded. Total each category based on a 30-day month.

3. To select a type of graph to be drawn with *Visualizer,* use <Ô-O>, the options menu. Enter BARGRAPH <RETURN> as the type of graph to be drawn. To display the graph on the screen, enter GRAPH (or use <ESC> together with <Ô-G>).

4. To select a type of graph to be drawn with *Visualizer,* use <Ô-O>, the options menu. Enter STACKED BARS <RETURN> as the type of graph to

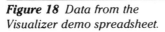

```
                                    Review/Graph            Escape : Main menu
--------A-------B------C---------D-----------E---------F---------G---------H---------
1  |      Acme Widgets, Inc. - records for total 1983-1984 revenues
2  |
3  |                    Sales      Cost      Gross     Taxes       Net
4  |-----------------------------------------------------------------------
5  |January    1983      700       350       350       52.5      297.5
6  |February             750       375       375       56.25     318.75
7  |March                900       500       400        60        340
8  |April               1300       750       550       82.5      467.5
9  |May                 1600       900       700       105        595
10 |June                1750      1000       750      112.5      637.5
11 |July                1800       850       950      142.5      807.5
12 |August              1700       800       900       135        765
13 |September           1300       700       600        90        510
14 |October             1200       650       550       82.5      467.5
15 |November            1100       550       550       82.5      467.5
16 |December            1300       650       650       97.5      552.5
17 |January    1984      550       300       250       37.5      212.5
18 |February             600       325       275       41.25     233.75
   |----------------------------------------------------------------------
A1

Enter Visualizer commands                                          ? for help
```

▲

Figure 18 *Data from the
Visualizer demo spreadsheet.*

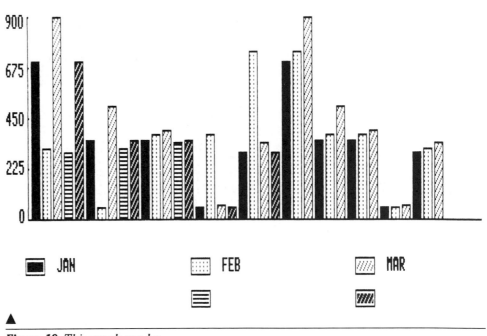

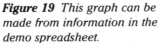

▲

Figure 19 *This graph can be
made from information in the
demo spreadsheet.*

be drawn. To display the graph on the screen, enter GRAPH (or use
<ESC> together with < ⌂ -G>).

5. To label a graph, first use < ⌂ -O>, the options menu. Choose ENTER
    from the menu, so that you can enter the label you wish. After you have
    typed ENTER, choose LABEL, then highlight *A*. This sequence will attach
    a label to data range *A*. Clear the range of data. Now choose the data in
    D5–H5. (To do this, use < ⌂ -A> to place data in Range A; then highlight,
    beginning at D5 and continuing through H5). Now graph this data and
    notice both the graph and the label.

6. The *Visualizer* demo spreadsheet has data for your experimentation (Figure 18). Use the data to produce the graph in Figure 19, which illustrates how data from different ranges can be integrated. You will need to highlight selected data, place data in appropriate data ranges, choose *Enter* and *Label data,* and choose *BarGraph.* You will need to use the < Ĉ -O> menu for these transactions.

7. Using the *Cities* database from Chapter 6 (Box 3), create a spreadsheet analysis, decade by decade since 1950, of the five most rapidly growing cities. Include data for the overall population growth of the U.S. over the same time. Show percentages of growth by decade, as well as the actual size of each city at the beginning of each decade.

8. Using the AppleWorks word processor, write a brief analysis of a city of your choice. Include in it select data from the *Cities* database, and an analysis of growth by comparison to the U.S. from the spreadsheet.

References

Hannah, L. (1985–86). Social studies, spreadsheets, and the quality of life. *The Computing Teacher, 13,* 13–15.

Joshi, B. D. (1986–87). *Lotus 1-2-3:* A tool for scientific problem solving. *Journal of Computers in Mathematics and Science Teaching, 6,* 28–36, 43.

Luehrmann, A. (1986). Spreadsheets: More than just finance. *The Computing Teacher, 13,* 24–28.

Wells, G., & Berger, C. (1986–87). Teacher/student-developed spreadsheet simulations: A population growth example. *Journal of Computers in Mathematics and Science Teaching, 5,* 34–40.

▲ ▶ ▼ ◀ ▲ ▶ ▼ ◀ ▲ ▶ ▼ ◀ ▲ ▶ ▼ ◀ ▲ ▶ ▼ ◀ ▲ ▶

Activity Organizing Data for a Spreadsheet

Type	Preparatory
Objective	Organize data and summarize results of data analysis
Prerequisite(s)	Work with tables and, possibly, a calculator
Materials Needed	Worksheet Calculator
Activity	Students will organize data so that it can be easily read and interpreted. Suppose the class has been divided into four teams for a fund-raising sale. The data on the following worksheet show the teams (and members' names) and the amounts sold and money collected. The students should place the data into a table and summarize the data into total team sales. After examining the totals, they can determine the winning team; they can use either the table provided in the spreadsheet or one of their own creation.
Variation(s)	Suppose that Jones enters the class on the third day of the contest, and is assigned to Team II. How should the winning team now be determined? Suppose that Ana was sick for the duration of the contest. So that her team is not penalized for her lack of sales, how should the winning team now be determined?

Exploration

Name

Organizing Data for a Spreadsheet Worksheet

Team I

Jane		Jerry		Ana		Tony		Bill	
sold	$56.30	sold	$41.90	sold	$10.50	sold	$17.95	sold	$22.10
cash	$42.10	cash	$36.10	cash	$ 8.90	cash	$ 9.90	cash	$19.50

Team II

Phil		Carlos		Maria		Sandy		Susan	
sold	$ 9.50	sold	$55.60	sold	$24.95	sold	$29.00	sold	$30.50
cash	$ 9.50	cash	$40.00	cash	$20.00	cash	$29.00	cash	$25.00

Team III

Penny		Toni		Tommy		Marcia		Eddie	
sold	$15.40	sold	$14.90	sold	$78.00	sold	$30.50	sold	$44.00
cash	$12.00	cash	$14.90	cash	$75.00	cash	$28.40	cash	$30.00

Team IV

Sandy		Bob		Rich		Edyth		Barbara	
sold	$50.00	sold	$30.95	sold	$19.95	sold	$30.00	sold	$23.70
cash	$50.00	cash	$24.00	cash	$15.00	cash	$15.00	cash	$21.00

Organize the data into the following table. Total each team's contribution and determine the winner.

Person's name	Team I		Team II		Team III		Team IV	
	Sold	Cash	Sold	Cash	Sold	Cash	Sold	Cash
1.								
2.								
3.								
4.								
5.								

Totals

Variation(s) Suppose that Bobby came into the class on the second day of the contest and was added to Team I. He sold $24.59 and had cash of $20.00. How could the winner be determined?

Suppose that Sandy (of Team IV) became ill and was unable to participate; thus, Team IV had only four members. How could the winner be determined?

Suppose that Bobby joined Team I *and* Sandy did not participate at all. How could the winner be determined?

Problem Solving with Spreadsheets Worksheet I

1. A man and his grandson have the same birthday. For six birthdays in a row the man's age is a whole-number multiple of the grandson's. How old is each at the sixth of these birthdays?

Grandpa's Age	Grandson's Age	Whole Numbers
0	0	
1	1	1
2	2	1
3	3	1
4	4	1
5	5	1

A disk copy of a form for use with a spreadsheet, entitled *Grpa.grson,* is provided in the *Applications Disk.* Insert numbers into the form on the disk, study the pattern of numbers produced, then try new numbers after you think about the meaning of the results. (A final solution is also provided under *Sol.grpa.grson* on the *Applications Disk.*)

2. Mary's older brother (John) and Jim's older sister (Ana) both work at QueenBurger. Their hours and pay are as follows:

Name	Hours Worked	Pay
John	15	$59.25
Ana	12	$49.20

Mary says that her brother is better paid. Jim argues, however, that his sister gets better wages. How can we know who is right? (Is a spreadsheet useful or necessary here? Why or why not?)

Exploration

Problem Solving with Spreadsheets Worksheet II

1. In a school's math contest, 10 problems were given. Each contestant gained 5 points for each right answer but lost 3 points for each wrong answer. How many problems were correctly solved by pupils who received a final score of 34 points? Of 10 points?

    A partial solution, which shows a pattern that will help solve the problem, is printed below.

Number of Problems Right	Number of Problems Wrong	Points for Right Answer(s)	Points Off for Wrong Answer(s)	Total Points
1	9	5	27	−22
2	8	10	24	−14
3	7	15	21	−6
4				
5				
6				
7				
8				
9				
10	0	50	0	50

2. A cyclist is supposed to be at a destination at a specified time. It is known that if he travels at a speed of 15 km per hour, he will arrive an hour early, and if his speed is 10 km per hour, he will be an hour late. At what speed should he travel in order to arrive on time?

    Set up a spreadsheet to help solve this problem.

Activity   Suggestion for the Cyclist Problem

Data that provides a solution to Part 2 of the previous exploration, is given below. Have the students interpret the numbers along the side columns and find the pattern that allows them to determine the solution. Explain what the numbers across the top mean. Explain what the numbers down the left side mean.

	9	10	11	12	13	14	15	16
1.5	13.5	15	16.5	18	19.5	21	22.5	24
2	18	20	22	24	26	28	30	32
2.5	22.5	25	27.5	30	32.5	35	37.5	40
3	27	30	33	36	39	42	45	48
3.5	31.5	35	38.5	42	45.5	49	52.5	56
4	36	40	44	48	52	56	60	64
4.5	40.5	45	49.5	54	58.5	63	67.5	72
5	45	50	55	60	65	70	75	80
5.5	49.5	55	60.5	66	71.5	77	82.5	88
6	54	60	66	72	78	84	90	96
6.5	58.5	65	71.5	78	84.5	91	97.5	104
7	63	70	77	84	91	98	105	112
7.5	67.5	75	82.5	90	97.5	105	112.5	120

An important activity related to this exercise is to have the students draw a graph of the data and read possible solutions from the graph. This helps them develop their visual ability as a problem-solving tool.

Chapter 8

Other Tool Uses
of the Computer

▲ ▶ ▼ ◀ ▲ ▶ ▼ ◀ ▲ ▶ ▼ ◀ ▲ ▶ ▼ ◀ ▲ ▶ ▼ ◀ ▲ ▶

Objectives

▶ Identify uses of graphics packages
▶ Identify uses of telecommunication, and the hardware and software it uses
▶ Give examples of networks and their uses
▶ Identify various tool uses of computers other than word processing, databases, spreadsheets, telecommunication, networking, and desktop publishing
▶ Identify uses of the computer for voice and music synthesis, for scientific instrumentation, and for interactive video disks

There are several popular types of computer-tool software, some specialized, others of general use. Accounting aids and inventory systems, which are important to business, are specialized tool software. Of more general use are telecommunication, desktop publishing, and networking software. In this chapter, telecommunication, networks, graphics uses, voice and music generation, and desktop publishing are discussed. Other uses in music, science, and storytelling are mentioned.

Graphics Utilities

Graphics can be used for *visual communication.* There are educational uses for a number of *graphics packages* or *tablets,* particularly the programs that allow the user to create and manipulate shapes and perspectives. The computer's use as a tool is enhanced by the ease with which spatial and visual phenomena can be manipulated, and by the ease with which those phenomena can be integrated into verbal communications.

Graphics Tablets

Visual displays and motion graphics are valuable but their production is time-consuming. The computer tools for graphics production, measurement, and transformations are time-saving and convenient. Although they sacrifice the lifelike dynamics of motion graphics, their use as a learning tool is an important dimension

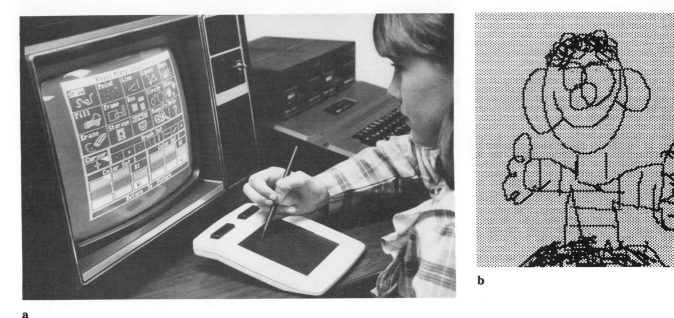

a

b

Figure 1 *(a) Koala Pad in use, and (b) a drawing of "Charlie" made by sixth-grade student with Koala Pad.*

of computer education. They can display a series of pictures as a vehicle for the teaching of creative writing, or they can aid in the illustration of a story.

The *Koala Pad* (see Figure 1) is an example of a graphics tabletlike "artist electronic sketch pad." It has a pad and a stylus for use in drawing and writing. It allows the artist to look at a magnified portion of a sketch and to edit that portion. Sketches and hand-written materials can be saved to disk, displayed on the screen, or printed as hardcopy. Figure 1 also shows a drawing made with a *Koala Pad.*

Graphics tablets can be used to illustrate stories written in a language arts class, or as a stimulus for the writing of stories. There are graphics tablets that facilitate the measurement of lengths, areas, and other dimensions, for scientific uses. There are even graphics tools that enable you to draw three-dimensional objects; in some cases the stylus can be passed over the object.

Zoom Graphics

Tools for producing hardcopy of screen graphics are useful. Although printing the graphics screen display onto paper is easy to do in some cases, it is not in others. Software such as *Zoom Graphics* add features such as rotation, enlargement, and isolation (or close-up) of the graphics screen. Such graphics can be used for screen displays or printouts. Special graphics transformation packages can do the following:

1. Enlarge a picture, possibly with a scaling factor to proportion height and width correctly
2. Rotate or flip a figure
3. Create a window on a particular portion of a picture, and print or enlarge that portion

Picture created with AppleMouse II and icons

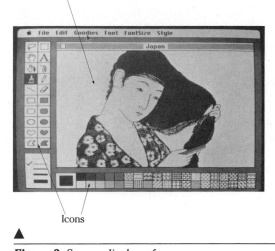

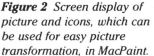

Icons

▲

Figure 2 *Screen display of picture and icons, which can be used for easy picture transformation, in MacPaint.*

4. Reverse the background so that a picture that has black writing on a white background is converted to (and printed as) one with white writing on a black background

Figure 2 shows a screen with icons that are used to produce and transform graphics with the software *MacPaint*.

Mouse-Produced Graphics

The Apple Macintosh provides sophisticated tools for drawing and writing. *MousePaint* is an Apple II+ or Apple IIe analog of *MacPaint*. *TopDraw* and *Paint Works* are similar packages for the Apple IIGS. Both systems use easily selected icons, controlled by a mouse (a hand-roller activation system), to provide tactile commands. Figure 3 shows an AppleMouse II. Figure 4 shows samples of sketches done by *MacPaint*. Many different fonts (character shapes) and sizes of letters can be used for typing on a picture. Filling areas with colors and patterns is easily accomplished. Among other things you may observe are shading and outlining (with differing line widths). Finally, all patterns and outcomes in the figure are produced by *MacPaint*. To sketch, the user manipulates an AppleMouse II and presses buttons to select features and locations. The Apple IIGS is getting more and more programs that give the Apple IIGS Mac-like capabilities, for example, *PaintWorks Plus* and *PaintWorks Gold*.

PaintWorks Plus/Gold (Activision) For the Apple IIGS, *PaintWorks Plus* is a program that is very similar to the popular *MacPaint* for the Macintosh; *PaintWorks Gold* is a more advanced version of this program. These make full use of and nicely illustrate the windows, dialog boxes, QuickDraw II, and many of the other tool boxes described in Appendix F. You may select from 16 colors and 16 patterns at any one time. Drawings can be a combination of these colors and patterns. You can also go to the Color Palette Dialog Box to mix your own colors. Although you can have only

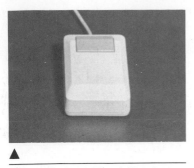

Figure 3 *AppleMouse II to be used with programs such as MacPaint.*

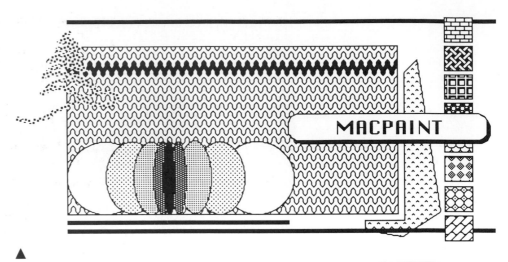

Figure 4 *Sketches generated by MacPaint.*

16 colors at one time, there are 4096 colors from which you can choose. Shapes to choose include rectangle, rounded rectangle, oval, freeform shape, polygon, and straight line. Each can be hollow or filled. A goodies section lets you select a grid or FatBits, among other choices. The FatBits allow for blowups of the screen so that you can view or color each individual dot on the screen. By using FatBits, you can make very detailed drawings. Other options include the capability of moving the drawings.

You can integrate text with your graphics. For the text, you choose from different fonts, including Courier, Dover, Geneva, Helvetica, or Hollywood. Your text can be bold, italic, underlined, outlined, or shadowed. You can also choose the size of the letters.

Editing features include cutting, pasting, copying, inverting, flipping horizontally, flipping vertically, and rotating by quarter turns. *PaintWorks Gold* also allows you to make rotations in one-degree increments and change perspectives. You can save, manipulate, resave, and print out pictures. If you have access to an ImageWriter II with a color ribbon, you can print the picture in color.

This software could be very useful for artwork, spatial development, transformational geometry, or just plain fun. It should be an active part of an educational program.

Light Pens

Used to touch the video screen, **light pens** can identify specific locations on the screen or point to sections of a display. They can be particularly useful for young children and handicapped people. They also can be used for complicated graphics.

Telecommunication

Telecommunication is a rapidly expanding part of computer education, with the potential of becoming one of its most important applications. To get started in telecommunication, you need a **modem** connected to your computer and a telephone line and communication software. The software may be packaged with a modem. Your local computer store can suggest a particular package. Computerized telecommunication is essentially the transfer of data over distances, via telephone lines or other transmission forms, such as satellites. Two telecommunication activities are valuable in education: using electronic bulletin boards and accessing databases.

Many computer stores, computer clubs (or users groups), and many school systems have **electronic bulletin boards.** These bulletin boards allow you to send and receive **electronic mail** (or E-mail), transfer data, read pertinent news, or more generally communicate with others. In most cases local bulletin boards are free of charge, as they are intended to promote communication among members and to develop interest in furthering computing and telecommunication.

The second type of telecommunication is database access; many databases are available. These services often use *Tymnet* and *Telenet,* which are nationally based networks that have local telephone numbers in major urban centers. Through such services you can perform various types of research: get up-to-date financial information, including current purchasing and selling prices and analysis of stocks (*Dow Jones*); conduct literature searches (*Dialog*); do comparison shopping, book travel reservations, gather news and information (*The Source*); and call up useful education systems (*Plato*). *Plato* is a large, computer-based educational system that is available via telecommunications for some microcomputer systems; it can also be used with clusters of terminals. Numerous educational programs are available through *Plato*.

Some of these are a part of a commercial information service, others act more in the public domain, in their accessibility and purpose. Examples of the commercial information services are *The Source, CompuServe, Dow-Jones News,* and *GEnie.* Each provides E-mail, searchable databases, news and weather, and other on-line uses. For many educators, CompuServe is a most interesting and cost-efficient commercial service. Typically an initial membership fee is charged, together with an hourly rate for use of the service. The speed at which data can be accessed is a factor in cost, as is, for several of the sources, the time of day the service is used. For example, during late evening hours when the service is less used, the cost is typically greatly reduced.

The many uses for these telecommunications activities include,

- ▶ Research of reference sources for all sorts of bibliographic material
- ▶ Find and print out references on any topic; use this capability, for example, for term papers
- ▶ Send electronic mail or receive it
- ▶ Share test-item banks
- ▶ Establish and communicate with electronic pen pals
- ▶ Communicate with students in another country, so that a language or social-studies class can learn a different language and culture on a first-hand basis
- ▶ Down-load records or files from a centralized unit such as a district office, or up-load these records or files (*Down-load* means to load information from another computer "down" to yours; *Up-load* means to load "up" to another computer from yours)
- ▶ Use a school system's bulletin board for messages, day-to-day information, notices of job availability, memos, etc.
- ▶ Down-load public-domain software
- ▶ Tap into the stock market or similar sources, so that a social-studies class can study such economic phenomena

Telecommunication Hardware

Modems (the word is an acronym for *modulate–demodulate*) come in two types. One is the direct-connect modem, which plugs into telephone jacks. Advantages of the direct-connect modem are that many different computers can use them

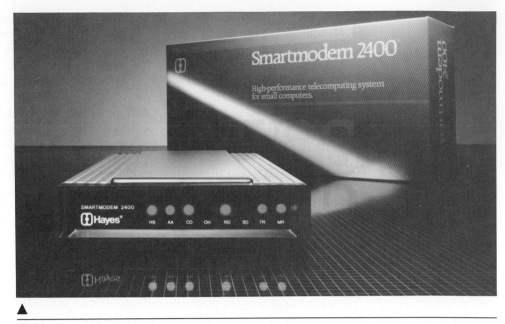

Figure 5 *A direct-connect modem.*

and their transmission of data is reliable. An alternate to the direct-connect type is the acoustic coupler, which the user operates by placing a telephone receiver in a pair of cups, with the mouthpiece in one cup and the earpiece in the other. Figure 5 shows a direct-connect modem. The price of a modem ranges from $100 to $2000; the cost is approximately proportional to the transmission speed. The transmission speed ranges from 110 bits per second (about one-third of a regular double-spaced page per minute) to 300 bits per second (about one typical page of type per minute), to 2400 bits per second (about 10 pages per minute).

Telecommunication Software

Telecommunication software is a program that controls the communication; it is either in ROM or loaded into the computer (see Appendix F). The software contains the **protocol,** the instructions that determine the nature of the communication process. This includes the speed of transmission, the time at which each computer is permitted to transmit, whether data is sent one character at a time or in packets, and the transmission format. If the computers involved use different protocols, the communication cannot take place.

Telecommunication has a range of forms. These include electronic mail (E-mail), bulletin boards, terminal emulation, file transferring, and information utilities. In terminal emulation, two computers are connected; one computer becomes a keyboard and screen for the other computer and can perform simple operations. Telecommunication software makes possible the down-loading of files, the placement of files from some other source into memory and possibly onto a disk. It also permits up-loading, the transfer of a file from your computer to another computer. This capability of file transfers between distant points suggests a substantial benefit for business, education, and government. The potential time savings of sending a letter, a research paper, an important blueprint, or the like by telephone line rather than by mail could be important.

A bulletin board may be a simple menu of news, information, and options available to interested users. Figure 6 is a sample of a bulletin board in a school

```
              BULLETIN BOARD MENU


       [1]    Normal board...........................
       [2]    Education board.......................
       [3]    Computer Education and
              Technology (teachers only)
       [4]    The Luker Enforcer..................
       [5]    The Note Passer (Students)
       [6]    The professor
       [7]    Science Teachers
       [8]    Computer News Magazine
       [9]    Syntax Helper
```

▲

Figure 6 *A typical bulletin board menu.*

```
  List of supported commands
  ---------------------------------------------
  1, 2, 3, 4, 5, 6, 7, 8, 9 Boards B for Menu
  ---------------------------------------------
  (R)ead ! Y -> Your statistics
  (S)end ! F -> Feedback
  mail ! D -> Get free downloads
  T = Time # --> Upload to system
  $ = News              U --> Get a user listing
  I = Info              O --> Off/Bye/Terminate
  C = Chat              V --> Change video width
  N = Nulls             H --> Get detailed help
  G --------------> General file menu
  E --------------> Educational file menu
  8 --------------> Computer News
```

▲

Figure 7 *Typical introduction screen for a bulletin board.*

system. As the users' interests change, other options may be added to keep the bulletin board current with their needs. Figure 7 shows an introductory screen supported by one school system. This screen permits the users to go directly to the board above or to (R)ead their own mail. With a bulletin board system, particularly a public-domain bulletin board, your computer can monitor incoming calls or other transmitted messages. Typically the software would need to contain an automatic answering capability, and a recording device to read and down-load the message. With this arrangement, you can read messages and respond to them. These bulletin-board systems may handle open-access messages as well as private messages.

Bulletin boards and other telecommunication forms permit you to overcome the difficulty that can occur when users try to transmit data from one type of computer to another that uses a different disk operating system. For example, what is saved on an IBM-formatted disk cannot be loaded into an Apple computer, or visa versa. However, bulletin boards or similar techniques allow you to send data (such as ASCII code) from an Apple to an IBM. Thus, if your friend has written a document on an IBM word processor and you want to edit it on your Apple, your friend could transmit it by telecommunication methods but could not simply give it to you on a disk.

Networks

Networks are connected computers, designed to share capabilities. The most practical form of networking for educational use is the **Local Area Network,** LAN, with which computers can be linked with other computing equipment, such as other computers, printers, servers, storage disks, and so forth, in a localized area, such as within a room, building, or school campus. A LAN may follow any of a variety of topologies, or connection schemes. Two of them are shown in Figure 8*a* and Figure 8*b*. The network in Figure 8*a* is called a **ring network,** as the picture demonstrates. Figure 8*b* is a **star network.** Again the picture shows why it is so named. In the star network, the computer in the center is called a file server, or simply the server. A **file server** controls a hard disk, printer, or other peripherals,

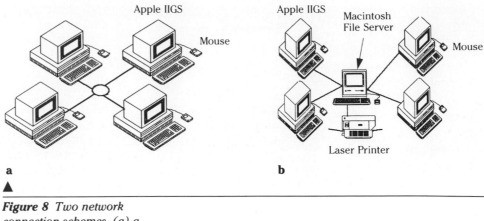

a   **b**

▲

Figure 8 *Two network connection schemes. (a) a ring network. (b) a star network.*

and is tied to a network. For example, it allows data to be shared among the computers in a room.

The AppleTalk network is appropriate for use with Apple computers. With this network you can connect up to 32 devices, which share peripherals such as fixed disk drives and printers (such as a laser printer) so that they can communicate with each other. These devices can, if the appropriate licenses are purchased, share software such as desktop publishing, word processing, CAD/CAM, and integrated software (in which word processing, databases, spreadsheets, graphics packages, and telecommunication are combined into one package). Figure 9 shows four Apple Macintoshes sharing a LaserWriter printer. When first invented, the AppleTalk network allowed several Macintosh computers to be wired together so that they could share peripherals. Now, the AppleShare software makes it possible to share common hard-disk drives as well; one of the Macintoshes is used as a file server. It is also possible to connect MS-DOS computers (for example, IBM and IBM compatibles) into this system; they can then be served by and use printers with the Macintosh file server. An APPLE IIe and an APPLE IIGS, with appropriate hardware and software configurations (AppleTalk Ports for the IIGS and Apple II Workstation Cards for the Apple IIe), can now be a part of an AppleTalk network. Figure 10 shows a star

Figure 9 *Apple Macintoshes and Apple IIGS's sharing a LaserWriter printer.*

▼

Figure 10 *A star network in which a Macintosh is the server; four Apple IIGS's and a LaserWriter printer are connected.*

▼

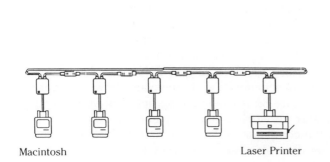

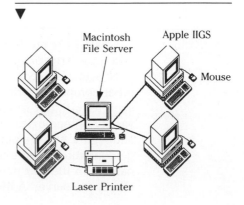

network with a Macintosh as the server and four Apple IIGS's with an available LaserWriter printer.

Advantages of Networks

Networks allow you to access printers and hard-disk drives directly, so that you don't have to move to a computer that is connected to a printer or hard-disk drive. Thus, only one or two high-quality printers can replace several low- to medium-quality printers in, for example, a lab setting. Computer science or computer applications teachers can also distribute needed software immediately over the network, so that they don't have to pass out disks at the beginning of a class and collect them at the end. Another financial savings is that a single fixed or hard-disk drive can be used, rather than individual disk drives and masses of floppy disks.

Uses of Networks in the Classroom

Apple Computer, Inc. has released new software and hardware to use with networks. For example, a student–teacher network management program, called *Aristotle,* is available to manage the programs that a file server makes available to members of a class. It keeps records on the progress and re-entry points of class members.

Figure 11 shows four Apple IIGS's being served by a Macintosh. The network includes both a printer and a fixed or hard-disk drive. Note that each Apple IIGS does not need a floppy disk drive, because the fixed disk drive can serve all of them. However, any of the Apple IIGS's could have its own disk drive, in addition to the fixed disk drive.

Several different types of networks are possible. Figure 12 shows ring and star networks with useful peripherals. Because of the flexibility of arrangements, each practitioner can set up the system that is best for their individual classroom or school. For example, the first arrangement shows that each of the four (or ten or twenty) computers can be connected to a server, through which software can be distributed, processing controlled, and peripherals shared. The server could also save files on a hard disk, or print whatever is needed from any of the other computers. Both ring and star networks allow data to be transmitted to many computers

Figure 11 *A network of four Apple IIGS's, a printer, and a fixed or hard-disk drive, served by a Macintosh.*

▼

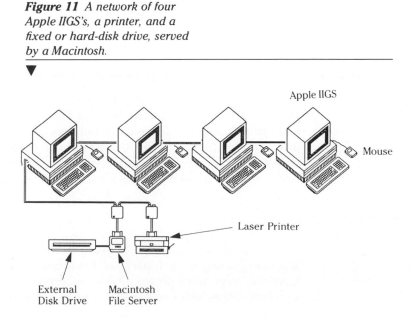

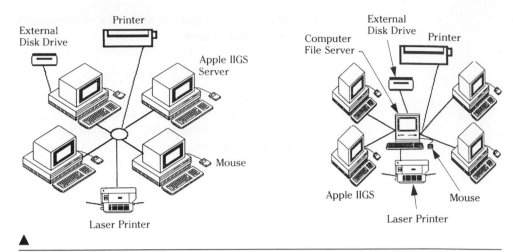

▲

Figure 12 *Ring and star*
networks with peripherals.

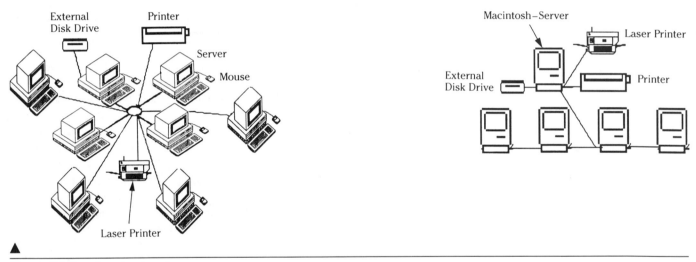

▲

Figure 13 *Developed networks,*
with extensive peripherals.

and peripherals; the star network controls transmission to individual computers, and the ring network makes data available to all.

Figure 13 shows even more realistic arrangements of computer networks. Each shows more than one printer, so that high-quality hard copy, a quick draft, or a good print, can all be made. Each network of Figure 13 contains both a hard-disk drive and internal drives for the individual computers. The networks shown here only begin to hint at the possibilities for networking in a classroom. Typically, all computers in the room may be a part of the network.

Integrated Packages

An **integrated package** is one package equivalent to two or more separate software packages; each part can function either independently or together. For example, some word processors can incorporate spreadsheet financial statements into text. Other word processors cannot use spreadsheet files. AppleWorks is an integrated package that contains a word processor, a database management system, a spreadsheet, and a desktop manager. The word processor incorporates most features of the more advanced stand-alone word processors. The database management system is sophisticated. The desktop manager, the housekeeper that integrates the other three components, is easy and user-friendly.

Suppose that names, addresses, telephone numbers, and other data are stored in a file. A letter needs to be sent to specific people in your address file. An integrated system would allow you to print personalized letters and address labels for each individual. Further, it would allow you to select just that information from the data file that you wish to use. For example, telephone numbers could be omitted from the data file, so that only the name, address, and zip code are printed on the address labels.

As another example, suppose that you must prepare a report for a meeting. This report needs to have a financial statement, a set of data to support a recommendation, and a memorandum. The word processor of an integrated system could be used for the memorandum, the spreadsheet for the financial records, and the database system for the data listing. The CUT and PASTE or PRINT TO commands of the integrated system make it possible to include the financial report and data listing at the appropriate place. The management component lets you bring onto the desktop, files for word processing, spreadsheets, and databases. Once they are on the desktop they may be used or left there for later use.

AppleWorks GS

AppleWorks GS (Claris Corp.) is an integrated software package consisting of six programs: a word processor, a spreadsheet, a database, a graphics package, a page maker, and telecommunications. Files generated by *AppleWorks* or *PaintWorks Plus/Gold* can be used with *AppleWorks GS*. The graphics program of *AppleWorks GS* adds the feature of object-oriented drawing, which considerably increases the flexibility with which individual shapes can be manipulated. Objects can be placed in "front" or "back" of other objects, and then reversed. Many objects can be placed in a linear ordering, from front to back, or vice versa.

Without leaving the program, the user can pass information from one application to another. For example, the page maker can put together text and graphics. Data from the spreadsheet can be graphed immediately through use of the graphics program. Labels can be generated from the database and addresses merged into the word processor, so that form letters can be sent. Files can be transferred to another site through the telecommunication program. *AppleWorks GS* shows enormous potential as an educational tool.

Other Software that Integrates Text and Graphics

Many other software packages can combine text and graphics. A few that are now commercially available are discussed below.

StoryTree (Scholastic)   One nice writing tool that lets your students compose stories and build branching into their stories is *StoryTree*. Using it, students can design branches that either the user chooses or that occur by chance. The students can also weight the chances of branching, so that the story will branch one way a particular percentage of the time and the rest of the time will branch the other way. For example, 25 percent of the time, the story will branch to option *A,* and 75 percent of the time, to option *B*. Students should learn to design structure charts, such as those described in Chapter 3, to build their options, so that they can see the possibilities that can be embedded in one story. This program will also yield printouts of their stories.

The Newsroom (Springboard), Print Shop (Broderbund), and the Certificate Maker (Springboard)   Similar in function, these programs are very popular. They help you or your students construct printouts with integrated text and graphics. *The Newsroom* helps with constructing a newspaper or newsletter. *Print Shop* helps in creating posters, banners, holiday cards, and various displays. *Certificate Maker* can make certificates to honor your or your students' latest accomplishments. For each program, you or your students construct the contents. When connected to appropriate printers, such as the ImageWriter II, some of the latest versions let you or your students develop color graphics displays.

Multiscribe GS and TopDraw (Style Ware)   *Multiscribe GS* is a word processor that allows graphics to be integrated with the text. Coordinated with *Multiscribe GS* is *TopDraw,* an excellent graphics package that has many nice features. These were the forerunners along with AppleWorks for the AppleWorks GS. The AppleWorks GS includes these capabilities but requires considerable memory. If you do not have the needed amount of memory (minimum 1025K), you might want to use the earlier versions of *Multiscribe* and *TopDraw.*

Auditory Communication

The computer can also use sound as a tool to learning. Voice and music synthesizers are two ways in which the computer can provide auditory communication.

Voice Synthesizers

Voice synthesizers can be programmed to speak words as if a person were saying them. There are several types of voice synthesizers. One uses digitized speech: human voice sounds (whole words or phrases) are prerecorded. Another recognizes familiar typed words and pronounces them. Each has its own strengths and weaknesses. The prerecorded-voice type gives sounds like a real human being, but requires a substantial amount of computer memory. Recognition of typed words does not use a lot of computer memory, but the pronunciations sound like a computer.

Voice synthesizers give information in a form so that the user, perhaps a young or blind person, need not read information. To develop their writing skills, such students can type in words or stories that they want to hear. To take advantage of voice synthesizers, multilingual programs can speak words in one language and show them on the screen in two languages. They also can use voice synthesizers to demonstrate and repeat words in a variety of languages.

More talking software available for the Apple IIGS include *Smooth Talker* (First Byte) and *Kid Talk* (First Byte), each of which repeat written words and stories that students have typed. Others are *First Letters and Words* (First Byte), which introduces young children to the world of letters and words, *Speller Bee* (First Byte), a coaching program to improve spelling, *Math Talk* (First Byte) and *Math Talk Fractions* (First Byte).

Music Synthesizers

Auditory communication can also be made through effective use of **music synthesizers.** Some synthesizers come with a number of voices, so that students can hear first individual parts, then the parts together. Students composing music can also use synthesizers: they can write a part, then edit it—adding, deleting, changing the timing, and combining it with other parts. Combined with any of the following software, music synthesizers could be a fun and useful addition to a music course or to any other course that studies sound (physics, for example).

The Music Studio (Activision)   Currently available for the Apple IIGS, this software allows you to listen to, transform, or construct music. A special version nicely portrays uses of the tool boxes described in Appendix F: it makes strong use of pull-down and pop-up menus, for example. You may load songs (selected from the large number that come with the software) or you may load sounds (selected from classical, jazz, and rock instruments, or voices). Choices for classical instruments are those most often found in an orchestra, including violin, viola, cello, string bass, flute, oboe, clarinet, bassoon, harp, piano, guitar, celeste, or pizzicato. Choices for jazz instruments include piano, string bass, alto sax, tenor sax, two sets of drum kits, plucked bass, and three sets of guitars. Rock instrumentation includes many of the sounds used in rock music.

You can also create your own sounds. You can compose and transpose music, vary the timing, adjust the loudness, and listen to it being played by various instruments. There is also the option of seeing the score move while you hear the sound. This excellent tool helps students in creating, editing, appending, and synthesizing music. You can also add lyrics and get printouts of the score if you have an ImageWriter II.

Music Construction Set   This software allows for the user to hear the music as the score moves. Like the previously mentioned software, this program enables you to load a file, play and edit it, replay it, save the revised score, and print the score.

Using the Computer for Instrumentation

An interesting application of the computer is as an instrument for *collecting* data. Various devices that interface with the computer can collect data from real settings. For example, a device that can capture a sound wave and give a spectrum analysis allows students to study acoustical and electrical waveforms. Other devices allow students to perform laboratory experiments in harmonic motion (with a pendulum), acceleration due to gravity, and the relationship between light intensity and distance from the source. Similarly, students can conduct heat experiments, in topics such as the cooling curves of paraffin and mothballs, thermal radiation, and the relationship between temperature and the depth of fluids. Students can conduct experiments in human physiology, to determine measurements such as skin measurements, respiration rate, and heart rate, and lie detection. This direction shows much potential for education. For further information contact Cambridge Development Laboratory, 100 Fifth Avenue, Waltham, MA 02154.

The *Science Toolkit* (Broderbund) can turn your computer into a science lab. Measure and record the temperature, speed, response time, and many other aspects of phenomena in the world about you. The system includes four on-screen instruments, with temperature and light probes, and an interface module that plays into the joystick port (see Appendix F). It also has enhancements to detect and record speed and motion.

Interactive Video Disks

Interactive video disks are showing much potential for education. Because the video disks are interfaced with and controlled by the computer, the capabilities of both movies and computers can be utilized.

One such project is the Interactive Media Science Project at Florida State University. This project is developing materials, for middle-school science students, that blend science content, processes, and skills while focusing on appropriate problems of science, technology, and society. The materials are focused around meaningful problem situations. Students are given a problem. They then can choose from a menu of options the means that they will use to research the problem. They can go to a database for information. They can call up visual resources of still or motion images, with the added benefit of sound. Students can make and test conjectures, and employ process skills such as experimenting, observing, measuring, and inferring.

Students direct their own learning, rather than following a predetermined linear route. Students can investigate any lesson in any order, and they can easily exit from a lesson and go to another. They also actively participate in decision making.

The prototype hardware system is based on the Apple IIGS microcomputer with one megabyte random access memory (RAM) (see Appendix F), and is jointly supported by the National Science Foundation and Houghton Mifflin Publishing Company, who is publishing an interrelated but independent textbook series. The content is intended to be a sequence of three one-year courses or levels. Each level will integrate concepts from the various sciences, but will emphasize a particular science: physical science, life science, or earth and space science.

▶ ▲ ◀ ▼ ▶ ▲ ◀ ▼ ▶ ▲ ◀ ▼ ▶ ▲ ◀ ▼ ▶ ▲ ◀ ▼ ▶ ▲

Summary

This chapter provided an overview of educational uses of the computer as a tool. Computers can be used for verbal communication via word processors, visual communication via graphics capabilities, and auditory communication via voice and music synthesizers. Spreadsheets and database managers allow you to compile and manipulate information; some peripherals actually collect data. Telecommunications capabilities allow for transfer of information, database access, and personal communication (electronic mail, bulletin boards) via telephone lines.

Software discussed in this chapter:

Koala Pad	*Print Shop*
Zoom Graphics	*Certificate Maker*
MousePaint	*Smooth Talker*
MacPaint	*First Letters and Words*
Multiscribe GS	*Kid Talk*
PaintWorks	*Speller Bee*
TopDraw	*Math Talk*
PaintWorks Plus/Gold	*Math Talk Fractions*
Aristotle	*Music Studio*
AppleWorks	*Music Construction Set*
AppleWorks GS	*Science Toolkit*
StoryTree	
Newsroom	

Important Terms

Bit map	Icon
Down-load	Instrumentation
Electronic mail	Integrated software
Field	Interactive Media Science Project
Field length	Light pen
File	Modem
File server	Music synthesizer
Graphics tablet	Up-load

References

Anderson-Inman, L. (1987, April). Telecomputing a chain story. *The Computing Teacher, 14,* 37–39.

Anderson-Inman, L. (1987, November). The reading–writing connection: Classroom applications for the computer, Part I. *The Computing Teacher, 14,* 23–26.

Butler, G., & Jobe, H. M. (1987). The Australian-American connection. *The Computer Teacher, 14,* 25–26.

Dodge, B., & Dodge, J. (1987). Selecting telecommunications software for educational settings. *The Computing Teacher, 14,* 10–12, 32.

Harris, B., Arntsen, M. K., Thurman, R., & Merrill, P. F. (1987, October). Computers, gifted students and the development of an elementary school newspaper. *The Computing Teacher, 15,* 11–13.

Krueger, S. (1987, June). Brontosaurus meets the computer. *The Computing Teacher, 14,* 13–15.

Lindstrom, B. (1989, January). AppleWorks GS. *A+,* pp. 30–34.

McLaughlin, B. (1989, January). AppleWorks GS and beyond. *A+,* pp. 35–39.

Riel, M. (1987, April). The intercultural learning network. *The Computing Teacher, 14,* 27–30.

Sayers, D., & Brown, K. (1987, April). Bilingual education and telecommunications: A perfect fit. *The Computing Teacher, 14,* 23–24.

Schiffman, S. S. (1986, May). Productivity tools for the classroom. *The Computing Teacher, 13,* 27–31.

▶ ▲ ◀ ▼ ▶ ▶ ▲ ◀ ▼ ▶ ▶ ▲ ◀ ▼ ▶ ▶ ▲ ◀ ▼ ▶ ▶ ▲ ◀ ▼ ▶ ▶ ▲

Activity Koala Pad Activities

Type   Machine

Objective   Apply problem-solving strategies to the construction of visual displays

Prerequisite(s) Some eye-to-hand coordination

Materials Needed Koala Pad
                     Koala software
                     Stylus

Activity   From the menu (see the figure) on the software that comes with the Koala Pad, your students can select a pen (thin- or thick-stroked), a shape (rectangle, circle, lines, or freehand), and a color or colors. They also need to decide whether to frame and/or fill the shape.

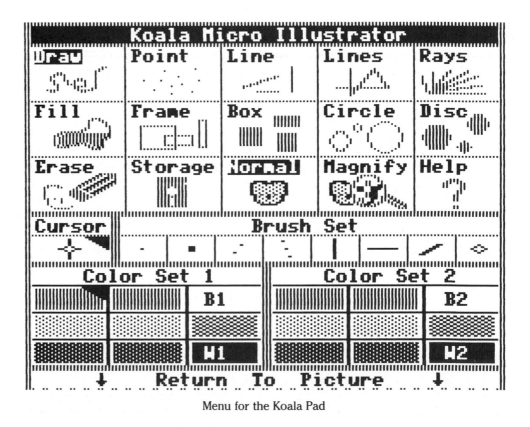

Menu for the Koala Pad

Have the students simply move the stylus on the Koala Pad until the cursor or blinking cross is at the position of their choice on the menu; they then press the button on the top left of the Koala Pad.

Pictures drawn with the Koala Pad are shown on the next page; drawing them uses such problem-solving strategies as decomposing and recombining. Figures can be broken into simple shapes such as rectangles, circles, or lines; the length of a line segment can be approximated; and variables, such as the number of regions and the types of shadings, can be controlled and isolated.

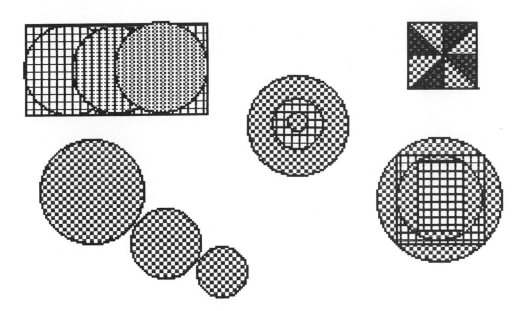

Figures drawn with the Koala Pad

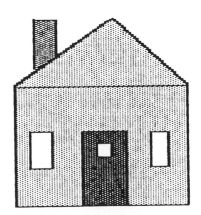

House drawn by the Koala Pad

Give your students adequate time for some free play; then guide them through the construction of the house (see the figure). Then give them a picture to construct. Finally, ask them to create an original picture.

One example is the construction of the house as drawn. First, move the cursor to FRAME on the menu and press the button on the Koala Pad. Choose a color and brush stroke. Now, to move to the drawing board, press the button on the Koala Pad or <RETURN>. Select the upper left corner of the basic house construction (the basic rectangle). Then move the stylus to the lower right corner of the location to trace the outline of the house and press the button on the Koala Pad to form a rectangle. Again using the FRAME, locate the doors and windows.

To build the roof, go back to the menu, move the cursor to the LINE selection, and press the button. Return to the drawing pad, estimate the center of the house (half way across the house) and the distance to the top of the roof, and mark that point on the Koala Pad. Next move the stylus to one side of the house frame, such as the upper left corner, and press the button on the Koala Pad. Return the stylus to the top of the roof and press the button again. Move the stylus to the upper right corner of the house frame and once more press the button.

Now to build the chimney. Press LINES on the menu, estimate on the drawing pad where the lower part of the chimney would come on the roof, and press the button. Now move the stylus straight up to where the top of the chimney should be and again press the button. Next move horizontally across the width of the chimney and press the button. Finally, move the stylus directly below the last point to the location on the roof and again press the Koala Pad button. The frame of the house is now built.

Now to shade the house. First, return to the menu and move the stylus to the FILL command, press the button on the Koala Pad, and select a color. Return to the drawing, place the stylus in the region to be colored, and press the button. Using the same color, or returning to the menu to change colors, move the stylus to each region and color it. Now the house is finished.

Variation(s)   Make creative drawings through original constructions, again emphasizing problem-solving strategies. Other alternatives include employing different graphics programs such as *Applemouse* to make similar drawings.

Activity   Code Contest

Type	Machine
Objective	To code or decode a message sent via telecommunications, look for a pattern or sequence
Prerequisite(s)	Previous coding experiences in BASIC
Materials Needed	Modem connected to computer and telephone line
	Modem connected to computer and telephone line at other school(s)
	File of coded message

Activity

Students will write a message, rewrite it in a code of their choice, and challenge students at other schools to decode their message. This should be a class project, with all students working together.

First, have your students devise a code that uses either numbers or letters. If they have trouble creating a code, they can consult one of the many children's books with ideas for codes. (Note that codes using pictures would not be suitable.) Encourage them to employ a pattern in their code, but it should not be an obvious one, such as the backwards alphabet. Then have them compose a message in their code, perhaps including an invitation to a party. Once coded, the message should be written into a text file, using the following program:

```
10 LET D$ = CHR$(4)
20 PRINT D$;"OPEN MESSAGE"
30 INPUT "PLEASE TYPE YOUR MESSAGE, ";M$
40 PRINT D$;"WRITE MESSAGE"
50 PRINT M$
60 PRINT D$;"CLOSE MESSAGE"
70 END
```

The message will be saved as a text file under the name MESSAGE when this short program is run.

Arrange for other schools to call your computer at a certain time. Once the computers at both schools are connected, load your text file. The other school can then retrieve and save the file and disconnect. Their classes should then attempt to solve your message. The school or class to first decode your message and send the decoded message back to the original computer wins.

Variation(s)

Similar techniques can be employed for writing and sending electronic letters, and for transmitting computer programs. A student can write a program; a student at another school can then run the program, debug or modify it, and return it.

Activity   Electronic Scavenger Hunt

Type	Machine
Level	Intermediate
Objective	To solve an electronic scavenger hunt, apply the techniques of working backwards and looking for a sequence
Prerequisite(s)	Experiences with actual scavenger hunts
Materials Needed	Modem connected to computers at several schools Support software Printer
Activity	To solve a mystery, students will access text files at a determined number of locations, to receive clues that must be arranged in a particular sequence. Clues are stored at each location and can be printed out. By studying the printout, students decide on a logical sequence. To test a sequence students will call up clues, one at a time, in what they think is the correct sequence, for example, MYSTERY1. If this clue is in the correct sequence, it will be printed out. If not, the message "FILE DOES NOT EXIST" will be given. Clues are stored at each location, not only under the game title, such as MYSTERY, but also with a sequence clue, such as MYSTERY1 CLUE1. Students will have a printout with all clues in the correct sequence when they solve the mystery. To create a text file, use suggestions in the CODE CONTEST.

Activity   Electronic Brain Bowl

Type	Machine
Level	Intermediate
Objective	Solve problems in shortest length of time
Prerequisite(s)	Doing similar types of problems without telecommunications
Materials Needed	Question bank in specific subject areas or in general knowledge Modem connected to computers and telephone lines at several schools
Activity	Students at several schools compete, either as individuals or in groups, to answer questions contained in the source computer. Using their school or class computer, students phone the source computer to get one question at a time, disconnect while they discuss the question, then reconnect to give their answer. If they are correct, they receive another question. Points are awarded for each section of correctly answered questions.

Activity Electronic Bulletin Boards

Type	Machine
Level	Intermediate
Objective	Apply skills in working backwards and decomposing/recombining to the use of electronic mail communications in an electronic bulletin board
Prerequisite(s)	Experience in writing and working with electronic bulletin boards
Materials Needed	Modem Appropriate sign-on to an electronic bulletin board
Activity	A number of school districts are now forming and using electronic bulletin boards. Students can enhance their problem-solving skills through the use of such electronic bulletin boards. The following are some suggestions of experiences that students from several schools can jointly apply to the use of electronic mail.

1. Have the students create and maintain a chain letter. Each time the students enter the chain letter mailbox, they add a paragraph so that the letter "hangs together." They could agree upon a maximum length—each time a paragraph is added, another paragraph is deleted.
2. Students can create and maintain a chain graphics program similar to the chain letter except that they add (and delete) modules to create an interesting graphic that "hangs together." Before program files can be transferred, they must be converted to text files. To do this, add a few lines at the beginning of the procedure:

```
1 D$ = CHR$(4) : N$ = "PROGRAM NAME": REM USE
  APPROPRIATE PROGRAM NAME
2 PRINT D$;"OPEN ";N$
3 PRINT D$;"WRITE ";N$
4 LIST 6 - 100000: REM USE APPROPRIATE LINE NUMBERS
  THAT LIST THE PROGRAM
5 PRINT D$;"CLOSE ";N$
```

3. Have the students debug somebody's program. Or have them leave a program they are working on in an electronic mailbox so that students at another school can debug it and return it to the electronic mailbox.
4. Students can find penpals with common interests and communicate through the electronic mail.

Part Three

Educational Uses of the Computer

▶ ▲ ◀ ▼ ▶ ▲ ◀ ▼ ▶ ▲ ◀ ▼ ▶ ▲ ◀ ▼ ▶ ▲ ◀ ▼ ▶ ▲

The computer revolution has come to the school! A majority of schools in the United States now have at least one microcomputer—many have five, fifty, or more. Using these computers effectively is a major concern of teachers and administrators. In Part One, we showed you how to control the machine. In Part Two, you examined the role of the computer as a tool. In Part Three, you will examine the computer as an instructional tool.

Instructional computer programs usually are categorized as drill and practice, simulations, or tutorials. Drill and practice programs come in many formats, from onscreen representations of traditional workbooks to fast-paced games with animated graphics; they are examined in Chapter 9. Instructional software used to develop visual imagery and spatial perception through the manipulation of graphics that represent concepts, is discussed in Chapter 10. Computer simulations, discussed in Chapter 11, are often used in the classroom to place students in situations that are too expensive, dangerous, inconvenient, complex, or time-consuming to be experienced firsthand. Tutorial programs emphasizing the development of concepts, generalizations, and algorithms are presented in Chapter 12.

Using computer-managed instruction to assist you with many of the day-to-day chores in the classroom is explored in Chapter 13. Evaluation of software for the applications described in Chapters 9 through 13 is explained in Chapter 14.

Chapter 15 examines trends and issues in computer education. Societal and career changes are considered. We discuss the integration of the computer into the school and the idea of computer literacy. Finally, we examine the role of intelligent machines.

Throughout these chapters we will refer to a number of commercially available programs. Their names, distributors, and distributors' addresses are listed in Appendix K.

Chapter 9

Drill and Practice

▶ ▲ ◀ ▼ ▶ ▲ ◀ ▼ ▶ ▲ ◀ ▼ ▶ ▲ ◀ ▼ ▶ ▲ ◀ ▼ ▶ ▲ ◀

Objectives

▶ Identify features of a drill and practice program
▶ Describe features of drill and practice programs and identify uses for each feature
▶ Modify existing drill and practice programs

Computer-assisted instruction is categorized into several types. One of these is drill and practice. Skill development, which is a part of most disciplines, is often associated with drill and practice. In this chapter, we relate drill and practice to skill development, and provide a model for teaching strategies for the development of skills.

If you have available the *MECC Elementary Volume 7* program, insert it and choose (6) SHAPES. Then play the game. Observe the nature of activities to be practiced, and keep in mind the types of skills being developed.

If you have available the *Clock* program, this might be a good time to examine it. Notice how such a program is designed. Try making errors; see how the errors are handled, what types of feedback you are given, and overall design. Figure 1 shows a *Clock* screen display.

Characterizing Drill and Practice Programs

Drill and practice programs function mainly to develop *skills*. Skills are characterized by speed and accuracy. Thus, the timing of operation of a computer can be used in posing exercises, keeping track of how long it takes for students to respond, and providing feedback. A computer is a patient teacher. It can pose exercises that develop accuracy, and supply enough exercises that response patterns are strengthened. Exercise sets to shape behavior can be posed. For example, the computer can keep records for the number of correct and incorrect responses. It can make branch decisions according to these values, and it can repeat questions that are missed. Because it can so easily repeat items, the computer is well suited for the development of accurate response patterns.

Immediate Feedback

According to some psychological and educational theories, a prime factor in the development of skill is that of immediate feedback. Computers can be programmed to note an incorrect response immediately and to provide **corrective feedback** promptly, so that a habit of incorrect responses does not form. To encourage correct response patterns, **positive reinforcement** can be programmed into a lesson: the computer can be programmed to provide praise and make encouraging remarks.

Student Controls the Pace

Learners differ in the speed with which they process information. For example, some learners are able to read and comprehend a screen of directions rapidly. Others, however, need to read, reread, and even ponder statements. Flexibility for the students to move at their own speed is important in certain forms of computer-assisted instruction, particularly in parts of a drill and practice program.

Figure 1 *Screen display of Clock.*

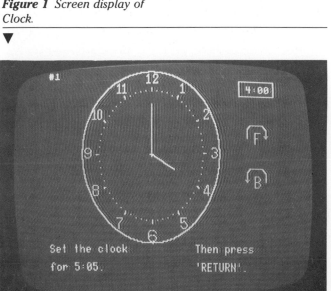

Strategies for Teaching and Learning Skills

Todd's (1972) theoretical studies offer a system for the teaching of skills. His work suggests ways in which instructors can branch in response to students' answers. Specific aspects of drill and practice are initiated by a "teacher," whereas other aspects are student responsibilities.

The concept follows the game theory: moves that lead to certain results are made. A **move** is an action or statement involved in the teaching and learning of a skill, as in introducing the skill or demonstrating the skill. **Strategies** are sequenced moves, such as introduction, motivation, and demonstration. Thus, skill development and the associated drill and practice involve two types of strategies: teaching (drilling) strategies and practicing strategies. The teaching moves are shown in Box 1.

The moves in Box 1 may be combined into planned sequences (a teaching strategy is thereby created). If you have it available, explore *Olympic Decathlon* now. Think about the moves in the program. Determine the parts that demonstrate the different moves: motivation, introduction, demonstration, and so on. After working through it, determine the precise teaching strategy. Figure 2 shows two screen displays. Whether you have the program or not, determine the purposes (moves) that these two screen displays represent.

Another example of a teaching strategy is preparing a student to learn the skill of word processing. A motivation move could show the comparative ease with which a letter can be produced through word processing, as opposed to hand writing or use of an electric typewriter. An introduction move could show, in overview fashion, that the steps of processing a document include

1. Entering manuscript
2. Correcting errors
3. Making block moves
4. Page formatting
5. Producing a hardcopy

Finally, a demonstration move showing how to make a transition from *entry mode* to *edit mode* would also teach the commands of the text editor.

Figure 2 *Screen displays from Olympic Decathlon.*

▼

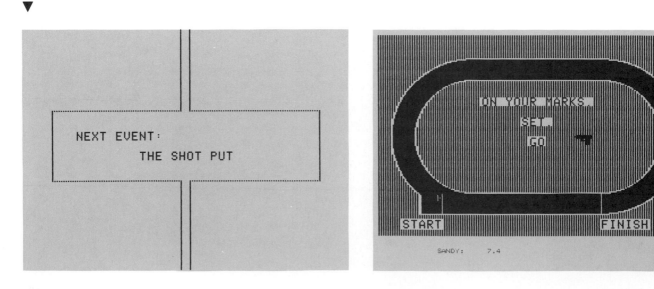

Box 1   Teacher-Initiated Moves in Drill and Practice

▶ *Motivation:* persuading the learner to work toward the skill
▶ *Introduction:* providing a mental set, a predisposition toward understanding of some aspect of a skill
▶ *Assertion:* tying skills to related generalizations, by applying the generalization to specific steps
▶ *Demonstration:* showing the parts of an algorithm or step-by-step process
▶ *Analogy:* to maximize transfer of learning, compare and contrast an unknown skill and mastered skill

---

Student practice is a crucial element to the development of speed and accuracy. Practice naturally entails at least two stages. First is the development of accuracy; that is, proper execution of the steps. For example, when you learn to play a new song on a piano, you can practice isolated segments of the piece, so that you can first establish the sequence and timing of those notes. After the segments are mastered, the song as a whole can be played.

The second phase of practicing the piano piece involves achieving the speed, or better, the proper tempo. In this phase, the learner uses **repetitive practice.** This practice entails making sure that timing and synchronization are stabilized. (In different examples, the intent of repetitive practice is to increase speed while maintaining accuracy; consider, for example, the achievement of typewriting skills.) Box 2 shows moves that a student uses in developing a skill.

In the *MECC Music* drill and practice program, students are asked to identify the note of a measure that is being played incorrectly. After answering, they are given the opportunity to compare the written notes and their answer with the notes being played (Figure 3). Learners who review and compare in this way are using an error-correcting move to determine why they were wrong.

The language-arts software *Plurals and Possessives* involves the learner in a clarification move. In one exercise, two clowns are shown with two balloons each. If the student incorrectly uses the phrase *The Clown's Balloons* to describe the

Figure 3 Screen display of MECC Music drill and practice program.

▼

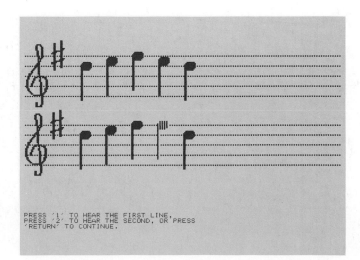

> **Box 2   Moves that a Learner Uses in Drill and Practice**
>
> ▶   *Assertion:* stating or summarizing the principle from which the steps are derived
> ▶   *Application:* regulating the selection of the appropriate skill(s)
> ▶   *Answer checking:* assuring that the results are correct
> ▶   *Error correcting:* locating and debugging the steps of the process, so that correct answers result
> ▶   *Clarification:* organizing (chunking) the steps into structures so that learning and retention are easy
> ▶   *Practice:* executing the steps in enough examples to assure speed and accuracy at a high level (massed practice)

picture, the program helps the student to clarify the rules of grammar and punctuation, and shapes the student's learning: pictures illustrating the question and the student's answer are shown side by side (see Figure 4).

In the early phases of the development of a skill, assertion and clarification moves occur often. Practice, answer checking, and error correcting occur frequently after the initial work has been completed. Finally, application and practice moves complete the development of a skill. Application may be profitably incorporated late in the learning sequence so that the new skill can be compared with other skills. Also, the appropriate uses of the skill and its limitations are clarified in application moves.

The concepts of massed practice and varied, or distributed, practice are appropriately applied in drill and practice programs. **Massed practice** involves many repetitions of the task in a short period of time; it is appropriate to do soon after accuracy is gained. It improves speed and stabilizes accuracy. **Distributed practice** involves the continuation of practice over time. It is mainly for the maintenance of the skill.

Figure 4 *Screen display of The Clown's Balloons from Plurals and Possessives.*

▼

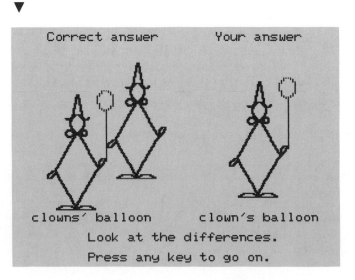

Correct answer   Your answer

clowns' balloon   clown's balloon

Look at the differences.

Press any key to go on.

Features of Drill and Practice Programs

These programs offer several features that aid in the teaching and the learning processes. Two factors that can help learners are the order in which questions are asked (that order can be randomly generated or patterned) and the use of timing mechanisms. Teachers can be aided by computerized records of the students' responses.

Randomly Generated versus Patterned Ordering of Questions

Randomly presented questions provide variety to the practice of a skill. Initial **varied practice** sets the range of the questions, then exercises are randomly generated. This type of practice is appropriate for learners who are mastering (getting skillful and appropriately speedy at) the skill. However, randomly generated questions are appropriate only to certain parts of drill and practice experience, whereas patterned exercises are more appropriate to others. For example, for use after a certain degree of speed and accuracy is achieved, systematic exercises may be more appropriate than random ones. Consider, for example, the learning of words in a spelling list (or new vocabulary words in a second language). Using a computer to select out troublesome words and to discard from the practice set those already mastered may be a more efficient drill format than a random selection of words. Such a creation of a convergent set of practice exercises is a feature that makes drill and practice software more versatile than comparable software with only randomly generated exercises.

Timing Mechanisms

Some drill and practice software provide **timing loops** to control the speed at which drills are performed. Speed is sometimes one of the critical variables in skill development, but timing mechanisms are necessary in some situations and unnecessary (even undesirable) in others. In essence, the prevalent method of creating timing loops is to have the computer count (to itself). By varying the interval of time that is consumed in counting, the time allowed for the response is varied. This embedding of timing loops within programs is done sometimes meaningfully, inappropriately at others. The user who is alert to concepts of programming can choose alternatives. It is easy to replace one timing mechanism with another. The substitution of a user-controlled command can remove the issue of timing if desired; the user simply chooses whether to go ahead or remain on a particular exercise.

Important considerations with respect to machine pacing include the following:

1. It is effective if the user controls the pace during the accuracy-development phase.
2. The machine can control the pace during speed-development conditions.
3. Machine speed should increase only with increasing student speed; an accuracy factor to maintain balance between speed and accuracy is helpful.
4. The speed of the directions and skill-demonstration phases should be controlled by the speed of learning.
5. It should be possible for the learner to restudy steps in the demonstration and clarification phases.
6. Missed questions should be presented a second time.

Records of Students' Responses

Various ways and reasons for keeping records exist. Some of these are examined in the software discussion in Chapter 14. Records of students' responses can be used to

1. Provide feedback to students
2. Develop future questions or problems appropriate for students' needs
3. Diagnose students' attainment of various difficulty levels
4. Assign grades

Records of students' responses can be kept in various forms, including

1. A secured file on external storage (on disk, for example) that requires a password for access
2. A value of a variable of the program that is output at a particular point in the program's execution
3. A value of a program's variable that is available upon specific (teacher) request, or that of a knowledgeable user

As an example of the last of these, the *Clock* program includes a CONTROL-KEY feature that calls the number of correct analog-clock–digital-clock matches achieved by the student. A screen display of a record of a student's responses is shown in Figure 5. Note that, in contrast, other pictures of *Clock* do not show the record of responses; hence these records are secured from the student during practice sessions.

Uses of Drill and Practice Programs

The purpose of drill and practice varies among content areas. For example, speed of calculations and accuracy of results have traditionally been sought in arithmetic and science exercises. On the other hand, social-studies skills may involve association of states and capitals, countries and capitals, or dates and events.

Figure 5 *Clock program's response record.*

▼

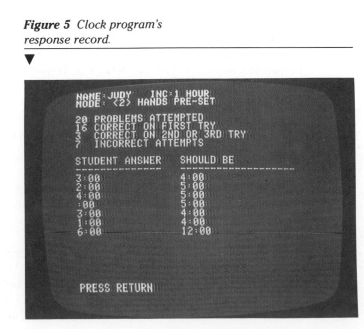

Spelling and pronunciation skills tend to be accuracy-oriented rather than speed-oriented. Physical education and music exercises might focus on the development of accurate timing, with speed being less important than precision in timing. In contrast, in events such as the 100-meter dash, speed of execution is the critical variable.

Among the uses of computers as tools for the development of skills, the common factor is the **dynamics** that can be achieved. Textbooks cannot capture the dynamics in the way a computer can. On the other hand, using a computer is an ineffective substitute for actually playing (and practicing) a musical instrument or running a 100-meter dash.

The choice of the model to use in drill and practice is, obviously, dependent on the skill being developed. Consider a computer program that provides practice in telling time, for example. The model presented by the computer in *Clock* is functionally a more dynamic one than a clock. The differences include,

1. The hands of a real clock cannot readily be set to a particular time.
2. Producing random selections from a chosen category of intervals of time (for example, 5-minute intervals) is not a feasible drill on a real clock.
3. The computer can set the digital version and check the student's setting of the clock, and vice versa.
4. The computer can reveal the correct setting on either clock if the student has trouble setting one version correctly.
5. The time intervals to practice may be selected (hours only; half-hours; quarter-hours; multiples of 5 minutes; individual minute intervals).

Generality: Ability to Adapt to Different Needs

In the use (and purchase) of software, **generality** is an important feature. This has been pointed out throughout the programming chapters and is even more important (or at least as important) in software usage. It is not advisable to purchase a piece of software that can be used but once or a few times, even for several students. Programs that can be *modified* to increase the number of times they are useful are better buys. For example, a drill and practice program that has a fixed spelling list is quite specific by comparison to one that has a changeable spelling list. Likewise, a program that allows practice on states and capitals of a region is less flexible than one that has all states and capitals, or countries and capitals, or more generally any matched pair.

Code that is easy to modify involves READ, DATA, and PRINT statements. Programs that have many interactive components with these types of statements are the most easily modified. However, the program or disk **protection** schemes used by many commercial producers of software do not allow program listing, so modification of those programs is blocked. This is a factor to consider in software purchase. During examination of software, think about whether modification can be imagined. Further, to test the feasibility of modifying the interactive components, attempt to LIST the program. If LISTing is possible, more general use can be made of the software and its value increases.

Allowing More than One Correct Answer; Allowing Spelling Variations

Under certain conditions, more than one answer to a question is correct. For example, a question about the first president of the United States can be correctly answered by "Washington" or "George Washington." Programming and software should be designed to accommodate multiple correct responses when appropriate. In other conditions, correct spelling might or might not be an important factor in an answer (for example, a difficult proper name). It may be desired for students to know the capital (Tallahassee) of a state, or the state (Massachusetts) having a particular capital, before they can spell the words. In such cases, the program would appropriately test to see if a response were reasonable.

Using a Menu

From the *Applications Disk,* type RUN STATES.CAPITALS. We can practice the states by region, one region at a time, from the following menu:

```
<1>NORTHEAST
<2>SOUTHEAST
<3>MIDWEST
<4>SOUTHWEST
<5>NORTHWEST
```

Figure 6 *(a) Pictures, (b) Words, and (c) Shapes from MECC Elementary Volume 7.*

▼

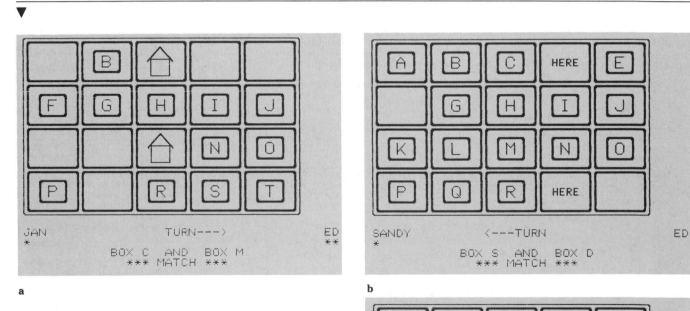

a

b

c

Note that after you have chosen an option, the states and capitals of that region can be practiced in either of two forms: given state, input capital; given capital, input state. Think about the characteristics of *States.capitals.* Does it permit spelling variations? reversibility? What other characteristics are present?

Now, insert *MECC Elementary Volume 7.* Experiment with (4) PICTURES, (5) WORDS, and (6) SHAPES. See if practice helps to increase accuracy. Now try to produce an organizational scheme that helps to increase associational memory. Work again to see if your accuracy improves (Figure 6).

Preparing One's Own Materials

The preparation of materials for use in computer education can take several forms. It is important to note that using materials other than the software is essential to understanding. Computer usage (including programming) is a *tool* for complete understanding. It *supplements* those proven activities that we currently use to accomplish objectives. Thus, class handouts, notes, and specifically designed activities that maximize the learning achieved from the computerized activity, are necessary and appropriate.

Preparing computer software by modifying existing software is also an important part of preparing one's own materials.

The principles in Box 3 provide some guidance for drill and practice activities. The approach to teaching specific skills is in sharp contrast to the teaching of concepts, principles, visualizations, and problem solving, as will be evident in later chapters. These principles suggest ways in which skills can be developed and strongly suggest that the skills should be an outgrowth of conceptual development.

Applications in Available Software

The following software illustrate the concepts discussed in this chapter.

Magic Spells (The Learning Company)   To help readers in grades one–six sharpen their spelling skills, they must recognize, unscramble, and spell flashed words while they take a journey through the Magic Kingdom.

M—SS—NG L—NKS (Sunburst)   These are a series of language games in which passages from books have missing letters or missing words. Students (grade three through adult) will enjoy these games. There are several programs, each with several passages, in the series. The students can gain a lot of practice in using word recognition, contextual cues, and systematic trial and error, to reason out the missing letters and words. At the end of each game, students get feedback concerning their performance.

Stickybear Series (Weekly Reader)   Some of the most advanced animated graphics available for your microcomputer illustrate ducks quacking, trains chugging, and motors putt-putting, as letters of the alphabet are portrayed as large graphic characters, accompanied by animated pictures and sounds of objects whose names start with the pictured letter. Colorful groups of big moving objects—trucks, trains, planes, and more—teach numbers, counting, and simple arithmetic. Colorful animated graphics also represent opposites and shapes. These materials are for the primary level; *Class Packs* of four disks (*ABC, Numbers, Opposites,* and *Shapes*) and a teacher's guide are included.

Box 3   Principles for Skill Development

1. Seek mastery of facts and algorithms only when they are well understood as ideas.
2. Practice association, facts, and algorithms in a scheduled fashion. Practice new skills a few at a time but often, and do frequent reviews of masterted skills. Include both massed and distributed practice in the schedule.
3. Use associations, facts, and algorithms in a variety of ways and settings.
4. Encourage students during practice, provide praise for good effort, and chart progress toward mastery.
5. Provide activities and practice that improve timing or tempo development, when appropriate. Also provide feedback on timing or tempo development when practiced.
6. Give feedback immediately and provide corrective measures when improvements in accuracy are required.
7. Minimize penalty for error while providing praise proportional to progress.
8. Set specific goals for skill mastery, maintain high expectations of goal achievement, and provide support (moral and otherwise) as students work toward mastery.

How the West Was One + Three × Four (Sunburst)   This drill and practice exercise (for grades four through adult) uses three spinners to generate three numbers. The student uses basic operations to combine those numbers to produce a specified number. Using a stagecoach and a steam engine, students progress along a game board. And, of course, if the student lands on the appropriate place, he or she can take shortcuts on faster paths; hence, some strategy can be used. Students really like this program.

Word Spinner (The Learning Company)   This program develops spelling skills through a game format that encourages students (grades 1 through 5) to explore word patterns and experiment with rhyme. It also improves game-playing strategies and performance.

Comments from Research

Initially the most common use of computers was for drill and practice. However, there seems to be considerable controversy over whether this is the most effective use of the limited number of computers available to students. Trumbull (1986) noted that the use of drill-and-practice programs taught students that computers are boring. On the other hand, Yates (1983) argued for the use of drill-and-practice programs. Using computers does seem to contribute to the development of specific skills and/or knowledge. However, there is still a serious, fundamental question about the focus of our educational system. See Chapter 15 for further discussion of this question.

▶ ▲ ◀ ▼ ▶ ▲ ◀ ▼ ▶ ▲ ◀ ▼ ▶ ▲ ◀ ▼ ▶ ▲ ◀ ▼ ▶ ▲

Summary

This chapter discussed drill and practice as a form of learning often associated with skill development. Because becoming skillful in a practice area is the goal, the speed and the accuracy of results are usually important variables. Computers can effectively present varied practice exercises and monitor the results for accuracy. Further, after a required degree of accuracy has been achieved, massed practice can be provided for the development of speed.

A model for the strategies used in the teaching and learning of skills, is useful to the designing (and evaluating) of drill and practice software. The model suggests that there are three phases in skill development. The initiation phase establishes the goal and provides demonstrative examples. The debugging or perfecting phase provides varied practice for developing the skill. Finally, the practicing phase provides massed practice for developing speed and/or accuracy when appropriate.

The following programs were referred to in this chapter:

MECC Elementary Volume 7	*Magic Spells*
Clock	*M—SS—NG L—NKS*
Olympic Decathlon	*Stickybear Series*
MECC Music	*How the West Was One + Three × Four*
Plurals and Possessives	*Word Spinner*
States.capitals	

Important Terms

Analogy	Massed practice
Answer checking	Motivation
Application	Move
Assertion	Positive reinforcement
Clarification	Practice
Corrective feedback	Protection
Demonstration	Repetitive practice
Distributed practice	Reversibility
Dynamics	Strategy
Error correcting	Timing loop
Generality	Varied practice
Introduction	

Exercises

1. Using *States.capitals,* relate Miller's Number (see Chapter 2) to the process of learning all 50 state capitals.

2. In modifying *States.capitals,* on the *Applications Disk,* replace the list of states and their capitals with a list of countries and capital cities of South America. Save the modified program to the disk (under a new name).

3. To modify *Scramble,* on the *Applications Disk,* replace the current list of spelling words. Save the modified program to the disk (under a new name).

4. Examine three (or more) drill and practice programs. Answer the following questions about them:
   a. Is a goal-setting and demonstration phase provided?
   b. Is a debugging or perfecting phase provided?
   c. Is a perfecting and practicing phase provided?

References

Ashlock, R. B., & Washbon, C. A. (1978). Games: Practice activities for the basic facts. In Suydam, M. N., & Reys, R. E. (Eds.). *Developing computational skills: The 1978 yearbook, The National Council of Teachers of Mathematics* (pp. 39–50).

Cooney, T. J., Davis, E. J., & Henderson, K. B. (1975). *Dynamics of teaching secondary school mathematics.* Prospect Heights, IL: Waveland Press.

Davis, E. J. (1978). Suggestions for teaching basic facts of arithmetic. In Suydam, M. N., & Reys, R. E. (Eds.). *Developing computational skills: The 1978 yearbook, The National Council of Teachers of Mathematics.*

Smith, B. O., & Meux, M. O. (1967). *A study of the strategies of teaching.* Urbana, IL: University of Illinois Press.

Thornburg, D. D., & Davidson, J. (1987). Debating drill and practice. *A+, 5,* 44–52.

Todd, H. W. (1972). *Moves and strategies in a skill venture in secondary school mathematics.* Ph.D. dissertation. Urbana, IL: University of Illinois.

Trumbull, D. J. (1986). Games children play: A cautionary tale. *Educational Leadership, 43*(6): 18–21.

Yates, D. S. (1983). In defense of CAI: Is drill-and-practice a dirty word? *Curriculum Review, 22*(5): 55–57.

Chapter 10

Visualization and Imagery Development

▶ ▲ ◀ ▼ ▶ ▲ ◀ ▼ ▶ ▲ ◀ ▼ ▶ ▲ ◀ ▼ ▶ ▲ ◀ ▼ ▶ ▲

Objectives

▶ Identify computer software that can be used as part of the process of developing concepts
▶ Identify computer software to develop students' visualization skills
▶ Use computer software for developing visualization in the problem-solving process
▶ Describe examples of ways to select and use programs in the classroom to develop visualization
▶ Describe ways of using graphics programs in instruction

Many people have complained that most educational software is mainly electronic page turning, that its emphasis is on drill and practice of skills, and that the potential of the computer is greatly underused. Graphics is rarely an integral part of the instructional content, and too little concern is given to conceptual development and the integration of computer experiences into the overall educational environment. Our first introduction to computer-assisted instruction has been through drill and practice, a base familiar to many people. The following chapters build less familiar ideas into a more complete conceptual scheme of the uses of a computer's potential.

Technology opens the doors for new types of learning, such as visual thinking and imagery development, a learning style that is important to many people and that deserves development in others. To visualize a situation or relationship is to form an image of something unseen—an abstraction. **Visualization** is closely tied to concept formation, which is the formation of understanding of an idea. Readiness activities to develop concepts encourage appropriate visualization of the underlying ideas. Educators are increasing their attention to nonverbal—visual and perceptual—learning.

This chapter examines visualization and imagery development. The next chapters show how simulation and tutorial programs can use highly creative graphics, to effectively apply visualization and imagery processes; the resulting interactive learning environment allows students to experiment with such ideas as trying different language combinations, conducting science experiments, and examining the interactions of variables. The realism of dynamic visual feedback can help the students refocus their thinking and experiment, until their imagery develops fully and they are able to work independently.

A picture is worth a thousand words, so they say. From ancient times, when communication was recorded in pictographs, to today, when traffic and information symbols are an international language, pictures have been an important part of communication. Words are different from language to language, but pictures transcend language.

In *Experiences in Visual Thinking,* McKim (1972) commented,

> Visual thinking pervades all human activity, from the abstract and theoretical to the down-to-earth and everyday. An astronomer ponders a mysterious cosmic event; a football coach considers a new strategy; a motorist maneuvers his car along an unfamiliar freeway: all thinking visually. . . . Surgeons think visually to perform an operation; chemists to construct molecular models; mathematicians to consider abstract space–time relationships; engineers to design circuits, structures, and mechanisms; businessmen to organize and schedule work; architects to coordinate function with beauty; carpenters and mechanics to translate plans into things [p. 6].

Computer graphics has the potential to communicate a vast amount of information in a single display. It can be dynamic, bringing the time and motion of the world about us into a program, and making concepts true to life. Fifteen years ago, most computer-formed graphics was generated by typed characters. Today, detailed color images are routinely presented through high-resolution computer graphics. Educators can take full advantage of capabilities such as the illustration of actions, such as walking and running; the changing of an item's state, such as taking apart, putting together, and changing size, orientation, and perspectives; and the representation of information in forms such as graphs of data and maps.

As a first experience, boot up the *Applications Disk* and type:

```
RUN TRANSFORM
```

In this program, you attempt to match two randomly selected shapes. If you think you can match the shapes, then use game paddles or keyboard inputs to manipulate one of the shapes, through slides, turns, flips, and dilations (stretching or shrinking). See Figure 1 for sample displays. As you match the shapes, think about your thinking processes—what you see in your mind and how you process the thoughts. For example, you may find yourself flipping or turning pictures around in your mind.

If you have available the *Perception* program, work with it at this time as an example of a commercial program that illustrates concepts of visualization. There are several programs that incorporate visualization concepts on the *Perception* disk. *Perception II* has a partially covered shape, with a window that slides down the video screen, so that you see part of the shape at one time. Then four figures are given; you choose the one that matches the obscured one. Figure 2 shows a sample sequence.

Perception I, on the same disk, shows two line segments at various locations within a three-dimensional figure. You use game paddles to adjust the length of one of the line segments to make it appear to be the same length as the other (Figure 3).

Perception III, on the same disk, displays one shape to be compared to five other shapes of various sizes. The objective is to select the one of the five shapes that matches the first shape. The user can choose whether to display the shapes simultaneously or individually, and regulate the length of time in which they are displayed (six to thirty seconds) (Figure 4). Again, as you work, be aware of your thinking processes.

Computer graphics has much to offer education. Graphics can simulate events, visually present experiments, show time–motion phenomena, transform objects and show them from different perspectives, and present data and statistics visually

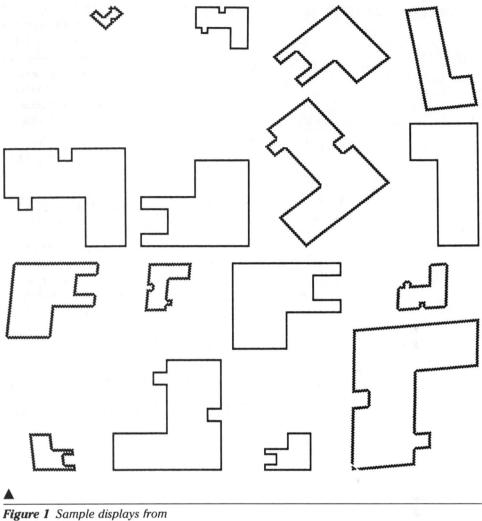

▲

Figure 1 *Sample displays from Transform, a shape-matching program.*

and dynamically. Graphics can do this while under the user's control and manipulation; this is virtually impossible in other media. Instructional software can encourage conceptual development and visualization skills. Computer graphics can help develop problem-solving skills. See the related activities ("Transforming Shapes" and the "Shape Construction Set") at the end of the chapter.

Concept Formulation

People frequently confuse **concepts** and **skills.** Concepts and skills, in fact, are very different, and are developed in quite different ways. Skills help us *perform* certain tasks, whereas concepts help us *understand* those tasks. As a simple example, consider the sum 3 + 4. Getting the correct answer, particularly with speed and accuracy, would be a skill, whereas taking three objects and four objects and putting them together to get a total of seven objects would be demonstrating the concept. Children often are pressed to perform skills when they have not yet developed the underlying concepts.

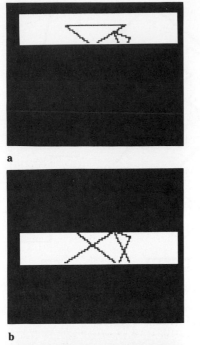

a

b

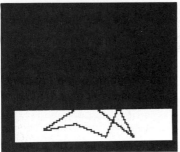

c

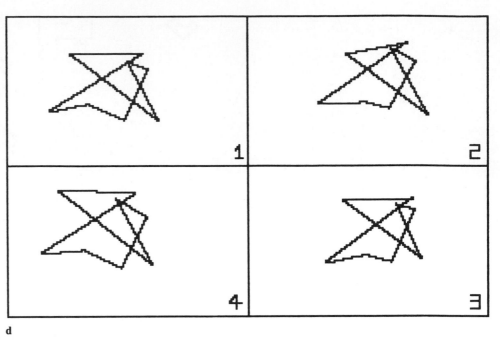

d

▲

Figure 2 *A sequence of motions as a slit is slid down the screen, revealing parts of a figure in (a), (b), and (c); (d) are options from which you choose the figure you saw. This is from Perception II.*

Computer programs designed to drill and practice skills often stress speed and accuracy. They should be used only for skill development and should not be confused with programs designed to develop concepts, which should be more visual and transformational, as in *Transform*. As visualization processes are learned, the environment must be free of tension; there should be no timer. On the other hand, as the student grows comfortable with the concept being taught, he or she may wish to keep score; this is an option with *Transform*.

Dynamic and Static Imagery

It is important to distinguish between static and dynamic imagery; pictures can be **dynamic** (in motion) or **static** (still). Dynamic pictures demonstrate actions, such as running, walking, taking an object apart, putting objects together to form a new object, or changing perspectives. Static pictures are still, such as a representation of the concept of *five* or *cat,* and lack transformational abilities. Dynamic imagery is the mental transformation of an object from one state to another and perhaps back. Dynamic imagery is thus connected with reversible conditions, such as running to and running away from, or putting together and taking apart (3 + 4 and 7 − 3). Static imagery, on the other hand, is short term, lacking the reversible conditions. If a state changes, a person with static imagery will be unable to make the connection between the states.

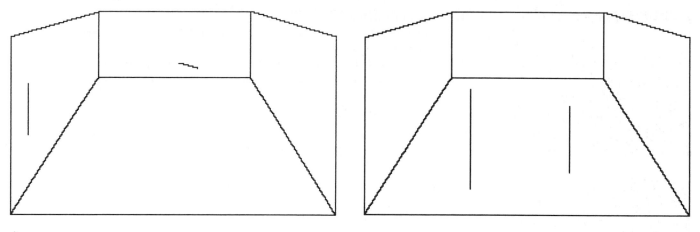

▲

Figure 3 *Examples of lengths to be matched, according to variations in perspective, in Perception I.*

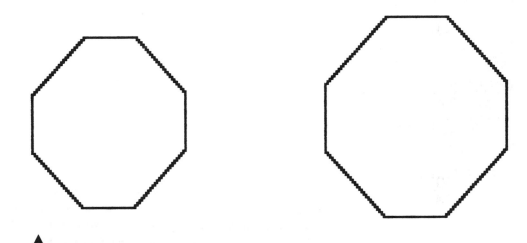

▲

Figure 4 *Example of Perception III, where one figure (on the left) and possible matching figures are displayed sequentially; you select the match.*

Imagery and Achievement

Students' low mathematics scores are often a concern. Dynamic imagery, visualization, and spatial development are promising aids to a conceptual understanding of mathematics (or science and other disciplines). Many cognitive and affective qualities that are highly correlated with mathematical achievement are right-hemisphere functions. These qualities, which tend to solidify at middle-school age, include

1. Visual perception
2. Spatial ability (the ability to turn models around in one's head and to change perspectives)

3. Problem-solving abilities
4. Conservation abilities (particularly, the ability to conserve area and volume is highly correlated with mathematical achievement)
5. Field dependence and independence (field independence is often measured as the ability to find a simple figure embedded in a complex figure)
6. Student attitudes and self-concept
7. Academic motivation

We have discussed the **bimodal functioning** of the brain: right-hemisphere functioning is spatial, holistic, tactual, intuitive, synthesizing; whereas, left-hemisphere functioning is verbal, sequential, linear, deductive, analytical. Too little attention is given to right-hemisphere development or bimodal coordination, such as using visualization to understand underlying principles and then relating those principles to skills. One goal of education is to fully develop the brain, and to develop bidirectional communication between the left and right hemispheres so that the functioning of both is enhanced.

The first three qualities in the list are to right-hemisphere activity. Conservation tasks (number 4 on the list) test whether one's visual-spatial notions (right-hemisphere activity) are coordinated with logical thinking (left-hemisphere activity). The measure of **field independence** (5) tests one's ability to coordinate visual-spatial abilities with analytical abilities—that is, the ability to coordinate between right- and left-hemisphere processing. The sixth and seventh qualities deal with the affective domain, or attitudes and values, related to right-hemisphere processing. Hence, each of the qualities that is highly correlated with mathematical achievement involves the ability to achieve coordination of the right and left hemispheres.

Imagery development relates not only to mathematics and science, but also to many other subject areas. For example, language should be associated with mental pictures of objects or actions (think of *dog* or *running*). As language is acquired, the child's thinking patterns shift slowly to a left-hemisphere orientation. Right-hemisphere cognitive potential is as important for problem solving as are language skills and is necessary but alone not sufficient for creative thinking.

Other subject areas require imagery development. Art obviously involves the creation of visual images relating to mental images. Music creates all kinds of images, through patterning, repetition, and counterpoints. Physical education relates body-movement concepts—such as *above, below, before*, and *after*—to mental images. Social studies investigates relationships among various phenomena and uses data to represent social issues, such as economic trends and political theories; visual representation of those data can be shown through graphs—bar, circular, line, and pictorial representations.

Visualization Implications for Software

Software should allow students to transform figures and shapes, and to repeat a process until they have developed the dynamic imagery. You cannot assume, because students have seen or performed actions once, that they have developed dynamic imagery.

An implication of our list of cognitive and affective qualities is that such qualities as *field dependence* and *independence* should be considered as software is constructed, selected, and used. Some of your students will be field dependent, and consequently will get lost in highly complex screen displays.

Integrating Computers into Curricula

Coordinating off-machine and on-machine activities is very important. In the development of concepts, particularly for young children, **haptic** experiences (the touch and manipulation of objects, often without sight) are often useful. Learning through body movements, such as walking turtle paths, is also conceptually sound. Concept formation progresses first from haptic experiences and body movements, to children's drawing pictures of objects and actions, and then to their manipulating or transforming pictures on a video screen. Through these experiences, children form images to reflect on as they develop more abstract and symbolic thinking. *Reflective abstraction* plays an essential role here as the children reflect back on their haptic experiences and body movements and build connections with video screen images and their own mental images.

Using Spatial Experiences to Develop Problem-Solving Abilities

Spatial experiences with instruction will improve students' problem-solving abilities. At least initially, problem solving involves right-hemisphere processing. Hence, the processing is likely to be nonlinear. Critical ideas must be broken down and search strategies used to relate the problem to a simpler or known problem. We will examine the use of spatial relations and picture drawing as a part of problem solving.

Spatial Development

Sense perception (sight, smell, taste, touch, hearing) is an important part of **spatial development,** which includes the development of awareness of states of being (above/below/between, closer to/farther away), states of transformation (moving closer to/farther away, rotating, changing perspectives), estimation (as of angles and distances), and discrimination (as among various shapes and figures). The video screen for a computer is a highly perceptual instrument because of its potential for highly interactive motion graphics.

Piaget and Inhelder (1967) emphasized that spatial development is constructed through actions rather than through perception alone. Two concepts that they stressed were assimilation and accommodation. **Assimilation** is the process in which the objects and information are incorporated into existing behavior patterns. **Accommodation** is the reorganizing or transforming of existing patterns to adjust to information just received through assimilation. Piaget and Inhelder claimed that a child does not learn about space through perceptions alone, but rather through actions also. Keeping these ideas in mind, reflect on the thinking processes that occurred as you worked through the *Transform* program.

Spatial experiences in play, such as working with blocks, erector sets, construction activities, and sports, are believed to be necessary for children. Through working with these materials, children form mental pictures of spatial activities: taking apart, putting together, and changing perspectives. (Interestingly, these early experiences are connected with sex differences. Young boys typically have more spatial experiences than do girls. Evidence suggests that because visualization and spatial experiences influence spatial abilities, such experience helps to eliminate sex differences in spatial abilities. Lack of spatial abilities may result in math anxiety; so girls need spatial experiences at least as much as do boys.)

Picture Drawing

Drawing pictures that represent ideas in a problem helps develop good problem-solving skills. As you draw a picture you confront your own imagery of the problem and its possible solutions. You should be able to analyze it from different points of view, take it apart, put it together. In the process the solution often appears. For example, when playing computer adventure or mystery games, such as the commercial programs *Cranston Manor* or *Snooper Troops,* the user finds it helpful to map out various objects and locations.

Visualization and Prepared Computer Materials

Earlier we discussed the importance of visualization processes. Now we need to consider ways in which computer graphics in prepared programs can be used to develop those skills.

Embodiments versus Embellishments

Prepared computer materials may use graphics for either embodiments or embellishments. An **embodiment** is a model or physical representation of an abstract idea. For example, three cubes can represent the number three, a physical model can be used to represent a molecular structure, or an object or actions can be used to represent words.

Embellishments, on the other hand, are decorations. A number of current computer programs have very active graphics that are mainly embellishments and not embodiments. Sometimes the embellishments are very motivational, like a graph showing the percentage of correct answers; other times they become very distracting. Recall that some people are not strongly field independent (that is, they are less able to focus on the specific ideas under study and become distracted by the overall display). Graphics can be distractors rather than enhancers.

Transforming Images

Motion graphics can be very effective for illustrating the **transformation** of a situation from one state to another. Consider the *Transform* program introduced at the beginning of this chapter. Transformations have a number of applications for visualization and computer graphics in a variety of fields. Examples of transformations include the putting together of ten separate blocks to form one block of size *ten,* the motion of a projectile when shot at a target, the motion of a swinging pendulum, the interactions of various molecular structures, the motion of two cars traveling at different speeds, or the changing perspectives of a rotating three-dimensional object. Notice that the concepts are carefully depicted by the graphics' presentation of changes from one state to another. For example, Figure 5 illustrates several perspectives from which a simple frame house can be viewed. The commercial program *Flight Simulator II* depicts the changing of perspectives that a pilot experiences when flying an airplane, as shown in Figure 6.

Representing Data

Would you rather see a table or a graph of a set of data? A table can give you specific numbers; by looking at it, you can see general trends. However, graphs, such as those produced by the *Color Average* program (see *Applications Disk*), allow you to visualize relationships, such as the average of a set of numbers. In Figure 7, the dotted line shows the average height of the rectangles. Compare the sum of the distances above the line to the sum of the distances below the line. Does the use of graphics help you to visualize the average?

As our ability to understand and interpret complex relationships among data

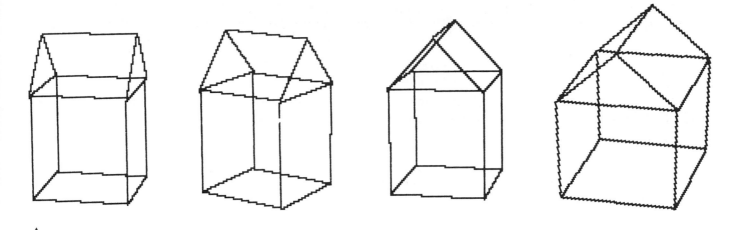

▲

Figure 5 *Views of a simple frame house from several perspectives.*

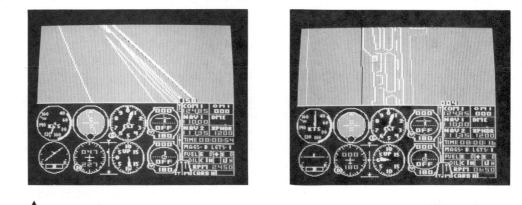

▲

Figure 6 *Screen displays showing different perspectives shown to the user "flying" with the Flight Simulator II.*

increases, our thinking processes become more advanced. As students grow into more formal ways of thinking, they should learn to isolate and control variables, find correlations between those variables, systematically examine combinations of variables, and use proportional reasoning.

Computer graphics can be used for representing embodiments, transforming images from one state to another, and representing data. Each of these is important in the development of both conceptual and visualization processes.

Evaluating and Using Computer Materials for Concept and Visualization Development

Guiding principles for the selection and use of software related to concept and visualization development are presented in Box 1. These principles are explored through four commercially available programs, *Rocky's Boots, Sentences, Micro-dynamo,* and *Flight Simulator II.*

Box 1   Principles for the Selection and Use of Computer Materials for Visualization and Concept Development

1. Use graphics for embodiments rather than embellishments (*embodiment*).

2. Allow the user to transform the graphics from one state to other state(s) when dynamic relationships are involved (*transformation*).

3. Keep the figures simple, so that students can focus on the essence of the ideas (*field dependence* and *independence*).

4. Allow the user to have the control to repeat the illustrated process over and over (*assimilation/accommodation*).

5. Encourage visualization and isolation of each critical variable of the situation (*processing complex data*).

6. Encourage visualizations of the relationships and interactions of any variables (*processing complex data*).

7. Provide opportunities for and encourage both girls and boys to participate actively in using conceptual and visualization materials (*sex differences in spatial development*).

Rocky's Boots allows users to build electrical circuits and relate them to logic connectives. The user is allowed to move from room to room on the display screen. In each room, there are various connectors with which the user can build combinations of electrical circuits. The user can also transfer connectors from one room to another. The embodiments are the circuits and how they behave. Thus they demonstrate principle 1: they are accurate and represent real situations. The user is allowed to transform the graphics from one state to another (for example, circuits that are disconnected can be connected in some combination). The program thus uses principle 2. The displays are free from extraneous distractors (principle 3). The users can repeat the process as often as they wish before moving to the next stage (principle 4). Boys and girls alike can enjoy this program (principle 7). Figure

Figure 7 *Screen display of Color Average demonstrates visual representation of numeric data.*

▼

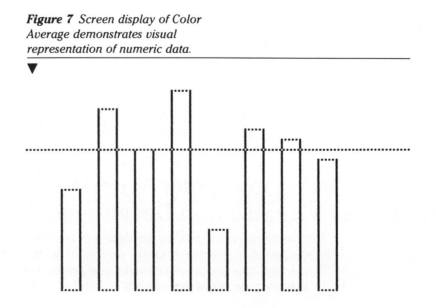

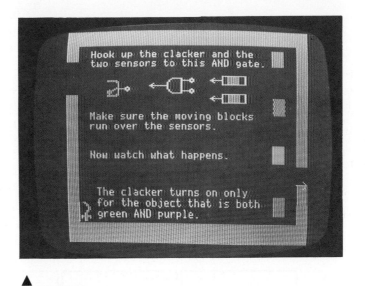

▲

Figure 8 *Screen display of*
Rocky's Boots.

8 shows sample displays. (But remember, these are static and you need actually to work through the program to understand it.)

A program on the *Plato* system that also illustrates the principles nicely is *Sentences.* It is designed so that children can easily make up sentences and see the action in the sentences carried out through the graphics. To give input, students can either type the sentence through the keyboard or use the touch panel to touch the words to be used one at a time. For example, suppose the user inputs the sentence, "The rabbit jumps over the tree house." A graphics display then illustrates a rabbit jumping over a tree house. Figure 9 shows this sentence and a variety of others with corresponding displays. In this figure, the panel of words to be chosen from remains on the screen as each sentence is created.

Sentences illustrates an embodiment (principle 1), and the action carried out is directly related to the embodiment. By inputting the words desired, students are able to transform the graphics (principle 2). The figures are simple (principle 3). The student can repeat the action as often as is desired (principle 4). Variables in this program include the type of noun, verb, adjective (if any), indirect object (if any), and direct object. Students can isolate, control, and visualize the effects of individual variables and their interactions (principles 5 and 6). Girls and boys alike should be attracted to the program (principle 7).

Another example is *Micro-dynamo.* In these materials, interactions of different variables over the same time period are studied. For example, the phenomena involved with flu are studied. The variables studied include,

▶ SICK = the number of sick people
▶ SUSC = the number of susceptible people
▶ INFEC = the number of infected people
▶ RECOV = the number of recovered people

The graphics are embodiments of graphs of relationships (principle 1). They are transformed only when the values for the variables are changed (principle 2). The figures are simple and use color effectively, so people can follow them (principle 3). The process can be repeated over and over, and new values can be tried for each variable (principle 4). The individual variables are displayed over a common

Figure 9 *Four sample sentences*
and corresponding displays
created with Sentences. The word
panel is the same for each
sentence.

▼

```
The rabbit jumps over the tree house. ok
```

to	from	over	the
🏠 house	🐇 rabbit	🚗 car	🐱 cat
🧍 girl	🧒 boy	🐕 dog	🌳 tree
carries	runs	jumps	walks

```
Help available
```

```
The rabbit house jumps over the tree house. ok
```

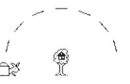

```
The boy walks the dog to the house. ok
```

```
The car carries the house to the tree house. ok
```

time interval. Students can change conditions relating to these variables and see other possible outcomes (principles 5 and 6). Boys and girls alike should enjoy working with this program (principle 7).

Flight Simulator II also satisfies many of the principles. The graphics are embodiments, both of the instruments involved and of the three-dimensional scenes viewed out the window (principle 1). To perform transformations, the user can change directions, increase speed, change the flaps, and so on (principle 2). The pictures are a bit complex and care must be given to focus upon individual parts (but principle 3 is still met). By repeating the process with the same conditions again, the user can control the program, but because the airplane is in motion, the repetition is different from that in *Rocky's Boots* (principle 4). Effects of critical variables are demonstrated through the graphics displays; for example, changing direction results in a changed picture (principle 5). Interactions of variables are also demonstrated graphically; for example, the interaction of changing flaps and speed can be investigated—the results, including crashing, are displayed visually (principle 6). Girls and boys alike can explore this program (principle 7). This program was not designed for conceptual or visual development; it was developed as a training simulation for novice pilots. It is discussed further in Chapter 11.

Graphics Applications

You should take advantage of the graphics capabilities of the computer in various subject areas. Not only can you use prepared materials for specific topics, but you can also use Computer-Aided Design/Computer-Aided Manufacture (**CAD/CAM**) packages. These packages are prepared so that input data—such as locations, dimensions, and shapes—are then represented by graphics. The graphics can be manipulated so that perspectives, shapes, dimensions, and so on, change. CAD/CAM packages are gaining importance in a number of fields such as architecture, engineering, urban planning, and art. As a teacher, you have the task to develop career awareness for your students, and computer graphics can be helpful in building this awareness.

Art and Design

Computer graphics offers much to the art field. Graphics patterns can be generated by the use of artistic concepts. Both still and motion pictures can be generated through computers using output devices such as plotters, video tapes, films, and photographs. CAD/CAM packages for three-dimensional graphics initially approximate a shape. After viewing the shape from different perspectives, the user modifies the shape, reexamines it, modifies it again, and so on. Such techniques can be used for designing automobiles, aircraft, ships, furniture, and shoes, as well as for art and engineering.

Business

With the availability of computer graphics, businesses are using charts and graphs to convey information. Data can easily be converted to charts and graphs and thus expressed visually.

Housing

Included in the category of housing are such fields as architecture, interior design, and urban planning. CAD/CAM graphics packages can be very helpful in teaching these topics. Computer graphics can generate floor plans, blueprints, and sketches, and can take into account various constraints, such as adjacency requirements (what needs to be next to what), dimensional limitations and objectives, ratio requirements (how much of the space should be used for what), shape specifications, natural and artificial lighting, interior and exterior view, and interior and exterior visual privacy.

Urban planning also uses computer graphics. Uses include the generation of maps of street incidents (crimes), traffic accidents, auto thefts, and neighborhood business districts. Large databases on each of the factors are used in their creation; the information is cross-referenced for use in the compilation of various maps.

Languages

Graphics can be used to represent words and actions, as was done in *Sentences* (another example is the *SRA Sentence Animator*). The opposite of this program also could be constructed: the child views the animation and then creates a sentence that represents the action.

Another linguistic use of computers is to have the children create and save graphic screen displays, and then write a story in which they build the pictured item. The students can thus be motivated to develop their creative writing skills.

Mathematics

Many of the programming activities discussed in this book can lead to the understanding of mathematical concepts. Even more interesting is to study the mathematics underlying the graphics packages and see how the use of graphics applies to a wide range of topics, such as linear algebra and linear transformations.

Music

Musical patterns, such as chords, scales, rhythms, and songs, can be represented by graphics patterns, such as those in the demonstration programs for the *Alf Music Synthesizer;* those patterns can then be made concrete. The coordination of graphics and sound is an exciting capability.

Physical Education

Graphics can be used to enhance the understanding of body movements; particular emphasis can be placed on direction (such as *above, below, inside, outside*), gaming strategies, tournament charting, health factors, and body parts.

Science

Graphics can present many scientific concepts in the concrete and can help students represent data and make projections. Graphics simulations can demonstrate scientific relationships. Detailed electronic drawings, constructed through computer graphics, can provide global overviews from which specific regions can be isolated and enlarged.

Simulation Training

Computer simulations can be used in training exercises such as for flying an airplane or driving a car. The simulations can be very lifelike. Interesting simulations with appropriate feedback systems can provide more efficient and safer training than can real experiences.

Social Studies

Graphs and maps can demonstrate the influence of variables on, for example, a flu epidemic, inflation rates, population growths, or drug addiction.

Applications to Available Software

The following software illustrate concepts discussed in this chapter.

Safari Search   This program by Sunburst is problem-solving software. It has activities to promote thinking and strategy development, ranging from simple search processes to complex reasoning processes. Inference and selected patterns of inference, as well as the processes of collecting, organizing, and using information, are experienced in a set of varied games. A five-by-five board of boxes contains the hidden goal, finding an animal. This grid also contains clues; the difficulty of the game depends on the types of clues provided. In easier games, the clues allow the user to make quick inferences; in others, a complex pattern of clues is needed for the user to make the final inferences.

Figure 10 shows an example of a Safari Search activity. To find an animal in the Seal Search game, you receive *warm* or *hot* clues that hint at how close to the seal's cell you are. As the pattern of clues unfolds, a student can deduce the exact location of the seal. Where would you say the seal is hidden in our example?

The *Safari Search* games do embody the problem-solving concepts being learned. As can be seen from Figure 10, they meaningfully contribute to the development of search strategies and organizational techniques. By judiciously choosing cells, students can isolate critical variables of the puzzle. By seeing *warm* and *hot* on the screen, a young child can process the meaning of the clues and discern complex patterns built by several clues. By playing with varied, related games, students are likely to assimilate broader visual patterning. The students' growth from basic to general pattern-search strategies is aided by the activities.

Figure 10 *A Safari Search activity.*

▼

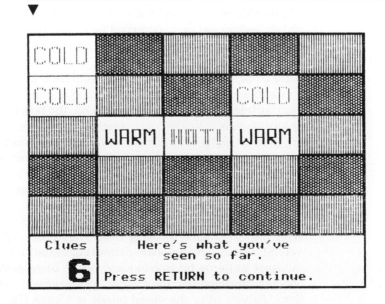

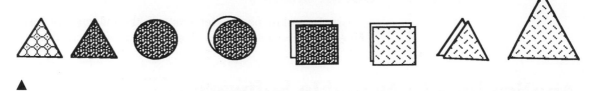

Figure 11 *A pattern sequence in High Wire Logic.*

High Wire Logic   This program by Sunburst is a computerization of "logical blocks"—a means of applying principles of logic. Essential concepts of computer education/science and science are taught. The objects used in the program have the following characteristics: color, fill (shading), size, and shape. Several types of games are included on the *High Wire Logic* disk. In playing one of the games, students alternate in selecting blocks that have exactly two characteristics that are alike. Another game requires students to sequence blocks so that three of their characteristics are always preserved in consecutive blocks; another game sets up a pattern in a matrix and students insert missing elements in the pattern. "Seeing" the properties of objects in a sequence helps students to develop important concepts (*variable, alike,* and *different*) used in the processing of data. While isolating critical variables, these sequences focus on what is constant amid several differences, a problem-solving strategy. For example, in Figure 11, there is one difference between an object and the next object.

In Search of the Most Amazing Thing   This software by Spinnaker involves students in problem solving in an "adventure-game" environment. A player tries to use clues to find the "most amazing thing" (at one point a golden metallic ball . . . but it changes through the ages). Students experience keeping records, drawing and using maps, drawing conclusions and inferences, and experimenting throughout their work with this software. Visualizations of location and relative position is a necessary part of *In Search of . . . .* By experimenting and analyzing examples, students assimilate the methods by which "location data" can be organized. Drawing maps and recording information on them is one example of a cluster of the organizational methods that can be assimilated. Having to keep their drawings simple and record only important facts helps young students attend to the essence of the ideas, and thereby increases their field independence.

Gnee or Not Gnee   This Sunburst program is a series of concept-acquisition tasks, applicable to science, English (including reading), mathematics, and social studies. Appropriate for grades three through six, the tasks include the presentation of three or four objects with a set of common characteristics (to be observed); other objects are then presented for comparison. In some games, students discover the rule; in some games, students create rules; and in others, higher-order rules are given through examples and students construct other examples to fit the rules. Analogy is an important heuristic taught in this series of games. Two examples are provided in Figure 12. The first part of Figure 12 illustrates activities used to develop and test various imagery skills. Can a youngster focus on essential ideas in the patterns? With the experience of using many, many sets of visual analogies, do students assimilate and accommodate patterns of visual relationships? Can critical variables in visual patterns be isolated and used? *Gnee or Not Gnee* contains a wealth of concept development and imagery development activities addressing these questions. As you solve the visual puzzle of Figure 12a, are you noting the differences

▲

Figure 12 *Two activities from*
Gnee or Not Gnee.

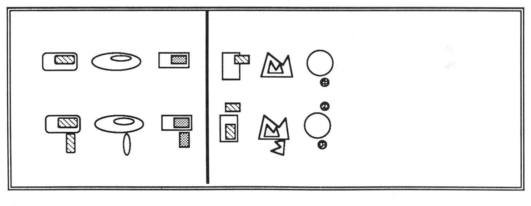

▲

Figure 13 *A solution to the*
visual analogy problem in the
Gnee or Not Gnee discussion.

and similarities between the top row and the bottom row? Can you describe how they are alike? How they are different? (See Figure 13.)

Patterns similar to those in Figure 12 are presented, then students are asked to draw the element that would logically occur next in the pattern. For example, the objects in part **a** are presented as a pattern, then the upper row of three objects in part **b** is given. The object is to draw three objects, in the lower right portion of the diagram that logically continue the pattern. (What three things should be drawn in the box? A solution may be found at the end of the chapter.)

Verbal-analogy problems are also posed in *Gnee or Not Gnee.* In some forms of the game, two words may need to complete the pattern of analogy as in the above example. A solution may be *Short: Low.* Do you think there are two other words that fit the analogy also? Try to think of another pair of words.

Bumble Plot   This program by The Learning Company has five games, each with high graphic quality and strong imagery-development traits. Each game is designed to develop reasoning skills and lay the foundations for the learning of advanced concepts, and each teaches some basic concepts of a subject. The games require many reasoning skills, so that students develop spatial awareness, discover winning strategies, make predictions, and develop reasoning skills. Specific content introduced are positive and negative numbers, standard number-pair notation and the location of points in a coordinate system, and orientation on coordinate axes. The games progressively increase in challenge and sophistication; they are called *Trap and Guess, Bumblebug, Hidden Treasure, Bumble Art,* and *Roadblock. Bumble Plot* games present strong challenges for students to isolate critical variables and see the relationships among them. The visual material is essential to the concepts being developed, and presents a true embodiment of the ideas. The graphics are simple and to the point; the intellectual challenge is maintained. Excellent forms of visual feedback are provided.

Factory and **Super Factory**   Students in grades four through adult thoroughly enjoy these materials by Sunburst. In the construction of squares, *Factory* uses combinations of machines that paint strips (thick, medium, or thin), punch holes (of selected number and shape), and rotate elements. Sequencing the machines in proper order is very important. The computer can present challenges for students or they can challenge each other. To extend the concept, *Super Factory* has students construct cubes with different figures on the faces. If the materials are available, examine them to determine if the principles of visualization and concept development (Box 1) apply to them.

Geometry Supposer Series   Students (grades five through adult) use these materials to construct geometric figures—bisecting segments or angles and constructing specific triangles, squares, or circles. Students can also measure segments, angles, areas, or perimeters. One nice feature of some of these materials by Sunburst is the *repeat construction* feature: by pressing the space bar, the student can repeat a construction for a totally different figure. Students can make guesses and repeat the same constructions for several different figures to see if the guesses are correct. If these materials are available, compare the characteristics of these materials to the principles of visualization and concept development (Box 1); do they meet the test?

Green Globs and Graphing Equations   Using this Sunburst software, students, in grades nine through twelve, try to fit curves through given points on a grid. The goal is to cross as many points or globs as possible with one equation. An equation plotter allows students to experiment with plotting various equations. They can concentrate on linear or quadratic graphs, or they can select a more free form. In some sections, the computer generates a graph, and the student is to tell what equation is graphed. A graph for the guessed equation helps the student see how similar the graph of his or her equation is to the given graph. This exercise can give students a lot of practice at relating graphs and equations.

The *Green Globs* pop when an equation passes through their coordinates. They even have nice sound effects like a balloon popping. These problems can get rather challenging.

Finally, there is the *Tracker.* The student first inputs probes across the screen; feedback then indicates whether the probes intersect any points of a hidden graph of a specified equation. When the student thinks he or she has figured out the equation(s), he or she inputs a Tracker and can then see if it follows the path(s) of the hidden graph(s). A scoring system gives the students even more enticement. This exercise gives students a real challenge. Analyze this program according to the principles for visualization and concept development (Box 1).

Compu-Teach Series   Compu-Teach (by Compu-Teach) has several programs that are worth reviewing. They are making a real effort to put out quality educational software that makes heavy use of good graphics and sound. Included in the series are **A B sCenes** (which presents pictures of objects that start with a letter the student had pressed), *ArithMATIC: COUNTING* (students type in a number between one and nine and the computer presents a picture of that number of objects), *Ruby the Scene Machine: The Farm* (the student can construct a farm scene), *Sentence Wizard* (a sentence is acted out), and *Word Pieces,* a language experience program for children aged 3–7 years. In using *Ruby the Scene Machine: The Farm,* the student can move a little man around the screen: the up/down and left/right keys locate a figure. Then students can choose from a rather wide list of possible figures, and the chosen figure suddenly appears. Using this process students can easily construct a farm scene. In using *Sentence Wizard* students supply a missing word to complete a sentence: if the guessed word is correct, the computer acts out the scene.

Apple Learning Series   One way of developing thinking in early childhood is to emphasize the building of mental images and the communication of them. In this spirit, Apple has put together a series of materials to help learning in early childhood. These materials include *Talking Textwriter* (published by Scholastic); *Sound Ideas* (Houghton Mifflin); *Muppet Workbook, Muppetville, Muppets on Stage,* and *Touch N'Write* (Sunburst); *Touch Window* (Personal Touch); *Echo II+, IIB* (Street Electronics); and *Teacher's Manual and Training Certificate* (Apple Computer Company). If interested in early childhood, you should check into these.

Mademoiselle Merveille Software   Another very interesting set of materials designed for early childhood is from Canada (DIL, Didacticiel International Et Laboratique). Through colorful graphics and music, these programs (whose title could be translated as "Miss Marvel") enable children to increase their reading, math, and language skills before they have mastered letters and numbers. Using either a keyboard or a graphics tablet (such as their WonderWorker), students develop the following skills: eye–hand coordination, visual and auditory discrimination, expanded speaking vocabulary, letter and number recognition, classification, sequencing, directional sense, understanding of spatial relationships, inferences, evaluation, creativity, memory, analogies, sharing, and so on. This series of ten different programs is best used with a teaching approach that includes circle discussions, three-dimensional manipulatives, and two-dimensional work on paper, as well as individual or small-group activity on the computer. A teacher's guide, with black-line masters and a four-color plastic 12″ × 12″ overlay to be used with a graphics tablet, is included.

Comments on Research

Research is beginning to study the effects of graphics as a teaching device. For example, McClurg and Chaille (1987) examined the effects of two computer games, *Factory* and *Stellar 7,* on fifth, seventh, and ninth grade students; they studied the effects of these games on the students' spatial ability. The experimental groups met for 45 minutes twice each week, for six weeks. Significant effects on the children's spatial ability were measured by the Mental Rotations Test, which was described in Shepard and Metzler (1971) and shown by McGee (1982) to be highly reliable.

Investigations by Forsyth and Lancy (1987) showed that games like treasure hunts similarly showed much potential in working with map skills. This study was conducted with American fourth- and fifth-grade students of normal intelligence. The students played the game for nine consecutive school days and were tested two weeks later. The study showed that students could identify places encountered in an adventure game and that students using a map were more successful at the task than those not using the map. Boys and girls both seemed to enjoy the game.

Other studies, for example, Lowery and Knirk (1982) and Gagnon (1983), support the view that video games have strong potential as an instructional tool. Care must be given to select appropriate games that will enhance the course of study.

▶ ▲ ◀ ▼ ▶ ▲ ◀ ▼ ▶ ▲ ◀ ▼ ▶ ▲ ◀ ▼ ▶ ▲ ◀ ▼ ▶ ▲

Summary

This chapter stressed the importance of developing visualization skills and of using computer graphics to encourage development of these skills. Connections among the skills of visualization, concept formation, and problem solving show how important it is to carefully integrate computer graphics into instructional materials. We suggested guiding principles that you can use in choosing, designing, and using computer materials in visualization and concept development. Finally, we explored the uses of computer graphics, visualization, and concept formation in a variety of fields.

Software discussed in this chapter:

Transform	*A B sCenes*
Perception	*ArithMATIC:Counting*
Flight Simulator II	*Ruby the Scene Machine: The Farm*
Color Average	*Sentence Wizard*
Rocky's Boots	*Word Pieces*
Sentences	*Talking Textwriter*
Micro-dynamo	*Sound Ideas*
CAD/CAM graphics packages	*Muppet Workbook*
SRA Sentence Animator	*Muppetville*
Safari Search	*Muppets on Stage*
High Wire Logic	*Touch N'Write*
In Search of the Most Amazing Thing	*Touch Window*
Gnee or Not Gnee	*Echo II +, IIB*
Bumble Plot	*Teacher's Manual and Training Certificate*
Factory	
Super Factory	*Mademoiselle Merveille* Software
Geometric Supposer Series	*Shape Construction Set*
Green Globs and Graphing Equations	

Important Terms

Accommodation	Field dependence/independence
Assimilation	Haptic
Bimodal functioning	Reflective abstraction
CAD/CAM	Skills
Concepts	Spatial development
Dynamic	Static
Embellishment	Transformation
Embodiment	Visualization

Exercises

1. Select an instructional area and identify at least ten ways in which visual experiences can enhance learning in each area.

2. For which of the examples you chose in (1) could you use computer graphics?

3. Identify cases in which the use of computer graphics would be far more effective than any other form.

4. Apply the principles in Box 1 to an appropriate instructional software package.

5. Identify several instructional software packages that use developing visualization skills to enhance problem-solving skills. What are the properties of each software package?

6. Solve puzzles in two of the following pieces of software: *Gnee or Not Gnee, Bumble Plot, In Search of the Most Amazing Thing, High Wire Logic,* and *Safari Search.* Which principles of imagery development (Box 1) did you observe in each package? In what ways were the principles' goals met or not met?

7. Solve puzzles in two of the following pieces of software: *Gnee or Not Gnee, Bumble Plot, In Search of the Most Amazing Thing, High Wire Logic,* and *Safari Search.* Which principles of imagery development (Box 1) were not followed by each package? What could be done "off computer" to incorporate these principles?

8. Examine *Visualizer* (discussed in Chapter 7) in terms of the principles of imagery development (Box 1).

References

Adams, S. (June 1985). Wander into wonderland! Adventure games take you on a vacation to a place as vivid as your imagination. *Family Computing,* 37–41.

Burton, E. (1977). *The new physical education for elementary school children.* Boston: Houghton Mifflin.

Dorval, M., & Pepin, M. (1986). Effect of playing a video game on a measure of spatial visualization. *Perceptual Motor Skills, 62,* 159–162.

Education Commission of the States. (1982). *Education for a high technology economy.* Materials prepared for governors' special briefings for the National Governors' Association Annual Meeting. Denver, CO: Education Commission of the States.

Flake, J. L. (1983). Brain hemispheric considerations for a developmental approach to diagnosing mathematics concepts for children. (*Research monograph.*) Kent, OH: Research Council for Diagnostic and Prescriptive Mathematics.

Forsyth, A., Jr., & Lancy, D. F. (1987). Simulated travel and place location learning in a computer adventure game. *Journal of Educational Computing Research, 3*(3), 377–394.

Gagnon, D. (1983). Videogames and spatial skills: Preliminary report. Unpublished paper. Harvard Graduate School of Education.

Greenfield, P. M. (1984). *Mind and media: The effects of television, video games and computers.* Cambridge: Harvard University Press.

Inhelder, B., & Piaget, J. (1958). *The growth of logical thinking: From childhood to adolescence.* New York: Basic Books.

Klein, E. (1985). Computer graphics, visual imagery, and spatial thought. In *Children and computers: New directions for child development.* San Francisco: Jossey-Bass Inc. *28,* 55–73.

Lancy, D. F., Cohen, H., Evans, B., Levine, N., & Nevin, M. L. (1986). Using the joystick as a tool to promote intellectual growth and social interaction. *The Quarterly Newsletter of the Laboratory of Comparative Human Cognition, 7*(4), 119–125.

Lowery, B. & Knirk, F. (1982). Micro-computer video games and spatial visualization acquisition. *Journal of Educational Technology Systems, 11*(2), 155–166.

McClurg, P. A., & Chaille, C. (1987). Computer games: Environments for developing spatial cognition? *Journal of Educational Computing Research, 3*(1), 95–111.

McGee, M. (1982). Spatial abilities: The influence of genetic factors. In *Spatial abilities-development and physiological foundation.* M. Potegal (Ed.). New York: Academic Press.

McKim, R. H. (1972). *Experiences in visual thinking.* Monterey, CA: Brooks/Cole.

Piaget, J., & Inhelder, B. (1967). *The child's conception of space.* New York: Basic Books.

Piaget, J., & Inhelder, B. (1971). *Mental imagery in the child.* New York: Basic Books.

Roberts, N., Anderson, D. F., Deal, R. M., Garet, M. S., & Shaffer, W. A. (1983). *Introduction to computer simulation: The system dynamics approach.* Reading, MA: Addison-Wesley.

Shepard, R., & Metzler, J. (1971). Mental rotation of three-dimensional objects. *Science, 191,* 952–954.

Sprung, B. (Ed.). (1983). *Perspectives on non-sexist early childhood education.* New York: Teachers College Press.

Suydam, M. N. (1980). Untangling clues from research on problem solving. In *Problem solving in school mathematics: The 1980 Yearbook. The National Council of Teachers of Mathematics.* Reston, VA: The National Council of Teachers of Mathematics.

Tobias, S. (1978). *Overcoming math anxiety.* New York: W. W. Norton.

Turkle, S. (1984). *The second self: Computers and the human spirit.* New York: Simon & Schuster.

Wheatley, G. H. (1978). *Wheatley Spatial Test.* Lafayette, IN: Purdue University.

Witkin, H. A. (1950). Individual differences in ease of perception of embedded figures. *Journal of Personality 19,* 1–15.

Witkin, H. A., Dye, R. B., Faterson, H. F., Goodenough, D. R., & Karp, S. A. (1962). *Psychological differentiation: Studies of development.* New York: John Wiley.

▶ ▲ ◀ ▼ ▶ ▲ ◀ ▼ ▶ ▲ ◀ ▼ ▶ ▲ ◀ ▼ ▶ ▲ ◀ ▼ ▶ ▲

Activity   Transforming Shapes

Type   Machine

Objective   Using a model, transform one shape to another; manipulate shapes on the video screen and in the mind

Prerequisite(s)   Previous activities in this unit

Materials Needed   *Transform* (Applications Disk)

Activity   By using transformations, students will attempt to superimpose computer images of one shape on top of another shape. Run *Transform* on the *Applications Disk* and read the directions. Your students can match two randomly selected shapes (see the figure). If the shapes cannot be matched, your students should quit and move on to another shape combination; recognizing shapes that cannot be matched is also important. Discuss with the students the idea that more than one sequence of moves can result in a match.

As the students get comfortable with this program, get hardcopy printouts of several collections of shapes and have students tell you the moves that will cause the shapes to match. This exercise will lead them to a more abstract level if they are ready to make the transfer. If they are not ready, suggest that they make paper pieces and go through the motions; this exercise still illustrates the transformations on a concrete level.

Note that a closely related activity is the Shape Construction Set activities. Also, alternative shapes can be constructed for *Transform;* the *Draw.MI* program on the

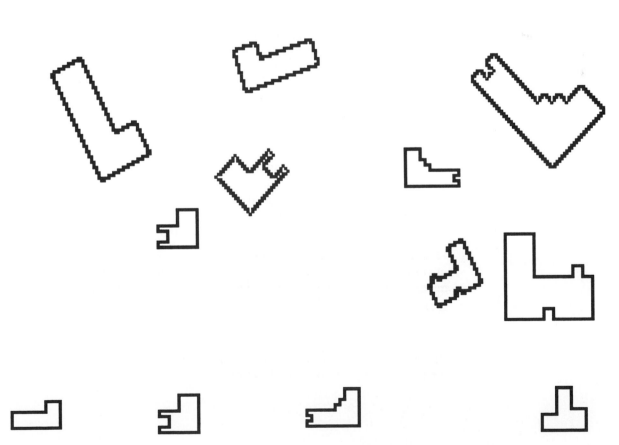

Applications Disk can make shapes and a shape table. The shape table constructed for the shape transform will also work for this program; the name of the shape table will match that listed in *Transform.*

Activity   Shape Construction Set Activities

Type   Machine

Objective   Use a model and decomposing/recombining strategies to develop and construct pictures

Prerequisite(s)   Experience with activities in Transformations

Materials needed   *Shape Construction Set* on the *Applications Disk* (Disk needs to remain in drive.) Worksheet

Activity   Making and manipulating shapes provides both fun and educational experiences for students. The *Shape Construction Set* is designed for those purposes. Students have the option to:

1. Make shapes
2. View shapes with different scales
3. Make a shape table (which is needed for using the shapes in a program or with the shape manipulator)
4. Manipulate shapes (through transformations) to make pictures

Additional options also exist to:

1. Retrieve previously saved screen displays
2. Save current screen displays

It would be best to copy this program, which comes in three parts—*Shape Construction Set, Draw.MI,* and *Shape Transform*—onto a separate disk. The disk should remain in the drive while the students are working with it. Initially, have the students experiment with the parts.

Making Shapes   To construct a shape, the user moves a cursor up, down, left, or right. The *Shape Construction Set* is menu-driven. With single keystrokes, students can make choices. Students can plot line segments or just move the cursor. In order to save a shape, the student must give it a name. Note that when a shape is saved on the disk, a second shape is also saved at the same time and has the same name as the first shape with an ".MI" attached. The second shape is a mirror image of the first shape, reflected across a vertical line through the initial starting point.

Viewing Shapes   Another option in the program allows students to view shapes of various sizes. They simply type in the name of the shape; in order to view the mirror image of the shape, they must add the ".MI" to the name.

Making a Shape Table   This program helps with the construction of a shape table. Actually it does most of the work. The user indicates how many shapes will be included in the shape table, what the names of the shapes are, and what the shape table is to be called. Be sure the disk in the drive has those shapes on it, and the program will do the rest of the work.

Manipulating the Shapes   In order to use the *Shape Transform* portion of the program, the user must first construct a shape table. An example of a shape table, *Blocks,* is included on the *Applications Disk.* When *Shape Transform* requests the name of a shape table, try *Blocks* or a student- or teacher-made shape table.

For the students to construct a shape table of their choice, they need to run the *Draw.MI* portion. With five shapes and their mirror images, they can select the option to make a shape table. If they plan to use their shape table with *Shape Transform,* they should so indicate when asked early in the program. The program will then automatically set the shape table up to be compatible with *Shape Transform.* It will expect names for the five shapes and will automatically load the mirror images in the right places. The students then name their shape table, which is now ready to use with *Shape Transform.*

Retrieving Previously Saved Screen Displays   Initially, no screen displays have been saved because that takes a lot of space on a disk. Once a screen display has been saved, it can easily be retrieved. By saving a screen display, students can continue working on a display for more than one session or they can use the display in other settings.

Saving Screen Displays   After loading a shape table, students making pictures can slide, flip, turn, or dilate the pieces. They can choose to save the screen display if they wish. (Note: Screen displays can fill up a disk rather quickly, so keep plenty of disks on hand.) To mix shapes from different tables, the students can make part of a picture with one combination of shapes in a table, save that screen display on the disk, and then run the program again; call up the new shape table and the previously saved screen display.

Several screen displays constructed by third-graders using the Shape Construction Set are shown in the following worksheet.

Exploration

Shape Construction Set Worksheet

Using the *Shape Construction Set* and the *Blocks* shape table on the *Applications Disk*, make these screen displays.

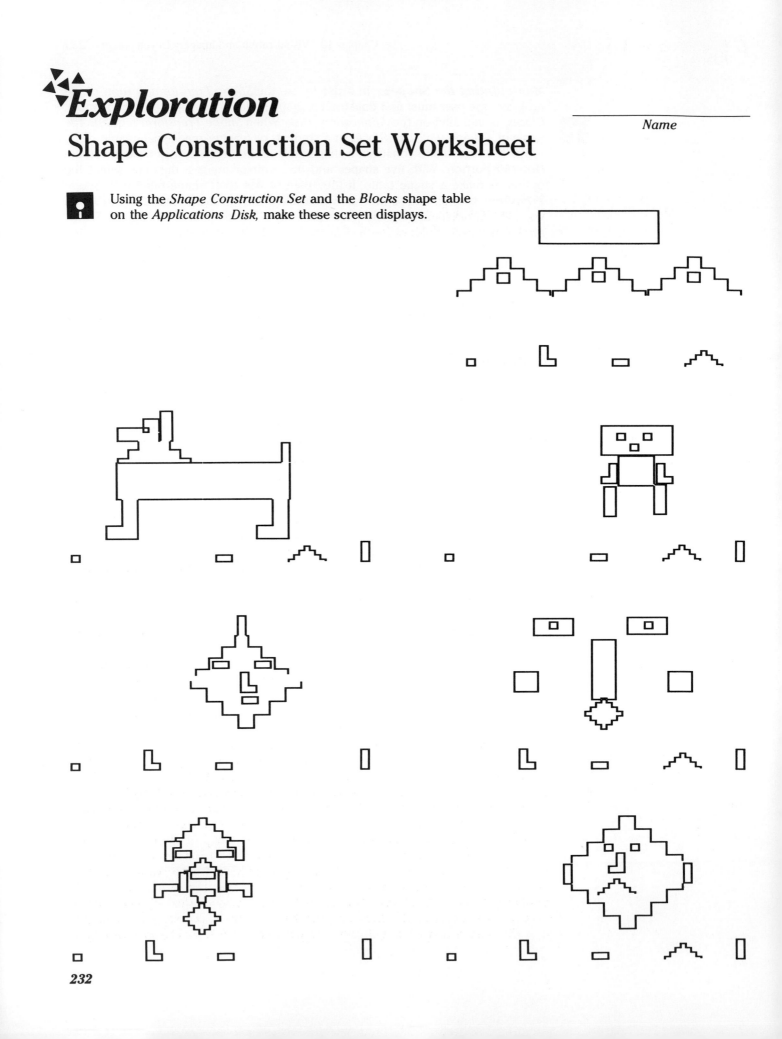

Chapter 11

Simulation

▶ ▲ ◀ ▼ ▶ ▲ ◀ ▼ ▶ ▲ ◀ ▼ ▶ ▲ ◀ ▼ ▶ ▲ ◀ ▼ ▶ ▲

Objectives

▶ Describe characteristics of a simulation
▶ Describe advantages of simulation use
▶ Give examples of simulations in various fields
▶ Describe effective uses of simulation in the classroom
▶ Analyze a simulation
▶ Identify sample simulations and relate to the above

Computer simulation offers much potential for education. A **simulation** is a representation of a real situation. You interact with the simulation: you make decisions, and consequences occur. Simulations can be used effectively to provide experiences that would not be possible otherwise, such as performing dangerous or ethically dubious experiments, flying airplanes with no prior experience, and ruling a kingdom.

First, if you have the materials described below, spend some time examining them so that you get a feel for simulations and how they behave. As you are examining these programs, observe what decisions you must make, what options you have, and what consequences result. Keep in mind the principles for visualization and conceptual development (Chapter 10).

In *Hammurabi,* a ruler of a kingdom must take decisions and take actions, such as buying or selling land and planting grain to keep the kingdom alive. *Rocky's Boots,* already described, is a simulation of electrical circuitry. In *Oregon Trail,* pioneers travel across the country battling obstacles, such as hostile Indians, starvation, and attacking wild animals. Figure 1 shows a sample screen display. *Pollute* simulates the polluting of water with industrial waste or sewage. Dumping rates, temperature, size of the water supply, and waste-treatment procedures can be input by the user. Feedback is given by both tables and graphs of the pollution level. See Figure 2 for a screen display. *Collide* simulates the collision of two masses. The user inputs the masses of the objects, their velocities, and their elasticity (coefficient of restitution). See Figure 3 for a sample screen display. *Micro-dynamo,* materials by Roberts et al. (1983), includes a number of simulations designed particularly for social studies and science classes. These materials study the effects of variables'

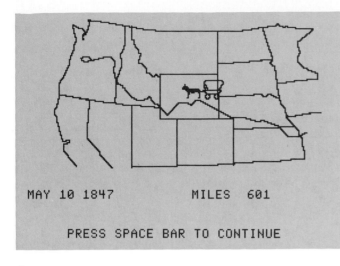

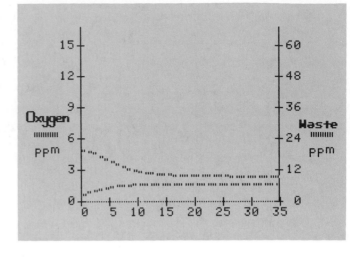

Figure 1 Screen display of Oregon Trail, showing progress of pioneers traveling across the country.

Figure 2 Screen display of Pollute, showing relationships between oxygen and waste levels.

interactions in a situation such as the *Flu* illustration described in Chapter 10. *Flight Simulator II* will be discussed in depth later in this chapter.

Microworlds are special cases of simulations. As you recall, microworlds are explorable and manipulable environments, in which simple and accessible demonstrations of a law are made through gaming activities that make the microworlds meaningful. Needed concepts can be defined within the experiences of the microworld.

Characterizing Simulation

A simulation is a **working analogy** of a real situation. For example, *Hammurabi* is a working analogy of a ruler making decisions about her or his kingdom. *Oregon Trail* is a working analogy of pioneers traveling across the country.

One of the important parts of a simulation is its **underlying model.** The underlying model determines the extent to which properties or relations in the simulation are similar to those of the real situation; in *Rocky's Boots* the underlying model is the logic of switching-circuit behavior. Once systems or measurements are observed, those observations can be used to predict the reactions of analogous systems. Thus simulations provide problem-solving experiences that can be related to other work.

Games versus Simulations

Games and simulations are alike in that both have rules governing their behavior, and you actively participate in both. Unlike most games, simulations are not necessarily competitive. Also, simulations are related to some real-world situation. Simulations usually are designed to teach information.

Probabilistic versus Deterministic

Is the winning of a game due to chance, skill, or both? A **probabilistic model** for a game or simulation is one whose outcomes are largely determined by chance. In a **deterministic model,** chance plays no part in determining the outcome.

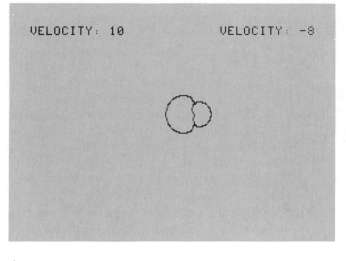

▲

Figure 3 *Screen display of
Collide, showing two particles
colliding with each other.*

Hammurabi, for example, has some random variables such as plagues or drought, which cause it to be somewhat probabilistic, whereas *Collide* is deterministic and will behave as the underlying models dictate.

Single-Step versus Multistep Simulations

In some simulations each step or decision is independent of the others. In others, each step is dependent on other decisions, and it is the combination and order of the decisions that determine the overall result. The former are **single-step** (input/output) **simulations;** the latter are **multistep** (interactive) **simulations.**

In *Hammurabi,* the outcome of each step is determined not only by that step, but also by the previous steps. *Rocky's Boots* uses both single- and multisteps: each single connection is a single step, whereas a complex accumulation of circuits is created through a multistep process. *Collide* is a single-step simulation: after the data are input, the action is determined by the underlying model, not by previous input.

Zero-Sum versus Non–Zero-Sum Games

In a **zero-sum game,** what one player wins the other player loses. Thus, the players' interests are diametrically opposed, and such games are often called *games of conflict.* A **non–zero-sum game** is not a direct conflict. For example, cooperative games or negotiated bargaining models are non–zero-sum games. In non–zero-sum games, all players may win. In *Rocky's Boots,* there are no winners or losers. In *Oregon Trail,* the goal is to complete the trip; there are many ways to fail, but you do not compete with other players.

Solving Problems versus Training

Some simulations ask the user to solve problems by creating a model and changing values of the variables; some provide practice or training in discovering and applying the underlying model. *Flight Simulator II* helps the student discover

---

Box 1   Components of a Simulation

1. Model representing an abstraction of the situation to be studied
2. Rules for behavior or interaction of the model
3. A means (for example, keyboard or game paddle) for the user to interact with and manipulate the model
4. Feedback, preferably realistic—to make the simulation come alive
5. A scoring device or means by which performance is rated
6. Feedback during the program concerning the user's behavior (optional)

---

and apply the underlying models, and hence gain training in the models. Box 1 summarizes the components of a simulation.

Using Simulations in the Classroom

Suppose you have only one computer and thirty students. What can you do? One excellent use of your computer is to involve the whole class in discussion and group decision making. Suppose you have thirty computers and thirty students; students can then work with a simulation individually.

Because simulations are designed to help students gain experience with a model, class discussions normally should accompany simulation. A unit of study can be built around one well-designed simulation, with additional resource materials, readings, field trips, and so on. Students can use the simulation for *exploratory investigation.* Classroom discussion of the related ideas can help students *formulate principles* about how the simulation behaves. The students then *operate from principles,* and use the principles to do intelligent *decision making.* Some applications of simulations are listed in Box 2.

Simulation can be used in a variety of ways. For example, a simulation can be used for forecasting or predicting, as in *Pollute.* A simulation can be used for demonstrating, experimenting, or conjecturing, as in *Rocky's Boots* and *Collide.* Simulations can be used for training personnel, as in *Flight Simulator II.* In each case, information is gathered, and decisions are made on the basis of previous training and available information. Consequences are shown, and additional decisions are made based on the consequences of earlier decisions. Through such experiences, students can gain skill in **decision making,** a very important goal of education.

Analyzing a Simulation

A simulation can be an excellent teaching tool. The learning that results from the use of the simulation, however, is dependent on the quality of the simulation. Box 3 shows factors that influence the educational value of the simulation. At the end of this chapter, there is a useful form for use in the analysis of simulations, especially in determining their educational value. In the next sections, this form is filled out as we make in-depth analyses of two simulations.

Oregon Trail Analysis

In *Oregon Trail,* you are given $900 to spend on a trip along the Oregon trail from Independence, Missouri, to Oregon City, Oregon, in 1847. Your family of five will cover the 2040-mile trail in five or six months—if you succeed. After spending

---

Box 2   Instructional Applications of Simulations

1. Simulations enable skills developed in a training situation to be transferred to the life situation.
2. Simulations provide a responsive environment and lead to relevant inquiry (what would happen if _____ ?).
3. Simulations telescope time.
4. Real laboratory settings might be difficult to obtain, expensive to maintain, or potentially dangerous; simulations can be less costly and safer.
5. Simulations allow the user opportunities for experiential learning, discovery, intuitive understanding, and practice of principles he or she has learned in courses, without censure or fear.
6. Users can learn to locate, analyze, and apply data in a meaningful context.
7. Simulations can make theory relevant and, by allowing students to discover the model behind the simulation, help them to synthesize classroom theory and relate it to reality.
8. Simulations can help the user gain intellectual control over her or his behavior.

$200 on a wagon, you must choose what qualities and quantities of food, ammunition, clothing, and miscellaneous supplies to take. Along the trail various events occur: hostile Indians or wild animals might descend on you, or you might run out of food or get sick. The effectiveness of this simulation is analyzed in Box 4.

Flight Simulator II Analysis

Flight Simulator II simulates the flying of an airplane. Its use of three-dimensional graphics is very effective; perspectives change as the plane changes orientations. The ground features, runways, and the horizon are normally visible. You can choose a view out the plane's forward windshield or you can look behind, to the left, or to the right of the plane. Figure 4 shows a sample screen display.

You, the pilot, have a choice of flying in easy mode or reality mode. The reality mode adds many complications, such as running out of gas or hitting bad weather. Also available are dusk flight, night flight, moderate weather flight, and the WWI Ace aerial battle game.

▲

Figure 4 *Screen display of Flight Simulator II.*

Box 3   Factors in Analyzing or Designing a Simulation

1. How does the user benefit from the simulation?
2. How valid is the simulation; that is, are important factors realistic?
3. When and how should the simulation be used?
4. What support materials would enhance the simulation?
5. How can the effects of the simulation be evaluated?
6. Can you interrupt the simulation and start again?
7. Does the simulation provide challenge and encourage curiosity and fantasy?
8. What is the overall quality of the simulation?

Box 4   Analysis of *Oregon Trail*

Name of the simulation: Oregon Trail
Subject area: Social studies   Instructional level: Upper elementary

1. ***What is the instructional objective of this simulation?*** This simulation is designed to teach students about applying problem-solving skills in making decisions. It is also designed to promote students' meaningful understanding of the factors (and their interrelationships) involved in the successful completion of a covered-wagon, cross-country journey in the nineteenth century.

2. ***How might this simulation be used?*** It could be used by a whole class or by individuals. It could be a part of a social studies unit in which students are studying America in the 1800s and the lives of the pioneers.

3. ***Can you restart the simulation if headed in a wrong direction?*** The user cannot restart it other than by breaking and rerunning the program.

4. ***With what age level(s) could this simulation be used effectively?*** It would be effective for upper-elementary grades.

5. ***Could this information be conveyed in another form?*** Other possibilities include writing and directing plays, watching films, and reading historical novels. These activities could give the students historical information, but would not give them the problem-solving experiences.

6. ***Does this simulation use probabilistic or deterministic models?*** Both probabilistic and deterministic models are used in this simulation. A basic deterministic model underlies the overall design. Attacks by Indians and diseases are randomly generated.

7. ***Is this a single-step (input/output) or multistep (interactive) simulation?*** It is a multistep simulation; earlier decisions affect the later decisions.

8. ***Is this a zero-sum or non–zero-sum simulation?*** It is not competitive among people, but you either make it to Oregon or die. Hence, in a sense it is both.

9. ***Is this simulation intended for solving problems or training?*** It is intended to teach problem-solving and decision-making skills.

10. ***Identify some of the choices and consequences:***

Choices	Consequences
How much money to spend for provisions	More expensive animals are healthier and travel faster
	Too few clothes lead to freezing in the mountains
	Need some miscellaneous supplies, such as medicine for sickness
	Need some money for on-trail emergencies
Whether to hunt, stop at next fort, or continue	Need to keep adequate food supply and provisions
Indians are ahead: whether to attack, continue, or circle your wagons	If attacked you may lose provisions or be killed

continued

Box 4   Analysis of *Oregon Trail* continued

Choices	Consequences
Whether to eat poorly, moderately, or well	Eating too poorly will lead to ill health: you might die Eating too well may use up your food: you might starve to death

11. ***Are feedback techniques effective? Do they provide motivation?*** The feedback techniques are both effective and motivational. Use of graphics and tables is very helpful.

12. ***Is there feedback on overall performance?*** No overall feedback is given other than your death or completion of the trip.

13. ***How valid is the simulation?*** Some aspects of this simulation might be valid, but a number of factors are not taken into consideration.

14. ***How effective is the use of graphics?*** The map of the trail and progress along the trail are effective, as is the motion of the deer or people across the screen. The aiming and shooting, however, are not properly synchronized.

15. ***What content can be learned from working with this simulation?*** Students learn about pioneer life in the mid-1800s and about decisions that people traveling the Oregon Trail had to make.

16. ***What support materials can enhance the simulation?*** United States maps and books about that period could enhance this simulation.

17. ***How can the effects of the simulation be evaluated?*** The effects of this program can be examined through informal student evaluations: Do they like it? Do they choose to go back and play it on their own? What are they learning from it? Are they developing problem-solving and decision-making skills? Are they getting better at it, thereby demonstrating that they are improving their ability to figure out the underlying model?

18. ***What changes can you suggest to make this simulation more effective?*** Synchronizing different effects in the shooting episodes would make it more effective in motivating youngsters.

19. ***Identify, if you can, an underlying mathematical model for this simulation. What are the key variables? How are their different values treated? Can you identify some assumptions that were made?*** Some of the mathematical models relate to ways in which money is spent and the maintenance of a proper balance of various provisions. Key variables include the amount of money you spend for provisions and your accuracy at shooting. If you refer back to the choices and consequences you've identified, you will see other variations involved.

20. ***What is the overall quality of the simulation?*** The simulation is fairly good. It is an appropriate length and difficulty level for upper-elementary school children, has fairly good graphics, and provides reasonable choices.

When the simulator is started, the plane is on the ground at Chicago's Meigs Field, a small airport located next to Lake Michigan. You can see the John Hancock Building ahead of you as you are facing north. You taxi, take off, climb (watch out . . . don't hit the Hancock Building), glide, turn, descend, and land. Other airports are available; their longitudes, latitudes, and altitudes are taken from factual data. Also prerecorded are sets of information from the New York/Boston, Seattle/Portland, and Los Angeles/San Diego areas.

Instruments important in this simulator include:

- ▶ Airspeed indicator
- ▶ Altitude indicator
- ▶ Altimeter
- ▶ Turn coordinator
- ▶ Heading indicator (directional gyro or gyrocompass)
- ▶ Vertical speed indicator

Keyboard inputs modify the flight controls, yoke, rudder pedals, throttle, flaps, and brakes.

An analysis of *Flight Simulator II* is given in Box 5.

Now that we have analyzed two simulations, we can describe some general principles about the instructional applications of simulations. (Also see Box 2, which lists some instructional applications of simulations.)

Using Simulations for Problem Solving

Many of the strategies for problem solving discussed elsewhere in this book can be applied to the use of simulations. When using a simulation, if you are confronted with a difficult problem, you break it down into simpler problems, isolate and control variables, explore and investigate the various parameters, and try to discover the underlying model that dictates behavior. Simulations can help students coordinate the right- and left-hemisphere functions of their brains. For example, in *Collide,* you can investigate what values can cause a mass to reverse direction after colliding with another mass. You can explore what values will result in both masses going in the same direction after the collision, or one or both masses standing still.

Making Your Own Simulation

The following steps for making your own simulation (not necessarily computerized) have been identified by Reese (1977):

1. Define the problem or situation
2. Decide how students can best experience it
3. Decide what grade or age level will use it
4. Set the teaching objectives
5. Get all the steps clear in your mind
6. Decide what pieces and component parts are needed
7. Decide how to set it up
8. Decide what the rules of play are and how a winner is determined
9. Clarify the debriefing (performance evaluation, feedback)
10. Make a working model
11. Field test the model
12. Revise the model as needed
13. Retest the model if major revisions were made

Box 5   Analysis of *Flight Simulator II*

Name of the simulation: Flight Simulator II
Subject area: Science or mathematics   Instructional level: High school

1. *What is the instructional objective of this simulation?* This simulation is designed to help the user gain skill in flying airplanes. It can also be used to help develop interest in the underlying concepts and principles involved, such as mathematics and science, as well as to enhance spatial abilities and visualization skills.

2. *How might this simulation be used?* The simulation could be used by individuals or groups to develop either of the objectives listed in (1). Content areas include the physics of aerodynamics, the mathematics of angles, the underlying matrices and transformational equations of three-dimensional transformational geometry, and the study of various cloud formations.

3. *Can you restart the simulation if the user is headed in a wrong direction?* Restart techniques are built into the program.

4. *With what age level(s) could this simulation be used effectively?* The program could be used by students over 11 years old.

5. *Could this information be conveyed in another form?* Simulation is the best means to convey this information. Reading a book or listening to lessons about flying would not be as effective. Actual flying is risky for a neophyte and is also expensive.

6. *Does this simulation use probabilistic or deterministic models?* This simulation is deterministic: the underlying mathematics and science models determine the results.

7. *Is this a single-step (input/output) or multistep (interactive) simulation?* This is a multistep simulation.

8. *Is this a zero-sum or non–zero-sum simulation?* Most of the simulation is designed for training, and hence is non-zero sum. The WWI Ace aerial battle game is zero sum.

9. *Is this simulation intended for solving problems or training?* The main intent of the program is to train novice pilots.

10. *Identify some of the choices and consequences:*

Choices	Consequences
Increasing the throttle and raising the elevators	Increases altitude
Banking to the left or right	Turns the plane to the left or right
Lowering flaps	Increases drag and lift
Raising nose of the plane	Avoids a dive
Pulling back the yoke	Pulls nose up; moves to a higher altitude
Pushing yoke away	Pitches nose down

11. *Are feedback techniques effective? Do they provide motivation?* The feedback techniques are very effective and motivational. The use of three-dimensional graphics helps make them exceptional.

12. *Is there feedback on overall performance?* Overall feedback is not given.

continued

Box 5   Analysis of *Flight Simulator II* continued

---

13. ***How valid is the simulation?*** The easy mode does not relate closely to reality, but is needed to help users learn the basic concepts. The reality mode is a more valid simulation.

14. ***How effective is the use of graphics?*** The graphics are effective. They also allow for exploring and demonstrating the interactions between speed, vertical velocity, elevation, and thrust.

15. ***What content can be learned from working with this simulation?*** Concepts with which students can become familiar include:

   ▶ Angles
   ▶ Spatial orientation
   ▶ Altitudes, latitudes, longitudes
   ▶ Geography
   ▶ Weather, including winds, moisture, temperature
   ▶ Clouds and their structure
   ▶ Wind vectors
   ▶ Aspects of navigation, including directional vectors
   ▶ Reading of instruments
   ▶ Reading of maps
   ▶ Changes of perspective
   ▶ Speed, acceleration, deceleration
   ▶ Weight and balance of aircraft
   ▶ Radio communications
   ▶ Axes of motion
   ▶ Physics of lift versus weight, thrust versus drag
   ▶ Lift-equation parameters: using flaps for descent, angle of attack, stalls and stall control

16. ***What support materials can enhance the simulation?*** A manual and maps are included with the program. Federal Aviation Administration materials and aeronautical charts also can be used.

17. ***How can the effects of the simulation be evaluated?*** The best way to evaluate flying skills is to fly a plane; however, this may not be practical. Instead, check students' ability to skillfully manipulate the simulation airplane to various locations, and to land, restart, and return. Informal student evaluation can be used to assess whether the program builds motivation for study of mathematics and science, and whether visualization skills are enhanced.

18. ***What changes can you suggest to make this simulation more effective?*** An audio option would enhance the program. The tracking and practice flight plans could be improved.

19. ***Identify, if you can, an underlying mathematical model for this simulation. What are the key variables? How are their different values treated? Can you identify some assumptions that were made?*** There are many underlying mathematical models involved here. The mathematics underlying aviation in a similar airplane has been built into this program. Considerable mathematics underlies the three-dimensional graphics. The laws of motion built into the simulation are examples of underlying assumptions in this program.

20. ***What is the overall quality of the simulation?*** Many of the aspects of the simulation are exceptional. There are some flaws. The option to track and print flight plans does not work correctly.

Reese also suggests the following guidelines for your own simulation or game:

▶ Do include motivational features
▶ Do look at the weak points as you test it
▶ Do ask yourself what the players' objectives are
▶ Do get class members involved
▶ Don't start with the pieces and try to make a game to fit
▶ Don't ignore the teaching objectives
▶ Don't make it too complicated
▶ Don't write incomplete or unclear directions

Simulation Software for Classroom Use

The following examples of available software demonstrate principles discussed in this chapter.

Decisions-Decisions

Simulation software can provide excellent opportunities for students to learn important concepts in social studies, as well as develop crucial decision-making skills. The *Decisions-Decisions* series of simulations (by Tom Snyder Productions) are intended for full-class discussion and use in decision making. Included in the series are the following set of simulations, ranging widely over social-studies topics: (1) *Television:* Study of Media Ethics, (2) *Immigration:* Maintaining the Open Door, (3) *Urbanization:* The Growth of Cities, (4) *Colonization:* Exploring the New World, (5) *Foreign Policy:* The Burdens of World Power, (6) *The Budget Process:* A Question of Balance, (7) *On the Campaign Trail:* Issues and Image in a Presidential Election, and (8) *The Revolutionary War:* Choosing Sides. Most of the simulations in the series work with one computer in a class; these are appropriate for ages 12 years–adult. The ideal grades are 7–12.

Television *The Study of Media Ethics* involves students in issues involving the media's responsibility. Students make decisions and see the effects of these decisions. Students act as the responsible decision-maker for a snack food company that is planning to underwrite a television show. Students consider the pressure brought to bear by a special-interest group who believe that the television program has excessive violence, and must decide whether to withdraw the financial agreement, edit the program (with the conflict this would cause with the producer), or stand behind the plan to sponsor the program. The simulation draws critical-thinking skills into play. Further, the same decisions can cause different results in different runnings. Thus the simulation is a multi-step, factually accurate one with an underlying probabilistic model. Within the facts, several different outcomes are obtainable with a specific sequence of decisions.

The Budget Process *A Question of Balance* simulates the process of developing a budget bill within the House of Representatives. It incorporates political science, economics, and current events concepts in a "balancing act" in which a budget bill, involving defense spendings, social programs spendings, and tax and inflation concepts, is brought forth. Winning support for the bill is an important consideration. Simulations allow students to see the effects of their manipulating variables one at a time or in combination. They see the effects of their decisions and can try to improve their eventual evaluation of the bill's effectiveness, the chance of it being passed, and the maintenance or improvement of their party's position of power. Again, a probabilistic model is used in a multi-step decision-making model. The simulation contains a concept-development mode with substantial problem-solving and critical-thinking requirements at its core.

Immigration   In using Maintaining the Open Door, students play the role of a president seeking re-election. At issue during the period leading to the primary election is the imminent landing of large numbers of refugees in several port cities. As a nation made of immigrants, to what extent does the United States still need to limit the number of people who want to settle on its banks? As students make critical decisions about the application of immigration policies, the effects achieved within the computer simulation are determined by the history of our immigration laws. The program is, therefore, partially deterministic. Yet multiple outcomes are possible so the simulation is useful for hours of experimentation.

Other simulations   Other simulations in the Decisions-Decisions series are similar. Most have probabilistic decision models, and are multi-step, zero-sum games. Most have a problem-solving goal that requires a substantial understanding of varied social-studies concepts (economics, history, political science, geology, civics, current events, and earth science). The software provides true simulations, with realistic analogies to actual situations; they are highly interactive.

The Other Side

This program (also by Tom Snyder Productions) is a separate simulation for the study of social issues. Ideally played by a small group of people, this dynamic interactive program involves participants in conflict resolution: they are put in competition for limited resources. An ideal way of using these simulations is to have one class or part of a class compete with another class or part of the class. In addition to its competitive spirit, the simulation leads participants to cooperate in building a bridge of peace. The basic goal of the simulation is the development of appropriate strategies for maintaining stable economies, military power and responsibility, and security, in spite of geopolitical and ideological differences. Peaceful coexistence and diplomacy are experienced. Students meet a new learning experience each time they play *The Other Side,* particularly if they switch from one side of the issues to the other side in subsequent games.

GeoWorld

This program uses databases as tools for simulation and problem solving. A highly graphic program shows the globe with accurate longitude and latitude, and placement of countries and resources. The concept of global education plays a part of this simulation. Major resources are critically placed and geologist's tools are available to test for these mineral resources. The program interfaces with AppleWorks, so that data collected from *GeoWorld* can be put into the database, the spreadsheet, or the word processor of AppleWorks. The reverse is also true, as data put into AppleWorks can be used in *GeoWorld.* This simulation is somewhat deterministic and somewhat probabilistic; it can be as multi-step as the exploration designed, and it has tremendous possibilities for open-ended, critical thinking. It incorporates imagery and simulations in a productive manner.

Problem Solving in Math

Problem solving in mathematics at grade levels 5–8 are contained in an "adventure game" simulation (Tom Snyder Productions) in which youngsters search to prove the existence of and find a hidden object. They encounter various sources of information as they meet various informants, who provide clues only if the user answers mathematical puzzles, ranging from simple to more complex problems. Tools are available in the adventure game so that you can abstract data from statements of informants and place them on a clipboard. Computational tools for operating on the data are also provided, and feedback on decisions is given. The graphics of the simulation are partially embellishments and partially embodiments. The simulation is primarily deterministic, as the same sequence of questions are always answered in the same way. This is not a difficulty, however, because students have their own data disk and do not have to repeat the same sequence of search. Imagery development through mapping skills is important to students' keeping track of their progress toward the goal.

Forecast!

Using this program by Mindscape, students (grades three and up) predict the weather; they employ the same methods used by professionals to track storm fronts and chart weather patterns. Five activities include "Weather Forecaster," "Weather Calculator," "Weather Keeper," "Weather Traveller," and "Weather Tracker." "Weather Forecaster" allows students to predict weather according to facts entered into the computer. "Weather Calculator" examines the types of measurement used in forecasting. "Weather Keeper" keeps a daily weather log. "Weather Traveller" offers glimpses of the weather for other parts of the country. "Weather Tracker" follows graphic trails of hurricanes and predicts where they will strike next. The materials include a teacher's guide and backup disk. If it is available, analyze this simulation.

Where in the World Is Carmen Sandiego? and Where in the USA Is Carmen Sandiego?

In their search for Carmen, students (grades seven through nine) follow an exciting trail through the great cities of the world. Adventure, mystery, and academic challenge make these excellent materials (published by Broderbund) for students to use in sharpening their reading comprehension, building a bank of factual information about a wide variety of countries and cultures, and developing their research skills, as they try to nab a notorious gang of thieves specializing in the theft of national treasures. If it is available, analyze this simulation.

Presidential Profiles

As American presidents introduce themselves to your classroom, (grades 5–12), four interactive exercises provide an in-depth study of each president. After students have selected a president, a portrait appears along with information about his political party, years in office, previous occupation, notable achievements, and the significant events that happened during the term(s). Games allow students to apply their knowledge as they identify a president from the provided clues, work with a timeline, or match up different presidents according to common factors. If it is available, analyze this simulation.

Unlocking the Map Code

Rand McNally gets into the educational software business through this package. Six lessons introduce students (grades four through six) to basic map and globe skills, including: "Land and Water Forms," "Interpreting Color and Map Symbols," "Direction," "Location," "Scale," and "Time." After learning about maps, the globe, and the compass, the students apply their knowledge in the "Simulated Flight Plan."

In using this simulation, your navigators fly a plane over mountains and oceans. The package includes colorful maps and graphics, a teacher's guide, and a reproducible student workbook. Analyze this simulation if it is available.

Crosscountry USA

Playing the role of truck drivers, students (grades four and up) travel cross-country. After collecting assigned items, they must arrive at a specified time at their final destination. This requires careful planning so that they take the fastest route and incur minimal expenses. In the process, students learn map reading, economic and political geography, and the country's major resources. The Didatech package includes a student manual, a teacher's guide, backup disk, political map of the United States of America, and 10 consumable maps for course-plotting. Class packs are available. If it is available, analyze this simulation.

Heart Lab

This Educational Activity simulation of a functioning human heart demonstrates various parts and functions of the heart: it shows the pumping action and traces the blood flow through the arteries, veins, and chambers. The package includes several items: a tutorial viewing the various vessels and chambers; a drill in which the student identifies the specific parts of the heart as shown by the computer; and a pulse-simulation exercise, in which the students enter their own pulse rates before and after exercise and observe visual evidence of varying pulse rates in the heart's action. If it is available, analyze this simulation.

Simulation Construction Kit

This program (Hartley's Courseware) allows you or your students (grades seven and up) to construct a simulation fairly easily, without having to do a lot of the programming. The program could be particularly useful for social studies. It provides only a limited use of variables, so its use for mathematics or science is limited, but programming in a usual programming language might be more useful for simulations that are heavily related to mathematics. This set comes with four disks, including a master disk and backup, a tutorial, and a sample simulation on ecological features of Big Trout National Park. In the program, building a construction involves six types of activities: writing text or formulas, inputting, branching, making graphics (with a nice graphics editor for static scenes), scoring, and ending. As they construct a simulation, students learn how to

1. Research the topic
2. Identify decisions and events
3. Determine a scoring system
4. Create a flow chart
5. Create the pictures
6. Enter the screens
7. Test and edit the simulation

The teacher's manual documents steps that students used in constructing the sample simulation. To see how the sample situation was put together, you or your students can use the editor to examine each frame of it. The documentation includes blackline masters of instructions for constructing and entering the simulation, so that the instructions can be copied for distribution to students. This kit basically takes care of much of the mechanics of the programming, but you or your students still need to perform the research and analysis needed to build a good thoughtful simulation. This is a nice tool.

▶ ▲ ◀ ▼ ▶ ▲ ◀ ▼ ▶ ▲ ◀ ▼ ▶ ▲ ◀ ▼ ▶ ▲ ◀ ▼ ▶ ▲

Summary

This chapter examined the role of simulation—its characteristics and uses. While they teach specific content, simulations can help students develop visualization and problem-solving processes. We discussed deterministic versus probabilistic, single-step versus multistep, and zero-sum versus non–zero-sum models, and examined whether the programs are used for solving problems or training. Two simulations were examined in depth. Simulations offer much potential for classroom uses. They can be used as a part of a curriculum unit; numerous supplementary materials can be included.

Software discussed in this chapter:

Hammurabi
Rocky's Boots
Oregon Trail
Pollute
Collide
Micro-dynamo
Flight Simulator II
Television
The Budget Process
Immigration
The Other Side
Problem Solving in Math

GeoWorld
Forecast!
Where in the World is Carmen Sandiego?
Where in the USA is Carmen Sandiego?
Presidential Profiles
Unlocking the Map Code
Crosscountry USA
Heart Lab
Simulation Construction Kit

Important Terms

Decision making
Deterministic model
Game
Multistep simulation
Non–zero-sum game
Probabilistic model

Simulation
Single-step simulation
Underlying model
Working analogy
Zero-sum game

Exercises

1. Classify each of the following as a simulation or a game:
    a. Basketball
    b. Chess
    c. "Monopoly"
    d. Hopscotch
    e. "Clue"
    f. "Life"
    g. Tennis
    h. Football
    i. *Space Invaders*
    j. *Pacman*

2. Which of the items in (1) are probabilistic? Deterministic? Give six other examples each of probabilistic and deterministic games or simulations.

3. Which of the items in (1) are single step? Multistep? Give six other examples of each.

4. Which of the items in (1) are zero sum? Non-zero sum? Give six other examples of each.

5. Analyze three commercially available simulations using the "Analysis of a Simulation" form at the end of this chapter. (You'll also find this form in a text file on the *Applications Disk.* If you have a word processor that uses text files, you may be able to use this form; change a few codings, if necessary, to match your word processor's system.)

References

Cruickshank, D. R. (1971). *Simulation as an instructional alternative in teacher preparation.* Stanford, CA: ERIC Clearinghouse on Teacher Education.

Evans, G. W., II, Wallace, G. F., & Sutherland, G. L. (1967). *Simulation using digital computers.* Englewood Cliffs, NJ: Prentice-Hall.

Julien, D. (1986). Adventure games as a continuing education exercise. *Library Software Review, 5*(1), 16–20.

McNergney, R., & Henson, S. (1985). Assessing professional decision-making abilities. *Educational Communication and Technology, 33*(3), 179–183.

Reese, J. (1977). *Simulation games and learning activities kit for the elementary school.* West Nyack, NY: Parker.

Roberts, N., Anderson, D. F., Deal, R. M., Garet, M. S., & Shaffer, W. A. (1983). *Introduction to computer simulation: The system dynamics approach.* Reading, MA: Addison-Wesley.

Tamaschiro, R. T. (1985). Build your own computer simulations. *The Computing Teacher, 13,* 36–42.

Vockell, E. L., & Rivers, R. H. (1984). *Computerized science simulations stimulus to generalized problem solving capabilities.* A paper presented at the Annual Convention of the American Education Research Association, New Orleans. ERIC ED 253 397.

Zuckerman, D. W., & Horn, R. E. (1970). *The guide to simulation games for education and training.* Cambridge, MA: Information Resources.

Analysis of a Simulation Form

Name of the simulation: _____

Subject area: _____   Instructional level: _____

1. *What is the instructional objective of this simulation?*

2. *How might this simulation be used?*

3. *Can you restart the simulation if you are headed in a wrong direction?*

4. *With what age level(s) could this simulation be used effectively?*

5. *Could this information be conveyed in another form?*

6. *Which does this simulation use, probabilistic or deterministic models?*

7. *Is this a single-step (input/output), or multistep (interactive) simulation?*

8. *Is this a zero-sum, or non–zero-sum simulation?*

9. *Is this simulation intended for solving problems, or training?*

10. *Identify some of the choices and consequences:*

    Choices   **Consequences**

continued

Analysis of a Simulation Form *continued*

11.   *Are feedback techniques effective? Do they provide motivation?*

12.   *Is there feedback on overall performance?*

13.   *How valid is the simulation?*

14.   *How effective is the use of graphics?*

15.   *What content can be learned from work with this simulation?*

16.   *What support materials can enhance the simulation?*

17.   *How can the effects of the simulation be evaluated?*

18.   *What changes can you suggest to make this simulation more effective?*

19.   *Identify, if you can, an underlying mathematical model for this simulation. What are the key variables? How are their different values treated? Can you identify some assumptions made?*

20.   *What is the overall quality of the simulation?*

Chapter 12

Tutorial Programs

▶ ▲ ◀ ▼ ▶ ▲ ◀ ▼ ▶ ▲ ◀ ▼ ▶ ▲ ◀ ▼ ▶ ▲ ◀ ▼ ▶ ▲

Objectives

- ▶ Describe the features of a tutorial
- ▶ Identify the components of effective instructional design
- ▶ To examine a tutorial program, apply components of instructional design
- ▶ Apply teaching/learning theory to tutorial design

Tutorial software teaches concepts and principles. Tutorial instruction is personal and interactive. Tutorials can be used to teach generalizations, to use prescriptions to develop skills, and to develop visualization, imagery, and problem solving.

We will examine three programs: *Sentences, Tenses,* and *Measurement.* If you have access to these programs, look at them to see how they perform.

Sentences was discussed in our examination of visualization and conceptual development. Concepts that could be learned from this program include those of *sentence, adjective, direct object,* and *action verbs.* Figure 1 shows how *Sentences* responds to several constructions. *Tenses* teaches past tense, present tense, future tense, and associated terms such as *yesterday, today,* and *tomorrow.* Figure 2 shows an instructional sequence.

Measurement demonstrates uses of scales and verniers. Prescriptions are given for finding complex lengths, combining units, and reading verniers. Figure 3 shows samples of displays.

Characterizing a Tutorial

The distinguishing characteristic of a *tutorial* is that it instructs—that is, it teaches new ideas. The word **tutor** implies a private teacher; it connotes a close, individual relationship between teacher and learner, as in the dialectic teaching of Socrates. In the simplistic form of tutorial programming, the learner is provided ideas, asked brief-answer questions about the ideas, and told whether each answer was right or wrong. More complex, ad hoc frame-oriented tutorial forms have also developed. In these, the author of the program attempts to anticipate all possible wrong responses and provide appropriate corrective feedback.

251

Type some words to make a sentence such as,

"The boy runs to the cat."

After you've made your sentence, press NEXT.

to	from	over	the
house	rabbit	car	cat
girl	boy	dog	tree
carries	runs	jumps	walks

a

Help available

The car rabbit carries the cat to the tree. no
         ******

b   Sorry, I do not understand that.

Boy walks dog. no
***   ***

c   Sorry, I do not understand that.

d   The girl carries the dog house to the car. ok

e   The girl carries the dog house from the car. ok

▲

Figure 1 Sample displays from Sentences show (a) directions. (b) The program does not understand the sentence. (c) The sentence is incomplete. Reversible actions are demonstrated in (d) "to the car" and (e) "from the car."

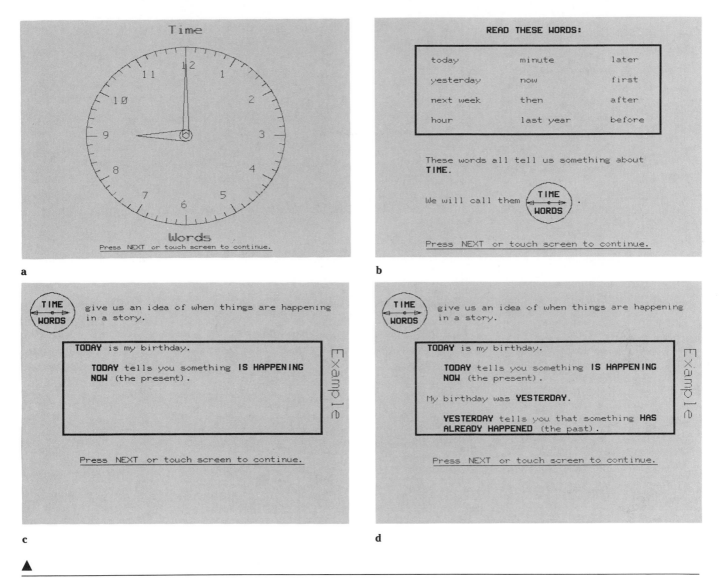

Figure 2 *Screen displays of Tenses show the sequence of instruction.*

In Intelligent Computer-Assisted Instruction, **ICAI,** a relational database of knowledge is typically part of the tutorial. **Expert systems** are generated via databases that apply experts' approach to a topic. Such systems should perform above the level of an existing human expert system. Applying rules of inference to the database of relational information, the program can add inferred information to the database. Using this information, its knowledge of the learner's interests, and the learner's patterns of responses to problems posed, a tutorial dialogue is led by the computer. Through the use of a dynamic database, students can actively control the gathering of information, try ideas, and explore learning, as if they were using an **intelligent library.** ICAI emphasizes learner control and databases that accept new information. Because it can construct a model of the student's knowledge, it can be cognitively more sophisticated than a program based on a textbook. Diagnosis can thus be a very effective part of tutorials.

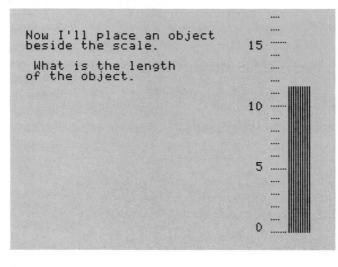

Figure 3 *Screen displays from Measurement.*

Tutorials are designed to teach concepts and principles. The term **concept** here means a word and all of its associations, such as examples, nonexamples, characterization, and definitions. **Principles** are either prescriptions or generalizations that are true. An example of a generalization is, "A set of words does not create a picture of action in *Sentences* unless it contains a noun, a transitive verb, and a direct object." **Prescriptions** give step-by-step directions for a task—for example, "In order to use a vernier caliper to find the length of an object, first use the larger scale to determine the length, then use the smaller scale, then add the two numbers together."

Tutorials can also teach processes, such as problem solving and visualization; they allow students to control the sequencing and opportunities for branching, in problem solving and visualization experiences. Developing these processes is at least as important as developing concepts, principles, and skills.

Examining Teaching/Learning Theory Relevant to Tutorials

The examination of learning theories from several orientations can help us understand various approaches to instructional tutorials. A learning theory should carefully model the way the human mind learns. However, each learning theory is only a simplified model, with all of its imperfections. A *Gestalt* theory would focus on large goals, and applications would provide experiences that would lead to flashes of insight. A *Skinnerean* model would ask questions in small steps with the goal of maintaining a low error rate, as used in the programmed-learning systems of the 1960s.

A particular teaching/learning theory is often selected because it is the most convenient one. It is generally easier to lead a learner to a goal; it is usually easier to tell a student an answer that he or she does not know than otherwise. But these methods do not necessarily serve the best interests of the learner. To give students answers, rather than to help them learn how to search for their own answers, can deprive them of meaningful learning. Instructional strategies should be designed to help develop both the student's thinking processes and her or his ability to learn how to learn. Bruner (1966) commented, "The tutor must correct the learner in a fashion that eventually makes it possible for the learner to take over the corrective function himself" (p. 53).

Gagné (1977) identified the following types of learning, which suggest several factors to consider as software is evaluated and constructed:

1. *Signal learning:* making a general, diffuse response to a signal
2. *Stimulus–response learning:* acquiring a precise response to a discriminated stimulus
3. *Chaining:* acquiring a chain of two or more stimulus–response connections
4. *Verbal association:* learning chains that are verbal
5. *Discrimination learning:* learning to make different identifying responses to many different stimuli that resemble each other in physical appearance
6. *Concept learning:* acquiring the capability to make a common response to a class of stimuli that differ from each other in some attribute(s)
7. *Rule learning:* responding to a class of stimuli with a class of performances
8. *Problem solving:* learning that requires thinking

Piaget (1969) has investigated children's thinking patterns. From these observations, he has deduced a number of principles. He identified the following set of development processes:

1. Experience
2. Social communication
3. Self-regulation
4. Maturation

Although **maturation** is out of the control of educators, the other features are within their control. An educational environment can allow active *experience* both off-machine and on-machine, the opportunity to discuss and refine ideas through **social communication,** and the setting for **self-regulation** or self-control over the learning process. Thus, Piagetian precepts relating to learning activities could provide guidance in the interface of computer activities with other learning experiences, so that when the student matures he or she has a framework to use in achieving tasks.

Refinements of Piaget's theory are now expressed in a *constructivist theory*, whose basic thesis is that students must construct their own knowledge. Forman and Pufall (1988) identify the following properties of constructivism:

1. Epistemic conflict
2. Self-reflection
3. Self-regulation

A conflict occurs, such as new knowledge that is not consistent with already known knowledge. Hence, to bring about a resolution, learning occurs that involves a reorganization of knowledge. Reflection is a means to explicitly construct or transform the learner's representation of reality. The restructuring needs to occur through self-regulation.

Not all people learn in the same way; no single theory applies to all people. Learning how to learn may be more important than specific content.

Another theory is that the question is not "How do people learn?" but rather "How do expert teachers teach?" Categories of teaching, such as using examples and nonexamples in the teaching of concepts, have been generated from observations of successful teachers. Such categories can be helpful in designing tutorials. Awareness of these categories can help students learn how to learn.

Learning/Teaching Theory in Instructional Design

Components of instructional design include the definition of objectives, motivation, prerequisite knowledge, instructional strategies, structure of the content or discipline, and evaluation. We will examine each of these.

Identifying Objectives

Just as in any other learning environment, the instructional objectives of computerized teaching state the expected outcomes of learning. For example, "use some words to make a sentence," "use the proper tense of words," or "find lengths of objects" are objectives indicating expected outcomes. Most of the reasons for using such objectives apply in computer-related education (both learning about computers and using computers to learn other subjects) just as in any other educational setting. Techniques for structuring sets of objectives and creating hierarchies of objectives apply equally. However, different objectives may be accomplished in an environment in which computers are available. Also, alternate means of accomplishing all objectives of the curriculum may be suggested. One approach is to develop many detailed, short-range objectives; another is to emphasize long-range objectives but allow the learner to create subobjectives.

Motivation

Clearly, motivation should not be neglected. In designing or evaluating curriculum materials, ask, "Why should my students want to learn that?" "Will my students see the relevance of the materials?" If you can show your students how a need is being met, they are more likely to be motivated.

Identifying Prerequisite Knowledge

Once objectives are structured, sequenced, and written, they provide a guide for the sequencing of instruction. For example, before exploring the meaning of a sentence in *Sentences,* a child should know what the individual terms—such as "house," "cat," "girl," "boy," or "walks"—mean. Before learning about scales in *Measurement,* the student should be able to estimate lengths.

In identifying the prerequisite knowledge of a specific objective or set of objectives, you should analyze the objective's content, developmental level, and imagery prerequisites. Ideally, tutorial software can contain experiences and learning patterns consistent with Piagetian ideals.

Analyzing Objectives

Tutorials can structure the learning sequence, and they can be tools for self-regulation in learning. For example, *Sentences* provides considerable opportunity for self-regulation. In using *Measurement,* the user can choose between two different experiences: learning concepts or principles, and practicing.

A behaviorist approach to the preparation of tutorial instruction would be,

1. Determine the terminal task
2. Analyze the task to determine the principles necessary (appropriate) to the resolution of the task
3. Determine the concepts that constitute the principles
4. Specify the associations necessary for building the concepts through tight sequences

This analysis provides a sequence through which the learner progresses to achieve the terminal task. Tutorials can both instruct and monitor.

However, laying out the content in such a thoroughly digested fashion is considered by some to be "programming the student." It might tend to reduce self-regulation and, to some extent, social communication. Instead, a tutorial can allow the user to design the structure with which the task is achieved. In this approach, the learner's options might include the following:

1. Simulation or imagery-developing experiences
2. "Helps" after setting and working on a subgoal
3. Ways of developing concepts and principles identified by the learner (student's construction of knowledge)
4. Alternatives that verify the solution

Thus, some teaching/learning theories suggest that exploration and responsibility for learning rest with the learner. Computer tutorials are particularly suited to self-pacing and personalized structuring, if the tutorials are menu-driven and give the student options for structuring his or her learning.

In some ways, the controversy involves the extent of user control versus the extent to which a lockstep approach to learning is used. Courseware that incorporates each of these learning theories might be developed. The advantage of tutorials is that the tools are now available for individual discovery; the factor of the *time it takes to construct knowledge* may be less an issue when users have more control. Also remember that the task analysis of processes, visualization, and problem solving are right-hemisphere processes and hence are nonlinear; thus, they can only take on meaning for students where the students put the knowledge together for themselves.

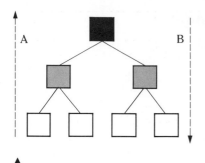

Figure 4 *Diagram of an analysis of tasks, showing two ways in which instruction can be sequenced. In A, sequencing and tasks can be chosen by the teacher to fit with a particular instructional goal; the alternative approach B is to allow the student to select the type and sequence of tasks.*

Instructional Strategies and Sequencing

Teaching/learning theories provide a variety of strategies for instruction. Figure 4 shows how task analysis can indicate different ways in which curricula can be sequenced.

In approach *A,* the type and sequence of learning activities are a smooth, uphill pattern: the teacher provides them and the learner follows them. In approach *B,* the activities and their sequencing are the learner's own choice, or the learner's choice as guided by the teacher. The goals differ. Approach *A* is directed at teaching specific content; approach *B* seeks to develop a set of processes related to the attainment and use of knowledge. Hence, some consistency between goal and method is seen; the latter can allow for the development of both content knowledge and processes.

The organization of content might vary from discipline to discipline. Some areas are suited to generalized instructional strategies; others can require learning that is content-specific. The strategies used in learning a language can vary considerably from those used in learning number and space concepts. This variance should be considered as instructional strategies are analyzed.

Evaluation

The evaluation of curriculum materials should be based on the objectives. Were the objectives achieved? Ways of measuring this achievement could be included in the instructional materials. Another important part of evaluation is determining whether the students want to use the materials. If appropriate motivation has been provided, the students should be interested in using the materials.

Knowledge and Process in Tutorials

Knowledge and *process* differ in form and acquisition method. Learning theory dictates the approach to learning that should be used for each. If acquiring knowledge is the goal, the focus frequently is on the concepts and principles. Principles are frequently taught in step-by-step procedures that use prescriptions to develop skills. Processes, on the other hand, include imagery development and problem solving. In addition, **algorithm production**—the act of forming a generalization—is a process.

Teaching Strategies

Concepts, skills, principles, and problem-solving processes are different types of knowledge. Thus, different strategies for learning and teaching them are appropriate. Being aware of different types of actions, or moves, and strategies will help the students develop learning strategies while they are learning content.

Concepts

One way to view a *concept* is as a word or phrase with all the appropriate associations of that word or phrase. For example, "noun" and its associations (such as "the name of a person, place, or thing," and "predicate noun") constitute the concept called *noun.*

Different types of concepts are identifiable. Right-hemisphere development may be involved in the thinker's ability to visualize and change a concept from one state

---

Box 1   Moves Used in Teaching Concepts

---

1. **Exemplifying** the concept (examples, nonexamples, and examples with explanations)
2. **Classifying** the concept (telling the class of concepts to which this concept belongs)
3. **Analyzing** the concept, by stating one or more subsets of the reference set
4. **Defining** the term that denotes the concept (describing the concept in equivalent terms)

---

to another. In other times, the left hemisphere plays a greater role, such as in discriminating between examples and nonexamples, defining, and characterizing. Any particular concept's relationship to right-hemisphere and left-hemisphere functions is inherent in the concept. Consider the following categories of concepts:

1. Concepts with static references, such as square, triangle, chair, noun, constitution, game, and ledger
2. Concepts with dynamic references, such as addition, going to/going from, velocity, defending, outlining, and planning
3. Concepts with value judgments, such as bad, good, just, unjust

Visualization of time and motion, so vital to daily life, is difficult to capture in a static model. (Hence, it is difficult to capture on a printed page.) Dynamic graphics allow the user to experience movement and the simulation of the passage of time.

Another view of *concept* is the associated models or sets of objects for which an *action* can be performed that will result in a particular outcome. The set of objects denoted by the concept is called the **reference set** of the concept. For example, the reference set of the concept *noun* is the set of all nouns.

This view suggests ways in which concepts can be taught; certain actions (**moves**) can be used to help students acquire a concept. They are shown in Box 1.

Providing examples and explaining why they are **examples** (or **nonexamples**) is a concrete way of teaching a concept. By contrast, stating the definition is *relatively abstract*. A **strategy** for teaching a concept is a sequence of actions or moves. For example, *computer program* might be a difficult concept for a person beginning to learn about computing. Seeing some examples (possibly in different languages) and talking about types of programs might make the concept easier to grasp.

Principles

Statements that can be judged to be true or false are generalizations. A *principle* here is a true generalization or a prescription. For example, "In order to get some action on the screen in *Sentences,* an object or noun, an action word or verb, and another object or direct object are needed" is a principle.

Because principles differ in form and substance from concepts, it is necessary to teach them differently. Principles *contain* concepts. The principle in our example contains the concepts *noun* and *verb*. Before you can grasp and use the principle, you must master these concepts. This does not mean that the concepts must be taught *before* the principle; they must be taught *with* the principle. Learning ability involves knowing what you need to know and when and how to learn it. Good tutorial software should allow the user to branch between locations so that additional experiences and explicit discussions of the concepts can be found.

What are the logical moves available for teaching a principle? Reexamine the generalization: "The total number of degrees of rotation of a closed turtle path is

---

Box 2   Moves Used in Teaching Principles

1. **Motivation** to learn the principle
2. **Assertion** by the teacher or the learner
3. **Instantiation** by providing examples
4. **Interpretation** by paraphrasing or developing constituent concepts
5. **Justification** through deductive or inductive reasoning
6. **Application** of the principle
7. **Counterexample** showing an instance in which a generalization is false

---

a multiple of 360 degrees." This is a statement; it contains concepts (*total number of degrees, closed turtle path,* and *multiple of 360 degrees*); it can be judged true or false. Examine the strategies we used in teaching this generalization in Chapter 2.

Box 2 illustrates actions and statements that are important to learning and teaching principles. The moves may be sequenced to create either **inductive** or **deductive** teaching strategies. For example, studying several instances of a principle, so that a pattern is identified and extended, is a form of discovery or inductive strategy. The extent to which the instances are provided or are learner-generated is indicative of the degree of guidance in the discovery. Deductive strategies, by contrast, typically begin with an assertion move (the principle is stated); the principle is justified or some applications of the principle are presented.

Note that these moves can be used to teach principles, to evaluate understanding of the principles, or to organize thought about principles. Principles frequently are converted into algorithms used for skill development. Having students learn to create (discover) principles, rather than teaching students to apply them, might be more important. For example, the essence of programming is writing (developing) the principle that is the crux of the program, so having students learn how to find that principle is the most important part of teaching programming.

Target Tasks

Consistent with the "principles" approach to constructing learning is the posing of target tasks. To initiate learning, a **target task** that presents a challenge is posed. If the learner successfully completes the challenge, no simpler task is provided. If not, a related, simpler task is provided or is developed by the learner. Thus, in a target-task approach to tutorials, the instructional sequences are employed only for those who need them.

Patterns are a main source of principles. Demonstrating the analysis of patterns and the derivation of principles teaches generalizing. Instantiation moves can lead to assertions: the learner must discover the generalization. In a guided discovery tutorial, instances of a rule are provided and the learner creates the generalization. The learner may be allowed to choose the degree of guidance. *Rocky's Boots* and *Sentences* allow the learners to choose whether or not they will practice, at many junctures. However, the practice provided is not necessarily patterned. Each learner must organize the experiences into patterns by her- or himself.

Skills

Another form of knowledge is that of skills. **Skills** typically apply to procedures followed to a conclusion; that is, they follow prescriptions. They tend to be algorithms: that is, step-by-step procedures that solve all exercises of a certain type.

Concepts, as we are viewing them, are sets of words and associations. In contrast, skills are procedures that are practiced to develop speed and accuracy.

When they are broken down into step-by-step processes, principles may suggest skills; however, principles contain more information about a task and less about how to perform it. Drill and practice programs are used more for teaching skills, whereas the functions of tutorials are more consistent with the teaching of concepts and generalizations. A well-integrated learning package ties these forms of learning into a linked sequence of knowledge acquisition.

Problem Solving

Typically, high-level use of knowledge is involved in problem solving. Problem solving includes the development of some process that achieves a goal. Problem solving differs from other knowledge forms. It involves the production of novel approaches to challenging situations; the drill and practice needed for the development of skills are not appropriate. Although concepts and principles are important in their own right and are crucial to problem solving, they do not alone represent problem solving. Learning the processes of problem solving is an important extension of concepts and principles, that may also add meaning to those concepts and principles.

Visualization

Tutorials should provide for the visualization of concepts and principles; the principles for the selection and use of visualization materials (discussed in Chapter 10) should be followed.

Essential Features of Tutorial Software

Tutorials are personalized and private. Successful tutorials can branch to accommodate different learners. Thus, for example, if one learner has developed a concept, that learner interacts with materials developing principles involving that concept. Another learner who has not yet developed the concept interacts further with materials involving the concept.

Branching

Suppose a learner has difficulty with an abstract idea. A tutorial that contains adequate branching would provide some concrete experiences, to build the basis on which the abstraction could be developed. Branching allows the user to select the appropriate means of learning, including self-pacing, self-regulation, and inductive or deductive learning strategies. Proper remediation loops, possibly a part of branching under machine or user control, provide a means by which holes in the knowledge base can be filled. The goal should be for the learner to select and control remediation. Guidance provided by corrective feedback includes computer-provided corrections to errors, remediation, and a means for self-evaluation.

Learning Styles

As concepts are developed and principles mastered, new ideas are best introduced at the learner's own pace. Most traditional media cannot adjust to different styles of learning, but current technology can. Although the most compatible learning style can be used alone, it is more valuable to use the compatible learning style as a bridge to less effective learning styles.

As you analyze tutorials, it is important to consider your students' learning styles. One classification of learning styles is **visual** versus **verbal.** Those whose strengths lie in visualizing and using visual skills may employ visual means to learn to reason verbally (and vice versa). For these students, the visual tool first is used, then it is gradually withdrawn as skill in verbal reasoning is developed.

Another classification of learning styles is reflective versus impulsive learning. The **reflective** learner gains an overview of the content to be learned, then learns each part individually, and then goes back to reexamine the overview and to study the coordination of the whole with its parts. The **impulsive** learner, on the other hand, works on the materials as they are presented and does not study the relationship of the parts to the whole. The reflective learner prefers freedom to control his or her learning, while the impulsive learner prefers that sequencing be already arranged in the most efficient way for learning.

User Controlled versus Sequenced Programs

Because tutorials are intended to expand the knowledge base, self-pacing and self-regulation are appropriate features. Allowing the user to reread a passage, review a graphic representation, and in general control the learning environment is desirable. In contrast, sequenced programs that use timed responses are appropriate for drill and practice.

Helps and Hints

There is a variety of helps and hints in software. Some of the powerful hint techniques were shown in Chapter 4. Strategies are a sequenced set of activities for learning, chosen by the teacher or program designer. These activities may include teaching moves, trial and error techniques, the use of models, and the like. (Models, important to problem solving and imagery development, are representations (frequently concrete) of situations.) Helps and hints are means toward developing strategies or parts of strategies.

Tutorials' Role in Well-Rounded Learning

A well-designed lesson integrates the most viable learning materials. The computer tutorial is but one of the possible components in the total design of the curriculum. Recall how we walked through the turtle path (Chapter 1). Experiences should flow from (1) interacting with physical materials to (2) interacting with computer materials to (3) abstracting the concepts and principles. In this sequence, experiences are the initiation point for social interaction and communication. Frequently, being able to discuss a topic (that is, to put knowledge into words), helps one to solidify and organize information for long-term storage.

Physical activity can make abstract concepts more concrete and relevant. Also, conceptual work with cognitive information is needed before, during, and after computer tutorials. Off-machine preparation and discussion can be more valuable than on-machine experiences. Software with good documentation often includes activities that are designed to correlate with the computer instruction.

Applications to Available Software

Some tutorials are being developed by WICAT and field-tested and marketed by IBM. These companies are working to develop comprehensive mathematics and language-education programs for grades 1–12. First, a careful analysis identifies the various content levels. Development and field testing of the materials then follows. In some cases rather sophisticated software evolves; for example, a proof-checker and an algebra toolkit utilities program (including a symbol manipulator and graphics plotter) have been developed. There are also reading comprehension and writing materials. Throughout these materials, a similar record keeping, pre- and post-testing materials, helps, and support printed materials are used to assist the teacher to incorporate the materials into his or her instruction.

Punctuation

Students can start with either the *Editor's Handbook* or *Punctuation Press.* The presentations in *Editor's Handbook* follow this format: rule or principle, example, three practice problems, then a choice of either more practice of that rule or continuation to a new rule. Examples of principles are:

1.   Start the names of days and months with a capital letter.
2.   Start the names of holidays and other special days with a capital letter.
3.   In a list of three or more things, separate the words with a comma (,).
4.   Put a comma (,) after the greeting and the closing in a friendly letter.

In using *Punctuation Press,* the student chooses between being a proofreader of capitals, proofreader of punctuation, copy editor, associate editor, or managing editor for a newspaper. Through the levels, the required skills become increasingly complex and an increasing number of rules must be correctly applied.

The initial goal is a properly edited article. An incorrectly edited article is not published. If the student only partially edits the article correctly, it is used on an interior page of the newspaper, with no graphic. If the article is correctly edited, it is placed on the front page of the newspaper and is given an accompanying graphic. The student can design the graphic from among various components of a face. Graphics, in this case, are strictly embellishments and not embodiments.

The materials allow for a lot of user control. As students go through the *Editor's Handbook* they can skip from rule to rule, if they choose. Or they can follow the standard form: rule, example, practice. They can choose the level of difficulty for editing, so that they can go back to an easier level or progress to a more difficult level as their needs dictate. By using such materials, students can learn how to regulate their own learning.

Vocabulary

These materials allow students to make words: they combine prefixes or suffixes with stem words. After completing a matrix of prefixes/suffixes and stem words, they determine if the results are real words and, reasoning by analogy, choose definitions from a list of possibilities. In the second part of each lesson, the students select a word from the given matrix to complete a sentence with a missing word. Crossword puzzles are used in the review exercises. In addition, the materials use stories to introduce new words so that students can learn their meanings from the context.

Combining Sentences

These materials reveal various principles for the combining of sentences, use dynamic visual displays to illustrate ways in which the principles can be applied to various sentences, and then give considerable practice in applying the principles. The students first apply the principles one by one, then synthesize and apply complex principles. An example of an application of these principles is the *GhostWriters Gallery*. Students choose paths as they read through a story, combine sentences at chosen points, and get a picture representative of the story at the end.

Reading for Meaning

These materials use two programs: *Reading More Than Words* and *Reading to Get Pictures*. In using the *Reading More Than Words* portion, students read stories and answer questions at the end. They then identify key words (at least two and no more than seven) that helped them understand the story. In using the *Reading to Get Pictures* portion, students first see four pictures; then they see one line of a story and indicate whether each of the four pictures could apply to that line. Another line is then shown, and again they indicate whether each of the four pictures applies to the developing story; and so on. As they are shown the story, they are to weed out inappropriate pictures, so that finally only one appropriate one remains. They also identify key words in the story as they go. These programs help students develop skills in focusing upon the key ideas and connecting mental images and words.

Math Concepts

These materials carefully use graphics to relate concrete models to numerical concepts. Models interweave throughout the materials. They include representations of number blocks, follow-the-dot schemes, pan balances, and linear and area models. Magic gardens also illustrate concepts of the number line. Mathematical concepts of whole numbers, fractions, decimals, and percentages develop around these models. The graphics are embodiments of the models. As mentioned earlier in the chapter, work with concrete materials should precede the use of these computer materials.

The magic garden is a particularly appealing game that weaves throughout the materials. In each game a segment of the number line is shown; it identifies some but not all numerical values and indicates a hole between two known values. The students are to input the numerical value for the hole. After the students guess the value, a hand comes out and plants a seed at the location of the guess. If the location is other than the hole (that is, the guess is incorrect), a leaf comes up from the seed. If the location is the proper coordinates for the hole, a pretty flower comes forth. These materials press the students to deal with much larger numbers, including hundreds of thousands, and more varied numbers, such as integers and decimals. Using the same models, these materials develop more complex mathematics.

Math concepts also includes units on geometry; these use the GeoDraw materials, which students can later encounter in their high-school geometry curriculum. Using GeoDraw, students can plot points, segments, lines, rays, N-gons, angles, circles, midpoints, parallels, and perpendiculars. They also can perform transformations and choose whether to keep or erase the pre-image, or original image, used in the transformation.

Geometry

The *Geometry* materials come in two major parts. One is the tutorial, through which students can move as quickly or as slowly as they want. The second part is the proof checker. This helps students develop skills in writing geometric proofs. A fixed list of axioms, postulates, and theorems are used. Using GeoDraw utilities for their geometric figures, students can make drawings and claim these as part of their proofs. Students can construct proofs in a variety of ways. Each line must supply a correct, logical inference before the student can continue to the next line. Each line consists of three parts: (1) a statement given for the specified figure, (2) a reference, which may be drawn from earlier statements, the given, or the graphic, and (3) the justification. A justification may be the application of an axiom, postulate, definition, or a previously proved theorem. Use of the proof checker clearly requires high-order thinking processes. See Flake (1988) for discussion of effectiveness of these programs with teacher education students.

General Comment

As quality materials continue to be developed and equipment stabilize, tutorial materials can be very useful for schools. They also can be extremely helpful for the general population. We all have learning holes. With the help of such materials, we can continue our education and maintain learning as a lifelong process to meet our ongoing needs. When students are going through school, they do not always feel the need to learn some things that might be critical for their lives. There are many adults whose geometry or reading skills are not up to par. Through the use of such computer materials, adults can still continue to learn and grow. Building a good library of quality materials is therefore critical to students of all ages.

The dichotomy between skills and problem solving is often less than constructive. Some people will not give time to skills because they want to spend all their time on problem solving. Too often, people will not devote time to problem solving because they only want to focus on skills: many people cannot solve problems because they have gotten lost in the skills. A major problem for those who only focus on skills is that their skills might become outdated and, if they have not developed their problem-solving processes, they will not be able to learn new materials and techniques. For example, some students wonder why they should spend a lot of time learning how to do long division, when for under $10 they can buy an electronic calculator that can do it far more accurately and more quickly than they ever could. The answer is that particular skills developed through appropriate conceptual development (as the ability to perform long division) allow the learner to apply the general problem-solving process to the development of new skills.

As software continues to evolve, there will be plenty of room for two approaches: those developing highly creative, imaginative software, as well as those following a more traditional structuring of content. Students need to learn how to work with and develop both problem-solving processes and appropriate skills. The appropriateness of skills will have to be continuously evaluated as technology continues to change our lives.

Summary

This chapter considered the unique characteristics of computer software tutorials, a form of computer-assisted instruction. Several teaching/learning theories were examined so we could see how tutorials can implement their approaches.

Teaching/learning strategies were detailed in Boxes 1 and 2. We described concepts and principles, and related these forms of knowledge to a general overview of expected educational outcomes, including the development of problem solving and skills. The distinctions between types of knowledge suggested differences in the moves that should be used in teaching them; we discussed strategies for teaching concepts or principles. The teaching/learning approach provided direction for the development and evaluation of computer software.

Software discussed in this chapter:

Sentences	*Vocabulary*
Tenses	*Combining Sentences*
Measurement	*Reading for Meaning*
Rocky's Boots	*Math Concepts*
Punctuation	*Geometry*

Important Terms

Algorithm production	ICAI	Problem solving
Analyzing	Impulsive	Reference set
Application	Inductive	Reflective
Assertion	Instantiation	Reflective abstraction
Classifying	Intelligent library	Self-regulation
Concept	Interpretation	Skills
Counterexample	Justification	Social communication
Deductive	Maturation	Strategy
Defining	Motivation	Target task
Examples	Move	Tutor
Exemplifying	Nonexamples	Verbal
Experience	Prescription	Visual
Expert system	Principle	Visualization

Exercises

1. Identify concepts being taught in a tutorial. List the concepts. Select one and specify what moves are used to teach it.

2. In a software program, identify whether concepts are static, dynamic, or value judgments.

3. Select a concept that is not thoroughly developed in a software program. Decide on a strategy for developing the concept and prepare a plan for revising the software to incorporate your strategy.

4. Find examples of principles taught in software.

5. Classify the principles that you identified in (4) by the ways they are being taught: exposition (strictly telling), structured discovery (leading learner to determine the underlying principle), or open-ended discovery.

6. Choose one principle that you identified in (4) and study how it is being taught. List the particular teaching moves sequentially. Are branching, feedback, and learning styles incorporated in the teaching strategy? Explain.

7. Examine an instructional program and identify the type of teaching taking place, according to the types described by Gagné.

References

Barr, A., & Feigenbaum, E. A. (1982). *The handbook of artificial intelligence.* Vol. 2. Los Altos, CA: William Kaufmann.

Bruner, J. (1966). *Toward a theory of instruction.* New York: W. W. Norton.

Cooney, T. J., Davis, E. J., & Henderson, K. B. (1983). *Dynamics of teaching secondary school mathematics.* Prospect Heights, IL: Waveland Press.

Flake, J. L. (1988). Using computers for developing proof skills. A paper presented at the Sixth International Congress on Mathematics Education. Budapest, Hungary.

Florida Beginning Teacher Program. (1983). *Domains of the Florida performance measurement system.* Coalition for the development of a performance evaluation system. Tallahassee, FL: Office of Teacher Education, Certification, and Inservice Staff Development, Florida Department of Education.

Forman, G. & Pufall, P. B. (Eds.). (1988). *Constructivism in the computer age.* Hillsdale, NJ: Lawrence Erlbaum Associates.

Forman, G. & Pufall, P. B. (1988). Constructivism in the computer age: A reconstructive epilogue. In Forman and Pufall (Eds.). *Constructivism in the computer age.* Hillsdale, NJ: Lawrence Erlbaum Associates.

Gagné, R. M. (1977). *The conditions of learning,* 3rd ed. New York: Holt, Rinehart & Winston.

Henderson, K. B. (1963). Research in teaching secondary school mathematics. In *Handbook on research on teaching,* Gage, N. L. (Ed.). Chicago: Rand McNally.

Morine, H., & Morine, G. (1973). *Discovery: A challenge to teachers.* Englewood Cliffs, NJ: Prentice-Hall.

Piaget, J. (1969). *Science of education and the psychology of the child.* New York: Grossman.

Shulman, L. S. (1968). Psychological controversies in the teaching of science and mathematics. *The Science Teacher 35,* 34–38.

Smith, B. O., & Meux, M. O. (1967). *A study of the strategies of teaching.* Urbana, IL: Bureau of Educational Research, College of Education, University of Illinois Press.

Wilkinson, A. C. (1983). *Classroom computers and cognitive science.* New York: Academic Press.

Wills, H. (1970). Generalizations. In *The teaching of secondary school mathematics: The Thirty-third Yearbook of The National Council of Teachers of Mathematics,* Rosskopf, M. (Ed.). Reston, VA: National Council of Teachers of Mathematics.

Chapter 13

The Computer as a Manager

▶ ▲ ◀ ▼ ▶ ▲ ◀ ▼ ▶ ▲ ◀ ▼ ▶ ▲ ◀ ▼ ▶ ▲ ◀ ▼ ▶ ▲ ▶

Objectives

▶ Describe ways in which the computer can be used for management of classroom activities

▶ Describe ways in which the computer can be used for management of administrative tasks

▶ Describe assumptions about learning on which computer-managed instruction is based

▶ Describe the features of a computer-managed instructional system

Most of us think of teachers as persons who work directly with students and facilitate their learning. In addition, however, teachers spend considerable time managing the instructional process. Teachers are responsible for preparing lesson plans; collecting attendance data; developing, administering, and scoring tests; analyzing student-performance data and prescribing the next appropriate instructional activity; completing periodic grade reports; and preparing reports for the central office.

Administrators also keep all sorts of records and need management systems. This chapter explores the use of the computer to do management tasks, including record keeping, other administrative applications, and computer-managed instruction. (See also electronic spreadsheets in Chapter 7.)

Computer-Managed Instruction

In **computer-managed instruction (CMI),** the computer is used to measure student performance, keep records of student progress, and prepare reports; teachers are thus free to spend more time helping students learn. Some programs simply keep track of students' off- and on-machine activities. Others are more extensive. In this section we will first examine the features of the more extensive uses of CMI. Then we will describe how teachers can use available software to help them manage classroom instruction more efficiently.

Underlying Assumptions

Because CMI is more than a collection of testing and record-keeping software, implementing CMI involves more than tacking technology onto an existing instructional program. The use of CMI is best based on two major concepts: **mastery learning** and **individualization.** The following points are adapted from a conceptualization first proposed by Baker (1978) and described more recently by Patterson and Patterson (1983).

Mastery Learning Proponents of mastery learning believe that nearly all children can learn if they are given enough time and provided with appropriate materials and quality instruction. The curriculum is divided into a sequence of measurable learning objectives. Students pursue a particular objective until they demonstrate mastery of it; they then proceed to the next objective in the sequence. The role of the teacher is to identify the objectives, determine an acceptable level of performance, and provide appropriate instruction until the student's performance reaches the mastery level.

In mastery learning, evaluation is criterion-referenced rather than norm-referenced. On a **criterion-referenced test,** a student's performance is compared with an acceptable level of performance. To indicate mastery of a particular objective, students may be expected to answer correctly 70 percent of the items covering that objective. On a **norm-referenced test** a student's performance is compared with the performance of other students. Student scores are usually reported in percentiles. A score in the 70th percentile means that the student performed better than 70 percent of the students in the same group.

Mastery learning does not require equal learning. Among students who attain mastery of a particular objective, many students extend their learning far beyond the minimum performance level defined as mastery. Mastery learning does not put a ceiling on what students can accomplish, but some students confuse the mastery of minimum standards with total mastery.

Individualization There are three characteristics of an individualized instructional program. The first is that students have the opportunity to learn at their own rates but cannot omit or repeat any part of the curriculum. Second, the instructional methods can differ for different students, depending on their individual learning styles and interests. Third, the curriculum can be individually tailored to meet a student's needs and goals. In practice, however, most individualized instructional programs allow students to proceed at their own pace through a common curriculum. Few programs tailor the curriculum to meet the individual needs of a student.

Mastery learning and individualization may exist independently of the other, and neither instructional program requires computerized management. However, the characteristics of mastery learning and individualization may provide a philosophical basis for the implementation of CMI.

Characteristics of a CMI System

Many instructional management systems, whether they are computerized or not, are based on the pretest-diagnosis-prescription-instruction-posttest model. The steps of this model are shown in Box 1. In this model, testing is seen as a support that teachers can use in making decisions about the appropriate instruction. The results of diagnostic testing are used by the teacher to determine each student's objectives (and perhaps those materials best suited to the student's learning style). The teacher analyzes the posttest results to determine if an objective has been mastered. Should subsequent instruction focus on the same objective but use different strategies, or is the student ready to move on to new material?

An instructional management system does not necessarily need to be computerized. In fact, many CMI projects have begun as individualization programs in which student performance data are recorded manually on printed forms or on wall charts. Frequently however, the record-keeping component of the program becomes too burdensome for the teachers. They find that they are spending more time administering and scoring tests than they are helping students learn. Faced with such a situation, some schools give up their individualized program, others hire aides to assist with the record keeping, and others use the computer to simplify the management tasks.

In general, there are three ways in which the computer can be used to manage the instructional process. At the minimum, the computer is used to keep records of students' progress. Students do most of their work with traditional instructional materials, except that students write their pre- and posttest responses on optical scanning sheets that are fed into a scanner for scoring. Then the data are transmitted to the computer for analysis and storage. Summary statistics for the whole class, as well as individual student records, can be printed out as needed—for parent-teacher conferences, reports to the central office, or the preparation of individual education plans and report cards.

The computer can also be used to generate and administer the pre- and posttests. The student can actually take the test on the computer. The computer can be programmed to analyze the students's response and, according to that analysis, select the next question. Students do not have to suffer through a test above their ability. The number of questions and the time spent in testing are minimized. In more sophisticated CMI systems, the computer can be programmed to prescribe instruction according to test results. For example, in using a computer-managed reading program, the student may be asked to read a specific story in the reading textbook and return to the computer to take a comprehension test.

Finally, the computer can be used to provide the instruction as well as to manage it. For example, the management component of the program can be linked to a tutorial program so that the level of each student's placement within the tutorial depends on previous test results. The tutorial is interactive, provides feedback about whether the student's answers are correct, and can branch to higher or lower levels of difficulty depending on the student's responses through *adaptive testing*.

In many CMI systems, however, the computer is used primarily for management. If the computer evaluates, scores, and reports, the teacher is free to make decisions about the appropriate instruction for each student.

Box 1 Implementing a CMI system

1. Identify the learning objectives.
2. Administer a pretest.
3. Diagnose areas of weakness.
4. Prescribe instruction.
    a. What are the learning objectives?
    b. In what sequence should they be taught?
    c. What materials should be used?
5. Provide instruction.
6. Administer test; repeat cycle if mastery is not achieved.

Should Your School Implement CMI?

Implementing a CMI system is a major decision that is usually considered at the school or district level. The main advantage of using CMI is that it relieves the teacher of time-consuming management and clerical tasks. However, CMI is not for everyone. The following questions (adapted in part from Patterson and Patterson, 1983, pp. 87–91) may help you decide whether CMI is right for your curriculum and your school.

Does Your Program's Philosophy Match the Learning-Theory Model Underlying CMI? As stated earlier, CMI can be based on concepts of mastery learning and individualization. Can your curriculum be organized so that students move at their own pace, pursuing an instructional objective until they demonstrate mastery of it? Can your objectives be organized sequentially so that prerequisite skills are learned first? Can mastery of your objectives be measured quantitatively? If so, then CMI may be worth considering. Not all educators agree, however, that objectives can be linearly sequenced or that students must master one objective before proceeding to another. If your curriculum is based on large group instruction that is presented to all students at the same time, if students are evaluated relative to other students' performance, or if your instructional decisions are based on data that cannot be quantified, then CMI may not be right for you.

Will CMI Be Cost Effective? Implementing a CMI system can be expected to cost more than using the traditional ways of managing instruction. If you choose to develop your own CMI program, the costs can be quite high. Teachers will spend many hours writing and sequencing objectives, writing pre- and posttest items, developing learning activities, and planning a record-keeping system. Then a technical consultant will be hired to write, test, and debug the computer program. To save money you can purchase a commercial CMI program, but it might not be flexible enough to meet your exact needs. You will need to consider not only software costs, but also the cost of the computer hardware and its maintenance. Also, teacher training may be needed to prepare teachers for using the CMI system. Can these additional costs be justified?

Will Using the Computer Save Time? Occasionally a CMI system is so poorly designed that data entry requires as much of the teacher's time as does keeping records manually. Or students' time may be wasted by their waiting in line for access to the computer terminals. Will CMI really make classroom management more efficient?

How Will Teachers Perceive Their Role?   In some districts that have implemented CMI, teachers believe that they have surrendered control of the learning process to the CMI system. In other cases, teachers have expressed the fear that their performance as a teacher might be inappropriately based on their students' progress. Districts that are considering implementing CMI should involve classroom teachers in the planning and decision making, and assure teachers that the data generated by the computer are intended to help them make instructional decisions, not to monitor their performance.

Will Education Be Improved?   Many argue that mastery learning and self-paced instruction better meet the needs of individual students, especially in remedial programs, than does traditional, large-group instruction. However, managing an individualized program is time-consuming. Will the computer facilitate management to the extent that students learn more in a specified amount of time?

Is the Instructional Level Appropriate?   Some educators caution that a curriculum involving heavy use of CMI tends to emphasize low-level skills, because knowledge such as geography facts, skill in computation, and reading comprehension is easier to measure with an objective test (and thus easier to test on the computer) than higher-level cognitive tasks such as critical analysis of an essay or problem solving. There are some commercially available CMI programs for elementary mathematics; however, most of them emphasize skills and ignore problem solving or conceptual development, and very few have taken into consideration the visualization factors highly correlated with mathematical achievement, that we mentioned in Chapter 10. Furthermore, many of these programs follow sequencing that is not consistent with children's learning. For example, many programs assume that a student should master nonregrouping problems before doing regrouping problems. But careful observation of children will show that such treatment is only setting up these children for future problems. To illustrate this point is a common mathematical problem. In adding two, two-digit numbers, a child thinks of it as two, one-digit problems, as shown below.

$$
\begin{array}{r} 1\,4 \\ +1\,3 \\ \hline 2\,7 \end{array}
\qquad
\begin{array}{r} 1\,4 \\ +1\,7 \\ \hline 211 \end{array}
$$

In the first case, adding $3 + 4 = 7$ and $1 + 1 = 2$ gives the correct answer, 27. But if the child is adding two one-digit numbers, he or she will also add $14 + 17$ as, $4 + 7 = 11$ and $1 + 1 = 2$. This extension of logic produces the wrong answer, 211. Artificial treatment of nonregrouping prior to regrouping can create such an erroneous logic.

Applications in Available Software

The following materials present principles discussed in this chapter.

Urban Reader

This comprehensive reading program, published by Educational Publishing Concepts, Inc., makes careful use of a detailed record-keeping system. To monitor the students' achievement, teachers may use the automatic tracking system. Students (grades 7–12) read stories and answer questions about the story at its end. After the student has achieved mastery of at least 70 percent of the questions over the stories in a unit, he or she automatically advances to the next level. This process continues until a student has read 70 percent of all of the stories. Teachers can manually override and adjust the student's level, but students do not have that option.

WICAT–IBM Materials

The WICAT–IBM materials have record-keeping systems, which were fully discussed in Chapter 12. The record-keeping system keeps track of the units completed and the time spent on them.

▶ ▲ ◀ ▼ ▶ ▲ ◀ ▼ ▶ ▲ ◀ ▼ ▶ ▲ ◀ ▼ ▶ ▲ ◀ ▼ ▶ ▲

Summary

In computer-managed instruction, the computer keeps records of student performance, administers and scores tests, and prepares reports. The computer can also provide instruction.

Most CMI programs are based on the assumption that mastery learning and individualization are desirable goals of instruction. The model used by most CMI systems includes six steps: (1) identify objectives, (2) administer pretest, (3) diagnose weaknesses, (4) prescribe instruction, (5) provide instruction, and (6) administer posttest. To decide if CMI is right for your school, you should consider whether your curriculum can be organized as a sequence of measurable learning objectives, whether the extra costs for software and hardware can be justified, whether CMI will really save time and free the teacher to teach, and whether students can be expected to learn more than they would by using traditional media. In selecting or designing a CMI system, you should consider whether the program is based on the best available research of students' learning processes and whether it provides opportunities for students to learn concepts and principles as well as skills.

Software discussed in this chapter:

Urban Reader
WICAT–IBM materials

Important Terms

Adaptive testing	Individualization
Computer-managed instruction (CMI)	Mastery learning
Criterion-referenced test	Norm-referenced test

Exercises

1. Obtain a copy of a commercial CMI program or visit a school that has implemented CMI.
   a. For which steps in the CMI model in Box 1 is the computer being used?
   b. What do you as a teacher like and dislike about the program you saw?
2. What advantage is there to using an integrated CMI program that administers, scores, and records test grades, rather than using separate testing and grade book programs?

References

Baker, F. (1978). *Computer managed instruction: Theory and practice.* Englewood Cliffs, NJ: Educational Technology Publications.

Patterson, J. L. & Patterson, J. H. (1983). *Putting computer power in the schools.* Englewood Cliffs, NJ: Prentice-Hall.

Wager, W. (1983). Microcomputers and the management of instruction. *Educational computer, 3,* 46–47, 71.

Chapter 14

Evaluating Software

▲ ▶ ▼ ◀ ▲ ▶ ▼ ◀ ▲ ▶ ▼ ◀ ▲ ▶ ▼ ◀ ▲ ▶ ▼ ◀ ▲ ▶

Objectives

▶ Identify criteria for the evaluation of instructional software
▶ Describe an appropriate review procedure
▶ Applying the review procedure, evaluate typical courseware

S uppose your school or department has budgeted $1500 to buy software, and
you have been asked to recommend purchases. You already have a good supply
of software for using the computer as a tool, and now you want to buy some
instructional software. You have catalogs from about ten software publishing companies listing hundreds of programs for your computer, with prices ranging from
$25 to over $500. But your school's experience in basing its software selection on
catalog descriptions has not been altogether successful. Of the six programs purchased last year, only one is in demand by students and teachers. The others seem
to be collecting dust in the closet.

This year you want to become more selective. When possible, you plan to order
software for a 30-day preview. And to decide on those that are worth previewing,
you want to read several reviews written by educators like yourself.

Where can you find reliable software reviews? What criteria are appropriate for
the evaluation of software? How can you proceed in reviewing educational software?

Why Do We Need to Review Software?

To decide whether the materials meet their instructional objectives and are
appropriate for their students, teachers, curriculum specialists, and school media
specialists review textbooks, films, reference books, and other curricular materials.
Because **courseware** (as computer software used for instruction is sometimes
called) is another medium for the presentation of instruction, educators need to
review it also before they can make decisions about what to purchase.

Selecting software to use in the classroom can be especially confusing and time
consuming. The quantity of software on the market is overwhelming and the quality

varies over a wide range. Not only do schools have limited budgets to buy software, but teachers have limited time to spend ordering, previewing, and returning software. In fact, only a few software publishers have a preview policy or offer a guarantee of satisfaction.

To assist each other in making well-informed decisions, educators are sharing their reviews through newsletters, journals, conferences, and informal networks. Most computing journals and an increasing number of professional education journals regularly publish software reviews. In addition, there are several new periodicals devoted exclusively to reviewing software. (Sources of published reviews are listed in Appendix J.) On a practical level, we want to learn to evaluate software for our own classroom use. However, we also have a responsibility as educators to share our experiences in a particular program and our professional evaluation of that program with our colleagues.

How Do We Recognize Quality Software?

Much of the early educational software presented a simple translation of textbooks and workbooks from the printed page to the computer screen. Critics charged that page-turning computer-assisted instruction was an unimaginative use of the powerful new technology. After making a sizable investment in computer hardware and software, educators expected more than electronic workbooks. Some of this early courseware was written by programmers who were technically skilled but knew little about learning theory and the interests and capabilities of children. Developing quality courseware is a complex task that should involve the expertise of both experienced educators and programmers.

Henry Olds (1983, p. 3) has identified four general features that characterize quality software:

1. It should be based on a carefully articulated theory about how children learn the particular content area.
2. It should reflect an understanding of the cognitive needs and capabilities of the intended learner.
3. It should be interactive, involving the learner in the learning process.
4. It should use the unique capabilities of the computer in truly functional ways, such as using graphics to represent an abstract concept.

Description before Evaluation

A **courseware** (or software) **review** includes both a thorough description and a careful evaluation of the software and accompanying materials. The **courseware description** specifies:

▶ Hardware requirements (type of computer, peripherals, memory)
▶ Software requirements (language, DOS)
▶ Subject area or topics
▶ Intended audience
▶ Instructional mode (drill and practice, tutorial, simulation, problem solving, visualization)
▶ Instructional objectives
▶ Prerequisite skills
▶ Supplementary materials (instruction manual, teacher's guide, followup activities)

- ► Publisher
- ► Warranty, backup policy
- ► Cost
- ► Other computer versions available

Usually the descriptive information can be obtained from the **documentation** (written instructions, manual, or user's guide) that accompanies the software. If the documentation is incomplete, the reviewer might need to run the program, to find or infer some of the descriptive information.

Evaluation Criteria

If the courseware description indicates that a program will run on your computer system, meet your instructional objectives, and perhaps be appropriate for your students, then the next step is a systematic evaluation. A **courseware evaluation** includes a rating of the software and its documentation, based on specific criteria and a discussion of the program's strengths and weaknesses. The specific criteria may vary among school districts, according to their particular needs and goals. The criteria will also vary among programs, according to the instructional mode. Simulations and tutorials, for example, are judged by different criteria. In general, however, an evaluation should consider the program's educational content and value, its mode of instruction, technical features, ease of use, degree of student interaction and motivation, record-keeping capability, and documentation. We will discuss each of these categories.

Educational Content and Value

In examining the program's content, a reviewer should consider these questions:

1. Are the instructional objectives of the courseware well defined? Does it seem to achieve its stated objectives? In some programs, the objectives are not specifically stated in the documentation, but may be easily inferred from the program itself. Some programs touch briefly on a number of objectives, whereas others cover one objective in depth. *Math Concepts,* for example, develops these elementary mathematics concepts in 22 lessons on one disk: before/after; between; less than/greater than; odd/even; place value; counting by 2's, 3's, 4's, 5's, and 10's; ordering numerals; reading decimal numerals; comparing decimals; rounding; and identifying primes. On the other hand, *Clock* is limited to teaching children how to tell time. The latter program is more likely to achieve its objectives.

2. Are the grade level and ability level of the intended students specified and is the program appropriate for them? Consider the intended students' reading level, typing ability, attention span, and prerequisite skills. In preschool programs that teach letter recognition, for example, graphics is a more appropriate form of feedback than are words. In using *Mathematics Assessment/Prescriptive Edu-disks,* to avoid the frustration that younger children may have in finding letters on the keyboard, students use the arrow keys to move the cursor to the correct answer and the space bar to select it. In the same program, however, children in first grade are expected to complete a 20-minute assessment test in one sitting.

3. Does the courseware have educational value? Is it important that it be taught in today's classroom? *Story Machine* allows beginning readers to write their own stories using a limited vocabulary of 44 words. The stu-

dent's story is then illustrated on the screen with animated graphics. However, the student's sentences must conform to the article/noun/verb or article/noun/verb/preposition/article/noun format. Nonconforming sentences are crossed out as if they are incorrect. The reviewer must evaluate whether the limitations in vocabulary and syntax restrict students' creativity, or whether the pictorial enactment of the story reinforces their writing and helps them learn new words.

4. Does the program use an appropriate method of presenting concepts? Is the presentation clear and logical? Are the examples nonambiguous? For example, to illustrate the concept of subtraction, an elementary mathematics tutorial shows pictures of objects being "taken away."

5. Is the courseware easily integrated with classwork and compatible with other materials? A geometry tutorial, *Euclid Tutor,* that guides students through the process of writing two-column proofs is not consistent with many geometry textbooks, because the postulates and theorems are worded differently and are presented in a different order. The *Game Show,* on the other hand, is easily integrated with classwork because a teacher can modify the questions and answers to correlate with the topic being studied.

6. Is the content accurate? Are there errors in spelling, punctuation, or grammar? Are there errors in fact? If the program is a simulation, does it give an accurate representation of the situation simulated? The simulation *Lemonade Stand* presents an oversimplified marketing situation because it assumes that the advertising and pricing decisions made by one lemonade-stand owner do not affect the business of a neighboring stand (Figure 1). Major mistakes in content are inexcusable, yet they do occur. For example, an early version of a science tutorial on color and light makes no distinction between the primary colors of paint and the primary colors of light; it assumes both are the same.

7. Is the courseware free of sexist, racial, and ethnic stereotypes?

8. Is the concept controversial? If so, is the presentation balanced?

Figure 1 *Screen display of Lemonade Stand.*

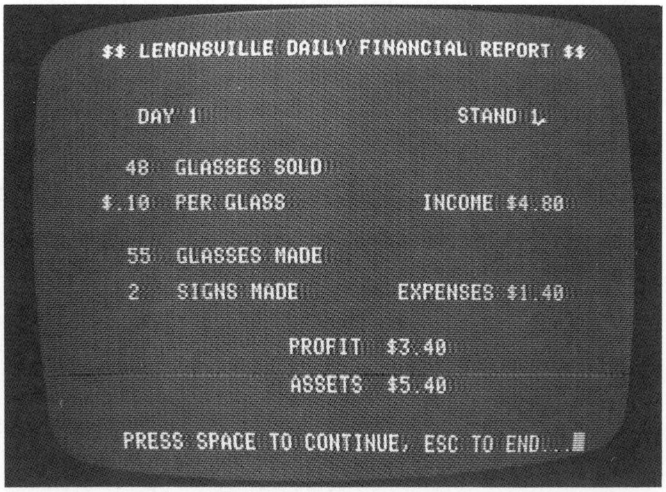

▼

```
$$ LEMONSVILLE DAILY FINANCIAL REPORT $$


    DAY 1                        STAND 1

    48  GLASSES SOLD
$ .10  PER GLASS               INCOME $4.80

    55  GLASSES MADE
     2  SIGNS MADE             EXPENSES $1.40

                    PROFIT  $3.40
                    ASSETS  $5.40

    PRESS SPACE TO CONTINUE, ESC TO END... ▊
```

Mode of Instruction

In considering a program's mode of instruction, you need to consider information discussed in earlier parts of this book. Is the program intended to teach concepts, principles, skills, visualization, and/or problem solving? Are the instructional materials (such as simulation, tutorial, drill and practice, visualization materials, and problem-solving materials) appropriate to the type of instruction?

1. If the materials are for developing problem-solving processes, are the students required to reason by analogy? To apply decomposition? To make generalizations? To apply recombination? To look for simpler, related problems? To reason by symmetry? To work backward to find the solution? See Chapter 4 for further discussions.

2. If the materials are for developing skills, is there motivation for students to develop the skills? Is there a statement of what is expected from the student? Are there assertions tying skills to related generalizations? Is there a demonstration showing the process? Is there a means by which students can build analogies, such as comparing and contrasting a skill and to develop a mastered skill, so that the transfer of learning is maximized? Are there means for regulating the selection of the appropriate skill(s)? Are answers checked, so that the attained results are known to be correct? Are there means by which students can correct errors in their own thinking; that is, can the users locate and debug the steps of their own process, so that they are assured of correct answers? Are there means for clarification of the process, for students to organize or chunk the steps into structures, so that learning and retention become easier? Are there ample means for practice? Are questions randomly generated? Are there timing mechanisms, if appropriate? Are records of students' responses generated? See Chapter 9 for further discussion.

3. If the materials are designed to develop visualization or conceptual processes, are graphics used for embodiments rather than embellishment? Can the student transform the graphics from one state to other state(s), when dynamic relationships are involved? Are the figures simple enough so that students can focus on the essence of the ideas? Can the student control the program so that he or she can repeat the process over and over? Will students be able to visualize and isolate any critical variables of the situation? Will the student be able to visualize the relationships and interactions of any variables? Are the materials appealing for both boys and girls? For further discussion see Chapter 10.

4. If the materials are simulations, what is the instructional objective of this simulation? How might the simulation be used? Can the student restart the simulation if he or she is headed in a wrong direction? Could the information be communicated just as effectively in another form? What are some of the choices and consequences? Are feedback techniques effective? Do they provide motivation? Is there feedback on overall performance? How valid is the simulation? How effective is the use of graphics? What content can students learn from working with this simulation? What support materials can enhance the simulation? How can the effects of the simulation be evaluated? What is the overall quality of the simulation? See Chapter 11 for further discussion.

5. If the materials are tutorials, can you identify the objectives? Is motivation created? Do the materials identify prerequisite knowledge? Are the objectives appropriately analyzed so that the most effective materials are used? Are appropriate instructional strategies and sequencing used? Are students allowed to control their progression through the materials? Is

content appropriately analyzed, so that concepts, principles, and skills are correctly identified? Are concepts exemplified, classified, analyzed, and/or defined? Are principles motivated through felt need? Are there assertions of principles? Are there adequate instances of the principles? Are there applications of the principles? See Chapter 12 for further discussion.

As you consider the questions raised here, be sure to review the information in the related chapters.

Technical Features

Educators and students expect instructional software to be as polished technically as professional business software and arcade games. Here are some factors to be considered.

1. Is the program free of programming errors? Is it **crashproof?** Can you recover if you accidentally hit <RESET>? In using *Bank Street Writer,* for example, if you try to print without having a printer attached, you can press <RESET> to regain control of the system. Pressing <RESET> at any other time does not damage the program or your text.
2. Are the screen layouts attractive, with no overcrowding and an easy-to-read typeface? Is the information presented screen by screen or do you have to scroll? Compare the two screens in Figure 2. Which is more attractive and easier to read?
3. Does the program have graphics, sound, and color? Are they well done technically? Do they avoid interrupting the flow of the program? Can the sound be turned off or used through headsets? Do these features add to the instructional value of the program? Are the graphics an embodiment of the underlying concepts or an embellishment? Are dynamic graphics used to represent dynamic ideas; static graphics, static ideas?

   Odell Lake, which simulates the environment of a fishing pond, uses animated graphics to show big fish eating smaller fish (Figure 3). *Clock*

Figure 2 *Which is easier to read?*

▼

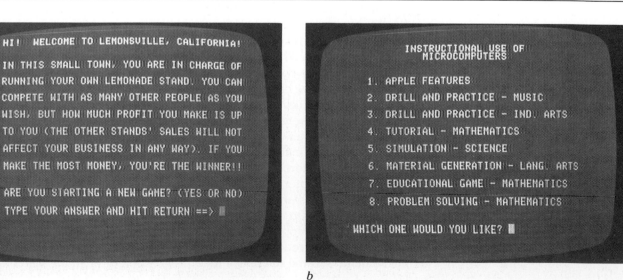

a

b

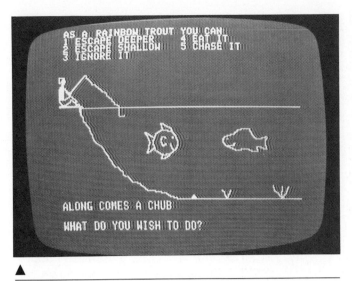

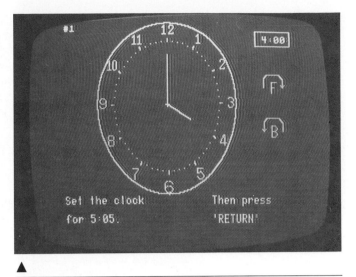

Figure 3 *Screen display of Odell Lake.*

Figure 4 *Screen display of Clock.*

allows students to adjust the hands of a clock to match a given time (Figure 4). As does that of a real clock, the minute hand revolves once for every hour. In the nuclear-reactor simulation *Three Mile Island,* dynamic graphics are used to represent the flow of water (see Figure 5). To illustrate the difference between *load* and *unload* in *Prefixes,* a dump truck moves across the screen and unloads its cargo (Figure 6). In *Elementary Math,* 28 blocks are partitioned onto 7 sets, to represent 28 divided by 7. In all of these examples, the graphics add to the instructional value: they illustrate or embody the underlying concept. In *Alligator Mix,* however, the arcadelike graphics add to the appeal of the math drill, but not to its instructional value. In addition, they can be distracting (Figure 7).

Figure 5 *Screen display of Three Mile Island.*

Figure 6 *Screen display of Prefixes.*

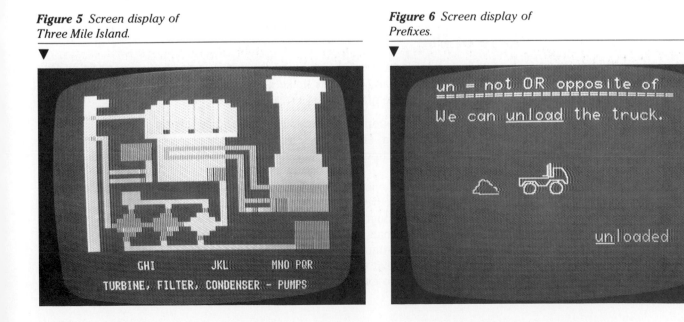

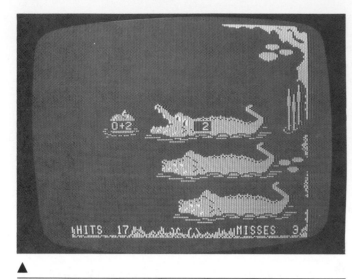

▲

Figure 7 *Alligator Mix uses arcadelike graphics to drill students in math facts.*

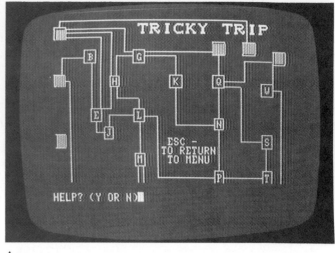

▲

Figure 8 *Screen display of Compu-solve.*

4. Does the program provide for individual needs: can it branch to hints, to review, or to a lower or higher level of difficulty, depending on the student's responses? In *Compu-solve,* a set of 10 problem-solving puzzles, the program flashes "HELP?" if you take too long to respond or respond incorrectly (Figure 8).
5. Is the program flexible; can it be easily modified?
   a. Can the teacher change the parameters of the program, such as the number of problems, the rate of presentation, or the level of difficulty? In *Alligator Mix,* an arcadelike math drill, the teacher can change the speed of the game and the difficulty of the problems presented.
   b. Can the teacher modify the content, such as the word lists in a spelling program?
   c. Can the teacher select specific lessons from a menu?

Ease of Use

Students and teachers rate courseware as easier to use, or more **user-friendly,** when the instructions and prompts make it clear what the student is expected to do next. Consider these questions:

1. Can students operate the program independently from the beginning, with a minimum of assistance from the teacher?
2. Are the instructions clear? Can they be skipped if users are familiar with the program?
3. Can students review the instructions at any time without starting the program over? Are frequently used keys explained at the top or bottom of the screen throughout the program? *Bank Street Writer,* for example, is easier to use than most word-processing programs because the commands are continuously displayed on the screen.
4. Can students exit the program at any time? Frequently, the <ESC> key is programmed to exit the program and return to the main menu.

5. Can students control the pace of the program? It is very frustrating, for example, to have the instructions displayed on the screen for a predetermined number of seconds. Fast readers become impatient waiting for the screen to advance and slow readers are frustrated when the screen clears before they have read it. To avoid this problem, most programs display PRESS ANY KEY TO CONTINUE at the bottom of the screen. Thus, the pace of the program is controlled by the user.

6. Are control keys used consistently? When information is entered from the keyboard, the <RETURN> key might or might not be required to signal the end of the input. To avoid confusion, use of <RETURN> should be consistent throughout the program.

7. When input is requested, does the student clearly understand what is expected? A program that asks for the selling price of a glass of lemonade, for example, should specify whether to answer in dollars or in cents. Similarly, a program should clarify whether to input ".05" or "5" for 5 cents.

8. Are common abbreviations accepted, such as Y, N, T, and F for "yes," "no," "true," and "false"?

9. How does the program handle inappropriate responses, input in the wrong form, or misspellings? A program that uses four designated keys (such as the arrow keys on the Apple IIe or IIc) to move up, down, right, and left should not respond when any other key is pressed or should display a reminder to press an arrow key. Some programs test whether the input is within an allowable range. In *Lemonade Stand,* if you try to sell your lemonade for less than one penny, the program responds, TRY A MORE REASONABLE SELLING PRICE.

10. Does the program accept variations of the correct answer? In mathematics, for example, the answers 0.6, .6, and .60 are equivalent and should be equally acceptable.

Student Interaction and Motivation

The quality of the interaction between student and software is very important in determining the success of a program. Consider the motivational features of the software and the usefulness of the feedback.

1. Is the student addressed by name in a personalized dialogue? Most students are pleased when the computer uses their name. However, some reviewers feel that computer–student dialogue should be avoided because it imparts human characteristics to a machine.

2. Do students find the program interesting and appealing, even with repeated use? *Dragon Games* consists of several language arts lessons in a game format (Figure 9). However, all of the lessons on the disk use exactly the same game board and there is no variation in the way the game proceeds. After playing once or twice, students lose interest because the outcome is predictable.

3. To maintain students' interest, does the program use appropriate motivational devices such as humor, surprise, variation? Are these devices appropriate to the intended age level?

4. Are students informed if their answers are right or wrong? Is the feedback immediate, or delayed until the end of the lesson? Is it specific to the question (TRY A SMALLER NUMBER) or general (WRONG)?

5. Is the tone of the feedback positive and constructive? Insulting, degrading, or threatening remarks are not acceptable for use in the classroom.

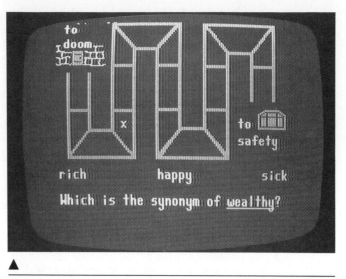

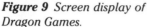

Figure 9 *Screen display of*
Dragon Games.

6. Does the feedback vary? Randomly generated positive reinforcement seems more personal than repetition of the same message after every correct response.
7. Does the feedback provide help, hints, or another chance?
8. Does the program avoid reinforcing incorrect responses? In *Dragon Games,* for example, losing a word game results in an animated picture of a fiery dragon, whereas winning is rewarded with a still picture of a closed treasure chest. Students are tempted to answer incorrectly even when they know the right answer because the fiery dragon is more interesting than the treasure chest.

Record-Keeping Capabilities

Some programs keep a record of students' responses and store the information on disk for later retrieval by the teacher. Or information may be stored so that students can continue a lesson at another time. Make these considerations in evaluating a program's record-keeping abilities.

1. Are student's records stored on disk for later retrieval?
   a. How many students' records may be stored? A management system limited to 25 students is not useful to a majority of teachers.
   b. How much information is stored: the number right and wrong, which answers were wrong, what the incorrect answer was? *Calendar Skills* records the incorrect answer to aid the teacher in diagnosing the reason for the error. The teacher can see, for example, that the student typed "Desember" instead of "December."
2. Is the record-keeping system easy for teachers to use? Teachers expect management systems to save them time, not to demand more time to learn their use.
3. Can the information be printed out? Is this feature optional?
4. Is reasonable security provided for the records, such as use of a control code or password? Is there a way to recover a forgotten password?

5. Are the records cumulative for each student, or do they reflect only the most recent computer session?
6. Are records of a partial lesson stored if a student leaves the lesson before it is finished?

Documentation

A reviewer should evaluate the documentation just as carefully as the software. The following questions should be answered.

1. Are the written instructions that accompany the software clear and easy to understand?
   a. Is the vocabulary unambiguous?
   b. Is the material well organized so that it is easy to find an answer to a specific question? Is there an index?
   c. Is the documentation comprehensive? Does it contain all the information that a teacher needs to use the program?
2. Does the documentation identify the intended users and the prerequisite skills they need?
3. To use the program, do teachers need the documentation, or is the program self-explanatory?
4. Are other support materials provided, such as tests or worksheets for noncomputer follow-up activities?
5. Do the support materials provide the teacher with suggestions for integrating the program into the classroom instruction?

Select Criteria Carefully

Certainly, no courseware has all the features we have discussed. Many well-designed, highly motivating educational programs have no record-keeping system, for example. Some sophisticated simulations require several hours to learn and cannot be described as "easy to use," yet are high in educational value. Part of the reviewer's task is to select the relevant criteria for the program being evaluated.

Review Procedure

Many resource centers and school districts have developed software-review forms to guide educators in the review process. Review forms have been published by the National Council of Teachers of Mathematics, MicroSIFT, EPIE/Consumers Union, Minnesota Educational Computing Consortium, and by educational computing periodicals such as *The Computing Teacher, Electronic Learning,* and *Classroom Computer Learning.*

Some review forms list specific evaluation criteria and the reviewer rates the courseware on each criterion. Such a **checklist review form** is usually preferred when a school district has specific criteria on which to base its decision to purchase, or when the district wants to compare or rank similar software packages. Other forms are more open ended; they list general categories such as *Ease of use* and the reviewer describes the program's strengths and weaknesses in each category. This **open-ended review form** (see Box 1) is more informative than the checklist. It is easier to sense the reviewer's impression of the software from narrative comments than from numerical ratings. At the end of this chapter is an open-ended courseware review form that you can use to describe and evaluate instructional software. Other forms may be found in *Evaluation of Educational Software: A Guide to Guides* (Olds, 1983) and in the other references on p. 293.

Box 1   A Software Evaluation Walkthrough

Courseware Review Form

Title: *The Factory: Strategies in Problem Solving*

Publisher: *Sunburst Communications*   Copyright Date: *1983*

Subject Area: *Math, Science, Communications (Languages)* Cost: *$49.00*

Grade Level: *4–9*

Instructional mode (circle):

    Drill/Practice   Tutorial   (Simulation)   (Problem solving)

    Test/Diagnosis   Utility   Management   (Concept/Visualization)

Other:

System requirement (specify type of computer; memory required; disk, cassette tape, or ROM cartridge; language; operating system; peripherals needed; availability for other systems). Systems: *Apple II Family (II, II+, IIe, IIc, IIGS) 48 to 64 K; Atari, Commodore 64; TRS 80 Color, and IBM, IBM PC$_{JR}$ (64K minimum).*

Support materials (instructional manual, teacher's guide, follow-up activities): *Teacher's Guide and Activities are included in the package. It is of adequate quality, and permission to copy student worksheets is granted. The guide does present complete instructions for use, with suggestions about uses of* The Factory. *However, there is only a minimal amount of actual student activities with the package.*

Backup policy: *A backup diskette is provided at time of purchase. The statement is also made that permission is granted to load the program into multiple machines if the version that was purchased "loads completely."*

Instructional objectives: *To develop problem-solving strategies and visualization skills, including visual sequencing and patterning. (Specific objectives for the different levels of the games are stated.)*

Prerequisite skills: *None*

General description of the program: *A simulation of a factory,* The Factory *challenges a machine operator (you) to produce customized assembly lines to turn out customized products. You choose the sequence in which three machines are used (each machine may be used more than once, if desired) to create the visual image or pattern (blueprint) that could be produced (as, for example, in a block of wood). The general form of the screen and an example of a challenge are provided in Figure 10.*

    1.   ***Educational content and value:*** Is the content accurate? Clearly presented? Appropriate for the intended audience? Free of stereotypes? Important? Does the program seem to achieve its objectives? Is it easily integrated with classwork?   The Factory *does a very good job in teaching the problem-solving strategies it proposes to develop. A very well*

continued

Box 1   A Software Evaluation Walkthrough *continued*

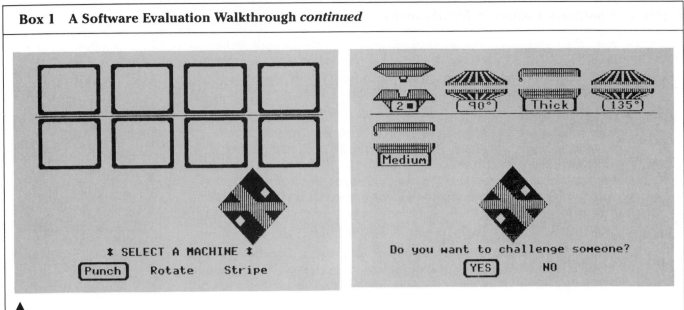

▲

Figure 10 *A sample challenge from The Factory.*

done visual-imagery development program, The Factory *actively involves students in challenging problems, from simple two- or three-step problems to more complex sequencing of up to eight steps. Three separate games are available; the first is introductory and instructional, the second has students experiment to create their own product (maybe challenging a friend to copy their pattern), and the third challenges them to reproduce a finished product.*

2. ***Mode of instruction:*** What is the program intended to teach: concepts, principles, skills, visualization, and/or problem solving? Is the appropriate form of instruction (such as simulation, tutorial, drill and practice, visualization materials, problem-solving materials) being used?   *A major strength of* The Factory *is its creative,* problem-solving *mode of instruction, with superior visualization and imagery development. A good selection of problem-solving heuristics are used, from working backwards to simplifying the problem to seeing multiple solutions. Likewise, a good cross-section of visualization skills are developed, from spatial development to the transformation of images to embodiments of important spatial relations such as sequencing. Students can isolate and control individual variables such as turning, punching circular or square holes, and stripping thin, medium, or thick strips. Students can repeat the process until they get it right.*

3. ***Technical features:*** Did you have any technical problems with the program? Is the layout visually attractive? Are graphics, color, and sound used effectively to enhance instruction? Could you modify the program? *Technical features of* The Factory *are quite good; there are no troublesome operational difficulties. The layout is simple, attractive, and colorful. It enhances the proposed learning experience and contributes to*

continued

Box 1   A Software Evaluation Walkthrough *continued*

---

concept development. The graphics are integral to the purpose of the program, and facilitate the development of problem-solving strategies, both in practice and feedback. Sound is available but may be inactivated if desired. The sound does not seem to contribute to the program's purpose.

4. **Ease of use:** Are the instructions clear? Can students operate the program easily? Control the pace? Review the instructions? End the program? How is inappropriate input handled? *The program is easy to use, both for the younger and the more experienced user. From the very introduction to the most complex challenges, the user is in control. Returning to directions, choosing new challenges (or exiting), seeking feedback, and reviewing examples are all easy to do.*

5. **Motivation:** Does the program hold students' interest? Do students want to use it again? Does the program vary when repeated? *The format and intellectual/visual challenges of* The Factory *are very motivating to most users. It can be viewed as a "fun activity;" however, the type of learning is substantial and subtle. Some educators, however, might not appreciate the nature of the learning goals it provides, as they are not the "drill-and-practice" type of the three R's.*

6. **Feedback:** Is the feedback positive and constructive? Appropriate for the grade level? Immediate? Varied? Does it provide help or an explanation? *Feedback is provided. It shows a machine sequence and its final product for comparison, a subtle but effective visual feedback.*

7. **Record keeping:** Are students' records stored on disk for later retrieval? What information is stored? For how many students? Is the record-keeping system easy to use? Is it reasonably secure? *The Factory does not have a record-keeping component.*

8. **Documentation:** Are the written instructions clear? Well organized? Comprehensive? Are the objectives, prerequisites, and intended audience specified? *The documentation is clear, simple, and complete. Objectives, prerequisites, intended audience, and a variety of other information are provided. However, the audience is probably not so specific and limited as the documentation suggests. In spite of the fact that the documentation meets the general requirements, it could be more suggestive of the wide range of activities and uses of* The Factory. *It could be considerably more complete and user-oriented.*

9. **Summary and recommendations:** What are the program's strengths? What are its weaknesses? Does it take advantage of the computer's capabilities? Does it involve the learner in the learning process? How does it compare to others with similar objectives? Would you buy and use it?
   The major strengths of The Factory *are:*
   a. *Excellent problem-solving and visualization orientations.*
   b. *Excellent range of activities and challenge (including creativity) for students.*
   c. *Built-in problem-solving strategies, including finding a simpler problem and finding a more elegant solution.*

continued

Box 1   A Software Evaluation Walkthrough *continued*

    d.   *Useful sound feedback.*
    e.   *Nice interaction with the user and high degree of user control.*

The major weaknesses of The Factory *are:*
    a.   *Some educators would view left-hemispheric activities as the sole*
        responsibility of education. Such educators would not seek
        the goals of this program.
    b.   *A record-keeping system could be a good diagnostic tool for*
        development of spatial development.
    c.   *Transformations possible on spatial objects could be enhanced to*
        include some more reflections (not limited to rotations and
        combinations of rotations) and translation.

The graphic capabilities of the computer are utilized well in The Factory.
In this respect, the program is exemplary. No others on the market can be
compared with it for the same purpose, in terms of simplicity, challenge,
simulation, or development of problem-solving strategies.

Software Reviews

Pollard (1989) identified 10 top sources for information on the quality of various software. These sources are listed below; their addresses are listed in Appendix J.

Educational Software Preview Guide	*Curriculum Software Guides*
Only the Best	*Technology in the Curriculum*
The Educational Software Selector	*MicroSIFT*
Software Reviews on File	*Micro*
The Chime Newsletter	*Computer Courseware Evaluations*

In using published reviews, a reader who is familiar with other software packages that have similar objectives can compare them with the package under review. Such a comparison is particularly useful if the other software is relatively well known. The reviewer should be careful, however, not to assume that others' instructional needs are identical to his or her own.

In addition, a reviewer should observe several students of the appropriate age using the software. If possible, the courseware should be used in a typical classroom situation. Frequently, teachers discover that students do not respond to the program as they had anticipated. Do the students understand the directions? Are they eager to use the program? How long does it take them to complete a typical lesson? What features of the program create frustrations for them? What comments do the students make about the program?

In making your final evaluation of the program, recall the four general features that characterize quality software. In particular, does the program take advantage of the unique capabilities of the computer? What advantage does it have over a textbook, a workbook, a game board, or a personal tutor? Is it truly interactive, involving the learner in the learning process? Is it sensitive to the needs and capabilities of the learner?

When you have completed your evaluation, share it with other teachers in your district or state through your professional organization or newsletter. If you return the software to the publisher, enclose a copy of your evaluation. Some modifications can be easily made, and you might find that your suggestions are incorporated in the next version of the program.

Courseware Review Form

Title: _____

Publisher: _____ Copyright date: _____

Subject area: _____ Cost: _____

Grade level: _____

Instructional mode (circle):

Drill / Practice   Tutorial   Simulation   Problem solving

Test / Diagnosis   Utility   Management   Concept / Visualization

Other:

System requirements (specify type of computer; memory required; disk, cassette tape, or ROM cartridge; language; operating system; peripherals needed; availability for other systems):

Support materials (instructional manual, teacher's guide, follow-up activities):

Backup policy:

Instructional objectives:

Prerequisite skills:

General description of the program:

1. *Educational content and value:* Is the content accurate? Clearly presented? Appropriate for the intended audience? Free of stereotypes? Important? Does the program seem to achieve its objectives? Is it easily integrated with classwork?

2. *Mode of instruction:* What is the program intended to teach: concepts, principles, skills, visualization, and/or problem solving? Is the appropriate form of instruction (such as simulation, tutorial, drill and practice, visualization materials, problem-solving materials) being used?

3. *Technical features:* Did you have any technical problems with the program? Is the layout visually attractive? Are graphics, color, and sound used effectively to enhance instruction? Could you modify the program?

continued

Courseware Review Form *continued*

4. *Ease of use:* Are the instructions clear? Can students operate the program easily? Control the pace? Review the instructions? End the program? How is inappropriate input handled?

5. *Motivation:* Does the program hold students' interest? Do students want to use it again? Does the program vary when repeated?

6. *Feedback:* Is the feedback positive and constructive? Appropriate for the grade level? Immediate? Varied? Does it provide help or an explanation?

7. *Record keeping:* Are students' records stored on disk for later retrieval? What information is stored? For how many students? Is the record-keeping system easy to use? Is it reasonably secure?

8. *Documentation:* Are the written instructions clear? Well organized? Comprehensive? Are the objectives, prerequisites, and intended audience specified?

9. *Summary and recommendations:* What are the program's strengths? What are its weaknesses? Does it take advantage of the computer's capabilities? Does it involve the learner in the learning process? How does it compare to others with similar objectives? Would you buy and use it?

▲ ▶ ▼ ◀ ▲ ▶ ▼ ◀ ▲ ▶ ▼ ◀ ▲ ▶ ▼ ◀ ▲ ▶ ▼ ◀ ▲ ▶

Summary

A courseware review includes both thorough description and careful evaluation of the software and its documentation. An evaluation includes a rating of the software package based on specific criteria and a discussion of the program's strengths and weaknesses. A reviewer should consider a program's educational content and value, technical features, ease of use, quality of interaction with students, record-keeping system, and documentation. After becoming familiar with a software package, a reviewer should run the program as both a successful and an unsuccessful student, observe students using the program, complete the review form, and, finally, note any discrepancies in the publisher's claims.

Software discussed in this chapter:

Math Concepts	*Three Mile Island*
Clock	*Prefixes*
Mathematics Assessment/	*Elementary Math*
Prescriptive Edu-disks	*Alligator Mix*
Story Machine	*Compu-solve*
Euclid Tutor	*Dragon Games*
Game Show	*Calendar Skills*
Lemonade Stand	*The Factory*
Bank Street Writer	
Odell Lake	

Important Terms

Checklist review form	Crashproof
Courseware	Documentation
Courseware description	Open-ended review form
Courseware evaluation	User-friendly
Courseware review	

Exercises

1. Survey the professional education journals in your field and determine which ones regularly publish software reviews.

2. What courseware-review journals are available at libraries or resource centers in your locale? What other sources of reviews are available locally?

3. Find three different published reviews of a particular instructional software package. Compare the three reviews. Which is the most informative? Why?

4. Use the Microcomputer Index on the *Dialog* database (available online at most college libraries) to find several reviews of *Bank Street Writer*.

5. Has your state, school district, or computer consortium developed its own review form and review procedure? If so, obtain copies to share with other members of the class.

6. Find out if there is a local resource center, library, or software store where teachers can go to preview instructional software.

7. Consult six catalogs of instructional software and determine the publisher's policy on backup or replacement disks, warranty, and preview; share your findings with your class.

8. Survey the software available at a school nearby. Ask the media specialists or teachers at the school which software is used regularly and which is not and why. Prepare a report and share it with your class.

9. Bring to class an example of courseware that uses graphics as an integral part of the instruction (embodiment) and an example of courseware that uses graphics only as an embellishment.

10. Bring to class an example of software that does not use the unique capabilities of the computer, but would be just as effective in another format: workbook, textbook, board game, flashcards, lecture, or classroom activity. What is the instructional objective? How would you design a computer-assisted instructional program to meet the same objective, that would also use the capabilities of the computer effectively?

11. Using the Courseware Review Form at the end of this chapter, review thoroughly a selected piece of courseware. Use the review procedure and criteria outlined in this chapter. Share the review with the members of your class. (A copy of the Courseware Review Form is included as a text file on the *Applications Disk*. If you have a word processor that uses text files, you can use this form with your word processor. You may need to change a few codings so that they match your word processor's codings.)

References

Anderson-Inman, L. (1987). Teaching for transfer: Integrating language arts software into the curriculum. *The Computer Teacher, 15,* 24–29, 38.

Bitter, G. G., & Wighton, D. (1987). The most important criteria used by the educational software evaluation consortium. *The Computing Teacher, 14,* 7–9.

Brown, S., Grossman, G. C., & Polson, N. (1984). Educational software reviews: Where are they? *The Computing Teacher, 12,* 33–37.

Kansky, R., Heck, W., & Johnson, J. (1981). *Guidelines for evaluating computerized instructional materials.* Reston, VA: National Council of Teachers of Mathematics.

Lathrop, A., & Goodson, B. (1983). *Courseware in the classroom.* Menlo Park, CA: Addison-Wesley.

Malnig, A. (1987). Choosing the right software. *A+, 5,* 28–34.

Olds, H. F., Jr. (1983). Evaluating the evaluation schemes. In N. B. James & I. Vaughan (Eds.), *Evaluation of educational software: A guide to guides.* Chelmsford, MA: The Northeast Regional Exchange.

Pollard, J. (1989, January). 10 top sources of reliable software information. *Learning,* 64–65.

Chapter 15

Trends and Issues in Computer Education

▲ ▶ ▼ ◀ ▲ ▶ ▼ ◀ ▲ ▶ ▼ ◀ ▲ ▶ ▼ ◀ ▲ ▶ ▼ ◀ ▲ ▶ ▼

Objectives

▶ Describe the influence of computers on our future
▶ Identify careers that will be heavily influenced by computers
▶ Describe various views of computer literacy
▶ Describe the roles of the computer as an integrated part of the curriculum and as a separate discipline
▶ Describe various equity issues related to educational uses of the computer
▶ Describe legal issues related to computers
▶ Identify characteristics of an intelligent machine and artificial intelligence

In this final chapter, we examine trends and issues in computer education. You, as a teacher, will want to know how your students and their lives will be affected by the computer. The influence of computers on society and careers is causing substantial changes. We will explore various points of view of computer literacy and the role of computers in schools. We will examine equity and legal issues. We will discuss the issues surrounding intelligent machines, which are, according to some, the next great wave of the future.

Influences of the Computer

The computer is a major influence both on society in general and on many of us as individuals. We will explore changes that it has brought to society and careers.

Changes in Society

According to a number of futurists, we are in the midst of a major societal revolution. They have identified the **computer revolution** (also called the *information revolution* or the *technological revolution*) as having a major effect on our society. In his best-selling book *The Third Wave,* Toffler (1980) identifies three major "waves" in our history:

1. The agricultural wave, from 8000 B.C. to around A.D. 1650 to 1759

2. The industrial wave, from the late 1700s or early 1800s to around the mid-1950s, which he says was "the same decade that saw the widespread introduction of the computer, commercial jet travel, the birth control pill, and many other high-impact innovations" (p. 14)
3. The wave we are in now (the **third wave**)

He also comments that the generation graduating from high school today is the first generation in American history to graduate less skilled than its parents; that is, because of the rapid changes in technology, today's generation is less prepared to face its future than were any of the previous generations.

Toffler claims that this third wave has four clusters of related industries, which are dictating the growth and are likely to be the dominant industries of the third wave. These industries are bringing shifts in economic power and in social and political alignments. The four main clusters he identifies are:

1. The electronics industries, including computers
2. The space industry
3. The ocean/sea development industries
4. The industries surrounding genetic engineering

He calls this new combination a *techno-sphere*. He says that we must resist the temptation to assume that tomorrow will be a mere extension of today. During the industrial wave, coal, steel, electricity, and rail transport were combined to form automobiles and a thousand other life-transforming products that could not have been predicted. So too, the real effects of current technological advance will not be evident until the new technologies are combined. The linking together of computers, electronics, new materials from outer space and the oceans, and genetic engineering—and using all of these, in turn, with the new energy base, of recycling energy such as solar energy—can create a dramatically new techno-sphere for a third-wave civilization.

Another futurist, the late Christopher Evans (1979), compares the computer revolution with the **industrial revolution.** He identifies four important features of the latter:

1. The scale and scope of change were huge—all aspects of life were affected
2. Changes took place with great rapidity, so that the entire society was altered within 100 years

3. Once the process of revolution was fully under way, no one could stop it or set it back against its course

4. Hardly anyone—certainly no one who could do anything about it—fore-saw its momentous coming

Evans believes that parallels between the computer revolution and the industrial revolution are substantial, with a contrast being the speed of the computer revolution. He predicts that the revolution will occur within 25 years; others have predicted an even shorter time span.

The best-selling book *Megatrends* (Naisbitt, 1982) identifies the shift from an industrial society to an information society as a major trend. Naisbitt claims that computer technology provides the same momentum to the information age as mechanization did to the industrial age. Further, he identifies three major stages of technology:

1. *Stage 1:* technology takes the path of least resistance; it appears in ways that are not threatening to people (for example, using microprocessors in toys)

2. *Stage 2:* technology is used to improve what we already have (for example, cars, manufacturing, sewing machines)

3. *Stage 3:* we create things suggested by the microprocessor itself—inventions and applications that were hitherto unimagined

There are many changes in store for the future. We should be careful to use our technological tools not only to do the same old thing, but also to explore new applications that will be even more powerful. That is where the real excitement lies.

Changes in Careers

Many careers are already in the process of change. Typewriters are being replaced by word processors. Professionals are finding themselves sitting in front of word processors and writing their own materials instead of talking into dictaphones. Architects, engineers, and artists are working with computer-aided design systems. Librarians now retrieve information and conduct literature searches online. People no longer assume that everyone works from 9 A.M. to 5 P.M. in an office; a number of people work at home and send information to the office via modem. Robots are assembling cars—and even computers.

Naisbitt and Evans predict other changes in the way we work. Naisbitt predicts the smashing of the management pyramid, in which the boss is at the top, his or her assistants report to him or her, their assistants report to them, and so on. He claims that "the failure of hierarchies to solve society's problems forced people to talk to one another—and that was the beginning of networks" (p. 191). He says that society is moving from the hierarchical structure to a networking structure, in which people are talking to each other and are sharing ideas, information, and resources.

Evans (1979) predicts that computers will contribute to the decline of the professions—nonprofessionals will have access to computer programs containing the collected wisdom of professions. For example, computers might be able to diagnose a person's physical problems better than many physicians can. Whether the authority of the professionals will decline is debatable, but most futurists agree that the professionals' role will change. Doctors, lawyers, and teachers will not be the sources of knowledge so much as the experts at integrating the knowledge and applying it to individual situations. Through telecommunications, large amounts of information are available to anyone.

Consider, as an example, the role of the teacher. Twenty years ago, people were concerned that machines were going to replace the teacher. Today, it is clear that the machines are not going to replace the teacher, but rather that the teacher's role will be redefined. The teacher will become more a facilitator of learning and less a disburser of knowledge. Using computers, different students can work at different rates and do different kinds of tasks. Thus, the teacher must become an expert diagnostician, helping to channel students to various sources of knowledge according to the students' needs. To build readiness and imagery for a discussion in social studies or science, for example, a student may be assigned to use a specific computer simulation.

Naisbitt claims that the greater the high technology, the greater the "high touch." In other words, the greater the use of machines, the greater is the need of human beings to be in touch with each other. The need for contact with people became clear in the early 1970s, when the developers of the *Plato* system (a large computer-based educational system with terminals all over the country) designed a feature called the TALK command. The command allows a user to TALK with any other user. It was not originally intended to be a major feature of the system, but once people caught on to it, it became very popular. In the early years, often someone working at a *Plato* terminal in Champaign, Illinois, would be TALKing with someone in Princeton, New Jersey. The need for contact with people came through loud and clear as use of the TALK command grew. Today the TALK command on networks like *The Source* and *Compuserve* is among the most popular features, even though the charges per hour are not nominal. This ease of communication allows specialists in any field to keep in close contact and therefore easily exchange materials, verbal and graphic. (It should also be pointed out that FAX systems, for facsimiles, have sprouted throughout the country nearly overnight.)

Computer Literacy

Now that we have discussed potential influences on our society and changes in careers, we examine computer literacy. One goal of education is to prepare students to cope with situations they encounter in life. Consequently, schools have a responsibility to teach skills that are useful to such tasks as comparison shopping, balancing a checkbook, reading a road map, completing an employment application, driving a car, and preparing for a future career. With the advent of the computer revolution, schools are adding computer literacy, or computer awareness, to the list of knowledge that all students should gain.

What Is Computer Literacy?

Of all the uses of computers, which ones should all students learn to do comfortably and successfully? These questions have stimulated controversy among educators. Some people equate computer literacy with the ability to select and use commercial software. Their argument is that the average person does not need to know how a computer works, what RAM is, or how to write a computer program. They compare using a computer to driving a car—in order to drive, one does not need to know how a car works, what a manifold is, or how to do a tune-up.

On the other hand, some people equate computer literacy with knowledge of programming. Their argument is that in order for a person to use the computer to solve problems, that person needs to have the flexibility and control that a knowledge of programming provides. In short, knowledge is power.

Borrowing from both points of view, the National Science Board Commission on Precollege Education in Mathematics, Science, and Technology (1983) identified the following set of competencies to be expected of all students:

1. Basic knowledge of how computers work and of common computer terminology, including a general understanding of the various applications of computers
2. Experience in using the computer as a tool, which should include experiences in the use of standard applications software such as word processing systems and filing systems
3. Familiarity with one high-level computer language and ability to use that language as a means of interacting with the device
4. Ability to use a computer language to do problem-solving tasks in the context of normal academic experiences and at a level that reflects the individual student's level of ability
5. General understanding of the problems and issues confronting both individuals and society as a whole in the use of computers, including the social and economic effects of computers, the history and development of computing, and the ethics involved in computer automation

Those students showing a special interest in and ability for computing and those who might pursue further study in scientific and technical fields should also,

1. Have a thorough knowledge of how computers work, including an indepth understanding of varied computer applications and automated information sources
2. Have experience in using the computer as a tool, with particular emphasis on applications such as text editing, computer-assisted composition, computer-based statistical analysis, simulation, data logging and manipulation, . . . and use of common computer utilities
3. Be able to use at least two computer languages in the context of other academic experiences, with an emphasis on appropriate problem-solving skills and development of readable, structured programs [p. 100]

One of the major controversies in the development of computer-literacy curricula is whether all students should learn programming. Note that the National Science Board recommends that all students become familiar with a computer language so that they can use the computer to solve specific problems that arise in their schoolwork. Learning to program also helps students to develop skills in visualization and logical reasoning. Furthermore, students who learn programming also learn about the capabilities and limitations of the computer and the ways in which the computer processes information.

In describing the computer revolution, Evans (1979) stated, "We move from the amplification and emancipation of the power of muscles to the amplification and emancipation of the power of the brain" (p. x). It is the time to develop minds. Teaching students to develop problem-solving abilities may be the most important function of our educational system.

Should Teachers Learn to Program?

Many teachers may not need to learn programming, but, in our experience, they want to because their students are programming and asking questions. (A recent survey in a computer education class indicated that nearly all of the teachers, including early childhood and elementary teachers, were taking the course because they felt pressure to learn programming so that they could respond to students' questions.)

Is Computer Literacy Different for Teachers than for Students?

Certainly teachers should have at least the level of literacy that students are expected to have. Are there additional areas with which teachers should be familiar? At a minimum, teachers should:

1. Understand the variety of ways in which computers can be used in education
2. Be familiar with the wide range of educational software available
3. Be able to apply appropriate criteria for the selection and evaluation of software
4. Be able to integrate the uses of the computer into their curriculum
5. Be able to customize modifiable software to meet specific objectives
6. Be familiar with the resources (periodicals, resource centers, user groups) that can provide more information as needed

Further, the National Science Board Commission (1983) identified the following basic educational applications of computers (p. 53):

1. Microworlds, which are cybernetic environments within which elements may be combined according to given rules
2. Educational games, including adventure games, which develop reading comprehension and problem-solving skills
3. Microcomputer-based instrumentation systems that permit explorations of real-world phenomena
4. Databases that increase the amount of information available to students
5. Tools, including graph-plotting routines, word processing, spreadsheet programs, and general-purpose problem solvers
6. Special-purpose computer languages, like Logo, which permit the creation of learning environments that foster development of the child's intellect
7. Simulations, which create flexible universes within which the student can experimentally discover properties of the real world
8. Discovery learning in mathematics, which provides an active and self-directed learning environment within which the student can discover properties of mathematical functions and operations

As they integrate technology with their instruction, teachers should know how to make full use of this new technology and provide role models for their students. A mathematics teacher can integrate a three-dimensional flight simulator or a curve plotter with his or her mathematics instruction. A science or social studies teacher can integrate simulations of physical or social phenomena into those courses; the social studies teacher also can discuss futurists' thoughts concerning the effects of computers on society. The home economics teacher can use programs to prepare menus and plan appropriate nutrition, or can use a graphics package for interior design. The art teacher can make effective use of graphics packages to guide her or his students in creating new designs on the computer. The industrial arts teacher can use graphics packages to create drafting designs. The music teacher can use the music synthesizer to illustrate subroutines to set up rounds, such as "Row, Row, Row Your Boat." Rounds are similar to some of the loops or recursions we illustrated in the early part of this book. The English teacher can find creative ways of using the computer to enhance written communication. Yes, it would appear that in some areas of computer literacy, teachers should know beyond what their students know. It is our students who will be creating a whole new synthesis in society with this new technology. They will go beyond us, but we must set them on the path.

There have been a number of calls for improving the quality of education for all children. To gain a better understanding of the potential of new interactive technologies to improve learning, the House Committee on Education and Labor and its Subcommittee on Select Education requested the U.S. Congress, Office of Technology Assessment to conduct a study, which was reported in 1988. The most important finding was that computers with all their power are not self-implementing, but that in the hands of creative and technically competent teachers, computers can provide a new world of teaching opportunities. The following findings concern the teacher's role:

▶ Despite the presence of computers in almost all K through 12 schools nationwide, only half of the nation's teachers report that they have used computers in instruction.

▶ Few teachers have found ways to exploit the enormous potential that interactive technologies offer.

▶ Most teachers want to use technology.

▶ The process by which teachers appropriate technology is more complex than that by which teachers adopt other changes.

▶ Teachers use computers in ways that work best with their own teaching styles and methods, but these styles evolve as teachers gain more computer experience.

▶ The very opportunities opened by the computer can create more work for the teacher, and thus make the job harder initially.

▶ The teacher-reform movement has created special challenges and opportunities for the application of technology to education.

▶ Preservice technology training, while important in giving prospective teachers facility with the computer, only serves as an introduction.

▶ The federal government's role in training teachers to use technology has been a limited one, although federal support was important in creating a "first wave" of computer-using educators.

▶ Any further investment in technology for education must factor in teacher training and support, whether that effort is focused on a few specialized teachers or on all teachers.

▶ School administrators must support and encourage teachers to use technology throughout the curriculum.

▶ Efforts to support teachers require attention to more than immediate needs and current practice (pp. 87–88).

Strengths and Weaknesses of Different Programming Languages

Computer scientists have much to say about which computer languages are the most appropriate for students to learn. During the past 20 years, at least six languages have been proclaimed as being the best. Languages that are best for beginners might not be best for the experienced user. The following are a few characteristics that might be considered:

1. *Is the language conducive to structured programming?* Logo and Pascal are designed to force writers to use structured programming but BASIC can also be structured.

2. *Do the variables need to be spelled out initially?* This capability could be good for experienced programmers and for students preparing to become serious programmers, because it forces students to plan their programs carefully. Such a formal approach can become very discouraging for beginners, however, because they are forced to formalize many concepts

before they have constructed an intuition for them. Pascal requires that variables be specified, but BASIC and Logo do not.

3. *Does the language include graphics capabilities?* For the experienced programmer whose interest is in processing a large amount of data or in symbol manipulation, graphics may not be important; but for a beginning student, graphics is extremely motivational. Logo, of course, has easy, powerful graphics. The Apple implementations of BASIC and Pascal also have graphics.

4. *Are there capabilities for local and global variables?* This capability can make things easier for both the novice and the experienced programmer. Logo and Pascal have this capability, but BASIC does not.

5. *Is immediate mode accessible?* For the beginner this is important because it allows the user to build his or her intuitions and to try ideas easily. Logo and BASIC have this feature, but many versions of Pascal do not.

6. *Is the operating system fairly simple to use?* The Apple BASIC operating system is simple and straightforward. The Logo system is more complicated because there are both an execution mode and an editing mode. The Pascal operating system is complex and has several modes.

7. *Is it easy to edit programs?* The Logo and Pascal editors are simple to use and have easy ways to add and delete. BASIC, on the other hand, is cumbersome and awkward.

Logo is one of the best languages for the beginner because it has many of these features. However, as long as BASIC is the dominant language for microcomputers, it cannot be ignored. Pascal is the computer scientists' choice for those planning to be serious programmers. We recommend that first experiences be with Logo and believe that elementary-school students should have access to it. We suggest that BASIC be taught only as a second language and in a structured form. Pascal is recommended for the high-school advanced-placement course in computer science.

Integration of the Computer into the Schools

A number of issues concerning the integration of the computer into the school need to be considered. We now examine the issues of integrated versus separate curriculum, isolation versus cooperation, the use of computers in a laboratory versus in individual classrooms, uses of networking, and staff development.

Integrated versus Separate Curricula

A number of schools are deciding to open a new area in computer literacy, computer education, or computer science. The strengths and weaknesses of this approach should be considered.

In an integrated curriculum, we should look for interweaving threads. In his Pulitzer Prize-winning book *Gödel, Escher, Bach,* Hofstadter (1979), a computer scientist, identified a number of interrelationships between the works of Gödel, a mathematician; Escher, an artist and mathematician; and Bach, a musical composer. Some of those threads relate to those woven through this book, including:

1. The conflict between the finite and the infinite
2. Recursion
3. Modularization
4. Chunking
5. Mental and visual imagery

Imagine the uses of simultaneous applications of the concepts *finite* and *infinite* in music that continues on and on, yet recycles through the same loops. Think about drawings of stairs that are going up and yet bending back under themselves, as in the Escher drawings. Imagine the ways in which recursion is used in music, mathematics, and Escher's art. Think of ways in which modularization can be used in music and art. Similarly, think of ways in which chunking can be used in music composition, artistic design, and mathematics. Art, music, and mathematics are all highly related to imagery, sometimes visual and sometimes auditory.

Developing graphics and simulation techniques is exciting for students; through these they develop the desire to learn the underlying mathematics, science, data structures, assembly language, and so on. To understand how to create their own three-dimensional flight simulators, they would need this information and would learn through their perception of these needs. This approach can bring students back into the mathematics and science classes. The computer can also be used to provide other motivation for learning mathematics and science.

The National Science Board Commission (1983) stressed, "Appropriate instruction in technology should be integrated into the curriculum for grades K through 12. Doing so will serve to strengthen the teaching of science, mathematics and computer literacy" (p. 101). Furthermore, they stressed (pp. 101–102) that through learning about technology, students should gain skills in:

1. Formulating and solving problems and identifying alternative solutions to problems
2. Making connections between theory and practice, building and testing models
3. Examining trade-offs, performing risk analysis, synthesizing, and designing
4. Using the concepts of feedback and stability

Of course, computers draw upon mathematics and science and offer much to those disciplines; computers also can contribute to other subject areas—the skills listed above apply to social studies, art, music, and other areas.

Some schools choose to have a separate program in computer science, in which students spend a year learning each of several languages. We believe that this approach does not provide as much growth as do other options. Languages are simply sets of symbols with perhaps a few differentiating concepts. The second language usually is easier to learn than the first because learning the first requires also the understanding of programming concepts. We believe it is not the language but the underlying concepts and problem-solving skills that are most important.

Another alternative that some are proposing is to teach virtually theoretical computer science, including switching circuits, indepth work with data structures—stacks, queues, and linked lists, computer architecture, and assembly language. Mathematics and science teachers teach most of the computer-programming classes in high schools, but qualified teachers would be needed to teach these computer science courses. There has been a severe shortage of teachers for mathematics and science, because people have found that it is more remunerative to pursue careers in computers outside education. Hence, getting well-qualified teachers for these courses is nontrivial.

We have mentioned here the arguments for integrating computers into existing classes, or creating new curricula consisting of a series of programming languages or a theoretical computer-science series. Each school must determine the approach that will work best for it.

Isolation versus Cooperation

It is sometimes believed that computers isolate people from each other; yet this generation of computers is in many ways encouraging people to interact. Students work together developing programming skills (as any Logo teacher will testify), playing games, interacting with simulations, and so on. This is a great improvement from each person being whipped through his or her paces in the former programmed-learning variation of computer-assisted instruction.

Computer-Related Hardware

For use with computers, two types of electronic equipment are worthy of consideration. These pieces of equipment open wide possibilities for expanding and exploiting the functions of computers.

Computer Projection Systems   A variety of projection systems are now available; their quality has dramatically improved over a short time. Some systems, generally referred to as *data display systems,* may be used on an overhead projector, to project the computer's display onto a screen. The resolution is quite good, though color is not yet available. The price for such units is approximately $750. These tools are useful for presentations and discussions when computers are being used with large groups. Used to project computer simulations, for example, these devices can involve a full class of students in group problem-solving activities.

Interactive Video Systems   Although this book focuses on computing and therefore cannot describe the implications of interactive video systems in much detail, the idea must be introduced. Briefly, computers can control video systems (for example, video disks) so that interaction can occur—the computer can respond to questions being asked about active video material and seek information in integrated systems. This is a significant area of development and study that should be explored. Suffice it to say that the potential use of such systems in education are great and that combining computers with video systems opens possibilities for events that now are only imaginable.

Word Processing and Integrated Software Packages

Word Processors   Among the more prominent word-processing programs available today are *Microsoft Word,* available for the Macintosh and IBM, and *WordPerfect* for IBM and Apple IIc, e, and GS. These word processors are among the most highly rated. They include features that substantially extend the concept of word processing. Each has an associated dictionary for spelling checks, and, to personalize letters and other communications; each can electronically integrate names, addresses, and other information into a document. Advanced formatting capabilities include the use of electronic cut-and-paste, to combine text and graphics in the same document; text and graphics can even be placed side-by-side on a line (this may seem simple but has not been). *WordPerfect* includes a thesaurus for the presentation of synonyms. *Microsoft Word* has a "Page Preview" that essentially provides a view of the page's layout, prior to printing. Each of these word processors can also transfer data to such other systems as desktop-publishing software. Though this description omits many other features that are of equal significance, it illustrates the direction in which word processors are going.

Integrated Software Packages   Integrated software packages somewhat like the AppleWorks program (see Chapters 5–8) are available on many different computer systems, some having more advanced features than those in AppleWorks. For example, *Microsoft Works* for the Macintosh and IBM and *PFS: First Choice* for the IBM family are particularly easy to use, flexible integrated systems with word processing, spreadsheets, and databases at their core. Each has advanced features superior to others on the market. For example, *Microsoft Works* uses icons and pull-down windows for ease and simplicity; *PFS: First Choice* contains a "business graphics" component (like the *Visualizer* addition to AppleWorks) and a thesaurus and spelling-checker component. Each contains electronic communications software.

Computers in Laboratories versus in Classrooms

Many schools are setting up computer laboratories, which provide a pleasant environment in which students can learn. A class can go to the laboratory and work together. Sometimes, however, when the teacher wants to demonstrate ideas, one machine is quite enough; using one machine in a classroom instead of having to move to a lab, can make it easier to integrate computers into instruction. Ideally, schools should have both a laboratory with a cluster of machines, and a single machine with an overhead display device in each classroom for demonstration purposes. It can be helpful to have a few computers in the classroom for students to use individually or in small groups. (It should be noted that group size was investigated by Cox and Berger (1985), who found that groups of three to four seemed to be optimal for use with problem solving.) Not all schools can afford such arrangements. A compromise option is to have a few computers available on movable carts to use in classrooms as they are needed, but for them to be clustered in a laboratory at other times.

Networking

Several computers can share a disk drive on a host computer at the teacher station. The teacher can download programs to each student station, and students can save from their terminal to the host disk drive. The host drive may be a regular floppy-disk drive or a hard-disk drive. One of the main advantages of networking is that one piece of software can be downloaded to serve a number of computers. An advantage of networking with floppy-disk drives is that it is cheaper; only one or two drives are needed for a laboratory of 15–30 terminals. An advantage of networking with a hard-disk drive is the amount of memory (20–80 megabytes) available; also, hard disks are more reliable than floppy disks. A disadvantage of networking is that many programs cannot be downloaded or cannot be saved on a hard-disk drive unless a special license fee is paid for a networkable version. In summary, networking is advisable in only certain situations. Networking is primarily appropriate for classes in which everyone uses the same application.

Staff Development

Staff development must be viewed as a long-range process. First, teachers must become comfortable with the computer. Second, teachers must examine what the computer can do for their students. Third, teachers should learn what the computer can do for the teachers themselves; it can, for example, increase their own problem-solving, logical, and visualization processes.

Evaluations of the Effectiveness of Computers in Education

A number of recent studies have raised questions concerning the effectiveness of computers in education. These evaluation procedures and their findings both seem to contain considerable variations.

Large-Scale Evaluations

Computers have now been in schools long enough that some large-scale evaluations are surfacing. For example, in 1984–85, the New York City Board of Education (1986) conducted a large-scale evaluation of a number of computer projects, including a Logo computer language for grades kindergarten through two, a word-processing program for grades seven through nine, and a computer literacy program involving basic computer knowledge and career information, for grades three through nine. Unfortunately their testing instruments did not seem to accurately measure the children's abilities, so many results were inconclusive.

Another study conducted in New York City made systematic observations over the course of a semester of the behavior of 212 subjects with some language or cognitive impairment (de Bernard & Ferber, 1986). These observations involved environments in which microcomputers were used with either instructional software or Logo, and the teacher mediated learning (had control). They found relationships between the subject's age and level of cognitive distancing; that is, the discrepancy between a child's actual mental age and the level that he or she could reach in solving problems with assistance was related for all ages. Their results suggested a strong relationship between the students' level of cognitive development and their ability to profit from Logo instruction. They also found that teachers initiated more interactions with children at the lowest level of distancing than with those at higher levels; there was more interaction between students in Logo than in either the teacher-directed or the other instructional software groups.

Another large-scale evaluation project was conducted by Carmichael and others (1985) in Ontario, Canada. This study involved 433 students in 18 classrooms that involved 13 different teachers. Students worked in either a classroom containing one to five computers over the entire school year, or a computer laboratory. Logo and word processing were studied extensively. Their findings indicate that creative use of computers fosters the development of independent and original thinking and encourages extensive social interaction among students. Students become more willing to share, refine, and revise their ideas. They also experienced an increase in self-esteem and confidence if they have a significant amount of control over their learning.

Reflections on Evaluation Systems

Our uses for the computer and our measures of its use seem to vary considerably. The first New York study seemed to be measuring specific outcomes, while the second New York study and the Ontario study seemed to be describing what is happening. As we grow in our understanding of ways in which this machine can radically change the whole way we teach and learn, we should be careful not to limit our expectations to specific outcomes, as our only measure of its potential. The computer holds the potential to change not only *how* we learn and *what* we learn, but also the entire learning environment and overall educational system.

Careful reflections by Johanson (1988) suggest that we should be very cautious in making premature generalizations about uses of computers. He has identified the following hypotheses:

1. A cognitive chain of consequences exists; students are not progressing to the end of the chain, but could.
2. Applications represent a more likely arena than programming in which to look for the desired cognitive outcomes.
3. The research on cognitive outcomes of programming has been poorly conceptualized.
4. Research has been unsophisticated and done at the wrong age level.
5. The anticipation of cognitive benefits constitutes a resurrection of the discredited concept of mental discipline.
6. Problem solving, higher-order thinking, divergent thinking and other goals of programming instruction are discontinuous with the regular curriculum and are unlikely to be achieved.
7. Problem solving and higher-order thinking may be domain-specific.
8. Failure to find the desired effects of programming, such as higher-order thinking, problem solving, and enhanced metacognition, have been due to a lack of curricular sophistication. Objectives related to such outcomes have not been adequately inherent in the experimental treatments (pp. 4–11).

Social Issues Related to Logo

The issue of whether heavy emphasis should be placed upon applications software or on Logo will not be settled at this point. However, issues that are related to Logo learning, including social issues and aspects of information-processing styles, need to be considered here. For example, in conclusions similar to those of the Carmichael and others (1985) study, Ginther and Williamson (1985) claim that there are some important personal and social benefits from Logo instruction. Guntermann and Tovar (1987), examining the use of Logo for collaborative learning with problem-solving experiences, suggested that computer use for instructional purpose is as successful with small groups of children as with individuals. Trowbridge and Durnin (1984) found that group-based computer learning was superior to individual computer learning, provided that the size of the group did not exceed three students. De Bernard and Ferber (1986) found that the teacher-initiated behavior was highest in interactions for the Logo groups across age groups.

Vygotsky (1978) conceptualized the "zone of proximal development" as the region of skillfulness that lies between the child's independent functioning and the child's functioning with social support. He portrays this zone as occurring in a child who has partly mastered a skill, but can act more effectively with the assistance of a more skilled peer or adult. Children working together on Logo projects may generate far more dynamic outcomes than have yet been measured. De Bernard and Ferber (1986) used Vygotsky's theories in their observations and analyses.

Other Cognitive Aspects

Relationships between students' information-processing styles and Logo programming skills were examined by Bradley (1985). She found strong correlations between successful use of top-down processing and success with Logo, holistic processing, field-independence tendencies, and general achievement.

It might be that if students creatively use the *microworld* concept along with tools or subprocedures already available to them, that this creative endeavor might have a greater impact than the children's having to create all the subprocedures from scratch. Students "cut and paste" tools together in an appropriate sequencing, possibly even passing variables. In this case the children are oscillating between the structured world that they do not yet understand and the unstructured world to which they are bringing organization. This in fact may be the way that a constructivist approach to teaching may be operationalized.

Pea (1984) raised a number of questions concerning ways in which computers can be used as intelligent tutoring systems and learning devices that help students construct their own knowledge. He identified the importance of "integrating the powerful information-processing systems of the computer with the frail information-processing system of the human mind" (p. 13). He also points out:

> One consequence of the information age is that what children will have to know to learn and develop will be drastically different from what our educational system now provides. Today, we spend decades learning the three R's and memorizing facts that are often outdated. A culture pervaded by AI-based [Artificial intelligence-based] developmental tools (for all the basics, and thinking tools in creative processes such as design and invention) will lead to new definitions of intelligence. These definitions may place a higher value on the skills that have long been the aid of liberal arts education: cognitive skills of information management; strategies for problem-solving that crosscut domains of knowledge; metacognitive skills such as planning, monitoring, and learning how to learn; and communication and critical inquiry skills. Teaching the basic facts of the disciplines will not be sufficient to provide for an educated citizenry that can use the thinking tools of this age, nor will it be feasible because of the information explosion (p. 19).

Equity Issues

In considering equity issues in education, we must examine access to computers and ways in which computers are used. A fundamental issue is whether the child controls the computer or the computer controls the child. Additionally, issues related to sex and socioeconomic status need particular consideration.

Sexual Equity

Modern women are moving into more creative and technical areas than did earlier generations. A number of women have found that their mathematics and science backgrounds fall far short of what is needed for the careers to which they aspire. Interest in computers often stimulates students' interest in mathematics, science, and languages. By encouraging students to work with computers at an early age, we can stimulate their interest in mathematics and science.

Girls as well as boys should be involved with computers as early as is reasonable. We have observed that in some schools, students are started with computers as early as second or third grade. At this age, the girls are as aggressive as the boys about getting their share of time at the computers. However, when students start to work with computers in middle school, in some cases girls appear to be more passive and to stay in the background, whereas the boys move ahead by demanding more computer time. Fortunately, some schools are reporting that their middle-school girls are just as aggressive about time at the computer as boys. One study reported that among entering freshmen at Berkeley, 49 percent of the males and 26 percent of the females had written computer programs (Luehrmann, 1984). Further examination of these inequities was conducted by Becker and Sterling (1987), Anderson (1987), and Schaefer and Sprigle (1988). These studies show that girls do have capabilities of effectively working with computers and should be strongly encouraged to be involved with the computer as early as possible. The seriousness of the equity concerns for women and minorities is examined in a number of current reports, such as Cole and Griffin (1987), National Research Council (1989), and the Task Force on Women, Minorities, and the Handicapped in Science and Technology (1988). These reports stress the importance of full equity in technology.

Socioeconomic Equity

Students from affluent homes are more likely to have their own home computers and hence have more hands-on time to develop programming and problem-solving skills. Students from economically deprived homes, however, usually are able to use computers only at school. In some school districts, the able students learn programming, whereas the less capable students spend their computer time using the drill and practice programs. Luehrmann (1984) reported that 35 percent of students in schools in minority neighborhoods and 18 percent of students in all schools spent their computer time on drill and practice; 10 percent of students in schools in minority neighborhoods and 23 percent of students in all schools spent their computer time on programming the computer. It appears that brighter or more affluent students are more likely to control the computer, whereas less bright or less affluent students are more likely to be controlled by the computer. Regardless of sex or socioeconomic status, students should have ample opportunity to use computers creatively.

Developing Software—Who Should Do It?

The typical developers of educational software are teachers, instructional designers, and computer specialists. Each has strengths; each has weaknesses. For example, quality instructional software cannot be produced by someone who knows a lot about children but very little about how to design materials or how to use computers. One cannot design quality educational software if one knows a lot about computers but very little about students and instructional-materials design. Quality instructional software cannot be designed by someone who knows about instructional design but knows little about the content to be taught, the potential of the computer, or students' thinking and learning processes.

The point is, to design effective instructional software you need to know a lot about how students think and learn, how to get the full effects of a computer, and how to put materials together. If we want to move away from programs that are only electronic page-turning, there is a need for a new professional who combines these capabilities. This need is part of Naisbitt's third wave of technology, which creates new employment from traditional components. Where such people will go from there depends upon how able they are at breaking out of the old ways of thinking and to what extent society will allow them to find new directions.

When a new dimension is added, as when a third is added to two dimensions, you get much more than the old space plus one more linear dimension. Instead you generate a totally new space. A strong background in educational applications, programming, logic concepts, and computer applications is essential to this new space that has been created.

Legal Issues: Privacy and Copyrights

Legal issues with respect to technology are a serious concern for all of us. Two major legal forms that need to be considered are privacy of information and copyrights.

Privacy

More and more data are being collected on each of us and are being filed in large databases. The **privacy** of such records should concern us. The questions of who should be allowed access to these data, how unauthorized uses can be stopped, and how we can be protected from having incorrect data filed about us, need serious thought. In education, grades could be changed, degrees awarded, and budgets modified through computer tampering.

Copyrights

Software distributors invest enormous amounts of time and money in the development of quality software. To secure their investments, they develop codes to protect against the copying of their materials. The effect has been like waving a red flag: it challenges a number of bright people who are determined to break codes. For every encode, there is a decode. The battle continues and students are the losers because large companies are not willing to invest in the development of software if they are afraid of having their materials stolen. Materials also have been grossly overpriced because the producers know that they have to make money from their first few copies.

Recreational Uses of the Computer

Many people have become hypnotized by video games. There must be reasons why people play the same video games over and over. People's wanting to play a game over and over is a very positive sign of the quality of the game. Some people think that well-designed games are forcing youngsters to integrate the functioning of the left and right hemispheres of their brains. Games that are highly visual and spatial involve strategies, and the discovery of underlying principles offers much learning to students. Youngsters who are growing up spending time actively involved with such games may be creating communication between their right and left hemispheres to a higher degree than did previous generations. To determine both the positive and negative aspects of this learning process, considerable research is needed in technology and brain functioning.

Intelligent Machines

The role of intelligent machines will complete our discussion of potential directions and influences of the computer age. We will examine the meaning of the term *intelligent machine* and will identify current applications in robotics and expert systems and areas that will need long-range research and development.

What Is an Intelligent Machine?

To answer the question of what is an **intelligent machine,** we will see what some of the specialists in the field have to say. **Artificial intelligence** is defined by Barr and Feigenbaum (1981) as,

> the part of computer science concerned with designing intelligent computer systems, that is systems that exhibit the characteristics we associate with intelligence in human behavior—understanding language, learning, reasoning, solving problems, and so on [p. 1].

Winston (1977) defined it as follows:

> Artificial intelligence is the study of ideas which enable computers to do the things that make people seem intelligent. But then, what is human intelligence? Is it the ability to reason? Is it the ability to acquire and apply knowledge? Is it the ability to manipulate and communicate ideas? Surely all of these abilities are part of what intelligence is, but they are not the whole of what can be said. Indeed, a definition in the usual sense seems impossible because intelligence appears to be an amalgam of so many information-processing and information-representation talents.
>
> Nevertheless, one can define the goals of the field of artificial intelligence: The central goals of artificial intelligence are to make computers more useful and to understand the principles which make intelligence possible [p. 1].

Topics included in the study of artificial intelligence are,

1. Methods of representing knowledge in the machine
2. Search strategies
3. Natural language processing
4. Robotics and vision

Two programs often cited as examples of artificial intelligence are *Animals* and *Eliza*. To teach the computer to become smarter, *Animals* asks for and analyzes input; Figure 1 shows a sample of the questions it asks. *Animals* is included on the *Logo Utilities Disk*. The computer asks you questions about an animal that you are thinking about until it either guesses the animal or eliminates all the possibilities it knows. If the program cannot guess your animal, it will then ask you to state a question that will distinguish your new animal from all the other animals that it knows. Subsequently, to update its information file, the computer will store this new question and its answer with the other questions. In the process, the computer becomes a little smarter each time: it learns new animals.

Eliza is a program in which you, the user, talk to a psychiatrist. *Eliza,* the

Figure 1 *Sample questions asked by Animals.*

▼

```
THINK OF AN ANIMAL.  I WILL
TRY TO GUESS IT BY ASKING QUESTIONS.

DOES IT HAVE FOUR LEGS?
DOES IT HAVE CLAWS?
CAN IT RUN?
DOES IT CRAWL?
IS IT A FISH?
OH WELL,  I WAS WRONG.  WHAT WAS IT?
PLEASE TYPE IN A QUESTION WHOSE ANSWER
IS "YES" FOR A SPIDER AND
"NO" FOR A FISH.
LET'S TRY AGAIN.
THINK OF AN ANIMAL.  I WILL
TRY TO GUESS IT BY ASKING QUESTIONS.

DOES IT HAVE FOUR LEGS?
DOES IT HAVE CLAWS?
CAN IT RUN?
DOES IT CRAWL?
DOES IT HAVE SIX LEGS?
IS IT A SPIDER?
LOOK HOW SMART I AM!
LET'S TRY AGAIN.
```

```
HELLO, I'M THE BRILLIANT PSYCHOANALYST.
PLEASE STATE YOUR PROBLEM AND I WILL TRY TO HELP YOU.
:I AM SCARED OF COMPUTERS.
DO YOU BELIEVE YOU ARE SCARED OF COMPUTERS?
:YES
I'M NOT SURE I BELIEVE THAT.
YOU SAY THAT YOU REALLY ARE AFRAID OF COMPUTERS?
:YES
ARE YOU REALLY BEING HONEST WITH ME?
:YES
I SEE.
:HOW DO I GET OVER MY FEAR OF COMPUTERS?
WHY DO YOU ASK?
:BECAUSE YOU ARE SUPPOSED TO HELP ME.
IS THAT THE ONLY REASON?
:NO, I WANT TO GET OVER MY FEAR OF COMPUTERS.
OK_I WON'T ARGUE WITH YOU.
:
EARLIER YOU SAID THAT YOU REALLY ARE AFRAID OF COMPUTERS. LET'S
DISCUSS THAT FURTHER.
:OK
WHY DID YOU SAY THAT YOU ARE SCARED OF COMPUTERS?
:BECAUSE I'M AFRAID THEY WILL TAKE OVER.
THAT'S A GOOD REASON.
:
```

▲

Figure 2 *Sample conversation with Eliza.*

psychiatrist, echoes back what you say. Figure 2 illustrates a typical dialogue. This program was created by Joseph Weizenbaum and is discussed, with reactions to it, in his *Computer Power and Human Reason* (1976). The program is designed to demonstrate an application of artificial intelligence to a language-analysis program. He commented:

> The program was constructed in a two-tier arrangement, the first tier consisting of the language analyzer and the second of a script. The script is a set of rules rather like those that might be given to an actor who is to use them to improvise around a certain theme [p. 3].

After a variation of this program, *Doctor,* was released, reactions were surprising. Weizenbaum commented that:

> A number of practicing psychiatrists seriously believed the DOCTOR computer program could grow into a nearly completely automatic form of psychotherapy. . . . I was startled to see how quickly and how very deeply people conversing with DOCTOR became emotionally involved with the computer and how unequivocally they anthropomorphized it. . . . Another widespread, and to me surprising, reaction to the ELIZA program was the spread of a belief that it demonstrated a general solution to the problem of computer understanding of natural language. In my paper, I had tried to say that no general solution to that problem was possible, i.e., that language is understood only in contextual frameworks, that even these can be shared by people to only a limited extent, and that consequently even people are not embodiments of any such general solution. But these conclusions were often ignored. In any case, ELIZA was such a small and simple step. Its contribution was, if any at all, only to vividly underline what many others had long ago discovered, namely, the importance of context to language understanding [pp. 5–7].

It should be noted that Weizenbaum gave the program the name of *Eliza* after Eliza Doolittle of *Pygmalion,* a story that concerned teaching a human being to speak "proper" English.

Weizenbaum further commented:

> But most existing programs, and especially the largest and most important ones, are not theory-based. . . . They are heuristic, not necessarily in the sense that they employ heuristic methods internally, but in that their construction is based on rules of thumb, stratagems that appear to "work" under most foreseen circumstances, and on other ad-hoc mechanisms that are added to them from time to time. My own program, ELIZA, was of precisely this type [p. 232].

Cognitive Science

As people want machines to become more and more intelligent, they also try to understand the workings of the human mind. The field of **cognitive science** is growing out of psychology and artificial intelligence. This is an example of a new discipline developing from two other disciplines.

You might find *Classroom Computers and Cognitive Science* (Wilkinson, 1983) interesting. An outgrowth of a National Institute of Education study, this book describes several aspects of uses of computers and cognitive development. It discusses the role of cognitive models in the development of intelligent computer-assisted instruction, natural-language and related programs, and programming languages for the novice.

Robotics

One of the major applications of artificial intelligence is **robotics.** The industrial revolution brought forth the innovative concept of mass production. Human beings became part of assembly lines and did the same job over and over. We know that computers are far better at repetition than are human beings. One of the reasons that the American automobile industry has had serious difficulty in recent years is that they cannot compete with the Japanese industry, which is already using robots to do the assembly line work: The robots are able to produce automobiles that are less expensive and more reliable. This is a definite part of the trend moving from the industrial revolution to the technologic revolution. Some people believe that we should not waste human resources to do work that machines can do. Robotic applications are continuing to grow. Perhaps soon robots will be able to clean our houses and cook for us.

Knowledge Engineering through Expert Systems

Another growing aspect of artificial intelligence (AI) is **knowledge engineering** through the development of **expert systems.** Barr and Feigenbaum (1982) defined expert systems in the following way:

> Over the past decade, many of the fundamental AI techniques . . . on search, knowledge representation, and natural-language processing have been applied in the form of *expert systems,* that is, computer systems that can help solve complex, real-world problems in specific scientific, engineering, and medical specialties. These systems are most strongly characterized by their use of large bodies of domain knowledge—facts and procedures, gleaned from human experts, that have proved useful for solving typical problems in their domain. Expert-systems research promises to lead to AI applications of great economic and social impact.
>
> Representing and using the various types of knowledge that characterize expertise constitute one principal focus of expert-systems research. Among the things that might be useful for an expert system to know about are:
>
> 1. Facts about the domain: "The shin bone is connected to the ankle bone" or, more typical of human experts, "The automatic choke on '77 Chevys often gets stuck on cold mornings"
> 2. Hard-and-fast rules or procedures: "Always unplug the set before you stick a screwdriver into the back"

3. Problem situations and what might be good things to try to do when you are in them (heuristics): "If it won't start but you are getting a spark, check the fuel line"
4. Global strategies: differential diagnosis
5. A "theory" of the domain: a causal explanation of how an internal-combustion engine works [pp. 79, 81]

Hemispheric Brain Research and Intelligent Machines

Much work done in artificial intelligence is limited to manipulating strings and language; these activities are more closely related to the left than to the right hemisphere of the brain. Thus far, the people in artificial intelligence are ignoring the bimodal brain research. Considerable evidence suggests that the right hemisphere plays an important role in human intelligence. Until right-hemisphere processes are integrated with artificial intelligence, true intelligence might not be achieved.

Perhaps the greatest potential of artificial intelligence in education lies in the construction of highly intelligent video games. Such games will be far more sophisticated than today's simple games. They will have sophisticated underlying models that will incorporate higher computer speed and memory, and they'll make use of highly sophisticated graphics capabilities and reasoning power. Such games could bring about whole-brain coordination of the user.

Logo as an Application of Artificial Intelligence

Many researchers in artificial intelligence acknowledge that Logo is, thus far, the best application of artificial intelligence to education. As mentioned earlier in this book, Logo was created at the Artificial Intelligence Laboratory at the Massachusetts Institute of Technology. The computer is not intelligent, but, by teaching it new procedures, the user helps the machine to become intelligent. Winston (1977) commented:

> While looking at programs which solve problems expertly, it is natural to wonder if the ideas and metaphors employed can help make people better problem solvers. The answer may be Yes. People who write intelligent programs often feel that writing smart programs helps the programmer become smarter [p. 235].

As the focus of the revolution shifts from muscles to brains to creative uses of brains, we as educators are determining, willfully or otherwise, what our children can become. Whether they will be controlled by or will control machines may be in our hands.

▶ ▲ ◀ ▼ ▶ ▲ ◀ ▼ ▶ ▲ ◀ ▼ ▶ ▲ ◀ ▼ ▶ ▲ ◀ ▼ ▶

Summary

In this chapter, you gained perspective on the influences of the computer revolution on our society, the nature of computer literacy, the issues concerning implementation of the computer in our schools, and the potential of intelligent machines. A new discipline that can restructure current machines to achieve their full potential is emerging.

In this book, we started with turtlegraphics and used programming to introduce you to current machines and their uses. You learned a number of functional skills, including programming in Logo and tool uses such as word processing, databases, spreadsheets and integrated software, evaluating software, and examining the importance of problem solving and visualization. Finally, we talked about the future.

We realize that we are involved in a computer revolution that might change our society. The skills and abilities that our students will need in this new generation may require that we refocus our educational goals. Computers might provide a particularly effective means by which knowledge critical for the future can be developed.

Software discussed in this chapter:

Animals
Eliza

Important Terms

Artificial intelligence

Cognitive science

Computer revolution

Expert system

Industrial revolution

Intelligent machine

Knowledge engineering

Legal issues

Privacy

Robotics

Socioeconomic equity

Third wave

Exercises

1. Discuss new disciplines that are evolving because of technology.

2. Brainstorm to produce ideas for new uses of computers in school settings.

3. Brainstorm to produce ideas for new uses of computers in the home.

4. How does the "back-to-basics" movement in the school relate to the computer revolution? How does the "standards of excellence" concept relate to it?

5. Characterize intelligent machines.

6. What equity issues were discussed in this chapter? Can you think of others?

7. Identify at least ten careers that will be affected by the computer revolution.

8. Look back five years and compare life then to today. How many changes can you identify that are related to the computer revolution?

9. How has your life changed because of the computer revolution?

10. Look forward five years and identify ways in which you would like to have the computer revolution change your future.

11. Use books such as *The Micro Millenium* (Evans, 1979) to trace the historical development of computers.

12. Make a list of your anticipations for machine capabilities one, two, and five years from now.

References

Anderson, R. E. (1987). Females surpass males in computer problem solving: Findings from the Minnesota computer literacy assessment. *Journal of Educational Computing Research, 3*(1), 39–51.

Barr, A., & Feigenbaum, E. A. (eds.). (1981). *The handbook of artificial intelligence. Vol. 1.* Los Altos, CA: William Kaufmann.

Barr, A., & Feigenbaum, E. A. (Eds.). (1982). *The handbook of artificial intelligence. Vol. 2.* Los Altos, CA: William Kaufmann.

Becker, H. J., & Sterling, C. W. (1987). Equity in school computer use: National data and neglected considerations. *Journal of Educational Computing Research, 3*(3), 289–311.

Bradley, C. A. (1985). The relationship between students' information-processing styles and Logo programming. *Journal of Educational Computing Research, 1*(4), 427–433.

Carmichael, H. W., et al. (1985). Computers, children and classrooms: A multisite evaluation of the creative use of microcomputers by elementary school children. Final report. Toronto: Ontario Department of Education. (Available from Publication Centre, 880 Bay Street, 5th Floor, Toronto, Ontario, Canada M7A 1N8.) ERIC ED 268 994.

Cole, M. & Griffin, P. (Eds.). (1987). *Improving science and mathematics education for minorities and women: Contextual factors in education.* Madison, WI: Wisconsin Center for Education Research, University of Wisconsin.

Cox, D. A., & Berger, C. F. (1985). The importance of group size in the use of problem-solving skills on a microcomputer. *Journal of Educational Computing Research, 1*(4), 459–469.

de Bernard, A. E., & Ferber, G. P. (1986). The teaching/learning process of handicapped children in the microcomputer environment. A paper presented at the Annual Convention of the Council for Exceptional Children, New Orleans. ERIC ED 268 774.

Evans, C. (1979). *The micro millennium.* New York: Washington Square Press.

Feigenbaum, E. A., & McCorduck, P. (1983). *The fifth generation: Artificial intelligence and Japan's computer challenge to the world.* Reading, MA: Addison-Wesley.

Ginther, D. W., & Williamson, J. D. (1985). Learning Logo: What is really learned? *Computers in the Schools, 2/3,* 73–77.

Guntermann, E., & Tovar, M. (1987). Collaborative problem-solving with Logo: Effects of group size and group composition. *Journal of Educational Computing Research, 3*(3), 313–334.

Hofstadter, D. R., (1979). *Godel, Escher, Bach: An eternal golden braid.* New York: Vintage Books.

Johanson, R. P. (1988). Computers, cognition and curriculum: Retrospect and prospect. *Journal of Educational Computing Research, 4*(1), 1–30.

Kent, E. W. (1981). *The brains of men and machines.* Peterborough, NH: BYTE/McGraw-Hill.

Klopfer, L. E. (1986, Summer). Intelligent tutoring systems in science education: The coming generation of computer-based instructional programs. *Journal of Computers in Mathematics and Science Teaching,* pp. 16–23.

Luehrmann, A. (1984). *Educational computing for the 80's.* A presentation given at the Florida Computing Conference. Orlando, FL, February.

Naisbitt, J., (1982). *Megatrends: Ten new directions transforming our lives.* New York: Warner Books.

National Research Council. (1989). *Everybody counts: A report to the nation on the future of mathematics education.* Washington, DC: National Academy Press.

The National Science Board Commission on Precollege Education in Mathematics, Science and Technology. (1983). *Educating Americans for the 21st century: A plan of action for improving mathematics, science and technology education for all American elementary and secondary students so that their achievement is the best in the world by 1995.* A report to the American people and the National Science Board, Washington, DC: National Science Foundation.

Neighbours, D., & Slaton, F. (1987). Robots in my classroom. *The Computing Teacher, 14,* 24–28.

New York City Board of Education. (1986). School community education program in New York City. Brooklyn: Office of Educational Assessment. ERIC ED 278 131.

Norris, C. A. (1987). Human factors and computer interfaces: Implications for artificial intelligence. *The Computing Teacher, 15,* 23–25.

Pea, R. D. (1984). Integrating human and computer intelligence. Technical Report No. 32. New York: Center for Children and Technology. Bank Street College of Education. ERIC ED 257 449.

Piddock, P. (1987, February). Expert systems and education. *Computer Education,* 8–10.

Poirot, J. L., & Norris, C. A. (1987). Artificial intelligence applications in education. *The Computing Teacher, 15,* 8–10, 38.

Rambally, G. K. (1986). The AI approach to CAI. *The Computing Teacher, 13,* 39–42.

Schaefer, L., & Sprigle, J. E. (1988). Gender differences in the use of the Logo programming language. *Journal of Educational Computing Research, 4*(1), 49–55.

Sherwood, R. D., et al. (1987). New directions for videodiscs. *The Computing Teacher, 14,* 10–13.

Smith, R. L. (1986). Artificial intelligence. *Journal of Computers in Mathematics and Science Teaching, 5,* 67–68.

Stone, A. (1987). Action for equity. *The Computing Teacher, 14,* 54–55.

Thorkildsen, R., Lubke, M., Myette, B., & Parry, J. (1985–86). Artificial intelligence: Applications in education. *Educational Research Quarterly, 10,* 3–9.

The Task Force on Women, Minorities, and the Handicapped in Science and Technology. (1988). *Changing America: The new face of science and engineering. Interim Report.* Washington, DC: The Task Force on Women, Minorities, and the Handicapped in Science and Technology.

Toffler, A. (1980). *The third wave.* New York: Bantam Books.

Trowbridge, D., & Durnin, R. (1984). Results from an investigation of groups working at the computer. ERIC ED 238 724.

United States Congress, Office of Technology Assessment. (1988, September). *Power On! New tools for teaching and learning.* A report to the Office of Technology Assessment. Washington, DC: U.S. Government Printing Office.

Vygotsky, L. S. (1978). *Mind in society: The development of the higher psychological processes.* Cambridge, MA: Harvard University Press.

Weizenbaum, J. (1976). *Computer power and human reason: From judgment to calculation.* New York: W. H. Freeman.

Wilkinson, A. C. (Ed.). (1983). *Classroom computers and cognitive science.* New York: Academic Press.

Winston, P. H. (1977). *Artificial intelligence.* Reading, MA: Addison-Wesley.

Yazdani, M. (1986). Intelligent tutoring systems survey. *Artificial Intelligence Review.*

Appendix A

Operating the Computer Equipment

▶ ▼ ◀ ▲ ▶ ▼ ◀ ▲ ▶ ▼ ◀ ▲ ▶ ▼ ◀ ▲ ▶ ▼ ◀ ▲ ▶ ▼

To start working with computers, you need to know a few things about operating the equipment. The following are suggestions for the care and use of floppy disks and computer equipment.

Care and Use of Floppy Disks

Floppy disks require some special attention:

1. Hold the floppy disk by the upper corner, where the label is.
2. Do not bend, fold, or abuse the disk. Do not pile other materials on top of the disk. Use a felt-tip pen to write on the label. Do not remove the black paper jacket covering the disk. Do not touch the magnetic surface.
3. Do not place a floppy disk near heat or a magnetic field, as in a television or telephone.
4. Store the disk vertically in its paper jacket and in special boxes designed to minimize static electricity.
5. Avoid putting it in contact with smoke, chalk dust, and other dirt.

Turning the Computer On and Off

The on/off switch for the Apple II+, IIe, IIc, and IIGS is on the back left side. Reach back there and feel the switch (see Figure 2 on p. 3 in Chapter 1). Some people use an electric bar to turn the computer on and off, which saves wear and tear on the computer switch (Figure 1).

Now insert your disk into your disk drive; the label should appear on the right front, facing up (Figure 2). Shut the door to the disk drive (Figure 3). Turn on the television or monitor and the computer. You may hear a grinding, spinning, or clicking sound. The clicking sound is the appropriate sound; it means that the computer is reading the information on the disk. A red light on the disk drive also indicates that success. If the clicking sound does not occur within a few seconds, turn the machine off and take the disk out. Put the disk back in and try again. If again the clicking sound does not occur, your disk might not be appropriately formatted for the Apple system.

Suggestions for the Best Use of Your Equipment

Use your equipment with care. Here are some suggestions:

1. Do not open the door to the disk drive when the red light is on.
2. If you hear a grinding or spinning sound, hold down <CTRL> on the Apple II + or IIe; it is on the left side of the keyboard, in the second row up. If you are using the Apple IIc, press < ⌂ > on the bottom row and <CTRL> in the second row up on the left side. Also press <RESET>, which for the Apple II + or IIe is on the right side in the top row, and for the Apple IIc is on the left side in the top row (Figure 4). If this does not work, turn the machine off. Wait five seconds and turn it on again.
3. Sometimes an I/O (INPUT/OUTPUT) message or a * is displayed on the screen. This means that the computer is having trouble reading the disk or does not have enough memory for the program.
4. When you are finished, turn the machine off. Remove the disk from the drive and leave the door to the drive open. Be sure the television or monitor is turned off (if you use an electric bar, the monitor should be plugged into the bar).

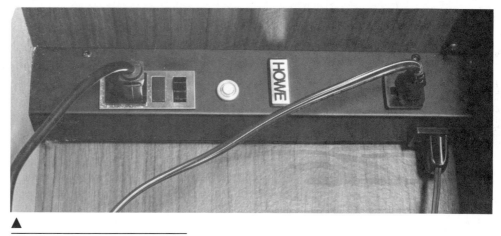

▲

Figure 1 *Sample electric bar to use for turning the computer on and off, saving wear on the computer switch.*

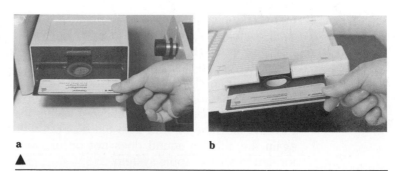

a   b
▲

Figure 2 *Inserting a disk into a disk drive for (a) the Apple II + and IIe and (b) the Apple IIc.*

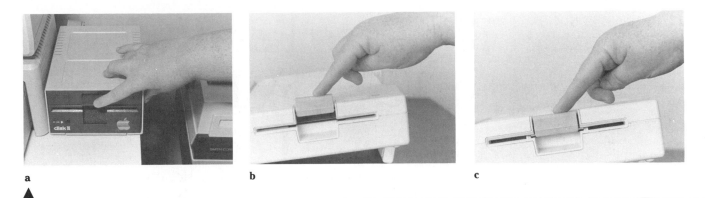

a   b   c

▲

Figure 3 *Shutting the disk drive door on the (a) Apple II+ or IIe and (b) Apple IIc. (c) Checking to be sure drive door is closed for the Apple IIc.*

a   b

c   d

▲

Figure 4 *<RESET> key for (a) the Apple II+, (b) the Apple IIe, (c) the Apple IIc, and (d) Apple IIGS.*

Appendix B

The Logo Editor for Terrapin, Logo Plus, and Apple Logo

▶ ▲ ◀ ▼ ▶ ▲ ◀ ▼ ▶ ▲ ◀ ▼ ▶ ▲ ◀ ▼ ▶ ▲ ◀ ▼ ▶ ▲ ◀

The Logo editor (for Terrapin, Logo Plus, and Apple Logo) helps you write procedures in Logo. To enter the editor, type

TO NAME   [You decide on what name you want; first character must be a letter, must have no spaces, and must not be a Logo primitive.]

When you are in the editor, you construct the program. After constructing the program, exit using either <CTRL-C> to define the procedure or <CTRL-G> to abort the procedure.

To move around in the editor, move the cursor up, down, left, and right:

↑   To move the cursor **up,** press the up arrow or hold down <CTRL> and press <P> (for *previous* line).

↓   To move the cursor **down,** press the down arrow or hold down <CTRL> and press <N> (for *next* line).

→   To move the cursor to the **right,** press the right arrow (right side, second row up on the keyboard).

←   To move the cursor to the **left,** press the left arrow (next to the right arrow key) (in Apple Logo, use <CTRL-B>).

To make corrections, use the following:

                 To insert new characters just start typing.

<CTRL-D>   To delete the character at the cursor, hold down <CTRL> and press <D>.

<CTRL-K>   To delete the remainder of the line to the right of the cursor, hold down <CTRL> and press <K>; for Terrapin Version 2.0 and Logo Plus, use <CTRL-X>.

<ESC>   <ESC>, found on the left side third row up on the keyboard, deletes the character immediately to the left of the cursor (in Apple Logo, use ←).

If you made any errors in your procedure or wish to make changes, use the editing commands. For example, you could use the editor to change the *Square* procedure using side measures of 50, to a *Square* using side measures of 100.

Appendix C

Using the Logo System in Terrapin, Logo Plus, and Apple Logo

▼ ▶ ▲ ◀ ▼ ▶ ▲ ◀ ▼ ▶ ▲ ◀ ▼ ▶ ▲ ◀ ▼ ▶ ▲ ◀ ▼ ▶ ▲ ◀ ▼ ▶ ▲

This appendix examines uses of the Logo System. Included are ways of loading/ reading and saving procedures and pictures, using screen-control commands, and printing pictures.

An operating system is a set of instructions that allows for operation of a computer system, in ways such as saving programs or pictures on a disk or retrieving such programs or pictures. To save programs, you must start with a prepared disk. If you are starting with a new disk, you will first need to initialize it (see Appendix G). If you have a disk already prepared for Applesoft BASIC, it can be used for Logo.

Put the Logo language disk into the disk drive and turn the machine on, or type

```
PR#6
```

if the disk control card (the card that controls the disk drive) is in slot 6.

Reading/Loading and Saving Procedures

To save a set of procedures on a disk, type

```
SAVE "NAME
```

where NAME is your program name—it must start with a letter, have no spaces, and not be a Logo primitive. To make sure the procedures were properly saved, type

```
CATALOG
```

which should list the files on the disk in the drive. You should see a name like

```
B 005 NAME.LOGO     [In Apple Logo, T 3 NAME.LOGO]
```

The .LOGO is Logo's way of filing the information. The B (T, in Apple Logo) indicates the type of file (in this case, B means binary file; in Apple Logo, T means text file). And the 005 tells how long the file is (3 tells how many blocks are used in NAME, in Apple Logo). Neither the B (T) nor the 005 (3) is typed in to read the file.

To retrieve a set of procedures previously saved under NAME (whatever name you used), type

```
READ "NAME     [LOAD "NAME, in Apple Logo]
```

Note that again the .LOGO is not used here. Logo keeps track of that part.

To save a screen display of graphics, type

```
SAVEPICT "NAME    [not a primitive in Apple Logo]
```

(Here NAME is the name of the picture. Do not use the same name you used previously.) Type

```
CATALOG
```

You should see on your catalog:

```
B 005 NAME.PICT
```

Again, you do not type .PICT; this is Logo's filing system. It distinguishes between saving procedures and saving pictures.

To retrieve a picture previously saved, type

```
READPICT "NAME     [not a primitive in Apple Logo]
```

If for some reason a file was not found, a message will come back stating:

```
FILE NOT FOUND
```

The name may have been typed incorrectly, or the file may not be on the disk.

To remove a file of procedures from the disk, type

```
ERASEFILE "NAME
```

To remove a picture file from the disk, type

```
ERASEPICT "NAME    [not a primitive in Apple Logo]
```

To remove a procedure from the computer memory, type

```
ERASE     procedurename     [abbreviated ER]
```

Screen Commands

Other commands, which do not affect the disk drive but do affect the screen, include:

<CTRL-F>	Allows you to view the full video screen (<CTRL-F> may not be available in Apple Logo. In some versions of Apple Logo, <CTRL-L> is equivalent to <CTRL-F>.)
<CTRL-S>	Allows you to switch back to the split screen, where text can be typed at the bottom of the graphics screen
<CTRL-T>	Allows you to get a page of text

Printing Out Programs and Pictures

When you work with programs or procedures, it is often helpful to get a listing of the statements in the procedures. To get a listing on the video screen, use the command:

PRINTOUT ALL   [abbreviated PO ALL; PO ALL is not available in Apple Logo]

which lists everything in your current workspace. If you wish to print out only one procedure, for example SQ, then type

PO SQ   [Apple Logo: PO "SQ]

You may also wish to print out a list of titles that you currently have in your workspace. In this case use

PRINTOUT TITLES   [abbreviated POTS]

which will give a listing of all procedures in the workspace at that time.

Often it is helpful to have a hardcopy of the procedure listings; to make a hardcopy, you need a printer attached to your computer. Assuming that the card connecting the computer with the printer is in slot 1 in the computer, you can first initialize the printer by typing

OUTDEV 1   [Apple Logo: .PRINTER 1]

where OUTDEV (.PRINTER, in Apple Logo) stands for output device in slot 1. After typing this, type as above either PO ALL, PO *procedurename*, or POTS. You should then get such a listing on the printer. To turn the printer off, type

OUTDEV 0   [Apple Logo: .PRINTER 0]

(Note that if this last line is not used the printer will continue printing.)

To get a printout of the picture on the screen, you will need to have a printer that does graphics displays—for example, an Epson MX80. There are many ways to get printouts of graphics displays and you may need to consult your manual for your particular combination. One of the most popular input/output cards is the Grappler interface card. If you have this card, be sure the picture is displayed on your video screen, then type

```
OUTDEV 1
(PRINT1 CHAR 9 "G CHAR 13)
OUTDEV 0     [This is not available in Apple Logo; you must use an analogous
               program from the Tool Kit.]
```

If you do not have the Grappler, or if you have a large number of computers but only a small number of printers, then use the SAVEPICT command, which saves the screen display on your disk. Then either use the READPICT command to load it at the computer with the printer, or use a commercial program that allows you to print out a graphics display from a saved screen display. (SAVEPICT and READPICT are not available in Apple Logo.)

Appendix D

Special Features of LogoWriter

▶ ▲ ◀ ▼ ▶ ▲ ◀ ▼ ▶ ▲ ◀ ▼ ▶ ▲ ◀ ▼ ▶ ▲ ◀ ▼ ▶ ▲

LogoWriter is a very interesting and unique version of Logo, thus this special appendix. LogoWriter includes nearly all the features of other versions of Logo and also includes its own special features. First, you will examine basic concepts, then special properties of LogoWriter.

One of the unusual properties of LogoWriter is that it comes in versions for many different machines, all of which you get when you purchase the software for a site license. Except for minor key strokes, the versions behave alike. At present, the machines include Apple IIe/c and the Apple IIGS, IBM PC, IBM PC_JR, and Commodore 64/128. The focus here is on the Apple; the IBM versions are given in parentheses.

The Basics

LogoWriter includes the basic features of earlier versions of Logo but makes them easier to use. Entering, saving, and exiting files, and editing and printing procedures and screens, are now simpler and more exciting tasks than they were in earlier versions of Logo.

Loading a File or Page

The term **page** is what many call a **file** or collection of related procedures. In this discussion *page* and *file* are used interchangeably.

To load a file into memory, turn on the computer with a LogoWriter language disk. The directions will tell you to press <RETURN> (or <ENTER>); do so. A *Contents Page* appears. Directions at the top tell you to move up/down arrows to select the page you want. (Note: the down arrow will, sometimes, go below the apparent bottom of the page. Just continue holding it down to see if there is more below.)

Once you find the file you want, simply press <RETURN> (or <ENTER>). The selected file will load into memory.

Saving and Exiting from a File or Page

In order to exit from a file, press the <ESC> key. This also automatically saves the file, clears the memory, and returns you to the *Contents Page*.

Creating a New File

To create a new file, go to the option of *New Page* on the Contents Page and select *New Page*. This will take you to a new page, which is not yet named. Use the primitive NAMEPAGE (abbreviated NP), to give the page a name starting with a quote; for example

```
NP "FUN
```

Using the Editor—Flipping the Page

To flip the page for the Apple, hold down the <⌂> key, then press F (abbreviated <⌂-F>). (For IBM, hold down the <CTRL> key, then press F, abbreviated as <CTRL-F>.) To move about the screen, use the up/down, left/right arrow keys. Use the backspace key to delete the character to the left of the cursor (on IBM use <DEL>).

Moving about the Screen

Note that the screen, both on the page and its flip side, has two portions separated by a line. The cursor moves about on the portion of the screen containing the cursor, but is not readily moved to the other portion. In order to move to the other portion, use either <⌂-U> (or <CTRL-U> for IBM) to move to the upper portion, or <⌂-D> (or <CTRL-D> for IBM) to move to the lower portion.

Stopping a Procedure in Process

To stop the execution of a procedure, use <⌂-S> (or <CTRL-BREAK> for IBM). The primitive STOP in a procedure stops the procedure after proper conditions have been met. The command STOPALL stops all procedures and brings all execution to a halt.

Printing Procedures/Screens

Your instructor will need to be sure your printer is coordinated with the form of LogoWriter you have. Manager disks for doing this come from LCSI.

To print a screen, be sure that the cursor is in the lower portion of the screen, then type: PRINTSCREEN.

To print the text for a page, be sure the cursor is in the lower portion of the screen, then type either PRINTTEXT or PRINTTEXT80 depending upon whether you want to print 40 or 80 character lines.

To list a set of procedures, first be sure the cursor is in the lower portion of the flip side of the page, then type either PRINTTEXT or PRINTTEXT80.

Unique Features of LogoWriter

LogoWriter has several features not available in other versions of Logo. Discussion of some of these features follows.

Integrating Text and Graphics

LogoWriter allows integration of text and graphics. Commands for putting text on the screen are PRINT, INSERT, SHOW, TYPE, and LABEL. Each of these commands will be described. The PRINT command will be of the form,

```
PRINT [HELLO, I LIKE COMPUTERS.]     [or]

PRINT :N    [where :N has some value]
```

This command prints text from the screen at the beginning of the line cursor. This primitive contains a carriage command (causing the cursor to move to the next line).

The INSERT primitive prints a word or list in the page or screen at the cursor's position, without a carriage return.

The SHOW primitive prints the text in the *Command Center* instead of on the page. Otherwise, it behaves like the PRINT command.

The TYPE primitive prints the word or list in the *Command Center;* a carriage return does not follow.

The LABEL primitive is used for integrating graphics and text. It behaves like the PRINT command, except it actually uses graphics displays for letters. Hence, the text is located on the screen by use of the turtlegraphics commands, such as FD or SETPOS.

Changing the Shape of the Turtle

Note on the *Contents Page* that there is a file called *Shapes*. Go to that page now if you haven't already. You will see a number of shape sections. Flip the page, and you will see a blow-up of one of the shapes. To advance through the shapes, press <♂> right arrow or left arrow (for IBM, use <CTRL> PgUp or PgDn).

To change the picture, use the up/down, left/right arrows to move the cursor. Using the <SPACE BAR> when the cursor is at a point will change the point to its reverse or opposite. This reverses the plotting of that dot—that is, a plotted dot becomes removed, or a blank becomes a plotted dot. This is how you can create your own picture. To leave the *Shapes* page, press <ESC>. This will return you to the *Contents Page*.

To change the shape of the turtle, now go to a page for writing procedures. Now, in either direct or indirect mode, type

```
SETSH N
```

where *N* is the number of the shape you want. Now to see your new shape, type

```
ST or SHOWTURTLE
```

Making Multiple Copies of the Turtle

To make multiple copies of the turtle on the screen, use the STAMP command. For example,

```
RG FD 50 STAMP RT 90 FD 50
```

resets (RG) the graphics to one turtle, the original turtle shape in home position, pointing up. The turtle moves forward (upward) and is stamped: a copy of it is left at that position. The turtle then turns right and moves forward 50. Stamp again, after plotting the turtle and before moving it. Another example for multiple stamping is:

```
REPEAT 6[STAMP FD 50 RT 60]
```

This causes a turtle to be stamped at each vertex of a hexagon.

Using Multiple Turtles

LogoWriter allows four turtles, numbered *0, 1, 2,* and *3,* to be used. They may all be the same shape, or they may each be a different shape. An important primitive for communicating with the turtles is the TELL command. You could give all of the turtles a command at once with

```
TELL ALL
```

You can communicate with one turtle, say turtle *2,* at a time with

```
TELL 2
```

You can communicate with several turtles at a time by using a list, for example,

```
TELL [1 2 3]
FD 50
```

The following is an example of using multiple turtles:

```
TELL ALL HT CT CG
TELL 0 SETSH 25 RT 45
TELL 1 SETSH 26 RT 135
TELL 2 SETSH 27 RT 225
TELL 3 SETSH 28 RT 315
TELL ALL ST FD 50
TELL [0 1 3] BK 25
```

Creating Motion Effects

Creating motion effects with LogoWriter is easy. To create motion, use turtles to move about on the screen. To avoid leaving a path, use PENUP. To leave a path, use PENDOWN. When the turtles are coordinated, each can represent a part of a total figure, so that when all turtles move together, the total figure is created.

Using Music/Sound Effects

The important primitive to give your masterpiece sound and/or music is the TONE command. It comes in the form of *tone frequency time;* for example,

```
TONE 415 30
TONE 523 120
```

The first number is the frequency, and the second number is the time or duration, measured in about 1/20th of a second. Table 1 gives a frequency table.

Tools

LogoWriter uses a concept of **tool** files, in which "tool procedures" are put into memory, without taking up space on the flip side of the page. Related commands are GETTOOLS, CLEARTOOLS, TOOLLIST, and STARTUP.

To develop a tool set, simply create a page and its procedures as usual; for example, let's call it *funtools.* Then develop another page, which we will call *fun.* The *fun* page will use the *funtools,* but will not list them on the flip side of the page *fun.* In order to call up the tools, use the command GETTOOLS followed by a quote mark and the name of the tools page; for example,

```
GETTOOLS "FUNTOOLS
```

Table 1 Frequency Table for LogoWriter			
Note	**Frequency, by Octave**		
B	123	247	494	988
A#	117	233	466	932
A	110	220	440	880
G#	104	208	415	830
G	98	196	392	784
F#	92	185	370	740
F	87	175	349	698
E	82	165	330	659
D#	78	156	311	622
D	73	147	294	587
C#	69	139	277	554
C	65	131	262	523 (middle C)

This loads the *tools* page into memory. To remove the tools, you must use the CLEARTOOLS command. The TOOLLIST will give you a list of tools currently in memory.

The STARTUP procedure is a unique feature of LogoWriter. When entering a page, a procedure named *startup* (if used) will automatically run. For example, it will run if the *fun* page has a startup procedure such as:

```
TO STARTUP
   GETTOOLS "FUNTOOLS
END
```

GETTOOLS places *funtools* automatically into memory. Of course, STARTUP has other uses as well; for example, if you want the disk to automatically load a set of procedures, use a page called *startup*. This page is then automatically loaded and processed.

Sequencing of Screens

The PRESCREEN and NEXTSCREEN primitives let you sequence some screens together in some order, perhaps to tell a story. With these you can create many interesting projects, including motion graphics, music or sound effects, interesting shapes, and stories.

Keyboards

Keyboard layouts for the different versions of LogoWriter are shown in Figures 1–4. The Commodore version is very similar to the other versions and uses a special function key.

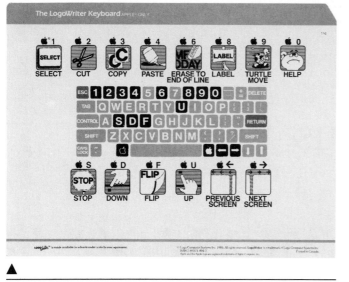

Figure 1 *Keyboard display for LogoWriter, Apple version.*

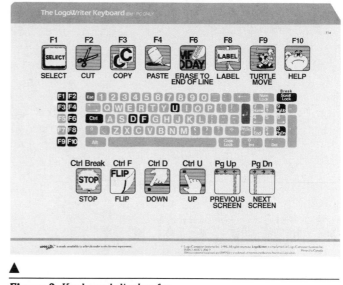

Figure 2 *Keyboard display for LogoWriter, IBM PC version.*

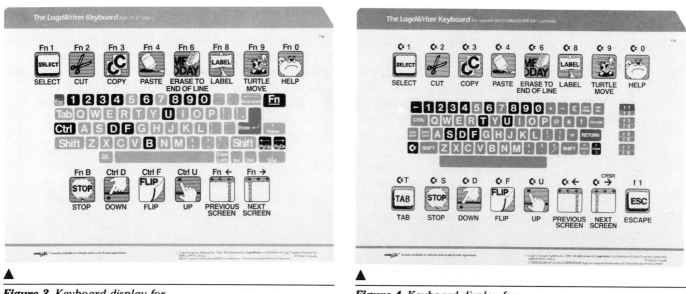

Figure 3 *Keyboard display for LogoWriter, IBM PC_{JR} version.*

Figure 4 *Keyboard display for LogoWriter, Commodore 64 version.*

Appendix E

Logo Plus

▶ ▲ ◀ ▼ ▶ ▲ ◀ ▼ ▶ ▲ ◀ ▼ ▶ ▲ ◀ ▼ ▶ ▲ ◀ ▼ ▶ ▲

L ogo Plus has features similar to LogoWriter. Integrating text and graphics, changing the shape of the turtle, creating motion effects, sequencing screens and startup are all possible in Logo Plus, as they are in LogoWriter. Logo Plus is also like Terrapin Logo in most respects. Disk operation, all commands of Terrapin, syntax, and the Utilities Disk are like those of Terrapin Logo. In addition to some of the properties of LogoWriter and Terrapin, Logo Plus also has other features:

▶ Graphics capabilities incorporating the commands HFLIP, VFLIP, ZOOM, and FILL
▶ Word and list operations: COUNT, ITEM, MEMBER?, WORD?, LIST, and LIST? allow decomposing and recombining words and lists
▶ Shape operations including CLEARSHAPES, COPYSHAPE, EDSHAPE, READ-SHAPE, SAVESHAPE, SETCOLOR, SETSIZE, STAMP, STAMPXY, TCOLOR, TOTALSHAPES, TSHAPE, TSIZE, which allow changing the turtle's shape and use shapes created for turtles within pictures
▶ Graphic Screen Text Commands: < ⌘ -W>, GCURSOR, DCURSORPOS, GMODE, GPRINT, GPRINT1, GREQUEST, GSTYLE, and GWRITE, which facilitate writing on the graphics screen
▶ Shape Editor commands: V, H, B, <CTRL-F>, <CTRL-S>, <CTRL-T>, <CTRL-C>, <CTRL-G>, which help in the creation of shapes for the turtle
▶ Disk and data file commands: SETDISK, BSAVE, BLOAD, APPEND, CLOSE, DISKREAD, DISKWRITE, EOF?, ONLINE, MAKEDIR, PREFIX, READFONT, SETPREFIX, VCAT, which serve for creating disk data files and operating with files on disk.

Shapes

In the Utilities file are shapes, and procedures for using and editing them. To get started with shapes, bring the shapes into memory: for Terrapin Logo, place the Utilities Disk into the disk drive and type READ "SETSHAPES; then type READ-SHAPE "VEHICLES (or READSHAPE "ANIMALS READSHAPE "AIRPLANES or READ-SHAPE "BIRDS). In Logo Plus on the 3.5 inch (smaller) disk, the Utilities are on the Logo Plus Disk. They are in the Utilities Directory, so VCAT "UTILITIES will let you see them. To bring them into memory and use them, type READ "UTILITIES/SET-SHAPES; then type READSHAPE "UTILITIES/VEHICLES (or READSHAPE "UTILITIES/ANIMALS READSHAPE "UTILITIES/AIRPLANES or READSHAPE "UTILITIES/BIRDS).

With the shapes in memory type SETSHAPE *n* (1, 2, 3 ...) to choose one of the various shapes to replace the turtle. If the turtle is showing (ST), the shape will show instead. Now it works just as the turtle did. Try such things as:

```
TO SQPLACE
   SETSHAPE 1 PU ST
   REPEAT 4[FD 70 RT 90 ST STAMP]
   HT
END

TO STY :N
   IF :N > 7 STOP
   GSTYLE :N GCURSOR 20 :N*2 GPRINT [SAIL]
   STY :N + 2
END

TO PLACEBOAT
   HT READSHAPES "SAILBOAT      [SAILBOAT you created is saved by typing
                                SAVESHAPES "SAILBOAT]
   SETSHAPE 1 PU HT
   SETCOLOR 5 PD STAMPXY 50 60 PU
   SETCOLOR 3 PD STAMPXY -50 60 PU HT
   LOCKHEADING SETH 85 SETCOLOR 1
   REPEAT 12 [FD 15 ST WAIT 10 HT WAIT 10] HT
   STY 1
END
```

These types of programs permit you to place copies of the shapes you choose at various places on the screen. In addition, illustrative programs on the Utilities Disk show how to make use of the shapes in programs. Included are BIRDS and TESTFLIGHT. To run the program BIRDS, READ "BIRDS from the Logo Plus Utilities (READ "UTILITIES/BIRDS from the Logo Plus Disk for the 3.5 inch disk). You must have the BIRDS shapes in memory. If they are not loaded automatically, type READSHAPES "BIRDS (READSHAPES "UTILITIES/BIRDS from the Logo Plus Disk for the 3.5 inch disk). Now everything is in memory so type FLY to see the bird soar. Another program is TESTFLIGHT. Follow the same sequence for TESTFLIGHT as for BIRDS. After everything is in memory, type TF to see the plane fly.

Text and Graphics

You can write on the graphics screen. Primitives for doing this are GCURSOR 5 10, which places the cursor at the fifth column and the tenth row on the graphics screen; GPRINT word/list prints the input on the graphics screen; GWRITE enters the graphics screen text editor (exit with <ESC>). An example will help:

```
GCURSOR 5 10 GPRINT [THE PICTURE IS A SAILBOAT]
```

Various styles (italics, underline, and bold) and fonts (Gothic, Roman, Colossal) are available for printing on the graphics screen. To use a different font, type READFONT "ROMAN. Then type GCURSOR 20 20 GPRINT [ROMAN] (With Logo Plus Utilities Disk in the drive).

The Screen

Three primitives (HFLIP, VFLIP, and FILL) are fun to use on the graphics screen, and these screen changes are unique to Logo Plus. HFLIP flips the graphics screen horizontally, VFLIP flips the graphics screen vertically, and FILL pours color into an enclosed region. Look at the following example:

```
TO FLIPPINGCO                        TO LSQ
    REPEAT 4[LSQ FD 60 RT 90]            REPEAT 4[FD 60 LT 90]
    WAIT 100                             PU LT 30 FD 10
    VFLIP WAIT 100                       PC 1 + RANDOM 3 PD FILL
    HFLIP                                PU BK 10 RT 30
END                                  END
```

The enclosed cross is filled with colors when the turtle is inside the enclosed region at FILL time. VFLIP flips the screen upside down. The HFLIP flips the screen horizontally.

Disk and Files

Logo Plus uses ProDOS, which helps you use and organize the disks. The main disk level operation is SETDISK 1 5, which "talks to the first 3.5 inch disk" and SETDISK 1 6 which "talks to the first 5.25 inch disk." MAKEDIR sets up a folder for storing files that are alike. Simply type MAKEDIR "foldername. It lets you save things in the folder, read from that folder and keep it out and opened. For example, to keep the folder out and open, SETDIR "foldername; to read from the folder, type READ "foldername/filename; and to save a file in a folder, type SAVE "foldername/filename. To see what is in a folder on a disk, type VCAT "foldername. Of course if you type SETDIR "foldername, the things you save or read are just those you put in the folder.

Figure 1 shows some shapes to make with the EDSHAPE 0 1 (or EDSHAPE 1 2 for a second shape) command. Just follow the directions on the screen. Once the turtle, house, fish, sailboat, and helicopter are made, you can make these combinations.

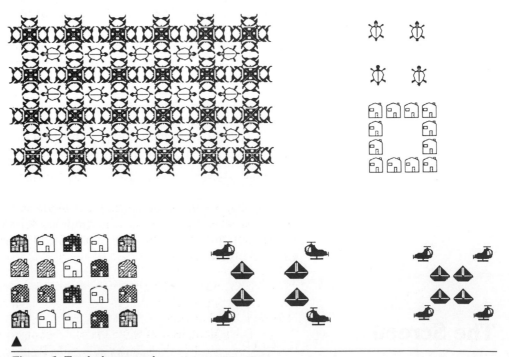

▲

Figure 1 *Turtleshapes and pictures to make in Logo Plus.*

Appendix F

What Is a Computer?

▼ ▶ ▲ ◀ ▼ ▶ ▲ ◀ ▼ ▶ ▲ ◀ ▼ ▶ ▲ ◀ ▼ ▶ ▲ ◀ ▼ ▶

Now that you have had some experience using the computer, you are ready to learn about the functioning of a computer and about computer terminology. This knowledge will help you to understand available literature on computers and to communicate with others about computers. Several states are now testing for computer literacy; one of the areas they often test is terminology. Hence, you should become familiar with the terminology. Another topic that many states are testing is history of computers. A brief overview is included here. After looking at computers in general, we look at the Apple IIGS in detail.

Background: 1642–1988

Before discussing the various parts of a computer and current technology, we briefly examine the evolution of technology, as shown in Box 1. The development of computing devices goes back to the mid-1600s and even farther if you consider the abacus. Techniques for dealing with large amounts of data began in the late 1800s as the U.S. Census Bureau began using punch cards. World War II aided the progress of computers; shortly after the war began, electronic computers began to appear. The development of transistors helped the electronic computers to become a reality. Punched cards were still the main medium for inputting data into computers. In the mid-1960s, the National Science Foundation in the United States supported the development of two major, large-scale instructional computing systems: the PLATO computer system, housed at the University of Illinois, and the TICCIT computer system, developed at the University of Texas and Brigham Young University. These systems led the way for instructional systems with interactive graphics.

In 1970, the development of the integrated circuit began. Through the use of large-scale integrated circuitry, the birth of single-board microcomputers was achieved in the mid-1970s. Since that time a number of computer companies have evolved, some of which have survived and a number of which plummeted. Two young men in their early- to mid-twenties founded a little company, Apple Computer, in 1977. By making a number of interactive-graphics, educational systems at a more affordable price than those of the earlier, larger systems, this company made serious inroads into education.

In 1981 a giant, IBM, entered the microcomputer business. With a new standard in the field, the MS DOS, it led the way for many other companies. Many IBM compatible machines came forth; some had strongly competitive prices. IBM and

Box 1	Getting a Perspective on Computers' History
1642	Blaise Pascal built an automatic device that could add or subtract by turning little wheels.
1831–1871	Charles Babbage created the analytic engine. Ada, the Countess of Lovelace, gave considerable support to Babbage's efforts.
1890	Herman Hollerith persuaded the U.S. Census Bureau to try punch cards, coding such personal information as age, sex, marital status, and race. Soon afterward, punched cards became a part of office machinery; Hollerith's small company later became International Business Machines (IBM).
1936	Turing's paper "On Computable Numbers" became available.
1939	Through research at AT&T, George Stibitz showed how calculations could be transmitted over telephone wires.
1946	ENIAC (Electronic Numerical Integrator and Calculator) appeared; it was a collection of 18,000 vacuum tubes, 70,000 resistors, 10,000 capacitors and 6,000 switches, and occupied the space of a two-car garage.
1946	Three scientists at Bell Labs invented a transistor.
1960s	Evolution of PLATO and TICCIT educational computer systems.
1970	Large-scale integration of circuits evolves.
1971	Intel Corp, a Silicon Valley company founded by Noyce, unveiled the microprocessor. It contained the entire central processing unit (CPU) of a simple computer on one chip.
1975	Circuits are integrated on a very large scale.
1977	The founding of Apple Computer, Inc. A few months later the Apple II (with ROM integer BASIC) emerges and begins a family of tremendously successful personal computers.
1979	Apple II Plus (with ROM floating-point Applesoft BASIC) is developed.
1980	Apple III is introduced.
1981	IBM personal computer appears.
1982	Apple IIe evolves.
1983	The ImageWriter and Apple III Plus are introduced.
1984	Macintosh develops.
1985	Apple IIc and the enhanced Apple IIe evolve.
1985	Apple introduces the LaserWriter.
1986	Apple introduces the Mac Plus.
1986	Apple IIGS evolves.
1987	Macintosh II and Macintosh SE develop and move toward compatibility between Macintosh, IBM/MS DOS, and the Apple II series.
1988	Apple IIc+ increases power of Apple IIc.

IBM compatibles rapidly became the standard for business. IBM decided to become an active part of education. The inroads of Apple Computer in education, however, made it difficult for IBM to gain as strong a position in education as it did in business. IBM then undertook serious research and development of educational software; the education community still has not felt the impact of this commitment.

Table 1	Apple Computers Sold, 1978–1984
Year	**Number of Apples Sold**
1978	7,600
1979	35,100
1980	78,100
1981	180,000
1982	Apple stopped public announcements of annual sales
1983 (June)	Millionth Apple II produced
1984 (Sept.)	Apple passes the $1 billion mark in its fiscal year
1984 (Nov.)	Two million Apple IIs sold

Table 2	Computers Used in Schools, 1981–1987
Year	**Number of Schools with Computers**
1981	15,318
1982	24,696
1983–84	55,768
1984–85	Over one million computers are in schools: about 15 million students and 500,000 teachers use computers as part of their instructional programs.
1987	Between 1.2 and 1.7 million computers in U.S. public schools. Over 95% of all elementary and secondary schools have at least one computer.

Meanwhile, Apple wanted to make a greater impact in business and released another pace-setter, the Macintosh, in 1984. Since then newer and better models of each machine have evolved. Three major forms currently exist: the Apple II series, the IBM/MS DOS personal computers, and the Macintosh series. One of Apple's latest releases, the Apple IIGS, kept the Apple II form, so that the large amount of Apple II software is upwardly compatible, but integrated many of the features of the Macintosh. Efforts toward making the three forms more compatible are now being made.

We are in the midst of a major revolution for which no one at this point knows the outcome. All signs, however, imply that computer uses in education will continue to grow and prosper.

Tables 1, 2, and 3, illustrate the growth of microcomputer's capabilities and their reach into educational settings during the past 10 years. Table 1 shows the escalation of the number of Apple microcomputers sold. In 1988, Apple sold 1,272,000 personal computers, and IBM sold 1,229,000 personal computers. Table 2 describes the increase in the number of computers in schools. Table 3 indicates the distribution of monies spent for computer equipment; keep in mind that the top two companies sell large computer systems as well as microcomputers.

Table 3	Sales of Computer Equipment for Winter, 1987	
Company	**Total Revenues**	**Percent Increase from Last Year**
IBM	$6.5 billion	6.5% (Including mainframes)
DEC	$2.4 billion	25. % (Including mainframes)
Apple	$575.3 million	41. %
Microsoft	$98.3 million	95. %
Lotus	$84.8 million	22. %
Intel	$395 million	40. %
Seagate	$267 million	110. %

Terminology of Parts of a Computer System

A **computer system** has four essential components: an **input device;** a **processing device;** a **memory device;** and an **output device.** Figure 1 shows three computer systems. Note that they vary in arrangement; however, each system has the four essential components. The **keyboard,** similar to that of a typewriter, is an input device. It allows you to type information and programs for the computer's use. The computer component includes a **central processing unit (CPU),** consisting of a **control unit** and an **arithmetic and logic unit (ALU),** and **memory.** Examples of output devices are **cathode ray tubes (CRTs)** and **printers.**

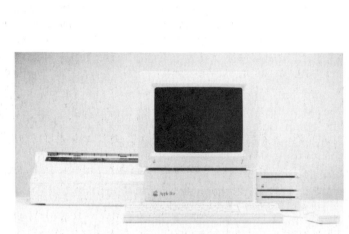

a

b

c

Figure 1 Sample computer systems: (a) Apple IIGS, (b) Apple Macintosh with optional disk drive and mouse on the right,(c) IBM PC with Brother printer and 8-inch disk drive on the side

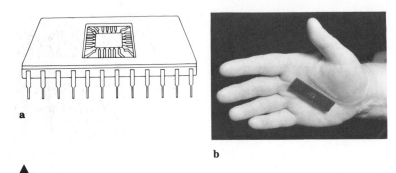

a

b

Figure 2 *(a) Sketch of CPU chip and (b) 6502 microprocessor for Apple IIe.*

The CPU of a microcomputer is its brains, in which data are processed. This unit contains the control unit, which coordinates and directs the processing, and the ALU, which performs the mathematical and logical operations. The CPU for the Apple II+ is smaller than a square centimeter. It is mounted in a silicon chip that is located in the main board of the computer. A CPU chip is shown in Figure 2.

6502 microprocessor
for Apple II+

ROM chips
for Apple II+

RAM chips
for Apple II+

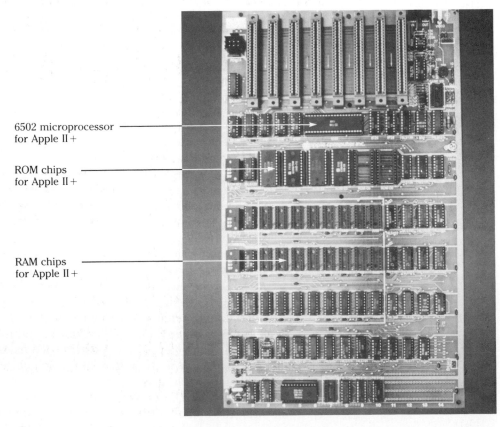

a

Figure 3 *Motherboards for (a) Apple II+, (b) Apple IIe, and (c) Apple IIGS.*

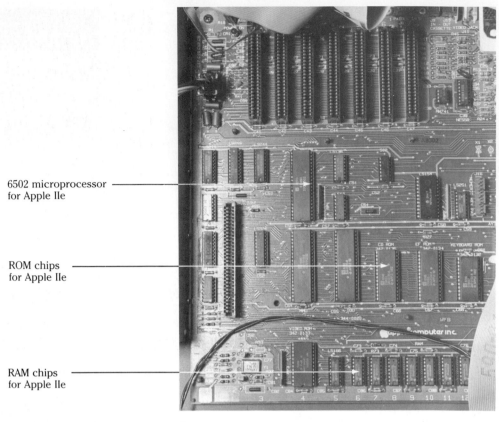

6502 microprocessor
for Apple IIe

ROM chips
for Apple IIe

RAM chips
for Apple IIe

b

Primary memory for microcomputers is **RAM** (Random Access Memory) and **ROM** (Read Only Memory). RAM is the computer's internal memory that is used for storage of data, programs, and in some instances, programming languages. It is *temporary:* it stores information during a particular function but can be erased when desired. It is automatically erased when the computer is turned off.

The amount of RAM available affects the possible uses of a computer. Typically, the Apple has 48K to 1250K of RAM. One **K (kilobyte)** of memory is 1000 (actually 1024; RAM is allocated in powers of 2) **bytes,** or **characters.** A byte is eight **bits.** A bit is a binary digit made up of zeros and ones, each of which corresponds to an electrical switch's being off or on.

ROM is permanent memory. It remains present and available even when a computer has been turned off and then back on. Typically, ROM contains important software. It may include one or more programming (high-level) languages such as BASIC, an assembler (low-level language), and other software for communication between the computer and peripherals such as the disk drive. Figure 3 shows the **motherboard,** the **main board** into which chips are plugged, for the Apple II+, Apple IIe, and Apple IIGS computers. It also pictures the RAM and ROM chips for these computers. Observe that as the Apple progressed from the II+ to the IIe to the IIGS, the boards have fewer and more compact chips, allowing for increased memory and capabilities.

Note that the CPU chip is larger than either the RAM chip or the ROM chip. However, the CPU is only a fraction of the chip. A large portion of the chip is made up of wiring that allows for communication between the CPU and other parts of the computer.

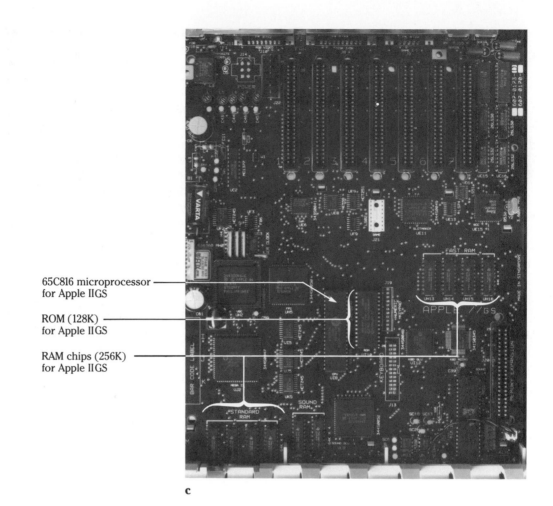

65C816 microprocessor
for Apple IIGS

ROM (128K)
for Apple IIGS

RAM chips (256K)
for Apple IIGS

c

Memory Size

The *size* or *capacity* of a computer is to some extent measured by the amount of RAM and ROM memory it supplies. At one time, a **mainframe** was defined as a computer with a range of RAM from 512K to 15 **megabytes** (a megabyte is one million bytes), the minicomputer had a range of 64K to 1 megabyte, and the microcomputer ranged from 4K to 64K; however, many microcomputers now have much larger memories. This distinction based on operating-memory capacity is disappearing with the development of microchips, because the memory capacity of these chips is increasing while their size is decreasing. Table 4 reveals the progression of increasing dynamic RAM.

Table 4	Increasing Capacity of Dynamic RAM, 1976–1985
Year	**Capacity**
1976	16K
1979	64K
1982	256K
1985	1 megabyte

Figure 3 shows motherboards for Apple II+, Apple IIe, and Apple IIGS. The Apple II+ provides 48K of RAM in the motherboard, contained in the twenty-four chips in three rows of eight chips each within the white square. Each chip thus has a capacity of 2K (but the memory must come with complete sets of eight chips of 16K of memory).

By contrast, the Apple IIe has 128K of primary memory stored on the eight chips located at the immediate front of the motherboard. These are 8K memory chips. In the years between the issuance of the Apple II+ and the Apple IIe, the capacity of a chip quadrupled (but the chips remained roughly the same size). (The Apple IIc comes with 128K of memory.) In that same time, in spite of the increase in capacity, the cost of the chip has decreased from more than $10 per chip to less than $2 per chip. The Apple IIGS comes with 256K in the motherboard and has expandable memory up to several megabytes.

Disk Operating Systems

The CPU is the center of data processing in a computer. It contains the ALU and the control units. Each serves processing functions: the ALU does the arithmetic and logic, and the control unit sequences the data and sends them to the next stage of processing or storage. The **disk operating system (DOS)** is a program written for the particular computer. Commands of DOS coordinate the interface of the disk drive with the computer and allow programs to be loaded from and saved to a floppy disk. To contrast the operation of the CPU with the disk operating system, first **boot** the DOS. "Booting DOS" means placing a disk with DOS on it into the disk drive and turning on the computer. This loads DOS computer software into RAM. To state it more accurately, part of the DOS is in ROM, which begins to load the remaining portion of DOS from the floppy disk into RAM memory. If you turn on the computer without an initialized disk in the drive and press <CTRL-RESET> or <⌘-RESET>, you will have the BASIC language available to you from ROM in the Apple, but you will not have the DOS available to you, because the remaining portion of DOS from the disk has not been added. Hence, you can write programs in BASIC, but you cannot store them or save them on a disk. In fact, part of the initializing process is adding that main portion of DOS to the new disk.

Apple Operating Systems

In the Apple system, DOS is loaded into RAM from the disk when the system is booted. However, to initiate the boot-up process, a relatively small portion of DOS resides in ROM. Logo, as well as most other languages, has a somewhat extended operating system.

DOS for the Apple computer is a set of machine language programs. Over the years, Apple has developed DOS 1.0, DOS 2.0, DOS 3.2, DOS 3.2.1, DOS 3.3, ProDOS8, ProDOS16 and GS/OS. The different numbers simply denote the sequence of development. The DOS family of operating systems is a sample of the many operating systems used by microcomputers. Other popular operating systems include CP/M and MS-DOS.

An operating system is (usually) a set of technical programs that directs the coordinated operation of a computer system. In particular, DOS establishes the rules for communication between the computer and the disk drive. It includes the vocabulary for this communication. Words such as

► CATALOG
► RUN FILENAME
► SAVE FILENAME

- DELETE FILENAME
- RENAME FILEN1, FILEN2
- LOCK FILENAME
- UNLOCK FILENAME

are all a part of the vocabulary for this communication. A listing of the DOS commands for the Apple family of computers is provided in Appendixes G and H (or in the Apple manuals).

Input Devices

The keyboard is the most widely used input device for microcomputers. The computer keyboard is similar to that of a standard typewriter. Figure 4 in Appendix A shows the keyboards of the Apple II +, IIe, IIc, and IIGS computers.

Extended forms of keyboards have special function keys that make data input easier. For example, a keypad for numerals and mathematical operations similar to that of a calculator is available. Such an extension may be a part of the keyboard or may be a special plug-in peripheral. Figure 4 shows the expansion interface slots, designed for plug-in additions to the Apple II series. Additional input devices include joysticks, game paddles, light pens, graphics tablets (for example, the *Koala Pad*), modems, Apple mouse, card readers, and sense sheets.

The **joysticks** and **game paddles** are peripherals for games and tactile computer exercises. The **light pen** provides input by contact with the screen. It may

8 slots numbered
0 through 7
for the Apple II +

Game paddle
connection

6502 microprocessor

a

Figure 4 *Expansion interface slots: (a) slots 0–7 (left to right) for Apple II +, (b) language card in slot 0 and disk drive controller card in slot 6, (c) slots for Apple IIGS, and (d) backview of ports for the Apple IIGS.*

Language card
allowing additional
memory beyond 48K
for the Apple II +

Slots for
additional cards

Power supply

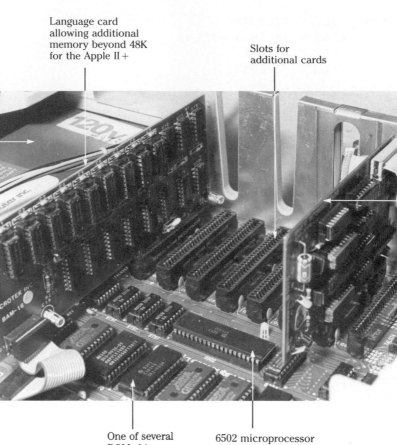

Card for disk
drive controller
in slot 6 for
Apple II +

One of several
ROM chips

6502 microprocessor
for Apple II +

b

Memory
expansion slot

General-purpose slots

c

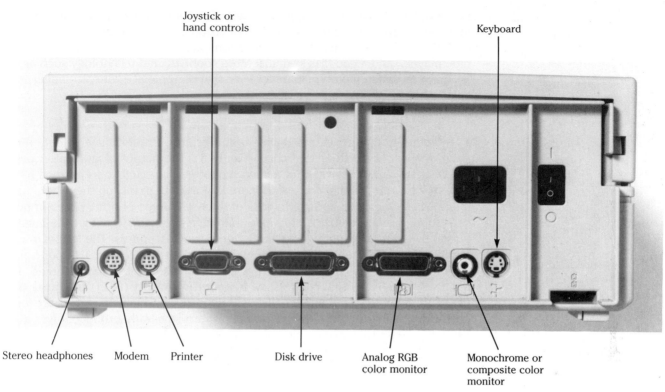

Joystick or
hand controls

Keyboard

Stereo headphones   Modem   Printer   Disk drive   Analog RGB   Monochrome or
                                                              color monitor   composite color
                                                                                  monitor

d

be used to touch the selection in a multiple-choice question, or to point to an object displayed on the screen. **Graphics tablets** may be used to draw pictures or to measure the dimensions of an object. The pictures may be digitized (translated to coordinate values) and used as a part of a program.

In contrast to the other devices, the **modem** is used for telecommunication. It allows data, such as electronic mail, to be transmitted. The **mouse** is a hand-held device that connects to the computer through a cord. It allows the user to make tactile control of operations such as the disk drive and drawing tools when appropriate software is installed. Another type of peripheral is the **card reader,** which senses patterns of holes and other markings in cards and stores these patterns as data. Similarly, computer (marked) **sense sheets** allow input of a hand-coded form to be sensed from the sheet. For example, many multiple-choice exams are answered on a marked sense sheet. The computer can read the answers and the student's name, correct tests, and store the score.

Output Devices

An output device is a peripheral that presents the results of computer operations. The most common output devices are CRTs, printer, and synthesizers. Printers and monitors (such as RGB monitors) are becoming more powerful; laser printers can produce typeset-quality type.

CRTs

The most predominant output device for microcomputers is the CRT (Cathode Ray Tube). Video screens are forms of CRTs. They may be regular television sets or specially designed **monitors.** For signal compatibility, television sets require

RF-modulators, whereas monitors do not. The more satisfactory, but sometimes more expensive, form is the monitor, a televisionlike piece of hardware that accepts output signals from special communications hardware such as computers, video tape players, and video disk systems. More sophisticated technology such as RGB, for high resolution pictures (graphics) like that of Apple IIGS, are also being added.

Printers

Another computer output device is the printer. Printers have widely diverse sizes, shapes, capabilities, and costs (Figure 5). The output of an **impact printer** is indistinguishable from that of a good typewriter; characters are formed by keys that strike through a film or cloth ribbon. **Dot-matrix print,** on the other hand, is made up of characters formed by sets of dots. This type of print varies in quality depending on the number of dots per character. One way to detect the quality of dot-matrix print is by noting whether letters have descenders. The letters *p, y,* and *q* normally are printed with parts below the line (the *descenders*). In poor-quality dot-matrix print, the descenders are absent and the print is hard to read. High-quality dot-matrix output comes from **near-letter quality** (NLQ) and **laser printers.** A third form of printer is the **thermal printer**, on which characters are formed on special heat-sensitive paper. Thermal printers generally produce lower-quality print. Figure 6 shows sample printouts.

Another factor to consider is a printer's **graphics capabilities.** Impact printers do not normally support graphics production. Dot-matrix printers can. If letter-quality print and graphics production from a printer are both desired, there may be a conflict of choice. Laser printers and NLQ (Near Letter Quality) printers do both. Also graphics can be constructed through skillful use of the period for daisy-wheel printers (by making a dot-matrix-like display using the period of the letter-quality printer).

a

b

c

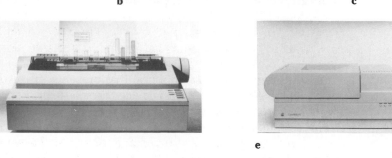

d　　　　　e

▲

Figure 5 *Printers: (a) Epson MX 100, (b) Okidata, (c) Brother, (d) Apple ImageWriter II, and (e) Apple LaserWriter II.*

```
Courier 12 pitch
Prestige 7 pitch
Prestige 10 pitch
LetterGothic 9.5 pitch
LetterGothic 10 pitch
Helvantic 12 pitch
Times Roman 8 pitch
Times Roman 10 pitch
Line Printer 8.5 pitch
PiFont 10 pitch
Bar3of9 12 pitch
Line Draw 10 pitch
Pica 16 pitch
Pica 14 pitch
Pica 12 pitch
Pica 8 pitch
Elite 10 pitch
Elite 15 pitch
Times Roman 12 pitch
Times  Roman  16  pitch
```
▲

Figure 6 *Printout of sample print types.*

Synthesizers

Synthesizers are computer devices that produce and control sound. The **voice synthesizer** produces and controls voicelike sounds, whereas the **music synthesizer** is used to compose music. The Apple IIGS sound chip with 15 sounds can be programmed to form synthesized voice or music.

CD ROM

One output device, the **CD ROM** (Compact Disc ROM), makes use of the new laser technology. Just as compact discs are making inroads in music, they are making a considerable difference in computers. A CD player connects to a computer via a controller card similar to many of the other types of controller cards. Large amounts of data can be compiled on a compact disc. For example, a CD-ROM hardware and software package for the IBM PC and compatibles is sold by Adventure Corps for $995; with the package, users have the entire 21 volumes of Grolier's Academic American Encyclopedia. Adventure's ROMulus CD-ROM drive has a data capacity of 540 megabytes per disc. The ROMulus player and controller are available separately for $849, and the Electronic Encyclopedia with access software is $199.

Another example of available CD-ROM discs is the Microsoft disc for $295, called the *Microsoft Bookshelf.* It contains a collection of 10 reference works, including the *1987 World Almanac and Book of Facts, The Chicago Manual of Style, Bartlett's Familiar Quotations, Roget's Thesaurus,* and the *US ZIP Code Directory.*

A third example is a prototype of a foreign language dictionary (developed by Software Mart) that includes text, graphics, and speech. The visual dictionary contains 1,660 terms in French and English plus 117 illustrations. The final version of the *Visual Dictionary CD ROM,* now available, includes 10,000 terms in French, Spanish, and English. Additional planned versions include six languages and as many as 1,000 images in the database, with an anticipated price of $500 to $1,000.

A fourth example of a CD ROM is the ERIC (Education Resources Information Center) resources. A current disc of ERIC citations from 1983 to 1987 is available, as well as two archival discs covering 1966 to 1982. Imagine how much easier it would be to use the computer to search for information rather than to look up each item by hand. Libraries can reduce large volumes of materials to a few small compact discs. Tools of the reference disc will be changing radically. The usual cost of an on-line search for ERIC is about $15–20 per hour, depending upon the service and time of day. Searching a database for one hour per week during a year costs a library $800 to $1,000. Yet, by using the CD ROM version, a library can allow unlimited access to ERIC over the course of a year for $1,200. Keeping that in mind, think about how technology can greatly improve the retrieval and management of the knowledge explosion that is occurring.

Local Area Network

Through Local Area Networking (LAN), the users can share interactive terminals tied to a mainframe, as in the PLATO and TICCIT computer systems. Many groups or companies want to connect their computers. Reasons for wanting to connect computers include information sharing, expanded database access, exchange of data, electronic mail, cost-effectiveness, and peripheral sharing.

One popular networking system is the AppleTalk system created by Apple. It can connect a number of computers. Work is ongoing to use **fiber optics** in the AppleTalk system. Fiber optics is a system for sending messages by laser lightwaves through ultra-thin glass fibers. Copper wires are the normal means for transmission of data, as through telephone communication. Now the telephone industry is moving to fiber optics, which offers the potential of optimal communications among computers, with clean, clear, error-free transmission. This technology could provide cheaper, faster access to all sorts of data.

Memory capacity and processors (particularly co-processors) are increasing the capability of computers to integrate various applications, including text and graphics. Clear examples of this include LogoWriter and various Macintosh, Apple IIGS, IBM systems and software.

Other Features

CPU Speed The CPU of a microcomputer performs approximately 500,000 additions and subtractions per second. This compares with arithmetic computations in excess of one million per second in some minicomputers. Mainframes may have multiprocessors. Thus, there may be the equivalent of several microprocessors serving together as the processing unit. In these mainframes, the number of operations per second may approach 100 million.

Storage Computers have hardware devices that help to overcome relatively limited internal memory. These vary in device type and storage method. Most microcomputers can use either a cassette recorder, cartridge, or disk drive. It is generally recognized that the disk drive is the more satisfactory storage device.

The most popular disk drives are those that use the floppy disk as the storage medium. **Hard disk** drives also are available. The hard disk drive can be physically about the same size as a floppy disk drive; it is several times as fast in loading and saving files. The hard disk drive cost is from four to seven times as much as for the soft disk drive. The storage capacity of the typical 5¼-inch floppy disk is approximately 150K, which is forty to fifty-five single-spaced, typed pages. In contrast, the approximate storage capacity for the hard disk is over 30,000K or 30 megabytes (30 million bytes). Table 5 shows relative prices and storage capacities.

Table 5   Average Price for Internal Hard Disk Subsystems for IBM and Compatibles

Amount of Storage	IBM PC, XT Systems	IBM AT Systems
20 MB	$ 440	$ 640
30 MB	$ 680	$ 860
40 MB	$ 780	$ 950
50 MB	$1,480	$2,080

Source: *Infoworld, Vol. 9, Issue 5, p. 15, Feb. 2, 1987.*

Languages   Microcomputers typically use fewer than a dozen computer languages, and they use them one at a time. In contrast, the minicomputer may have twenty to thirty languages available. A mainframe system typically has sixty to seventy accessible languages, which can function concurrently. A difference between mainframe languages and microcomputer languages involves translation. Many microcomputer languages are *interpretive languages* (instructions are translated to machine code, one line at a time, and immediately executed). In contrast, most versions of mainframe computer languages are *compiled languages* (where instructions are converted to machine code altogether and later executed) forms.

Maintenance   Computer maintenance is also a major concern for people who actively work with computers, particularly for those trying to keep a computer laboratory functioning. One method of maintenance is to simply exchange parts. If a part malfunctions, replace it with a working part. An extension of the idea is to "cannibalize" a system, using its parts to repair all other malfunctioning systems. If two machines malfunction, one in say, the disk drive, and the other in the monitor, the working parts of two machines can be combined into a working station.

Apple IIGS

The Apple IIGS is the latest member of the Apple II series. This machine differs from earlier Apple II's in several aspects, including display, keyboard layout, memory, microprocessor, and peripheral devices. Since this is the newest Apple, we have a greater in-depth examination of this machine here. Display features include the choice between 40- or 80-column output, four resolutions, and a number of different languages. The four color resolutions are low (16 colors, 40 by 48), high (6 colors, 280 by 192), double-high (16 colors, 140 by 192), and super-high (4 colors, 640 by 200; 16 colors, 320 by 200).

The attached keyboard allows for both uppercase and lowercase letters, and includes a numeric keypad. Users can choose keyboard layouts from standard, Dvorak (see Figure 7), and eight international keyboard layouts.

The Apple IIGS comes with standard memory of 256K—128K for Apple IIe emulation, 128K for improvements. Memory expansion cards allow for several megabytes of memory to be added in increments of 256K.

The Apple IIGS uses a 65C816 microprocessor. This microprocessor emulates the 6502 microprocessor, and hence the earlier Apple II. The 65C816 microprocessor is a 16-bit processor with a clock rate up to three times faster than the 8-bit processor on earlier models of the Apple II.

Diversity in peripheral devices is available in the Apple IIGS. There are 8 slots: 7 general purpose and 1 memory expansion card (see Figure 4c). Ports are in the back of the computer (see Figure 4d) to allow for connections of a serial printer,

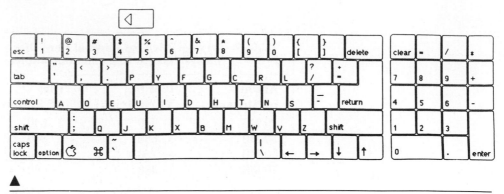

Figure 7 *Dvorak keyboard layout.*

modem, monochrome and analog RGB color monitors, 3.5-inch and 5.25-inch drives, mouse, joystick, hand controls, and AppleTalk. Use of the ports eliminates the expense of extra interface cards, but the slots allow the flexibility if you prefer interface cards. Without using interface cards, you can connect into an AppleTalk network.

In addition, the Apple IIGS includes a clock, desk accessories, and a 15-voice sound synthesizer. The desk accessories allow for applications such as a notepad, a calculator, and a clock. The sound synthesizer can produce a 15-voice orchestra or band or near human-voice sounds. A built-in headphone jack also allows the user to connect a headphone, a particularly important feature as computer-laboratory settings use sound-embellished programs.

Control Panel

The Apple IIGS has a control panel with a battery so that changes can be saved immediately after they are made; they are thus held in memory after the computer is turned off. To enter the control panel, press <⌕-CTRL-ESC>; that is, hold down the <⌕> key, the <CTRL> key, and then press the <ESC> key. If you are not in software that restricts access to the control panel and the computer is on, pressing this combination of keys lets you enter the control panel. Move the up arrow to the control panel and press <RETURN>. You will then see a display such as that in Figure 8.

The *display* allows you to select between color or monochrome monitor, 40- or 80-column displays, and various screen colors for the text, background, and the border. Up and down arrows allow you to choose features to be changed, and left and right arrows permit you to choose from the options. To make a change, press <RETURN>. To examine and leave the options unchanged, press the <ESC> key. You may also adjust the volume and the pitch of the synthesized sounds.

To determine the system's *speed,* you may choose between normal (like that in the Apple IIe) or fast, an added feature of the Apple IIGS. (Note: If you are playing music with LogoWriter or other versions of Logo, you may need to be sure the system speed is on normal, to supply the right sound effects.)

The *clock* allows you to set the calendar date and the time. The month, day, and year are presented in the format of your choice. The *time* allows for the hour, minute, and second to be shown, again in your choice of format, in an AM/PM or 24-hour clock.

Options gives choices for the display language, the keyboard layout, and a number of other alternatives. Display languages include American English, U.K. English, French, Danish, Spanish, Italian, German, and Swedish. There is a keyboard

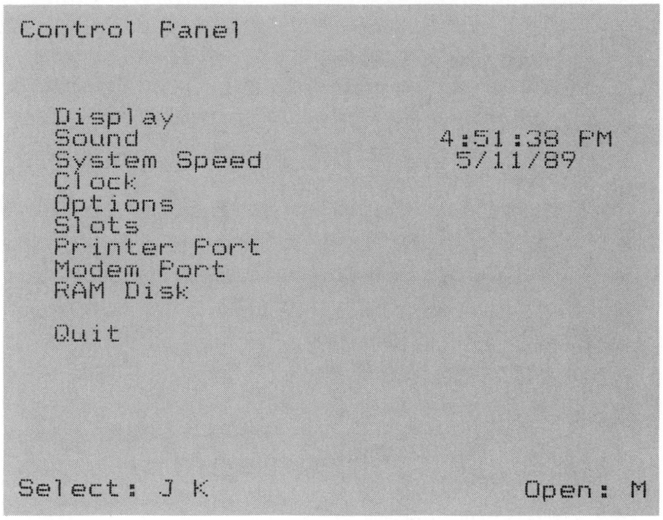

```
Control Panel


    Display
    Sound                           4:51:38 PM
    System Speed                    5/11/89
    Clock
    Options
    Slots
    Printer Port
    Modem Port
    RAM Disk

    Quit




Select: J K                              Open: M
```

▲

Figure 8 *Control panel for
Apple IIGS.*

layout choice for each of the above, as well as the Dvorak keyboard. The Dvorak is a keyboard designed for efficiency in typing; it breaks away from the QWERTY keyboard.

The *slots* option allows for selection of each port or slot. In each case you can choose between the original designation of the ports or the use of your own card. You also have a choice about setting the startup slot. Options for the startup slot are an assigned slot (1 through 7), the RAM disk, the ROM disk, or scan. In the last case, the computer first checks slot 6, drive 1 to see if there is a disk in that drive. If no disk is in slot 6, drive 1, then it goes to slot 5, drive 1.

The *printer* and *modem ports* allow you to set a number of different features that make your computer talk with your printer and modem.

The *RAM disk* lets you see how much available RAM is in the computer, and how much is in use. If enough memory exists, you can also set up a RAM disk.

A word of warning: all of the above options are readily available and if you have your own machine, you are certainly free to set your computer up however you want. However, if you are working in a community laboratory that many people share, please use common courtesy and not change commonly used settings (such as for the printer and modem, or even the time if it is correct). By all means go in and inspect the options. But it takes time to find the right combinations to make everything work in some of these settings. There should not be a battle every time you print a paper!

Other Features

QuickDraw II   QuickDraw II handles graphics for the Apple IIGS. Many of the other tools, such as the *Window Manager,* use QuickDraw II. QuickDraw II is very similar to the QuickDraw built into the Macintosh.

QuickDraw II includes routines for global environment, GrafPorts, drawing, pixel transfer, text drawing and measuring, cursor-handling, and customizing of QuickDraw II operations. It also permits the user to make calculations with rectangles, points, regions, and polygons. Utilities exist for mapping, scaling, and using random numbers. These routines allow a lot of flexibility in the use and manipu-

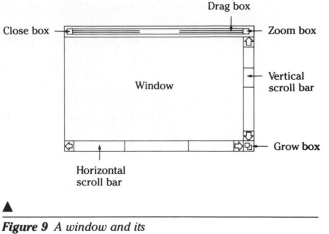

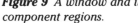

Figure 9 *A window and its component regions.*

lation of graphics. It is through these tools that complex drawings are made, moved, copied, dissected, and dilated. These features should be very useful to educational programs.

Sound Chip   The Ensoniq (DOC) digital oscillator chip and two 64K × 4 RAM chips allow for many new sound features used with the Apple IIGS. The Sound Manager contains all of the needed routines required to access the Ensoniq configuration. An oscillator is the basic sound-generating unit in the DOC. It contains 32 oscillators, each of which functions independently from all the other oscillators. The Free Form synthesizer uses a swap mode to generate sounds. A swap pair form a functional oscillator unit called a *generator.* There are fourteen generators in this sound system. Through this tool, appropriate sounds, music, and voice can add a lot to educational software.

Windows   A window is a display that presents information, such as a document, message, or graphic. Windows can be any size or shape, and an application can use one or many of them. The contents of windows vary, but most windows normally have the following common bars: title, close, size, and scroll (see Figure 9). You can use these tools to change the size of or move a window, close or activate a window, change the content of a window, or reshuffle the windows. A component region is a section that takes on a particular behavior, such as Drag region for dragging a menu down with a mouse; a Close region, for closing the frame; a Zoom region, for zooming in or out of the frame; or a Grow region, where the frame can be made larger or smaller by using the mouse to pull the frame out farther or back in closer.

References

Apple II/II + reference manual. (1979). Cupertino, CA: Apple Computer, Inc.

Apple II BASIC programming manual. (1978). Cupertino, CA: Apple Computer, Inc.

Apple IIe reference manual. (1983). Cupertino, CA: Apple Computer Inc.

Apple IIGS hardware reference. (1986). Cupertino, CA: Apple Computer, Inc.

Apple IIGS ProDOS 16 reference. (1986). Cupertino, CA: Apple Computer, Inc.

Apple IIGS toolbox reference, volumes 1 and 2. (1986). Cupertino, CA: Apple Computer, Inc.

The Applesoft tutorial. (1979). Cupertino, CA: Apple Computer, Inc.

BASIC programming reference manual: Applesoft II. (1978). Cupertino, CA: Apple Computer, Inc.

Demystifying computer languages: Special report. 1983. *Popular Computing, 2,* 80–163.

The DOS manual: Disk operating system. (1980). Cupertino, CA: Apple Computer, Inc.

The electronic encyclopedia. (1987). New York: Grolier Electronic Publishing, Inc.

Microsoft bookshelf. (1987). Redmond, WA: Microsoft.

Morabito, M. (1987, May/June). ERIC (Education Resources Information Center). *CD-ROM Review,* pp. 58–61.

Poole, L. (1981). *Apple II user's guide.* Berkeley, CA: Osborne/McGraw-Hill.

Strukhoff, R. (Ed.). (1987, May/June). *CD-ROM Review.* Entire issue.

Visual Dictionary. (1987). New York, NY: Facts on File.

Appendix G

Using the DOS 3.3 Apple Operating System

▶ ▲ ◀ ▼ ▶ ▲ ◀ ▼ ▶ ▲ ◀ ▼ ▶ ▲ ◀ ▼ ▶ ▲ ◀ ▼ ▶ ▲

To save programs for later changes, uses, and admiring reviews, use a floppy disk. Before using the floppy disk, however, you first need to initialize or orient your disk to the Apple system as described below.

Initializing a Disk

In order to use a disk, it must be oriented or initialized for the Apple system for DOS 3.3:

1. Activate or boot up (turn on) the computer using an initialized disk, such as the *Master Disk* that should have come with your system. Turn on the machine; then insert the *Master Disk,* close the door to the disk drive, and type:

   ```
   PR#6
   ```

   (PR stands for peripheral, the number following it stands for the slot number for the card interfacing the peripheral to the computer; if the disk drive controller card is in a slot other than 6, then use the appropriate slot number.) Rather than turning the machine off and back on frequently, type:

   ```
   PR#6
   ```

   instead.

2. Remove the *Master Disk* from the disk drive and replace it with the new disk. Remember to shut the door to the drive after you place the new disk in the drive. (Caution: do not insert the Applications Disk at this time. Initializing it would erase all the files on it!)

3. Now write an introductory *Hello* program. First type:

   ```
   NEW
   ```

   This removes any program left in memory. A sample program to write could be simply

   ```
   10 HOME
   20 PRINT "MARY DOE'S DISK"     [Use your own name.]
   ```

352

4. Now type:

```
INIT HELLO <RETURN>
```

The disk will then spin around (and perhaps make cracking noises) for about ninety seconds. When it stops it is initialized.

5. Just to check the disk, type PR#6 and see if the *Hello* program comes up. Now you can use the disk.

Saving Programs on the Disk

To save a program, first have the program typed into the computer. Then type:

```
SAVE Name
```

where the *Name* can be any string up to thirty characters that starts with a letter and uses no commas. Name the program something meaningful, so that you will remember later which program it represents. After initializing the disk, use it to save, load, and store programs.

Now write a program to save data on your disk. (First, start with a disk in the disk drive with the door shut, and either turn the machine on or type PR#6. This is important; otherwise you will not be able to save the program. We have watched students spend a lot of time typing in a program to save, but they have forgotten to first boot, that is, load initial instructions that set up the disk drive, and consequently have lost the whole program.) Consider the program:

```
10 GR
20 COLOR = 6
30 LET A = 20
40 LET B = 30
50 PLOT A,B
SAVE PUT THE POINT HERE
```

Loading Programs from the Disk

Using an initialized disk, put a copy of a program on a disk into the computer by typing

```
LOAD programname
```

This does not erase the program from the disk, but rather makes a copy of it. To examine the program, type

```
LIST
```

Other alternatives for looking at part of the program are

`LIST - n1`	Will list the program from the beginning up to the statement number n1
`LIST n1 -`	Will list from n1 to the end of the program
`LIST n1 - n2 or LIST n1,n2`	Will list from statement number n1 to n2
`<CTRL-S>`	Will stop the flow of printing on the screen as the lines are listed
`<CTRL-S>`	Used again, will allow for the flow to continue

After loading the program into memory, type

```
RUN
```

to see how the program executes. A different method for loading and running a program is simply to type

```
RUN programname
```

There the program is loaded and run in one command.

To see what programs are on a disk, type

```
CATALOG
```

The *Catalog* tells what programs and files are on the disk. A number of programs should be listed, such as:

```
A  003  COLOR DEMOSOFT
I  009  BIORHYTHM
B  006  FID
T  008  TEXT CREATED
```

The first letter, *A, B, I,* or *T,* tells what type the file is, the second item—for example, 003—tells how many *sectors* are used to store the program, and the third item gives the name of the file. The *A* means the *Applesoft BASIC computer language,* the *003* means the *first program listed takes up 3 sectors of storage,* and *Color demosoft* is the name of the program. The *I* means that the program is in *integer BASIC.* The *B* means the file is in *binary coding,* and the *T* means the file is a *TEXT file.*

Copying, Renaming, and Removing Programs

To copy a program from one disk to another, you can load the program from the original disk into the computer memory, exchange disks in the disk drive (remember to shut the door), then type

```
SAVE programname
```

(Appendix H discusses other methods to do this.)

To remove programs from your disk, type

```
DELETE programname
```

To change the name of a program on your disk, type

```
RENAME oldprogramname, newprogramname
```

Printing Program Listings

A printed copy of a program can be useful. Getting such a printout depends on the availability of a printer, the type of printer, and the type of connection used between the printer and the computer. Usually the card connecting the computer and the printer is placed in slot 1 of the computer. Be sure the printer is turned on, then type

    LOAD *programname*
    PR#1
    LIST

A listing of the program should appear. Then type

    PR#0

to turn the printer off. If these directions do not work, consult the manual for your printer.

Appendix H

Utility Programs on the DOS 3.3, ProDOS, and GS/OS Master Disk

▶ ▲ ◀ ▼ ▶ ▲ ◀ ▼ ▶ ▲ ◀ ▼ ▶ ▲ ◀ ▼ ▶ ▲ ◀ ▼ ▶ ▲

O n the DOS 3.3 *Master Disk* for the Apple, there are several very helpful programs with which you should become familiar. We will discuss them briefly; further discussion is given in the DOS manual.

Copya allows you to copy a complete disk. Caution: This program automatically initializes the disk onto which the copy will go, so do not use a disk on which you have programs that you wish to keep. When the disk is initialized, all programs originally on the disk are erased. *Fid* allows you to copy programs from one disk to a second disk. If you wish only to add programs to a currently initialized disk from another disk, and not to initialize a whole new disk, this is the program to use. *Muffin* allows you to copy programs from an old system (3.2) to a new system (3.3) disk.

When you use these programs you will be asked:

```
IN WHAT SLOT IS YOUR DISK?
```

In most cases, it will be in slot 6. You will also be asked:

```
WHICH DRIVE HAS THE ORIGINAL DISK?
```

In most cases, it will be in drive 1. You will then be asked:

```
WHICH DRIVE HAS THE COPY DISK?
```

The response to this will depend on whether you are using one or two drives. If you are using two drives, then the response will be *2* in most cases. If you are using one drive, then the response will be *1*. (Drive 1 is the drive you use to boot up the system.) The program will then ask:

```
DO YOU WANT PROMPTING?
```

If you are working with one drive, then your response will be YES. This allows information to be loaded into the computer memory from the original disk. You change disks, the information is stored on the second disk, you change disks again, information is loaded into the computer memory from the original disk, and so on. Both the *Fid* and *Muffin* programs will also ask:

```
WHAT FILE IS TO BE TRANSFERRED?
```

If you wish to transfer all files or a large number of files, respond to this question with a =. You will be asked:

```
DO YOU WANT TO BE PROMPTED?
```

If you are working with two disk drives and want all files transferred, then respond NO. If you are working with one disk drive or want only some of the files transferred, then respond YES or Y.

Another utility program on the *Master Disk* that is very helpful is the *Renumber* program. It has two uses: it allows you to renumber a program and it allows you to merge two programs. Try this:

```
RUN RENUMBER
```

Then suppose you wish to renumber a program starting with 100 and an increment of 10; you would type

```
& FIRST 100, INC 10
```

Suppose you wish to merge program *A* and program *B*. First make sure that the two programs have disjoint numbering. If they do not, then use the preceding routine to renumber them so that they do. Next:

```
LOAD PROGRAM A
&H
```

This puts the first program on hold. Now

```
LOAD PROGRAM B
&M
```

This merges the two programs.

Slots and Drives

One question that comes up quite early is about the **slot** and what **drive** that you are using. In order to answer this, you need to understand what these terms mean. With the older Apples, slot 6 is the slot normally used for the disk-drive controller for a 5.25-inch disk drive. A disk-drive controller is the card that connects the computer with the disk drive. The boot-up drive is drive *1*, the one that normally comes on when the computer is turned on. If there is a second drive, it is drive *2*.

Applied to the Apple IIGS, the question takes a little more understanding. If you are using disk-controller cards and slot 6, the above explanation applies. On the other hand, you may be using a 3.5-inch disk drive, for which card the customary slot is *5*. If you are working with two 3.5-inch disk drives, then the boot-up drive will be drive *1*, and the other one will be drive *2*.

In the Apple IIGS, ports in the back of the computer, including a smart port, can be used. By daisy-chaining several disk drives, the user can drive both 5.25-inch and 3.5-inch disks. The smart port, usually slot 5, reads the drives in an appointed order; from the control panel, it can be accessed by <&-CTRL-ESC>. (It is further discussed in Appendix G.) The normal use of slots and ports are described in Table 1.

Table 1	Slots and Ports
Slot	**Port**
Slot 1	Printer port
Slot 2	Modem port
Slot 3	Text display
Slot 4	Mouse port on keyboard
Slot 5	3.5-inch disk drive in disk drive port
Slot 6	5.25-inch disk drive in disk drive port*
Slot 7	AppleTalk in printer port or modem port

*Apple IIc has a built-in drive represented as slot 6 and drive 1.

In the Apple IIGS, the normal setup is to use one 3.5-inch drive and one 5.25-inch disk drive. This setup allows continued use of the large amount of software available on 5.25-inch disks. This setup also allows for use of the new software that is coming out in the 3.5-inch format.

A RAM drive can be set up in the Apple IIGS, if there is enough memory. As another drive, usually, but not always, the RAM drive takes on a designation of slot 5 and drive 2. When the machine is shut off whatever is in this drive will disappear. It can be particularly useful for either of two cases. In one case, a lot of data has to be available at one time, so materials are loaded into this RAM drive and called directly for use. In the other case, you might want to copy a 3.5-inch disk but have only one drive. You can copy the original disk into the RAM drive. Replace the original disk with the destination disk and copy from the RAM drive to the destination disk. Hence, you do not have to keep changing disks in the disk drive. At this time, using RAM is less expensive and more flexible than using additional disk drives.

ProDOS

Besides DOS 3.3, Apple has developed a more sophisticated operation system called ProDOS. ProDOS is mainly menu driven, so it is not only more sophisticated, but also is more user friendly than DOS 3.3. ProDOS has gone through several evolutions, from ProDOS (for Professional Disk Operating System) to ProDOS8 to ProDOS16 to GS/OS.

System Utilities

We examine the system utilities because there are a number of routines that can be useful to you. The systems continue to be up-dated so you will need to check your manuals for the most up-to-date information. In order to use system utilities you need to understand the following terms.

Volume name Each disk must have a volume name, for example, *Appleworks*. It should start with a slash "/" and end with a slash "/" with its name in between. Guidelines for naming a volume include

► Start the name with a letter.
► Don't use spaces.
► Don't make it longer than 15 characters.

An option also allows you to change the volume name.

Paths and Subdirectories ProDOS permits paths and subdirectories. This capability converts the directory of a disk from a linear path (as if all files were in a straight line) to a tree path (as if files were related) with group clusters. The latter allows for more chunking of files. Consider outlining topics for a paper. You should first identify key ideas, then develop each of the key ideas, such as:

          Major idea *A*
              Minor idea *A1*
                  Subminor idea A1.a
                  Subminor idea A1.b
                  Subminor idea A1.c
                  Subminor idea A1.d
              Minor idea *A2*
                  Subminor idea A2.a
                  Subminor idea A2.b
              Minor idea *A3*
          Major idea *B*
              Minor idea *B1*
              Minor idea *B2*
                  Subminor idea B2.a
                  Subminor idea B2.b
              Minor idea *B3*
          Major idea *C*
          Major idea *D*
              .
              .
              .

This outline could be converted to a tree structure, as discussed in Chapter 3 and illustrated in Figure 1. To assign a path to each subpart, use a slash "/" to separate each path and subpath. A sample path is

```
/A/A2/A2.b
```

Another sample path is

```
/B/B2/B2.a
```

Guidelines for naming paths include,

► Use a slash at the beginning of the pathname and to separate the individual names.
► Start each name with a letter.
► Don't make any name longer than 15 characters.
► You can use letters, numbers, and periods, but no other punctuation marks.

Formatting Disks If you have a new disk and want to use it for saving programs, you must first format the disk. An option to format the disk is available in the system

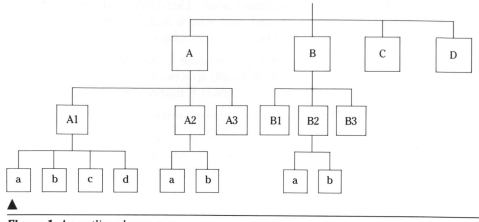

Figure 1 *An outline shown as a
tree structure.*

utilities. **Caution:** This erases all data! If you format a disk, there will be no data remaining on it. If there is data already on the disk, realize that formatting erases the data.

Copying Files versus Duplicating Disks   If you have files on one disk and want copies of them on another disk, you have two ways of copying them. One way is to use the *Copy Files* option. In order to use this, the disk that you are copying to *(the destination disk)* needs formatting first. This option will allow you to add files to a disk that may already have files. Also, you may copy only a few of the files from the first disk to the second, if you want, or you may copy all the files.

The second method of copying files to another disk is to use the Duplicate a Disk option. **Caution:** Duplicating a disk will erase data already on the destination disk! This routine initializes the destination disk and copies all files from the original disk to the destination disk.

Locking and Unlocking Files   Normally, if a new file is saved under a specific name that is already used for another file, the new file replaces the old file. Occasionally this process accidentally destroys files. One method to avoid this unintended loss is to protect files by locking them. However, if you are in the process of revising the file and are frequently changing it, you must often unlock the file. The option to lock or not lock files is available to you for your convenience. You must decide when it is useful and when it is not useful.

Appendix I

Special Features of AppleWorks

▶ ▲ ◀ ▼ ▶ ▲ ◀ ▼ ▶ ▲ ◀ ▼ ▶ ▲ ◀ ▼ ▶ ▲ ◀ ▼ ▶ ▲

Concept	Keystroke	Word Processor	Database	Spreadsheet
Arrange	\<Ó-A\>	NA	Arrange or sort category.	Arrange/assort rows.
Blank	\<Ó-B\>	NA	NA	Blank out cells.
Copy	\<Ó-C\>	Copy text.	Copy records.	Copy entries.
Delete	\<Ó-D\>	Delete text.	Delete records or report categories.	Delete columns/rows.
Edit, cursor switch	\<Ó-E\>	Insert/replace cursor switch.	Switch between insert/replace.	Switch between insert/replace.
Find	\<Ó-F\>	Find Marker/Page/Text.	Find records.	Find entries/text.
Group	\<Ó-G\>	NA	Add/remove group totals.	NA
Hard copy	\<Ó-H\>	Hard copy of current screen.	Print screen display.	Print current screen.
Insert	\<Ó-I\>	NA	Insert record or report category.	Insert rows/columns.
Justify or jump	\<Ó-J\>	NA	Justify report category.	Jump to other window.
Calculate	\<Ó-K\>	Calculates page breaks.	Define calculated report category.	Recalculate values.
Layout	\<Ó-L\>	NA	Change record layout.	Change cell layout.
Move	\<Ó-M\>	Moves text.	Moves record.	Move rows/columns.
Name change	\<Ó-N\>	Changes file name.	Change name of file/category.	Change name of file.
Options, printer	\<Ó-O\>	Printer options displayed.	Display print options.	Display print options.
Print	\<Ó-P\>	Prints text.	Go to report menu/print report.	Print worksheet.
Quick change	\<Ó-Q\>	Switches desktop files.	Switch to another desktop file.	Switch desktop files.
Replace or record selection	\<Ó-R\>	Replaces text.	Change rules of record selection.	NA
Save	\<Ó-S\>	Saves current file to disk.	Save file to disk.	Save current file to disk.
Tabs, totals, or titles	\<Ó-T\>	Sets tabs.	Add/remove report totals.	Set titles.
Edit cell content	\<Ó-U\>	NA	NA	Edit cell contents.
Value	\<Ó-V\>	NA	Set standard values.	Set standard values.
Window	\<Ó-W\>	NA	NA	Create windows.
Clear	\<Ó-Y\>	Clears to end of line.	Clear to end of entry.	Clear to end of cell.
Zoom	\<Ó-Z\>	Displays format setting.	Zoom: standard/multiple layout.	Zoom to formula display.
Ruler	\<Ó-1–9\>			
Help	\<Ó-?\>			
Cursor moves	\<Ó- \>			

Appendix J

Computer Programs and Software Reviews Mentioned in Text

▶ ▲ ◀ ▼ ▶ ▲ ◀ ▼ ▶ ▲ ◀ ▼ ▶ ▲ ◀ ▼ ▶ ▲ ◀ ▼ ▶ ▲

The following programs, procedures, and software are discussed in the text. The program or disk name is given first, the source is in parentheses, followed by the number(s) of the chapter(s) in which it is mentioned. A list of the software distributors and other resources follows this index. Then, we have listed sources of the software reviews discussed in Chapter 14.

Addresses of Distributors

Activision, Inc.
3885 Bohannon Drive
Menlo Park, CA 94025
(800) 227-9759 or (415) 329-0500

Addison-Wesley Publishing Company
One Jacob Way
Reading, MA 01867
(617) 944-3700

Adventure Corporation
P.O. Box 51125
Pacific Grove, CA 93950
(408) 375-2638

Apple Computer, Inc.
20525 Mariani Avenue
Cupertino, CA 95014
(408) 996-1010

Broderbund
17 Paul Drive
San Rafael, CA 94903-2101
(415) 479-1170

Cambridge Developmental Laboratory
36 Pleasant Street
Watertown, MA 02172
(617) 926-0869

CD-ROM Review
CW Communications/ Peterborough, Inc.
80 Elm St.
Peterborough, NH 03458

Claris
440 Clyde Avenue
Mountain View, CA 94043
(415) 962-8946

Classroom Computer Learning
Pitman Learning, Inc.
500 Harbor Blvd.
Belmont, CA 94002
(415) 592-7810

CompuServe
5000 Arlington Center Blvd.
P.O. Box 20212
Columbus, OH 43220

Compu-Teach, Inc.
240 Bradley St.
New Haven, CT
(203) 777-7738

Computer-Advanced Ideas
2550 Ninth Street
Oakland, CA 94607
(415) 526-9100

The Computing Teacher
The International Council on Computers in Education
University of Oregon
1787 Agate Street
Eugene, OR 97403
(503) 686-4414

Control Data Corporation
P.O. Box O
Minneapolis, MN 55440
(612) 853-8100

Control Data Corporation
Plato Computer-Based Education
308 N. Dale Street
St. Paul, MN 55103
(800) 328-4915

Developmental Learning Materials (DLM)
P.O. Box 4000
Allen, TX 75002
(214) 727-3346

Didatech
3812 William Street
Burnaby, BC
V5C 3H9 Canada
(604) 299-4435

Dow Jones News/Retrieval Services
P.O. Box 300
Princeton, NJ 08540
(800) 257-5114

Educational Activities, Inc.
P.O. Box 392
Freeport, NY 11520
(516) 223-4666

Educational Resources
2360 Hassell Road
Hoffman Estates, IL 60195
(800) 624-2926

EduWare Services, Inc.
28035 Dorothy Drive
Agoura, CA 91301
(818) 706-0661

Electronic Arts
1820 Gateway Drive
San Mateo, CA 94403
(415) 571-7171

Electronic Learning
Scholastic, Inc.
730 Broadway
New York, NY 10003
(212) 505-3000

EPIE Institute
63 Main Street
Southampton, NY 11968
(516) 283-4922

Family Guide to Educational Software
484 Sunrise Highway
Rockville Centre, NY 11570
(800) 848-0804

First Byte
3333 East Spring St.
Long Beach, CA 90806
(213) 595-7006

Frontier Software Company
P.O. Box 56505
Houston, TX 77227
(713) 963-0161

Grolier Electronic Publishing, Inc.
95 Madison Ave., Suite 1100
New York, NY 10016
(212) 696-9750

Hartley Courseware, Inc.
P.O. Box 431
Dimondale, MI 48821
(517) 646-6458

IBM Educational Systems
P.O. Box 2150
Atlanta, GA 30055
(404) 988-2532

Instant Software
Route 202
Peterborough, NH 03458
(603) 924-9261

Knowledge Index
(A service of Dialog Information Services)
3460 Hillview Avenue
Palo Alto, CA 94304
(800) 227-1927

Koala Technologies
A Pentron Company
269 Mt. Hermon Road
Scotts Valley, CA 95066
(408) 438-0946

Krell Software
1320 Stony Brook Road
Stony Brook, NY 11790
(516) 751-5139

LCSI
P.O. Box 162
High Gate Springs, VT 05460
(800) 321-LOGO

The Learning Company
6493 Kaiser Drive
Fremont, CA 94555
(415) 792-2101

Lego Systems, Inc.
555 Taylor Road
Enfield, CT 06082
(203) 749-2291

Microsoft
20700 Northup Way
Bellevue, WA 98004
(206) 828-8080

Minnesota Educational Computing Corporation (MECC)
2520 Broadway Drive
St. Paul, MN 55113
(612) 638-0627

Muse Software
347 N. Charles Avenue
Baltimore, MD 21201
(301) 659-7212

National Council of Teachers of Mathematics (NCTM)
1906 Association Drive
Reston, VA 22091
(703) 620-9840

On-Line Systems
See Sierra On-Line

Opportunities for Learning
20417 Nordhoff Street, Department 90
Chatsworth, CA 91311
(818) 341-2535

PBI Software, Inc.
1163 Triton Drive
Foster City, CA 94404
(415) 349-8765

Phoenix Software
6640 N. Sioux Avenue
Chicago, IL 60646
(312) 792-1227

Radio Shack
Education Division
Department 82-A-324
1300 One Tandy Center
Ft Worth, TX 76102
(817) 390-3011

Rand McNally & Co.
P.O. Box 7600
Chicago, IL 60680
(312) 673-9100

Reader's Digest
Educational Division
Pleasantville, NY 10570
(914) 769-7000

Scholastic Software
730 Broadway
New York, NY 10003
(212) 505-3000

Science Research Associates (SRA)
155 N. Wacker Drive
Chicago, IL 60707
(312) 984-7000

Sierra On-Line
Sierra On-Line Building
36575 Mudge Branch Road
Coarsegold, CA 93614
(209) 683-6858

Software Mart, Inc.
7419 Lakewood Drive
Austin, TX 78750
(512) 346-7887

Software Publishing Corporation
1901 Landings Drive
Mountain View, CA 94043
(415) 962-0191

The Source
1616 Anderson Road
McLean, VA 22102
(800) 336-3330

Spinnaker Software
215 First Street
Cambridge, MA 02143
(617) 494-1200

Springboard Software, Inc.
7808 Creekridge Circle
Minneapolis, MN 55435
(612) 944-3915

Styleware
440 Clyde Avenue
Mountain View, CA 94043
(415) 960-1500

SubLogic
713 Edgebrook Drive
Champaign, IL 61820
(217) 359-8482

Sunburst Communications
39 Washington Avenue
Pleasantville, NY 10570
(914) 769-5030

Terrapin, Inc.
678 Massachusetts Avenue
Cambridge, MA 02139
(617) 492-8816

Tom Snyder Productions
90 Sherman Street
Cambridge, MA 02140
(617) 876-4433

Visicorp
2895 Zanker Road
San Jose, CA 95134
(408) 946-9000

Software Reviews

Pollard (1989) identified 10 top sources for information on the quality of various software. These sources and their addresses are listed below.

Educational Software Preview Guide
ICCE, University of Oregon
1787 Agate St.
Eugene, OR 97403

Only the Best
Education News Service
P.O. Box 1789
Carmichael, CA 95609

The Educational Software Selector
EPIE Institute
P.O. Box 839
Water Mill, NY 11976

Sortware Reviews on File
Facts on File, Inc.
460 Park Ave. South
New York, NY 10016

The Chime Newsletter
Oklahoma State University
108 Gundersen
Stillwater, OR 74078-0146

Curriculum Software Guides
(Consult your Apple education representative.)

Technology in the Curriculum
California State Department of Education
P.O. Box 271
Sacramento, CA 95802-0271

MicroSIFT
Document Reproduction Services
Northwest Regional Educational Laboratory
101 S.W. Main St., Suite 500
Portland, OR 97204

Micro
Florida Center for Instructional Computing
University of South Florida
Tampa, FL 33620

Computer Courseware Evaluations
Learning Resources Distribution
10410 121st St.
Edmonton, Alberta T5N 1L2
Canada

Appendix K

Subject Areas and Computer Programs Mentioned in Text

▶ ▲ ◀ ▼ ▶ ▲ ◀ ▼ ▶ ▲ ◀ ▼ ▶ ▲ ◀ ▼ ▶ ▲ ◀ ▼ ▶ ▲

The following is a cross-listing of subject areas and some of the experiences and programs listed in the text. The experiences are listed by chapter. The program names are followed by the numbers of the chapters in which they are discussed.

Art

Many of the experiences in Chapters 1 through 4, 8, 10, and 15 can be applied to art.

AppleWorks GS (Claris), 8
MacPaint (Apple Computer), 8
Mademoiselle Merveille Software (DIL), 10
MousePaint (Apple Computer), 8
PaintWorks Plus/Gold (Activision), 8

Perception, Perception I, II, III (EduWare), 10
Print Shop (Broderbund), 8
Top Draw (StyleWare), 8
Transform (Author constructed), 10

Business Education

AppleWorks (Claris), 5, 6, 7, 8
AppleWorks GS (Claris), 8
Bank Street Writer (Broderbund), 5, 14
Color Average (Author constructed), 10

Data Manager II (Author constructed), 6
Homeword (Sierra On-Line), 5
Visualizer (PBI Software), 7, 8, 10

Computer Science

Many of the experiences in Chapters 1 through 8 and 15 can be applied to computer science.

Apple Logo Language (Apple Computer), 1
Krell Logo Language (Krell), 1
Rocky's Boots (The Learning Company), 4, 10, 11, 15

Rocky's Challenges (The Learning Company), 4
Terrapin Logo Language (Terrapin), 1

Foreign Language

Experiences in Chapters 4 and 8 discuss foreign languages.

Visual Dictionary (Software Mart), Appendix F

Visual Dictionary CD ROM (Software Mart), Appendix F

Information

Academic American Encyclopedia (Grolier), Appendix F

Adventure's ROMulus CD-ROM (Adventure), Appendix F

Microsoft Bookshelf (Microsoft), Appendix F

Visual Dictionary CD ROM (Software Mart), Appendix F

Language Education

Apple Learning Series (Apple Computer), 10

AppleWorks (Claris), 5, 8

AppleWorks GS (Claris), 8

Bank Street Writer (Broderbund), 5, 14

Certificate Maker (Springboard), 8

Combining Sentences (WICAT–IBM), 12

Compu-Teach Series (Compu-Teach), 10

First Letters and Words (First Byte), 8

Homeword (Sierra On-Line), 8

KidTalk (First Byte), 8

Mademoiselle Merveille Software (DIL), 10

Magic Spells (The Learning Company), 9

MECC Elementary Volume 7, Pictures, Words, Shapes (Minnesota Educational Computing Corporation), 9

M_SS_NG L_NKS (Sunburst), 9

MultiScribe GS (Activision), 8

Plurals and Possessives (Frontier Software), 9

Prefixes (Minnesota Educational Computing Corporation), 14

Print Shop (Broderbund), 8

Punctuation (WICAT—IBM), 12

Reading for Meaning (WICAT–IBM), 12

Scramble (Author constructed), 9

Sentence Animator (Science Research Associates), 10

Sentences (Control Data Corporation), 10, 12

Speller Bee (First Byte), 8

Stickybear Series (Weekly Reader), 9

Story Machine (Spinnaker), 14

StoryTree (Scholastic), 8

Tenses (Control Data Corporation), 12

The Clown's Balloons (Frontier Software), 9

The Newsroom (Springboard), 8

Urban Reader (Educational Publishing Concepts, Inc.), 13

Visual Dictionary (Software Mart), Appendix E

Vocabulary (WICAT—IBM), 12

Word Spinner (The Learning Company), 9

Logic

Rocky's Boots (The Learning Company), 4, 10, 11, 15

Rocky's Challenges (The Learning Company), 4

Mathematics

Many of the experiences in Chapters 1 through 4, and 6 through 12, and 15 relate to mathematics learning.

Alligator Mix (Developmental Learning Materials), 14

Bumble Plot (The Learning Company), 10

Cointoss (Author constructed), 4

Color Average (Author constructed), 10

Compu-solve (Educational Activities), 14

Compu-Teach Series (Compu-Teach), 10

Copopu (Author constructed), 3

Elementary Math (Muse), 14

Estimating Lengths (Author constructed), 12

Euclid Geometry Tutor (Radio Shack), 14

Factory (Sunburst), 10

Flight Simulator II (SubLogic), 10, 11

Geometric Supposer (Sunburst), 10

Geometry (WICAT—IBM), 12

Gertrude's Puzzles (The Learning Company), 4

Gertrude's Secrets (The Learning Company), 4

Green Globs and Graphing Equations (Sunburst), 10

Hammurabi (Public domain), 11

Mademoiselle Merveille Software (DIL), 10

Manypop (Author constructed), 3

Math Concepts (Hartley Courseware), 14

Math Concepts (WICAT—IBM), 12

Math Talk (First Byte), 8

Math Talk Fractions (First Byte), 8

Measurement (Cambridge Development Laboratory), 12

Micro-Dynamo (Addison-Wesley), 10, 11

Perception, Perception I, II, III (EduWare), 10

Robot Odyssey I (The Learning Company), 4
Rocky's Boots (The Learning Company), 4
Salaj (Author constructed), 3, 4
Simulation Construction Kit (Hartley's Courseware), 11
Super Factory (Sunburst), 10

The King's Rule (Sunburst), 4
The Pond (Sunburst), 4
The Royal Rules (Sunburst), 4
Transform (Author constructed), 10
Visualizer (PBI Software), 8, 10

Music

Experiences relating to music are discussed in Chapters 3, 8, 9, and 15.

MECC Music Drill and Practice Program (Minnesota Educational Computing Corporation), 9

Music Construction Set (Electronic Arts), 8
The Music Studio (Activision), 8

Physical Education

Many of the experiences relating body movements and actions on the screen are in Chapters 1, 2, and 10.

Olympic Decathlon (Microsoft), 9

Problem Solving

Many of the activities throughout Chapters 1 through 4 are focused on developing problem-solving processes. Chapters 5 through 15 also have numerous examples of problem solving.

Estimating Lengths (Author constructed), 11
Factory (Sunburst), 10
Gertrude's Puzzles (The Learning Company), 4
Gertrude's Secrets (The Learning Company), 4
Gnee or Not Gnee (Sunburst), 10
High Wire Logic (Sunburst), 10
In Search of the Most Amazing Thing (Spinnaker), 10
Robot Odyssey I (The Learning Company), 4

Rocky's Boots (The Learning Company), 4
Safari Search (Sunburst), 10
Simulation Construction Kit (Hartley's Courseware), 11
Snooper Troops (Spinnaker), 10
Super Factory (Sunburst), 10
The King's Rule (Sunburst), 4
The Pond (Sunburst), 4
The Royal Rules (Sunburst), 4

Science

Many of the experiences in Chapters 1 through 4, 7, 8, 10, 11, 12, and 15 relate to science.

Collide (Minnesota Educational Computing Corporation), 11
Data Manager II (Author constructed), 6
Estimating Lengths (Author constructed), 12
Factory (Sunburst), 10
Flight Simulator II (SubLogic), 10,11
Forecast! (CBS), 11
Gertrude's Puzzles (The Learning Company), 4
Gertrude's Secrets (The Learning Company), 4
Gnee or Not Gnee (Sunburst), 10
Heart Lab (Educational Activity), 11
High Wire Logic (Sunburst), 10
In Search of the Most Amazing Thing (Spinnaker), 10
Micro-Dynamo (Addison-Wesley), 10, 11
Odell Lake (MECC), 14

Perception, Perception I, II, III (EduWare), 10
Pollute (Minnesota Educational Computing Corporation), 11
Robot Odyssey I (The Learning Company), 4
Rocky's Boots (The Learning Company), 4
Science Toolkit (Broderbund), 8
Simulation Construction Kit (Hartley Courseware), 11
Super Factory (Sunburst), 10
The King's Rule (Sunburst), 4
The Pond (Sunburst), 4
The Royal Rules (Sunburst), 4
Three Mile Island (Muse), 14
Transform (Author constructed), 10

Social Studies

Teacher Utility

Glossary/ Index

Fid, 356

Field Any of the zones of information, such as name, address, and phone number, that are grouped together to form a record. 136

Field dependence The lack of ability to find a simple figure embedded in a complex figure. 212

Field independence The ability to find a simple figure embedded in a complex figure. 212

Field length The maximum number of characters that can be stored in a field. 136

File An organized collection of related information that can be treated as a unit. 136, 324

File server The center computer in a star network that controls a hard disk, printer, or other peripheral and is tied to the network. 179–80

Final, 69, 71, 74

Finite loop A loop that is executed a specific number of times. 36, 38

First Byte Company, 184

First Letters and Words (First Byte), 184

Flight Simulator II, 214, 219, 234–37, 241–42

Floppy Disk A circular mylar-coated disk used to store computer data for later use. 4

care and use of, 317

Flu, 234

Font, 175, 176

Food and Nutrients, 144

Forecast! (Mindscape), 245

Foreign language, programs for, 368

Formtools, 79

G

Game An activity involving active participation with rules governing its behavior and usually with winners and losers. 234–35

GAME, 75

Game paddles Hand-held computer input devices that consist of two separate dials, one on each paddle. In most applications, one dial moves a cursor or figure horizontally on the screen and the other vertically. 208, 341

Game Show, 278

Games, computer

guessing, 74–75

video, 309, 313

Games of conflict, 235

General Bear, 59–61

Generalization A statement that describes relationships among concepts; a nonprescriptive principle. 99, 102

GEnie system, 177

GeoDraw, 264–65

Geometric development, 8

Geometric Supposer Series, 224

Geometry (WICAT-IBM), 265

Geometry, and turtlegraphics, 27

GeoWorld, 244

Gertrude's Puzzles (The Learning Company), 111

Gertrude's Secrets (The Learning Company), 111

Gestalt theory, 255

GETTOOLS, 327–28

Gg, 74–75

Gnee or Not Gnee (Sunburst), 222–23

Gödel, Escher, Bach (Hofstadter), 301

GPRINT, 75

Grade book, 136, 157–59

Graphics

in Apple IIGS, 349–50

applications, 219–21

communication potential of, 208

drill and practice programs, 203

educational potential of 208–9

embodied versus embellished, 214–15

evaluation of, in software, 279–81

interactive, 68–70

light pens, 176

in Logo, 12–13

in math tutorials, 264

mouse-produced, 175–76

printouts of, 323

research on, 225–26

saving, 322

tablets, 173–74, 343

text and, in LogoWriter, 75

text integration, 176, 183–84, 325–26, 331

transformations of, 214

utilities, 173–76

as visual communication, 173

whole-brain development and, 27

zoom, 174–75

Graphics tablet Software that facilitates the creation and manipulation of computer-generated graphics. 343

Graphs, 163–64

Grappler interface card, 323

Green Globs and Graphing Equations (Sunburst), 224

H

Hammurabi, 233–35

Haptics Relating to the sense of touch. 212–13

Hard disk A permanent data storage device that is several times as fast in loading and saving files as a floppy disk and holds considerably more information. 346

Hard masters, 106

Head, 41–42

HEADING A Logo command that outputs the turtle's heading. 49

Health records, spreadsheets and, 154

Heart Lab (Educational Activity), 246

Help screen, 124, 127

Hemispheric brain functioning. *See* Bimodal brain functioning; Left-hemisphere brain functioning; Right-hemisphere brain functioning; Whole-brain coordination

Heuristics Thought processes that serve to guide, reveal, or suggest a possible course of action. 98–100

Hexagon, 20

Hi, 68, 75

HIDETURTLE (HT) A command in Logo that makes the turtle invisible. 38. *See also* **SHOWTURTLE**

High Wire Logic (Sunburst), 222

Hofstadter, D.R., 301

HOME A command in Logo that moves

the turtle to the center of the screen pointing up. 20, 44

Homeword, 122

House, 24

Housing, graphics for, 220

How the West Was Won + Three x Four (Sunburst), 222

HT. *See* **HIDETURTLE**

I

IBM, 333–35

ICAI Intelligent Computer-Assisted Instruction. A tutorial that includes a database of factual information and rules similar to an expert system. 253. *See also* **Expert System**

Icon A picture or graphic representing a computer command. 124, 175

IF . . . THEN . . . ELSE A Logo command that transfers control if the specified condition is true. Otherwise, the next line is executed. 81

IF . . . THEN STOP, 38

Imagery

achievement and, 211–12

aspects of, 7–8

development of, 7, 26, 207–8

explicit, 8

reflective versus anticipatory, 8

static versus dynamic, 4, 8, 210

transformations and, 8

See also **Visualization**

Immediate execution mode, 70. *See also* **Direct mode**

Immigration, 244

Impact print Print formed by a printer that mechanically presses the print element against paper to make an impression. 344

Impulsive A learning style in which the learner works on materials as they are presented and does not study the relationship of the parts to the whole. The opposite of **reflective**. 262

Indenting, 123

Indirect mode A mode of programming in which instructions typed at the keyboard are saved in memory as a program for later execution. Also called *programming mode.* 17–19. *See also* **Direct mode**

Individualization Instruction designed to match or strengthen individual learning styles. 269–70

Induction. *See* **Inductive reasoning**

Inductive reasoning The process of deriving a general conclusion by observing similarities and patterns in particular cases. 102, 105–6, 260

Industrial revolution Changes in society brought about by mass production and heavy emphasis on industry. 295

Infinite loop A loop that continues indefinitely. 36–38

Information, obtaining via databases, 177

Information age, 296–97

Information revolution. *See* **Computer revolution**

Inhelder, B., 213

Input device A peripheral device through which information is entered into the

MAKE A command in Logo that assigns a value to a variable name. The variable name must be a Logo word. 47
MAKE "NAME, 68
Manuals, software. *See* **Documentation**
Manypop, 81–82
Massachusetts Institute of Technology Artificial Intelligence Laboratory, 13, 25, 313
Massed practice In skill development, the working of many examples in a short period of time. A learning method appropriately used soon after accuracy has been gained. 198
Mastery learning Learning based on the division of a curriculum into a sequence of measurable learning objectives; students pursue a particular objective until they demonstrate mastery and then proceed to the next objective in the sequence. 269
Math Concepts (WICAT-IBM), 264, 277
Mathematics
   CMI programs for, 272
   graphics, 220
   imagery development and, 211–12
   programs, 74–75, 184, 369
   spreadsheets and, 154
   tutorials, 264
Mathematics Assessment Prescriptive Edu-Disks, 277
Math Talk (First Byte), 184
Math Talk Functions (First Byte), 184
Maturation The act or process of maturing (in a Piagetian sense, biologically). 255
Measurement, 251, 257
MECC Elementary Volume 7, 194, 202–3
MECC Music, 197
Mediated teaching, 49–50
Megabyte Approximately one million bytes, or 1000K, 339. *See also* **Byte; K**
Megatrends (Naisbitt), 296
Memory The part of the computer system in which data are stored. 336 *See also* **RAM; ROM**
Memory Device A device in which information is stored or manipulated. 336–40
Mental imagery. *See* Imagery
Microcomputer, history of, 333–35
Micro-dynamo, 217–18, 233
MicroSIFT, 285
Microsoft Bookshelf, 345
Microsoft Word, 303
Microsoft Works, 304
Microworld A simulated learning environment in which students control and manipulate various parameters so that they can explore relationships. The more complex microworlds are extensible, and thus allow students to use their own creativity to personalize and expand the microworld environment. 79–83, 234
Middle-out programming A combination of top-down programming and bottom-up programming, in which some planning of the big picture is being considered while individual parts are simultaneously planned. 106
Miller's number The number of items of information that a person can hold in

short-term memory at one time. The number is seven plus or minus two. 46
Mindscape Company, 245
Minnesota Educational Computing Corporation, 285
Minorities, and computers, 308
Mirror image. *See* **Reflect**
Modeling The process of translating from a real-world situation to an abstract or conceptual world. 100–101
Models
   CMI, 271
   drill and practice, 201
   educational use of, 6
   learning theory, 255
   problem-solving, 100–101
   simulation, 234–35
   to solve real-world problems, 98
Modem Peripheral device that is needed for communicating via telephone lines with other computers. 176, 177–78, 343
Modularization The process of breaking an entity into its component parts or separate modules. 41, 86
Monitor A televisionlike output device used for giving information. 4, 343. *See also* **Cathode ray tube**
Moresquares, 34, 36
Moresquares1 :Side, 36–37
Motherboard A computer's main circuit board, into which various other boards may be plugged. 338
Motion effects, 327
Motivation The creation of a felt need or desire for learning or doing. 197, 256, 260, 283
Mouse A desktop input device that controls cursor movement, giving the user an alternative to the keyboard; a mouse is usually used with specific software. 175, 343
MousePaint, 175
Move A type of action or statement involved in learning a skill. Different kinds of moves may be combined into a planned sequence to develop a teaching strategy. 196, 259–60
Move, 42, 69
MS DOS, 333, 335
M—ss—ng L—nks (Sunburst), 203
Muffin, 356
Multiscribe GS (Style Ware), 184
Multistep simulation Interactive simulation in which each step is dependent on the previous steps and in turn affects future steps. 235
Music
   coding, 83–85
   drill and practice in, 197
   graphics in, 220
   imagery and development in, 212
   in Logo, 77, 83–87
   programs, 184–85, 369
   structured, 86
   synthesizer, 184, 345
Music, 66, 82
MUSIC, 86
Music Construction Set, 185
The Music Studio (Activision), 185
Music synthesizer Peripheral device that plays electronic music. 184, 345
My Students Use Computers (Hunter), 140

N

Naisbitt, J., 296
NAME, 68, 320, 321–22
NAMEPAGE, 56, 325
Names, of variables, 35, 68
Naming, of procedures, 17. *See also* **TO**
National Council of Teachers of Mathematics, 285
National Science Board, Commission, 298–99, 302
Near-letter quality (NLQ) printer Printer that produces high-quality dot matrix output. 344
Network Connected computers, designed to share capabilities. 179
Networking, 304
NEW, 352
The Newsroom (Springboard), 184
New York City Board of Education, 305
NEXTSCREEN, 328
Nonexample A specific instance in which a particular principle does not apply. 235
Norm-referenced test A test in which a student's performance is compared with the performance of other students. 269
North America (Sunburst), 144
NOTRACE In Terrapin/Krell Logo, a command that turns off the trace function. Not available in Apple Logo. 44
NOWRAP In Terrapin/Krell Logo, a command that prevents turtlegraphics drawings from wrapping around the screen. Same as FENCE in Apple Logo. 38

O

Odell Lake, 280
Olds, Henry, 276
Olympic Decathlon, 196
On/off switch The switch that turns the computer on and off. 4, 317
Open-ended review form A form for reviewing software that allows for open-ended responses. 285–86
Operating system, 321. *See also* **Disk operating system**
Order of operations, 90
Oregon Trail, 233–36, 238–39
Orienting Starting a problem or finding questions that help with starting a problem. 101
Otherparallelsides, 109
The Other Side (Tom Snyder Productions), 244
OUTDEV, 323
Outlines, 359
Output device A peripheral device through which the results of a computer operation are expressed. The two most common output devices are the display screen and the printer. 4, 336, 343–47
Oval, 107–8
Owl, 106

P

Page, 324. *See also* **File**
PaintWorks Gold (Activision), 175–76